THE
INDIAN WARS
OF
THE WEST

Paul I. Wellman

Indian Head Books/New York

This edition published by Indian Head Books,
a division of Marboro Books Corp.

1992 Indian Head Books

ISBN 0-88029-834-0

Printed and bound in the United States of America

M 9 8 7 6 5 4 3

PREFACE

In the Old West the beginnings of the Machine Age encountered the last vestiges of the Stone Age. The white man had just embarked upon the great industrial era; the red man still used the flint arrow point.

Between these two extremes of human culture there was no common ground. The Indian could not understand the paleface's land hunger. To him the earth and its creatures belonged to all, the free gift of the Great Mystery. That one should build a fence around a little corner of it and say, "This is mine," was repugnant.

But the white man's greed was all-consuming. Seeing the fair land, he reached forth to take it. His conquest of the West was iniquitous in its conception and its execution. Not even the excuse that it permitted the spread of civilization was moral justification for it.

In the wars which inevitably followed, the Stone Age was foredoomed to defeat. The white man possessed the repeating rifle, the telegraph, and the railroad. The Indian had only his primitive weapons and his native courage. Remorselessly the Machine Age engulfed the Wilderness.

But not without a struggle. There was manhood in the red race. For decades the Indian fought a sometimes heroic, often spectacular, always futile war for the possession of his hunting grounds.

Historically we, as citizens of the United States, need to look back on the period of our conquest of the West with honest misgivings. Granted that the moralities under which nations are presumed to operate in this day had not yet been accepted, and that imperialism was the watchword of the era, not only for America but for every European nation as well, the record of our dealings with the Indians was shockingly bad.

We took advantage of our superior knowledge to cheat the natives of the wilderness at every turn. We made solemn agreements which we did not keep, because the Senate of the United States, that "greatest deliberative body in the world," had a habit of never getting around to ratifying the treaties which our military leaders and our peace commissions signed with the Indians. We displayed a childish inability to make our citizens obey their own laws. The Indian Bureau was corrupt and stupid, and surrounded by a swarm of grafting self-seekers. A few Indian Bureau employees were upright and intelligent in the old days, but these made only more dismal the spectacle of the venality of the rest.

When it came to fighting the Indians, we sometimes had men at the head of our military expeditions who were high-minded as well as brave. In fact this is the best part of the record. In general the officers of the United States Army, who had to fight the actual battles with the red men, were the best friends the red men had. But it is also a fact that some of our military commanders had just the opposite attitude, seeming to regard the Indian as less than human and worthy only of extermination.

As a result some ugly stories of inhumanity come down to us. Perhaps the cruelties of our Indian-killers were not as cold-blooded or scientifically planned as those of the Nazis. But they were brutally effective for all that. We did not put Indians in gas chambers or crematories. But we did shoot down defenseless men, women and children at places like Camp Grant, Sand Creek, and Wounded Knee. We did feed strychnine to red warriors. We did set whole villages of people out naked to freeze in the iron cold of Montana winters. And we did confine thousands in what amounted to concentration camps.

This book is a combined edition of two earlier volumes, *Death on the Prairie* and *Death in the Desert,* which I published in 1934 and 1935 respectively. The plan they followed is relatively simple. Two main theaters existed for the Western struggle—the plains country and the desert country, together with the mountainous areas which bordered on them. To follow out the devious courses of all the little, relatively unimportant clashes between the white men and the red men, would be manifestly impossible in the space permitted. Therefore I have sought to pursue only the main stream of the events, recording the most significant and important, yet attempting to give a coherent, moving picture of the wars for the West, insofar as it was in me to do it.

On the plains, the white man's great adversary was the Dakota Sioux. In the desert he was the Apache.

A word about the two peoples who furnished the backbone of the opposition to the advance of our frontier. In many respects they were the antitheses of one another. The Sioux were numerous, rich according to their standards, lordly and proud. The Apaches were relatively small in numbers, a poor people, living in bitter surroundings. The Sioux fought their wars for glory. The Apaches fought solely to kill their enemies.

The Dakota Sioux comprised the largest division of the great Siouan linguistic family which was second only to the Algonquin stock in numbers within the area of the present United States. The territory which the Dakota Sioux considered theirs extended from the Great Lakes to the Continental Divide, and from the Canadian border to the Platte River and beyond. Their numbers were upward of thirty thousand. From earliest times white men had traded with them and lived among them. Francis Parkman's classic "The Oregon Trail" is an account of a leisurely, pleasant summer he spent among the friendly Sioux in the days before they became the white man's bitter enemies.

Of the Sioux, Dr. Frederick W. Hodge wrote in his monumental "Handbook of American Indians," issued by the Bureau of American Ethnology: "The Dakota are universally conceded to be of the highest type, physically, mentally, and probably morally, of any of the western tribes. Their bravery has never been questioned by white or Indian, and they conquered or drove out every rival except the Chippewa." Parenthetically, it should be pointed out that the success of the Chippewa against the Sioux was due to the circumstance that they were the first to be supplied with firearms, by the French traders, and turned this advantage to good use during their wars.

The Sioux were handsome, well dressed, vigorous, and some of their leaders displayed great intellectual force. They had adapted themselves to their environment, and knew how to live in comfort in their tepees even on the rigorous plains. They were horsemen of unrivaled dash and skill and they were the equals if not the superiors of their white enemies in the use of their weapons. No higher tribute could have been paid them than that of General George Crook, himself a magnificent soldier, who called them "the finest light cavalry in the world." So much for the Sioux.

The Apaches were different. Centuries ago, out of the bleak wastes of the Arctic lands, a people began its southward march. It was a poor people, schooled by rigid adversity, used to the pang of hunger, the bite of the elements, the constant struggle for existence. Though lacking every form of material wealth, it was rich in courage and pride, a pride which found expression in its name for itself—*Tinde*, *Tinneh*, *Dine* or *N'de* in various dialects—which has always the same meaning wherever it is found, *The People*.

Filtering slowly southward these people debouched at last upon the Great Plains. Here for the first time they found some surcease from the pitiless fight for life. There was game in plenty, and the killing frost was left behind. Gradually, through the years, they moved farther and still farther southward. When the first precursors of the white race reached the plains they found the former children of the tundras living in a far-flung territory ranging from the Black Hills almost to the Sierra Madre. The first white explorers called them by various names, *Vaqueros*, *Escanjaques*, *Faraons* and *Padoucas*.[1]

Now new forces began to be felt by the Tinde. The Sioux, impelled by pressure from the east where the paleface was forcing the Chippewas westward, emerged in teeming numbers into the plains. From the west came another people, a hungry people, the Shoshoni race, out of the barren high reaches of the Rocky Mountain plateaus.

The impact of these two migrations occurred in the regions at that time north of the habitat of the People, but its repercussions were soon felt by them. Invincible in war, the Sioux drove the Shoshoni

---

[1] George E. Hyde ("Rangers and Regulars," p. 40) calls attention to the fact that *Padouca* was an early French name for Apache instead of Comanche as some writers have assumed. He cites Magry, writing in the 18th Century, who "speaks of the tribe who are called by the Spaniards Apaches but are known to the French as Padoucas."

back to their mountains—all but one branch, a numerous, wily, lethal division, which history was to call the Comanches.

These last moved southward to make room for the Sioux, and where they went they drove the Tinde out. An epic story might be written on the wars of that slow invasion, but no chronicler was present. We know only that some time within the last three hundred years this race which once called the Arctic tundras its home found itself forced farther and farther into the equally barren, though this time torrid, deserts of our Southwest.

And now a strange thing happened. In some manner, from the very ferocity of their surroundings, the People attained a ferocity of their own. The enervation of the sun, which subdued the Pueblos, the Pimas, and the Diggers, failed to tame the Tinde. Their warriors became lean, sun-baked, imbued with shocking cruelty and vitality, endowed with deadliness and malice beyond all other tribes of American Indians. So it was that, after centuries of wandering, they were named from their one outstanding trait, *Apache—Enemy*. And this is a connection in spirit with the Dakota of the north, for the word Sioux is a French-Canadian contraction of the Chippewa name *Nadowe-is-iw*, an adder—hence by metaphor, an enemy.

Other tribes enter into this chronicle. The Cheyennes, Nez Percés, Comanches, Kiowas, Arapahoes, Modocs, and Pueblos wrote chapters of history both stirring and tragic. But the Sioux and Apaches were ever the great adversaries.

The nadir of the American Indian may be said to have come in the 1920's. Then his was considered a "vanishing race" doomed to extinction like the bison. His land had almost all been taken from him, except that which appeared worthless, and even those lands he still possessed were being destroyed by over-grazing. He was poor, dispirited, and disease was widespread in every reservation.

But already, when the two books which comprise this volume were first published, the condition of the Indian was improving, although the start was slow and its results not at first so very evident. Intelligent white men at last awoke to what was happening. Organizations like the American Indian Defense Association were built, merging into the American Association on Indian Affairs which fought legal

battles for the Indians and carried on educational work in their behalf among the white people of the country.

In 1933 Franklin Delano Roosevelt took office as President and
appointed Harold Ickes Secretary of the Interior. For the first time
the full interest of a national administration and its Secretary of the
Interior were focussed on the Indian question. Mr. Ickes had been an
officer of the American Indian Rights Association. He chose for
Commissioner of Indian Affairs the man best qualified by knowledge,
experience and sympathetic understanding for the job—John Collier, who had been field secretary of the association of which Mr.
Ickes was an officer.

Together, with the never-failing interest and backing of President
Roosevelt, they accomplished a number of important things. The
Indian schools, which in many cases had been little more than prisons,
were reformed. The Soil Conservation Service was set to work re-
claiming the rapidly disintegrating Indian lands. The Indian Division of the C.C.C. worked on numerous projects for the benefit of
their own people. The Indian medical service, which already had
been given a good start toward renewed efficiency in the Hoover
administration, was extended and encouraged to grapple still more
strongly with the health problems. The Indians were confirmed in
their right to maintain their own cultures and their own traditions—
even their own religions—if they desired, as was the right of every
other American citizen. Finally, a great basic law was promulgated
by Franklin D. Roosevelt, as the result of the recommendations of
Harold Ickes and John Collier, and passed—the Indian Reorganization Act of 1934, which forbade further allotment and alienation of
Indian lands and property, empowered the tribes to organize local
governments and incorporate for their own interest, and extended to
them credit to buy livestock and machinery. This law was fought
bitterly by groups interested in the continued exploitation of the
Indians, and some tribes actually were convinced, against their own
best interests, that they should not enter into the reorganization.

But as a whole the picture for the Indian began to improve in a
way it had never improved before. Indians have received the train-
ing which enables them in thousands to take positions in the adminis-

tration of their own service they could never occupy before. Indian manufacture was safeguarded from white counterfeiters by the Arts and Crafts Board. Since 1934 the trend, whereby Indian land continually was taken over by white men, has not only been halted but reversed, so that Indian holdings are actually increasing. The population of Indians, which had fallen to 225,000 in 1925 and was still going down, is now around 400,000 and increasing.

All this, of course, has been achieved in the face of political opposition, an opposition which still continues in Congress and elsewhere. Oliver La Farge, in an essay of clarity and force, published under the title "As Long As the Grass Shall Grow," in 1940, summed it up thus:

"The picture is hopeful, and unfinished. Perhaps it will never be finished; it may be replaced once more by the old one. For there is always that incalculable force to whom the white men piously refer as the Great White Father, whom the Indians call simply Washington. He is, after all, only the composite expression of a hundred and thirty million of us Americans who are all too ready to forget entirely about a handful of people whom once we feared, then conquered, then planned to break."

That is the situation today. But this book is concerned with yesterday, when the issue of supremacy was being settled with flying bullets and arrows. Its purpose is to seek to picture for the reader the moving panorama of that struggle; to catch for him a little of the spirit of those days, the action, the vivid color, the heroism and the despair.

PAUL I. WELLMAN

ACKNOWLEDGMENTS

AN AUTHOR owes much to his friends—for their forbearance as much as for their help. In the first regard mine have been uniformly tolerant. In the latter respect many have rendered valuable assistance in the research, organization and final preparation of this volume. Particularly do I acknowledge my indebtedness to the following:

Stanley Vestal and the Houghton Mifflin Company, Boston, for permission to use quotations and references from Stanley Vestal's "Sitting Bull, Champion of the Sioux."

Charles Scribner's Sons, New York, for permission to quote and use material from George Bird Grinnell's "The Fighting Cheyennes."

Mrs. Olive K. Dixon, Amarillo, Texas, for permission to use data, names and incidents from her biography, "The Life of Billy Dixon."

The Bobbs-Merrill Company, Indianapolis, for permission to quote from Colonel Homer W. Wheeler's "Buffalo Days."

Mrs. Alice V. Schmidt, of Houston, and Charles A. Maddux, of Los Angeles, for permission to use material from John R. Cook's "The Border and the Buffalo."

Captain Robert G. Carter, U.S.A., retired, Washington, for information and the permission to use material from his "The Old Sergeant's Story; Winning the West from Indians and Bad Men in 1870–76."

A. C. McClurg and Company, Chicago, for the use of quotations and incidents from E. B. Bronson's "Reminiscences of a Ranchman."

Hunter-Trader-Trapper Company, Columbus, for permission to use certain statistics from E. A. Brininstool's "Fighting Red Cloud's Warriors."

The Century Company, New York, for quotations from magazine articles, "Besieged by the Utes," by Colonel E. V. Sumner, and "Chief Joseph, the Nez Percé," by Major C. E. S. Wood.

Mrs. Hortense Campbell Gibson, for sustained interest, voluminous correspondence in search of material, and other invaluable aid contributed.

Professor C. W. Grace for valuable photographs used.

The United States Department of War and the Bureau of American Ethnology for records and photographs generously furnished.

The State Historical Societies of Kansas, Nebraska, Minnesota, Arizona, New Mexico, and Texas, and the Library of Congress for their unfailing courtesy in tracing and lending material without which this volume could never have been completed.

PAUL I. WELLMAN

THE
INDIAN WARS
OF
THE WEST

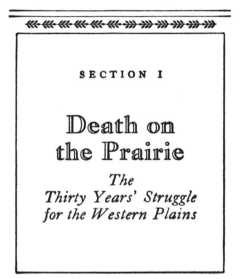

SECTION I

Death on the Prairie

The
*Thirty Years' Struggle
for the Western Plains*

CONTENTS FOR SECTION I

I.
MASSACRE IN MINNESOTA
1862–1863

II.
WAR SPREADS TO THE PLAINS
1864–1869

III.
THE STRICKEN FRONTIER
1864–1869

IV.
THE SOUTHERN TRIBES RISE
1873–1874

V.
THE STRUGGLE WITH THE SIOUX
1875–1877

ILLUSTRATIONS IN SECTION I

I

Massacre in Minnesota
1862-1863

1: THE STORM BREAKS

A SABBATH IN THE BACKWOODS

THE soft green hills of Minnesota lay placid in the August sun. Oak and birch and pine scarcely stirred in the breeze which brought a hint of coolness to the drowsy atmosphere, and the woodland lakes, which are the northland's chief charm, were barely ruffled.

Quiet was the forest which stretched its leagues on leagues of feathery tops to the northward. Even the birds were silent, for this was August. In the few small fields which the industry of the backwoodsmen had cleared out of the woods, no farmer moved. Scythe and hoe hung idle on their hooks. It was Sunday.

At the Lower Sioux Agency near Fort Ridgely, the morning of August 17, 1862, services were held as usual in the little Episcopal church. The rector addressed his simple words of faith to a mixed congregation—English and German farmers, a few agency employees and traders, and a handful of converted Sioux Indians. But his eyes probably wandered most frequently to a single dark figure which sat, morose and alone, in the shadows at the back of the church.

We have a photograph of him as he must have looked then— that silent communicant. He was a tall and splendid figure in his neat black broadcloth, with white collar and dark cravat; dressed as well as the best garbed white man among them. Only his head and feet were in sharp contrast. His feet were covered with doeskin moccasins, beaded according to the highest art of the Indian race. His head was bare and the swarthy bronze of his face was framed in two gleaming black braids of hair which swept downward over his shoulders, to fall across his broad chest in front.

If anybody in the church felt a shrinking from his dark presence, they gave no sign, for they all knew him. He was Little Crow, the great chief of the Santee Sioux, the steadfast friend of the white man, their guarantee of peace with the dark people of the forests.

The service ended. With perfect courtesy he greeted the white men and women assembled. Suavely he complimented the rector's eloquence; shook hands with everybody; strode out, mounted his horse and rode off—never to return.

Little Crow attended church that Sunday morning. By evening of the next day he was elbow-deep in the blood of those with whom he had worshipped.

THE BEGINNING OF THE MASSACRE

Why did Little Crow attend that last service? Nobody will ever know. Many have held it was for the purpose of cloaking the treachery which must already have been planned and ordered. But the reason may have been more human. Perhaps the dark chief came to be once more with the friends from whom he was to part forever.

Little Crow was an unusual Indian. He affected the white man's garb and ways, but was at heart an utter barbarian. His manners were those of a refined gentleman. His diplomatic talent and oratorical ability were very marked. And events were to prove him a patriot.

His friendship for the whites had once been genuine, but it was blasted long ago. An endless list of his people's grievances cried out to him. Rascally traders, using government red tape to withhold food from the starving red men, to sell them wormy flour and spoiled bacon at exorbitant prices; the seduction of Indian women by degenerate white men and the multiplication of half-breed children, a reproach and indignity to every honorable Sioux; Inkpaduta in the north, counting the spoils of his Spirit Lake raid and inciting to the war path; these and many other things fanned the smouldering flame.

Above all his tribe, Little Crow felt the wrong and the dishonor.

A son and grandson of chiefs, he had known the days of his people's glory. Then came the shameful Mendota Treaty of 1851, when the Sioux ceded most of their hunting grounds. He played his own part when, after a drunken fight with his brother, he nursed a crippled wrist and swore to banish firewater from the tribe. He sent for a Christian missionary to "teach the people the white man's way." Reverend Williamson, the man of God, won a place in Little Crow's heart, but now his goodness was all forgotten in the rascality of those other white men, the traders.

Only a week before the Sioux received the final insult. Their chiefs went to the agency to plead for the long-promised government stores. Andrew J. Myrick, a trader, listened with a sneer.

"If they're hungry, let them eat grass for all I care," was his callous reply.[1] The Sioux heard—and remembered.

. . . .

Forty miles from the agency three German farmers and the wife and daughter of one of them, sat at Sunday dinner. Four Indians entered the cabin. A crash of rifles, a flurry of knives—the happy dinner party lay dead. The Indians rode into the forest.

It was a signal. Up and down the Minnesota River stealthy bands of warriors set forth.

Monday dawned. With the first peep of the sun, the little community of traders at the Lower Agency was awakened by a gunshot, followed by a hideous war whoop. The people ran out of their homes into the streets to be shot down at their doors by Sioux posted in ambush. Myrick, whose cruel taunt had stirred the Indians' hatred, was killed in front of his store. When his body was found, days later, the mouth was stuffed full of grass.[2]

Other traders met ends as bloody. Francois La Bathe was slain on his counter. Henry Belland, James W. Lyndy and five other traders and clerks died similarly. Every soul in the agency would have perished but the Sioux began looting the ammunition stores and food boxes, permitting about fifty to reach the river. There a

[1] William Watts Folwell, "A History of Minnesota," p. 233, by permission of the Minnesota Historical Society.
[2] Folwell, "A History of Minnesota," p. 233.

heroic ferryman, Hubert Millier,[3] plied his boat until as he returned for the last load he was killed. Those cut off from crossing were all massacred and the Indians pursued the refugees, slaying seven more in the terrible fifteen-mile race to Fort Ridgely.

The arrival of the haggard vanguard of that fleeing band must have been a terrific shock to the people of the fort. The whole world was shocked by the events which followed.

The agency massacre was not the only tragedy of the morning.[4] While the Sioux were killing the traders, smaller parties swept through the surrounding settlements. The country was a shambles. The Indians took the farms as they came, slaughtering the men, carrying the young women off as captives, and butchering the children or allowing them to follow their mothers, according to the whim of the moment.

Lake Shetek and Renville County were especially bloody. In the first day alone more than two hundred white persons were killed in the vicinity of the Lower Agency. How anybody escaped is a mystery. Some of the experiences of the refugees are almost unbelievable. Tales of heroism also come down to us from that massacre. Men and women, even children, sacrificed themselves to save their friends.[5]

[3] The name is also given as Mauley.

[4] There are tales of frightful brutality during these raids. Governor Ramsey said in a speech: "But massacre itself had been mercy if it could have purchased exemption from the revolting circumstances with which it was accompanied— infants hewn into bloody chips of flesh, or nailed to doorposts to linger out their little lives in mortal agony . . . rape joined to murder in one awful tragedy . . . whole familes burned . . ."

It is only fair to the Indians to say that these atrocities occurred only in isolated instances if at all. Most of the settlers were mercifully killed at once. The Indian viewpoint is well summed up by Dr. Folwell: "From the white man's point of view these operations amounted simply to massacre, an atrocious and utterly unjustifiable butchery of unoffending citizens . . . The Indian, however, saw himself engaged in war, the most honorable of all pursuits, against men who, as he believed, had robbed him of his country and his freedom . . . He was making war on the white people in the same fashion in which he would have gone against the Chippewa or the Foxes. There are a few instances of . . . mutilation . . . There are also cases of tenderness and generosity to captives." ("A History of Minnesota," p. 125.)

[5] The story of 11-year-old Merton Eastlick and his devotion to his baby brother Johnny is worth re-telling. When the Indians struck Lake Shetek settlement, the Eastlick family hid with other settlers in the rushes of a stream bed. The Sioux found them, killed John Eastlick, the father, and three of the five boys. Mrs. East-

The exact number massacred will never be known. Minnesota state records list six hundred and forty-four.[6] There were hundreds, mostly women, taken captive. After the Battle of Wood Lake, two hundred and sixty-nine of these were recovered. Scores were rescued at other times. And the record of those who were never heard of again will never be complete.

CAPTAIN MARSH'S DEBACLE

And what were the soldiers at Fort Ridgely, fifteen miles from the Lower Agency, doing all this time?

Captain John S. Marsh, 5th Minnesota, was in command. As the first of the refugees burst into the fort with their frightened story, Marsh acted quickly. Sending a courier to Fort Snelling for help, he started promptly for the agency with forty-six men and

---

lick was captured. Before they found her, she hid her baby, Johnny, and charged his only surviving brother, Merton, never to leave him until he died. Mrs. Eastlick eventually escaped from the Indians and was found by August Garzine, a mail carrier, crazed with the belief that her whole family was dead. He took her to New Ulm. On the way, forty miles from the scene of the massacre, they found Merton and Johnny! The lad had carried the baby every foot of the way, hiding from Indians and subsisting on berries. He was an emaciated skeleton, with the flesh worn off his bare feet and was unable to speak for days afterward. But the baby was safe and sound.

[6] The Minnesota Historical Society's figures on the massacre are as follows:

Citizens Massacred

In Renville County (including reservations)	221
In Dakota Territory (including Big Stone Lake)	32
In Brown County (including Lake Shetek)	204
In all other frontier counties	187
	644

Soldiers Killed in Battle

Lower Sioux Ferry, Capt. Marsh's command	24
Ft. Ridgely and New Ulm	23
Wood Lake	17
Birch Coulie	26
Other engagements	23
	757

the post interpreter, Peter Quinn, leaving only a skeleton guard behind. They went in wagons but dismounted a mile from their destination. On the way they met a stream of fugitives. Here and there they passed dead bodies. They began to realize that they were in the midst of a great disaster—an Indian uprising of nightmare proportions.

Unused to Indian fighting but supremely confident, young Marsh led his men down to the ferry. The agency opposite was in flames. Not a soul could be seen. Had the Sioux left? No—at the very moment more than two hundred warriors were hiding behind saw logs and bushes with rifles cocked and aimed, ready to pull the triggers at a signal.

Now an Indian appeared among the burning buildings, walking toward the ferry. The soldiers recognized him—White Dog, a sub-chief and a frequent visitor at the fort. He motioned them to come across. Marsh hesitated. While he parleyed, a party of Sioux crossed unobserved farther down the river, and crept up on his flank.

Then White Dog made a gesture which must have been a signal. Clouds of smoke sprang up from a hundred apparently untenanted places. Marsh and his men suddenly found themselves fighting for their lives.

Half a dozen soldiers were killed in the first volley, including Quinn who was pierced by at least a dozen bullets. At the same moment the Indians on the flank opened fire. Marsh tried to charge into the thicket, saw it was useless, and ordered a volley fired instead. His men were falling fast. A retreat was finally ordered. They threw themselves into the timber near the river and for an hour fought an unequal battle with overwhelming numbers of Sioux, gradually retreating down the stream.

At length the captain decided to cross over. To show his men it was feasible, he tried to swim the swift current himself. The eddies caught him and he drowned—youthful, gallant, but utterly unfit to cope with Indian warriors.

The Sioux harried the rest of the soldiers almost to the fort. What was left of the command which had marched out so gallantly that morning, straggled in late in the evening. Of the forty-eight men who started, exactly half, including the captain, were dead.

HOW RUSTY CANNON SAVED FORT RIDGELY

That was a night of terror at Fort Ridgely. Lieutenant Thomas P. Gere, now commanding, had only a handful of soldiers left and scores of women and children to protect. The women hysterically begged their friends to shoot them rather than let the Indians get them. There were a dozen alarms which set the post frantic with fear. But nothing happened that night.

Next morning refugees still poured in, demoralized with fright. Should Little Crow attack now, nothing could prevent the massacre of every soul in the fort. But for some reason the attack was delayed. Why? The nervous young lieutenant paced the fort with anxious steps. About noon a challenge from a sentry changed to a shout of joy. Coming down a road from the north, at the double-quick, was a detachment of soldiers—Lieutenant Timothy J. Sheehan with the first reinforcements. Five hours later a second detachment came in from the south, after an all-night march of forty miles. There were more than two hundred and fifty refugees at the fort now. Among them were some resolute men who would make good fighters. Including these settlers, Sheehan, now the senior officer, marshaled about one hundred and eighty men, mostly raw recruits.

Still the Indians did not attack.[7] Every moment was used in strengthening the defenses.

Without warning on the morning of the 20th, a tall warrior, mounted on a splendid horse, rode up from the west and demanded a conference. It was Little Crow himself. He wanted to divert attention from his attack which was forming on the opposite side.

A sudden burst of firing announced the onslaught and the Sioux

---

[7] Sioux Indians afterward said Little Crow could not get his warriors to stop plundering long enough to follow him to the attack. Whatever the cause, the delay was fatal to the Indian plans.

leader rode for cover. With wild yells the Indians stormed the first line of defenses, outside the regular limits of the fort. Helter-skelter fled the soldiers for safety, with Sioux tomahawks flashing in their rear. So fierce was the charge that the redskins actually burst through the second line of defense, a row of log houses which formed the north wall of the fort and took possession of these barracks.

Still the defense reeled. Working like mad, Sheehan rallied his men on the parade ground. If they did not hold fast here, the fort was doomed. Two or three soldiers, hit, fell thrashing on the ground. The undisciplined troops began to waver. Simultaneously the Sioux came out from the buildings and formed for another charge. Sheehan's men began to retreat. The day seemed hopelessly lost.

And then came aid—aid so unexpected as to seem miraculous.

Among the few veteran soldiers at the fort was an old artillery sergeant with the unromantic name of Jones. Fort Ridgely had once been an artillery post and a few old cannon of various patterns and calibres were still parked there. Like all old gunners, Sergeant Jones loved his field pieces. To vary the monotony of garrison life, he had asked and received permission to drill some of the infantrymen in the principles of artillery practice. The soldiers took it up for fun. None of them had any idea that their lives and the lives of hundreds of others would ever hang upon their skill.

At this critical moment in the Sioux attack, Jones bethought himself of his amateur artillerymen and rusty old cannon. Here and there he hastily collected members of his gun squads and ran to where the ancient field pieces stood. There was some delay in getting things ready. The men were, after all, only infantrymen, and the old sergeant probably did some royal swearing before three guns were loaded. This was finished just as Sheehan's line began to melt before the Sioux fire and the threatened attack.

Now was the time. Everything depended upon the old artilleryman. His own wife and children were among the helpless non-combatants crowded in the south buildings of the fort.

"Aim in their center and fire as rapidly as possible," was the order.

Just as Sheehan, in despair, saw his recruits breaking for cover; just as Little Crow's warriors, with triumphant yells, began their final advance; just as the women in the south fort gave a concerted cry of terror, the ancient cannons spoke.

"Boom! Boom! Boom!"

Across the parade ground hurtled a heterogeneous collection of misfit cannon balls, canister and solid shot. Dismayed, the Indians halted.

Working like mad, the sergeant and his men rammed home a second round. Again the rusty field pieces spoke. It was too much for the Sioux. They could stand rifle fire—had done so right bravely. But the "wagon guns" appalled them. They wavered, began to retreat, and as a third discharge thundered among them, fled in panic, followed by the hysterical cheering of the soldiers.

Fort Ridgely was saved and Sergeant Jones was the hero of the day. The Sioux kept the fort surrounded, and even attempted another attack the following morning. But the age-worn cannon now were masters of the situation. Before the charge was well started, Sergeant Jones sent several shots among the hostiles and scattered them.[8] Little Crow had been wounded the first day. A sub-chief, Mankato, led that final abortive assault. The Indians quickly withdrew.

The defeat at Fort Ridgely was a solar-plexus blow to the Indians' hope of sweeping the white man out of Minnesota. They had suffered serious losses and the moral effect had been most discouraging.

[8] Jones was mentioned in the dispatches for his spectacular part in the battle. As for the modest hero himself, however, his only thought was of the workmanlike manner in which the guns were handled. In his terse report, still preserved, he stated that his amateur artillerymen and rusty cannon "gave much satisfaction . . . to all who witnessed the action."

2: THE WHITE MAN STRIKES BACK

THE DEFENSE OF NEW ULM

SHARING the post of greatest danger with Fort Ridgely was the little German frontier town of New Ulm, a few miles down the river. The morning after the agency massacre a small party of Indians were seen near the town but were driven off in a brief skirmish. Not much damage was done on either side but it threw New Ulm —already panic-stricken because of the inpouring hundreds of refugees with their tales of horror—into still greater terror.

Judge Charles E. Flandrau of the Supreme Court and ex-Sheriff Boardman of St. Peter rode with a company of volunteers to the threatened settlement. The Indians had gone when they arrived, and next day the town was not molested for Little Crow was busy with his attack on Fort Ridgely. But the Sioux had by no means forgotten New Ulm. In spite of their defeat at the fort they moved toward it. Early Saturday August 23rd, the smoke of burning buildings up the river showed that they were on their way.

Judge Flandrau, a man of great force of character, was elected commander of the defending forces. At the approach of the Sioux he formed his two hundred and fifty fighting men on the prairie a half mile west of the town. By ten o'clock they were skirmishing with Little Crow's advance guard.

Suddenly a brilliant spectacle unfolded itself. Five hundred Sioux warriors, with all the color of feathered head dresses, war paint and brilliant bead work, rode out of the woods and spread like a giant fan over the prairie. As they reached long rifle shot, they charged. The Sioux, yelling like fiends, looked so horrible that Flandrau's raw recruits began to retreat. A few more whoops and, in spite of the judge's efforts, the whole line fell back leaving the outer rows of houses of the town undefended. The Indians were soon shooting at New Ulm's citizens from the shelter of their own homes. Flandrau rode wildly up the hill and succeeded in rallying

34

his men. There they halted the Sioux advance. The crackling of rifle fire became incessant. The white men were hard pressed, but they held.

Then smoke came floating up from the lower end of the town. The Indians had slipped behind the defense and set some buildings ablaze. Now they advanced through the smoke. In a few minutes the whole lower part of New Ulm was burning. Bullets whined, in ever-increasing chorus, up the streets. Captain William Dodd, Flandrau's second in command, was killed. Captain Saunders was critically wounded with a ball through his body.

Under cover of the smoke, Little Crow massed his warriors in the shelter of some houses near the river. The charge in the morning had been so nearly a complete success that the Sioux believed a second attack would crush the whites. But by now New Ulm had been under fire for several hours and the men were steadying down.[1] The Sioux charge came, but a withering fire drove them back. Then, as the Indians withdrew, Flandrau led a fiery countercharge. It caught the Indians by surprise and drove them clear out of the city limits. Evening was falling and the firing shortly stopped.

During the night Flandrau ordered more than forty outlying buildings on the outskirts burned to the ground to prevent them from becoming rallying places for the savages on the morrow. A system of trenches was dug, and a large brick house made into a redoubt, garrisoned and munitioned. But there was no battle Sunday. The Sioux contented themselves with some long-range shooting. By noon Little Crow's warriors were in retreat.

SIBLEY TAKES COMMAND

Fort Ridgely and New Ulm definitely ended any probability that the Sioux would push the settlers out of eastern Minnesota. But Little Crow was not discouraged. The northeast, the north and

[1] "White men fight under a great disadvantage the first time they engage (the Indians). There is something so fiendish in their yells and terrifying in their appearance when in battle that it takes a good deal of time to overcome the sensation that it inspires"—Judge Flandrau's story of the battle.

even the south, down into Iowa where Inkpaduta had left a trail of blood years before at the Spirit Lake massacre, offered an un-limited field for his operations.

He withdrew his war parties into the wilderness for the present, content for a time to count his scalps and gloat over his booty. They had been repulsed, it is true, but, even so, the success of the week's raiding exceeded the Indians' most sanguine dreams. At one swoop the Sioux had won back much of their richest hunting country. Their camps were full of prisoners and plunder. Little Crow was a bigger man than ever among his people.

But a new figure was entering the picture. Colonel Henry H. Sibley, an old soldier in middle life, took command of the Minnesota troops. He had had wide experience, spoke French and the Dakota tongue and possessed a profound knowledge of Indian character.

Sibley reached the frontier in three days, and in four more his call for volunteers was answered by fourteen hundred men. They were raw, undisciplined and ill-equipped, but they were the only force on which Sibley could lay his hand. With them he marched toward Fort Ridgely. It took several days to reach the fort. On the way he kept his fatigue details busy burying the bodies of slaughtered settlers. He reached the fort on the afternoon of August 28th, to be received with wild joy by the people, who, he said, "seemed mad with excitement."

Next day he moved toward the Lower Agency, reaching it the last of August. His men buried Marsh's soldiers, together with more than twenty dead citizens. Traces of the handiwork of the Sioux were plentiful, but thus far not an Indian had been seen. Major J. R. Brown with two hundred men moved west along the river looking for hostiles and burying the dead. They camped at Birch Coulie the night of September 1st.

Little Crow was not asleep. His scouts watched, unseen, every movement of the army. Brown's movement was a beautiful oppor-tunity for the Sioux. As dawn broke there was a war whoop, fol-lowed by a sudden volley which swept into the camp from the birch woods near at hand. Dead and dying men, and kicking, screaming horses, littered the ground. The survivors of that deadly volley threw themselves behind their wagons and fought back. It was a short but terrific little battle. The Sioux poured into the camp such a storm of bullets that nearly every horse was killed or disabled, and annihilation threatened the whole command.

But Sibley at the agency heard the distant firing and marched immediately to Brown's assistance. The reinforcements reached Birch Coulie in the nick of time. As Sibley's column appeared, the Sioux withdrew up the valley. A picture of bloody wreckage was presented by Brown's camp. It was strewn with dead and dying men and horses. Some of the wagons were riddled like sieves. Of Brown's two hundred soldiers, twenty-four were dead and sixty-seven wounded, nearly fifty percent. Sibley retreated to Fort Ridgely to care for the wounded.

Birch Coulie wiped out the sting of New Ulm and Fort Ridgely for the Sioux. They considered honors even now. Sibley, on the other hand, saw that his raw levies were not ready for the job before them and went into camp to drill them into some sort of coherent military body. It was a big task and took time. Meanwhile Little Crow ranged far and wide.

He led one marauding expedition deep into northeastern Minnesota, with Hutchinson as its objective. Captain Richard Strout and a company of soldiers met him and were chased for miles, the Sioux almost riding into Cedar Mills on the strength of the wild retreat. But Hutchinson, now a fortified post like every frontier town, was too strong for the Indians. Little Crow, with more scalps and loot, returned to the old reservation camp.

THE BATTLE OF WOOD LAKE

While Sibley's army was learning its business, its commander took up wearisome days in a long-drawn negotiation with Little Crow. Hundreds of prisoners, mostly women and children, were in the hostile camp and great fear was held for their safety. Sibley, knowing Indians, feared that these helpless hostages would be murdered wholesale should he march against the Sioux.

The red chief proved more than his match in diplomacy, and Sibley finally gave up the negotiations.[2] Little Crow was making constant raids and keeping all Minnesota in an uproar. Finally, on September 18th, with sixteen hundred men and two pieces of artillery, Sibley marched northwest toward the Yellow Medicine River where the hostile village was reported to be.

Little Crow knew this march was in deadly earnest. He felt his handicaps. His warriors were fine natural fighters, but they completely lacked organization. They would not stand up to artillery fire. To maneuver them in battle was practically impossible. On the other hand, they were superior in mobility and were expert in scouting and ambush. In planning the fight with Sibley, the chief kept all these things in mind.

The road to the Sioux village lay through the deep timbered gorge of the Yellow Medicine. Sibley had to pass through it. As he marched past Wood Lake down this canyon, a volley of shots rang out half a mile ahead. Indians had fired into a party of foragers. Three men were down, one mortally wounded.

Major Welsh's command went at the double to the rescue. The foragers were saved, but heavy firing which broke out from the woods ahead showed that they were swarming with Sioux. Bullets were cutting the leaves from the trees overhead so that they fell in showers.

Little Crow had thrown a cloud of warriors across the road in front. Although the whites did not yet know it, two other large bodies of Indians lay hidden in ambush—one along the east side of the road, the other in a ravine to the right.

It was strange fighting for Sibley's men. The woods ahead looked deserted except for the spurts of rifle smoke and the sight of an occasional flitting figure. The constant piping of bullets overhead and the occasional smack as one found its mark, made the raw troops nervous. Welsh decided to charge. Into the woods went his

[2] Sibley was the center of a storm of abuse and criticism as he waited. The newspapers grew restive. One dubbed him "a snail who falls back on his authority and assumed dignity and refuses to march." Another referred to him as "the state undertaker with his company of grave diggers," an allusion to his burial of hundreds of dead settlers.

men but the foe they expected to meet had disappeared. Using the same tactics which were so fatal to Braddock a hundred years before, the Sioux slipped away from the direct front and poured in their fire from the flank. Welsh was forced to halt.

A staff officer came riding like the wind across the field with an order from Sibley to retire, but the stubborn major did not at once comply. Sibley sent another, this time peremptory, message to fall back at once. Then Welsh ordered a retreat.

Sibley's main body was formed on a low hill. Toward it Welsh started, carrying his wounded. The Sioux leaped in pursuit. There was a moment of hand-to-hand fighting. Then the soldiers began to run. Here was Little Crow's big chance. Had he been able to press home a charge at the backs of the fleeing troops, he might have cut Sibley's line in two. But Sibley rushed forward five companies under Colonel Marshall and the Indians were beaten back.

Then, too late, after the soldiers were formed and ready, the Sioux attacked in deadly earnest. For two hours they tried valorously to take the hill. Once a headlong charge on the extreme left came very near carrying home, but Major R. N. McLaren, with two companies of recruits, repulsed it.

Just then the Indians in the ravine were discovered. Backed by shells from the two guns, Marshall charged and drove them out. The Sioux had been roughly handled and were losing their zest for the fight. As the day wore on, the fire from the woods slackened. Finally, as if at a signal, the Indians disappeared.

Sibley, hampered by his many wounded, camped where he was.[3]

THE END OF LITTLE CROW

That must have been a gloomy night in the Sioux village. Little Crow recognized the completeness of his defeat in a final stand on a chosen battle ground. He could no longer hold his people together.

[3] An interesting sidelight, showing the character of Sibley, is the following: Several dead Sioux were found after the battle, although most of them were carried away. Next day Sibley published a general order expressing extreme pain and humiliation over the scalping of these Indians and threatening punishment for a repetition of the offense. "The bodies of the dead," read the order, "even of a savage enemy, shall not be subjected to indignities by civilized and Christian men."

The Sioux broke up their great camp and scattered all over the plains. Sibley said he permitted their escape because he knew that if pressed too closely they would slaughter their white captives. As a matter of fact, Little Crow did try hard to have the prisoners killed after the battle. But the chiefs saw their doom and wanted to soften the punishment. They refused. Little Crow's influence had ended.

Days passed. Through friendly Indians, Sibley got in touch with three trustworthy chiefs, offering amnesty and pardon if they would bring the prisoners to him. The offer was accepted. On the afternoon of September 26th, two hundred and sixty-nine captives were delivered, most of them women and children. All wore Indian clothing. There were some refined and educated women among them. Others were ignorant immigrant settlers. But their consideration for each other was beautiful to see as they helped the sick and assisted with the young children. Most of them cried with joy and relief. But some merely gave vacant stares. The scenes and experiences through which they had passed had left them dazed and stolid.

That night the rescued captives slept in the tents of the soldiers, the men taking the hard ground outside. They were sent down to Fort Ridgely the following day and their relatives—if any were left living—claimed them.

. . . .

The war in Minnesota was over. But there still remained to be written the punishment of its chief figures.

Sibley rounded up fifteen hundred of the Sioux and placed them in prisons at Fort Snelling and Mankato. The rest scattered far and wide over the plains, carrying the seeds of their grievance to the other tribes, the results of which will be noted later.

At a great court martial, three hundred and ninety-two prisoners, accused of extreme barbarity, were tried. Of these three hundred and seven were sentenced to death and sixteen to prison. President Lincoln commuted the death sentences of all but thirty-nine whose cruelties had been too clearly shown, and on December 28th a great concourse witnessed the execution of these unfortunates on a special gallows built for the purpose.

Little Crow was still at large. Although his followers had all deserted him, there were reports that he was gathering new strength and preparing for another invasion. Every day or so f esh rumors were printed in the newspapers and so much fear was attached to his name that it was practically impossible to get the settlers to return to their homes.

Nathan Lampson and his son Chauncey were deer hunting in the north woods on July 3rd, 1863. Stealing through the thickets, they surprised two Indians picking berries. Hostiles were still scattered all over the country. No Sioux was a friend. The elder Lampson fired, wounding one of the Indians. The other tried to help him on a horse. As the wounded Sioux attempted to fire at his father, Chauncey Lampson shot him dead. The other Indian mounted and escaped.

The Lampsons scalped the body and carted it to the neighboring town of Hutchinson. Nobody could identify it. Some claimed they noted a resemblance to Little Crow, but the complexion seemed too light. The mortifying corpse was thrown into the offal pit of a slaughter house.

Then came an unexpected revelation. A party of Indians was captured on Devil's Lake, among whom was a sixteen-year-old boy. He said he was a chief and asking for the commander of the troops by whom he was captured, made a statement of which the following is a part:

"I am the son of Little Crow; my name is Wo-wi-nap-sa. I am sixteen years old. . . . Father hid after the soldiers beat us last fall. He told me he could not fight against the white men, but would go below and steal horses from them . . . and then he would go away off. Father . . . wanted me to go with him to carry his bundles. . . . There were no horses . . . we were hungry . . . Father and I were picking red berries near Scattered Lake. . . . It was near night. He was hit the first time in the side, just above the hip. . . . He was shot the second time . . . in the side, near the shoulder. This was the shot that killed him. He told me he was killed and asked me for water. . . . He died immediately after."

Sibley read the statement and at once concluded that the Indian killed by the Lampsons was Little Crow. The corpse was hauled out of its noisome resting place and there was observed a mark of identification which could not be mistaken. A deformity of his right wrist, caused by a gunshot wound received in a family feud when he was a youth, was the mark.

So died Little Crow, at the height of his power the most feared red man in America; leader of the greatest massacre in history; a scholar and a gentleman after his way. He started on the white man's path but left it when his people's wrongs cried out to him. Reduced to stripping red berries to keep life in his frame, he was at last shot by wandering hunters and his body thrown into the stinking offal pit of a slaughter house.

II
War Spreads to the Plains
1864-1869

3: A CHIEF OF THE OGALALLAS

IN THE BEGINNING

LIFE was good on the high plains of the Dakotas before the white man came. The Teton Sioux wandered in leisurely, light hearted fashion wherever the whim moved them. Buffalo moved in dark masses on the grasslands; the Black Hills and the Rockies were populous with deer, beaver, bear and other game. The Sioux were great hunters, and starvation was usually far from their teepees. They were great warriors and near at hand were their traditional enemies, Crows, Pawnees, Flatheads, Shoshones and Blackfeet, who were so necessary to them, for how else should the Sioux braves win honor? Everything was ideally arranged for the simple happiness of this people. The skill of the squaws provided every necessity. The world was full of pleasant valleys; Wakan Tanka, the Great Mystery, smiled on his children.

In an Ogalalla teepee, about 1822, was born a baby boy. His father had no particular distinction, except that he died a drunkard. What the boy, Red Cloud, made of himself was due to his own personal traits, not to any family influence. There has never been a satisfactory explanation of how he got his name. No matter; he made it notable in history. His early years were typical of the boys of his tribe. He became a skillful hunter, a magnificent horseman, and could hold his own with any in feats of skill, speed, strength and agility. Very early he gained fame as a warrior and leader. Even in his early twenties he had his following.

The Teton Sioux loved fighting. Their five great tribes, the Ogalallas, Unkpapas, Sans Arcs, Brulés and Minneconjous, had frequent war parties in the field. Red Cloud had plenty of chances to distinguish himself.

The whole theory of war among the Sioux was different from that of the civilized white man. It resembled in many respects the feudal system of the middle ages. There was a certain wild chivalry, for example. A brave enemy was often spared rather than ruthlessly killed.[1] The warriors looked upon war as an opportunity to win honor. There was always greater rivalry to do some deed of daring, than merely to inflict damage upon the enemy.

Some of their exploits seem quixotic to our modern standards. The brave who charged into battle and struck his armed, unwounded enemy with his coup-stick or open hand, received more distinction for it than did the man who killed and scalped his enemy. The man who stole into a hostile camp and crept out leading a single horse whose lariat he had cut among the teepees was applauded more than the man who ran off a whole herd of ponies grazing unguarded outside of the village.

The analogy goes farther. Instead of definite military divisions, such as regiments, companies and squads, each with its appropriate officers, the Sioux fighting units were based on the prestige of various chiefs, much as medieval lords ranked according to the number of retainers they could muster. Renowned Sioux leaders had big bands of warriors. Each of these bands operated separately and retained the characteristics of an autonomous nation. It levied its own wars, moved to suit itself and was generally independent. Occasionally two or three bands would combine in a grand war party. But the idea of massing three or four thousand fighting men in the field and keeping them at it for months at a time was yet to come.

Living in this atmosphere of constant action, few of the Sioux noticed the black cloud, heavy with portent, which loomed on the horizon. The white man was beginning to seep across the plains in his strange, hysterical stampede over the mountains; was beginning to wander among the hills grubbing in the dirt, spoiling the little

[1] Sitting Bull's preservation of Frank Grouard and Little Assiniboine (Jumping Bull) are good examples of this frequent habit among the plains Indians. Yellow Nose, one of the most famous of the Northern Cheyenne warriors, was a Ute who had been captured and adopted into the tribe.

springs, for the dull yellow metal he prized above food and drink, above the love of his women, above honor even. There would be fighting—bitter, bloody fighting, not the glamorous, exciting battling of the Indian paladins—and the Sioux were to learn a new name, Red Cloud.

There had been war for some time in the south. The settlers in Kansas resented the presence of the Cheyennes and Kiowas on their frontier. The Indians were angered by the constant streams of immigrants who moved down the Santa Fé and Platte River trails on their way to California and Oregon. The caravans of covered wagons made much noise, what with the creaking wheels, the shouts of mule skinners, the cracking of whips, the bellowing of cattle, and the general hubbub which always accompanies the white man wherever he goes. As a result the buffalo and antelope moved out of the country. It was ruined as a hunting ground.

The exasperated Indians made more than one attack on these wagon trains. And the white men in revenge usually fired upon the next band they met—often killing Indians who knew nothing of any former attack and who approached them with the friendliest of intentions. This aroused still deeper enmity among the Indians and the vicious circle continued until all of western Kansas and Colorado were in a state of warfare.

In the summer of 1857, Colonel E. V. Sumner campaigned against the Cheyennes. There were several clashes with troops in later years. And on the morning of November 29th, 1864, Colonel J. M. Chivington, a fanatical ex-preacher, with a regiment of "hundred days men," led the notorious Sand Creek massacre, in which he destroyed the friendly Cheyenne villages of Black Kettle and White Antelope, although they were under the protection of Major Wynkoop of Fort Lyon.

The Sand Creek massacre had far-reaching effects. The Cheyennes carried the war pipe to the Sioux, and Sitting Bull and other Sioux chiefs smoked it with them.[2] But Red Cloud was already definitely on the war path. Streaming westward, harried out of Minnesota, had

---

[2] Stanley Vestal, "Sitting Bull, Champion of the Sioux," p. 70. References to this work hereafter are by permission of the publishers, Houghton Mifflin Co.

come the Santee Sioux by hundreds, telling of Little Crow's war and the causes of it. Red Cloud and the Tetons heard and sympathized.

When, in the summer of 1865, Major General G. M. Dodge, commanding the Department of the Missouri, sent four columns of troops up the Missouri to further punish the Santees, the Teton Sioux joined their relatives in the war. Red Cloud rode and skirmished with the soldiers under Generals Sully, Conner, Cole and Walker. He joined the Cheyennes in an attack on Colonel Sawyer's military train which was marching up the Niobrara River to open a wagon train to the Montana gold fields. The fight was inconclusive. Sawyer paid Red Cloud an indemnity of a wagon load of sugar, coffee and rice on his promise to withdraw. The chief was true to his promise but some other Sioux came up who had not shared in the provisions and the soldiers had to fight in spite of the indemnity.

The Harney-Sanborne Treaty was signed in 1865. Spotted Tail, Man-Afraid-of-His-Horses [3] and other chiefs conceded the white man a safe passage through their lands. Red Cloud was not present. He was in his teepee critically wounded by a Crow arrow. Shortly before, on a raid against the Crows, an arrow fired from ambush had struck him squarely in the middle of the back and passed completely through so that its barbed head stuck out from his breast. He was carried out of danger and a medicine man had tried to draw the arrow out. The feather at the back and the barbs in front prevented the shaft from being withdrawn. At length the medicine man had cut off the head, after which the arrow was drawn out. By a miracle no vital organs were pierced and Red Cloud eventually recovered.

He was set against allowing the provisions of the Harney-Sanborne Treaty to be carried out. More far-sighted than his fellows, he saw the inevitable disaster to his country if ever the white man were allowed to set foot firmly in it. With Red Cloud urging them on, the turbulent younger warriors of the Sioux kept up a series of dep-

[3] "His Sioux name, Tashunka Kokipapi, is not properly interpreted; it really means that the bearer was so potent in battle that the mere sight of his horses inspired fear."—Frederick W. Hodge, "Handbook of American Indians," Bureau of American Ethnology Bulletin 30.

redations which at length forced the government to send out a second treaty commission in the spring of 1866 to offer the Sioux new terms.

RED CLOUD'S DEFIANCE AND THE FOUNDING OF FORT PHIL KEARNY

The great council was held at Fort Laramie. Red Cloud was present. He was now the foremost warrior of his nation and his influence was steadily thrown against the white man's proposals.

A spectacular incident broke up the council, precipitated war, and made Red Cloud, for the time at least, supreme arbiter of his people. While the council was in session, a column of troops, led by General Henry B. Carrington, rode up. They were on the way to the Powder River country, in defiance of the very spirit of the peace council, to erect a row of forts, and apparently did not even know the council was in session.

Carrington rode up, dismounted, and was being introduced to the members of the commission, when Red Cloud dramatically leaped on the platform under the shade of the pine boughs, pointed to Carrington's colonel's shoulder straps [4] and shouted that he was the "White Eagle" who had come to steal a road through the Indians' land. The dramatic suddenness of the gesture riveted the attention of the Indians. Then he turned and, followed by every eye, sprang from the platform, ordered his teepees struck and led his band out on the prairie, openly announcing he was going on the war path.

That broke up the council. For some days the older chiefs of the other Sioux bands remained sullenly in conclave, but their young men were melting away like snow in summer, to join the standard raised in such spectacular manner by Red Cloud. Finally in sheer self-defense, to protect their own prestige, the older chiefs followed. Red Cloud was the greatest figure in the Sioux Nation. He had

[4] Although a general officer in the Civil War, Carrington held a colonelcy in the regular army. As everybody knows the colonel's insignia is a silver eagle on the shoulder strap. This was the figure to which Red Cloud alluded in his dramatic charge.

made the Sioux come to him. Now they looked to him for orders.

In the meantime Carrington marched into the Powder River country looking for a spot to erect a fort. The government wanted a string of posts built to protect the Bozeman trail over which thousands of emigrants were ready to travel to the new gold districts of Idaho and Montana. Carrington found an ideal location on the banks of Piney Creek, a branch of the Powder River and began construction of Fort Phil Kearny. Later a second post, known as Fort C. F. Smith was built ninety-one miles to the north.

The establishment of Fort Phil Kearny was equivalent to a declaration of war, if any such declaration was needed. Red Cloud smoked with many chiefs and tribes in those days. He was the prime mover in the hostilities against the white man. But there were many who saw eye to eye with him in the matter. Crazy Horse, the young paladin of the Ogalallas was one. There were Black Shield and High Backbone of the Minneconjous, who were just as eager as he to fight. They knew that the white man was eating up their land, driving away their buffalo, destroying their forests.

The Sioux gathered in magnificent response to Red Cloud's call. At times their huge encampment extended for miles up and down the Little Goose River. Estimates of as high as fifteen thousand Indians were made for this camp, with upward of four thousand fighting men. This number is probably too high. But, even so, it was the most imposing fighting force the Sioux had ever put into the field.

4: FORT PERILOUS

THE CIRCLE OF DEATH

No FINER natural cavalry ever existed than the Sioux, according to such authorities as General George Crook and General Frederick Benteen. Yet they were unfitted for conducting a sustained siege. Their ideas of organization were the most rudimentary, discipline was utterly lacking as our modern armies know it, and they had no knowledge of scientific warfare. In spite of this, the Sioux, largely because of the leadership of Red Cloud, besieged Fort Phil Kearny for more than two years. There are writers who have denied that Red Cloud played the dominating role ascribed to him in the campaign. It is true that Indians are prone to exaggerate not only their own importance but that of the leaders of their individual bands, so that it is often difficult to discover who was the actual commander in a given encounter. Still the impression of Red Cloud's importance and of the part he played is too well established to be dismissed from history.

General Carrington began building the fort on July 15th. Less than forty-eight hours later, at daybreak of the 17th, the Indians made their first attack. Part of the post horses were stampeded, and in a brisk little fight two soldiers were killed and three wounded. Later that day, the same war party scooped up the outfit of Louis Gazzous, a traveling sutler, and killed six men. In the next twelve days five wagon trains were attacked, fifteen men killed and much livestock run off. On July 24th Carrington wrote for reinforcements. He already knew the implacability of his enemy.

The Sioux did not formally invest the fort. But they planted scouting parties everywhere about it. The soldiers found they had a foe who never slept. Did a herder stray from his guard? He was cut off and killed. Did a sentry expose himself on the palisade during a moonlit night? A bullet from the bush laid him low. Did a detachment of soldiers set out without an imposing display of power? They straightway had to fight for their very existence.

Even during the long, bitter cold spells the Indians kept the circle of death about the post. That was not like the Sioux, whose custom was to withdraw to their camps during cold weather. Better than anything else that showed the grim purpose of their leader.

There was an atmosphere of constant dread about the fort, reflected in the letters the soldiers wrote home. And the feeling was justified by the circumstances. In the first five months from August 1st to December 31st the Sioux killed one hundred and fifty-four persons at or near Fort Phil Kearny, wounded twenty more and captured nearly seven hundred head of livestock. Fifty-one times they made hostile demonstrations.

In spite of this constant pressure the men worked on the building of the fort with dogged courage. The country about was hilly but barren, and the nearest forests from which stockade posts could be obtained were seven miles away. An enormous amount of wood was required for the huge rectangular palisade, sixteen hundred feet long by six hundred feet wide, to say nothing of the corral for several hundred horses and mules and the forty-two buildings in the post. Large parties continuously felled timber and hauled it to the fort. At times this "wood train" numbered one hundred and fifty men.

All through those five months not a man left the stockade without knowing that he might never see it again. They worked with their rifles close at hand and a guard stood constantly under arms. Even so, men were frequently cut off and killed. Sometimes soldiers disappeared and no trace of them was ever found. That meant one thing: they had been captured and carried away for torture.[1]

---

[1] "A favorite method of torture was to 'stake out' the victim. He was stripped of his clothing, laid on his back on the ground and his arms and legs, stretched to the utmost, were fastened by thongs to pins driven into the ground. In this state he was not only helpless, but almost motionless. All this time the Indians pleasantly talked to him. It was all a kind of a joke. Then a small fire was built near one of his feet. When that was so cooked as to have little sensation, another fire was built near the other foot; then the legs and arms and body until the whole person was crisped. Finally a small fire was built on the naked breast and kept up until life was extinct."—Colonel Richard I. Dodge, "Our Wild Indians," p. 526.

CAPTAIN FETTERMAN'S BOAST

Captain William J. Fetterman was a soldier by birth, instinct and profession. His Civil War record was brilliant. He went to Fort Phil Kearny because it promised plenty of action. From the first he disapproved of Carrington's cautious tactics. Fetterman arrived in November. On December 6th he had a chance at the action he craved and an opportunity to test the mettle of his tawny foe.

On that day frantic signalling from the lookout on near-looming Pilot Hill showed that the wood train was attacked two miles from the fort and forced to corral. Fetterman, with forty men, including Lieutenants Grummond, Bingham and Wands, and Captain Fred H. Brown, dashed to the rescue, while Carrington and twenty-five troopers rode over the Piney to take the Indians in the rear.

Down the valley galloped the eager Fetterman. Dust rose ahead and they saw horsemen—Sioux. Guns began to speak and bullets kicked up little clouds of dirt around their horses' feet. But Fetterman's carbines were crackling too. The Sioux whipped their horses and rode hard down the valley. Five miles Fetterman chased them, his men shooting but not hitting any of the Indians. The wood train made its way on in to the fort unmolested.

Thus far the affair was fun. The pursuit turned a spur of the Sullivant Hills and the fort was shut out of view. In a twinkling the whole aspect of things changed. The Sioux stopped running. Other mounted warriors joined them. And now, yelping and shooting, they turned and charged.

At the Indian rush some of Fetterman's troopers whirled their horses and spurred as hard as they could for safety. He had only about twenty-five men left and the Sioux were four to one, but he held his ground. It looked as if it would be hand-to-hand in a minute, with the odds in favor of the enemy, when there was a clatter of hoofs, and Carrington galloped around the spur at the head of his detachment.

Not knowing how many soldiers were following Carrington, the Sioux rode off. Fetterman was saved. But for the timely arrival of the post commander it would have been all over but the scalp dance. As it was, Lieutenant Bingham and Sergeant Rogers were dead. Lieutenant Grummond barely escaped with his life from the circle of barbaric foes. Five other soldiers were wounded.

It was a clever ambuscade and almost worked. The plan was a favorite one with the Sioux and Cheyennes—a small decoy party to lead the foe into the reach of the main body of warriors. In this case Indian lookouts were observed on the hills signalling the troop movements. Red Cloud's plans miscarried but were later put into effect.

As for the fire-eating Fetterman, it would be supposed that he should have derived some wisdom from the episode. But the opposite appears to have been the case. Only a short time after the fight he said: "Give me eighty men and I'll ride through the whole Sioux Nation."

If that remark ever got to Red Cloud's ears, it probably caused him considerable grim amusement.

WHERE IS FETTERMAN?

Two weeks passed. The morning of Friday, December 21st, dawned bright and cheery, the sun gleaming on the snow in the hills. Carrington surveyed the almost completed fort with a creator's pride. One more consignment of logs, he estimated, would finish the hospital building, the last structure to be built.

That morning a wood train of fifty-five men started to the hills. At eleven o'clock the Pilot Hill lookout began violently signalling. The wood train had been attacked again.

"Boots and Saddles," sounded the bugles. Carrington quickly told off forty-nine men from the 18th Infantry and twenty-seven from the 2nd Cavalry for the relief. He ordered Captain James Powell, experienced and cool-headed, to take command, but Fetterman came up and begged so hard for the assignment, urging his seniority, that the general gave in. Lieutenant Grummond volunteered to lead the cavalry. Captain Brown, soon to be transferred to Fort Laramie, asked to go along. He considered Indians a sort of game to be hunted

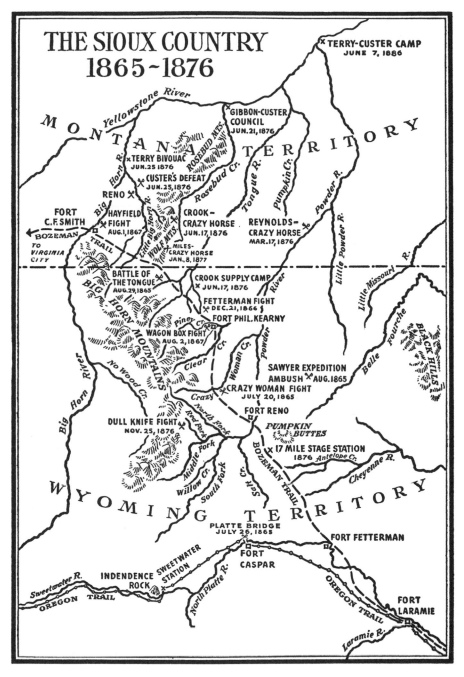

THE SIOUX COUNTRY
1865~1876

× TERRY-CUSTER CAMP
JUNE 7, 1886

M O N T A N A   T E R R I T O R Y

Yellowstone River

GIBBON-CUSTER
COUNCIL
JUN. 21, 1876

× TERRY BIVOUAC
JUN. 25 1876

× CUSTER'S DEFEAT
JUN. 25, 1876

RENO ×

FORT
C.F. SMITH

HAYFIELD
FIGHT
AUG. 1, 1867

CROOK—
CRAZY HORSE
JUN. 17, 1876

REYNOLDS—
CRAZY HORSE
MAR. 17, 1876

BOZEMAN

TO
VIRGINIA
CITY

MILES—
CRAZY HORSE
JAN. 8, 1877

BATTLE OF
THE TONGUE
AUG. 29, 1865

CROOK SUPPLY CAMP
× JUN. 17, 1876

FETTERMAN FIGHT
× DEC. 21, 1866

FORT PHIL. KEARNY

Piney Creek

WAGON BOX FIGHT
AUG. 2, 1867

Clear Cr.

BIG HORN MOUNTAINS

No Wood Cr.

Big Horn River

SAWYER EXPEDITION
AMBUSH × AUG. 1865

CRAZY WOMAN FIGHT
JULY 20, 1865

FORT RENO

DULL KNIFE FIGHT
NOV. 25, 1876

PUMPKIN
BUTTES

× 17 MILE STAGE STATION
1876 Antelope Cr.

BOZEMAN TRAIL

BLACK HILLS

Belle Fourche

Little Missouri R.

Little Powder R.

Powder R.

Pumpkin Cr.

Tongue R.

Rosebud Cr.

Cheyenne R.

W Y O M I N G   T E R R I T O R Y

PLATTE BRIDGE
JULY 26, 1865

FORT
CASPAR

FORT FETTERMAN

INDENDENCE
ROCK

SWEETWATER
STATION

Sweetwater R.

OREGON   TRAIL

North Platte R.

OREGON TRAIL

FORT
LARAMIE

Laramie R.

53

and was crazy "to get a scalp." A couple of old Indian fighters, Wheatley and Fisher, likewise went, with their new Henry breech-loading rifles which they "wanted to try on the red-skins." Every man was mounted, including the infantry, and they carried carbines and revolvers or Springfield muskets. Ammunition was low so they were not very well supplied. Still, they looked formidable enough as they rode out of the fort, eighty-one officers and men. Now was the time for Fetterman to "ride through the Sioux Nation."

Carrington, who knew his reckless subordinate, seems to have feared that some such thought was in his mind. He gave Fetterman specific orders: "Relieve the wood train, drive back the Indians but on no account pursue the Indians beyond Lodge Trail Ridge." To make sure he was not misunderstood, he repeated the orders to Grummond.

Instead of heading south of the Sullivant Hills where he heard the firing, Fetterman rode north of the hills toward Lodge Trail Ridge, which he occupied with his men in skirmish order shortly after noon. As he did so, the lookout signalled the wood train was no longer being attacked.

Now an alarming thing happened. Fetterman's command, after a brief halt on the ridge, disappeared on the other side. He had deliberately disobeyed orders.

. . . .

Fetterman perhaps merited all the censure that has been heaped on his head for that disobedience. But a wiser man than he might well have fallen victim to the uncanny skill of the trap which was prepared for him.

As he mounted the ridge he saw a handful of Indians below him, riding so daringly near that the hot impulse to pursue could not be denied. How was he to know that, in the ravines running from each side of the draw, hid the Sioux and Cheyennes in hundreds, their mounted men clustering at the mouth of the ravine, to close the door of the trap, while others in scores lay in the grass across the line of march?

The handful of warriors who so tantalized Fetterman were ten picked men, chosen as a high honor for this tremendously dangerous post. One of them was the famous Big Nose, brother of the great Cheyenne chief Little Wolf. As the soldiers started after the audacious decoys, Big Nose, greatly daring, whipped his horse back and forth in front of the troops, so close he seemed to be right among them, yet escaped from the hail of bullets unscathed.

At last the ten Indians divided into two groups, riding apart then criss-crossing. It was the signal to close in.

A wild whooping, a rush and the Cheyennes charged. Then the whole mass of Indians swept around the little band of soldiers. Some rode clear through the blue line. The troops grew rattled. Fetterman, Brown and the infantry stopped and became separated from Grummond's cavalry. These men died in the first fierce rush of the savages, stabbed and clubbed to death as they stood. But Grummond gathered his troopers around him on the ridge, surrounded by the yelling horde. Arrows glinted like a swarm of grasshoppers flashing across the sky.[2]

Suddenly, according to the Indian account, the officer commanding the cavalry (Grummond) went down, shot or beaten out of his saddle. The troopers grew panicky. Remorselessly the Indians followed them as they tried to retreat up the ridge. There was a final great rush, a desperate smother of flashing lances, tomahawks and clubs. Then all was quiet except for the whooping of the victors. Fetterman's command was dead to a man. His boast had proved empty and bitterly tragic.[3]

THE BLOODY TRAIL OF DISASTER

Back at the fort, Carrington, noting with alarm that Fetterman had disobeyed orders, looked around for somebody to send after him. Five minutes after the command disappeared heavy firing

[2] Most of the Indians in this battle were armed only with bows and arrows. A few had old smooth-bore muskets. A very few must have had rifles. Only six of Fetterman's men died from bullet wounds. The rest were killed by arrows, lances or clubs.

[3] George Bird Grinnell gives the Indian story of this battle in full, "The Fighting Cheyennes," pp. 230–235. References to and quotations from this book used hereafter are with the permission of and by arrangement with the publishers, Charles Scribner's Sons.

broke out. The roar of many guns was continuous and increased in volume. Everyone knew a hard battle was in progress. Surgeon Hines was sent with an orderly, with instructions to join Fetterman if possible. Hines quickly returned. There were too many Indians in the hills.

At that Carrington ordered Captain R. Ten Eyck, with every man who could be spared, to follow Fetterman. Followed by fifty-four soldiers, the captain galloped down the trail and began to ascend the ridge. It was noticed that the firing was diminishing in volume. What had happened? Were the Indians driven off? Or were the soldiers beaten? Carrington was nearly crazed with anxiety. He knew the men were ill supplied with ammunition. Then, just before Ten Eyck reached the summit, with three or four scattered shots the firing abruptly ceased altogether.

Ten Eyck in turn disappeared beyond the ridge. In a few minutes an orderly came spurring down the hill at the dead run. He rode into the fort with a message which filled every listener with dread.

"The valley on the other side of the ridge is filled with Indians, who are threatening me," wrote Ten Eyck. "The firing has stopped. No sign of Fetterman's command. Send a howitzer."

Back went the orderly with word that reinforcements were coming. Forty men followed hard at his heels. At the same time Carrington armed every noncombatant man in the post, even released prisoners from the guard house to man the palisades. No howitzer could be sent for lack of horses.

When Ten Eyck crossed the ridge, more than two thousand Indians were in the valley he estimated. There was no fighting going on. The warriors were dashing back and forth, yelling, their war bonnets flying in the breeze, the dust rising. It was cold. The temperature was falling, presaging the blizzard soon to come. Ten Eyck did not descend the hill until the reinforcements arrived. By that time the Indians were gone.

Cautiously Ten Eyck moved down the road. Quite without warning he came upon the ghastly evidence of a terrible disaster. In a little space enclosed by huge rocks were the bodies of Fetterman and Brown and forty-seven of their men. This was where the infantry had been overwhelmed. It was a horrible sight. The bodies of the dead were stripped, scalped, shot full of arrows and mutilated.[4]

Fetterman and Brown had bullet holes in their left temples from weapons held so close that the powder had burned their faces. They had "saved their last shots for themselves," to escape capture and torture.

Ten Eyck brought the forty-nine corpses to the fort in wagons. It was now bitter cold and night was setting in. With darkness, preparations were made to resist the expected Indian attack. Double guards were placed and in every barrack a non-commissioned officer and two men stood watch. The surviving officers did not sleep. But the night passed without attack.

Morning dawned cold and blustery with a blizzard threatening. Carrington, disregarding the advice of his officers, took eighty men and went to learn the fate of Grummond and the thirty-two missing men. As he left, he ordered every woman and child placed in the magazine with an officer sworn not to allow a single one to fall into the Indians' hands alive. If the Indians captured the fort, he was to blow up the magazine.

Evidences of the fight multiplied as Carrington reached the fatal ridge. Dead cavalry horses were scattered along the trail. Here and there they found bodies of slaughtered soldiers. A quarter of a mile beyond the scene of greatest carnage lay Grummond. Still farther were the corpses of a dozen men, grouped together with many empty cartridge shells about them. To one side were the dead frontiersmen, Wheatley and Fisher, with a heap of empty shells as evidence that they had sold their lives dearly.[5] All of the bodies were scalped and mutilated.

Every man was now accounted for. Eighty-one were dead. After the peace treaty the Indians admitted twelve killed and about sixty

[4] "Years afterwards the Sioux showed a rough, knotty war club of burr oak, driven full of nails and spikes, which had been used to beat the soldiers' brains out. It was still covered with brains and hair, glued to it in clotted blood." —J. P. Dunn, "Massacres of the Mountains," p. 495.

[5] "Within a few hundred feet of this position were found ten ponies and sixty-five great gouts of blood which had flowed from the death wounds of as many Indians. No ponies and no death spots were found anywhere else."—Dunn, "Massacres of the Mountains," p. 496.

wounded on their side. But years later the Cheyennes said that the dead warriors, laid out side by side, made two long rows, perhaps fifty or sixty men.[6]

There has been much dispute as to who led the Indians in this battle. Red Cloud said he commanded. High Backbone, the Minneconjou, has also been named as have Black Leg and Black Shield. But it is probable that the real commander of the Indians was Crazy Horse who was just beginning to build his reputation as the greatest fighter the Sioux Nation ever produced.

PORTUGEE PHILLIPS' RIDE

Carrington brought the dead back to the fort. That night the threatening sky fulfilled its portent. A terrific blizzard broke loose. The thermometer fell to thirty degrees below zero. Snow piled up so rapidly against the stockade that details of men had to work constantly to shovel it away lest it pile high enough to allow the Indians to climb over. Sentries could stand the intense cold only twenty minutes at a time. Even with quick reliefs there were many frozen feet, ears, noses and fingers.

But for the blizzard the Indians might have followed their advantage by attacking the fort itself. According to their own account this was a part of the plan.[7] To the people at the fort arrival of cold weather was providential.

Southward, two hundred and thirty-six miles, lay Fort Laramie, with reinforcements, ammunition and supplies. Word must be gotten through. There was no telegraph, so a courier had to take it. Carrington called for volunteers.

Several old plainsmen were in the post and many veteran soldiers, but they shook their heads. That ride, over a broken, snow-covered country, even in times of peace, meant almost certain death by freezing, with the temperature where it was and the blizzard raging so

---

[6] "There is scarcely a doubt that each of the sixty-five bloodspots on the field meant a dead Indian. Wounded Indians leave a battle field with wonderful celerity and one who cannot move until he has bled freely may safely be counted as dead or mortally wounded."—*Ibid.*, p. 500.

[7] Grinnell mentions this in "The Fighting Cheyennes," p. 227.

it was hard to see a hundred yards ahead. With the country swarming with hostile Indians the odds were a hundred to one against any man rash enough to attempt it.

But there was one man willing to take the risk. John Phillips, commonly known as "Portugee," was an Indian fighter, trapper and scout. He knew the country and offered to go.[8] Carrington gave him his own horse, a blooded Kentucky runner, the swiftest animal in the post. Wrapping himself in a huge buffalo coat, with a little hardtack for himself and a sack of grain for his horse, he passed out through a side gate into the swirling storm.

Nobody ever got the full details of that ride but it will always remain one of the epics of the West. At first he walked in the blackness of the night storm. For hours he led his horse, stopping at suspicious noises. He expected to be seen in the first half mile but no Indian yelled. With the howling wind whipping the snow around him, he mounted at last and spurred his horse along, across the Piney and past frozen Lake De Smet. Behind him the lights of the fort grew dim and disappeared.

Gallop—gallop—on through the storm, plunged Portugee Phillips. The miles fell behind him like the snowflakes he shook from his furry shoulders. The Indians were in their teepees, not dreaming that any white man would face the fury of this storm. And Portugee Phillips rode on and on.

Day dawned and still the wind whirled the snow. A short stop to feed his horse and cram a few crackers down his own throat, a handful of snow for a drink, and Portugee Phillips was in the saddle again. How he guided his horse across that wilderness, is explained only by the instinct which is sometimes possessed by those perfectly attuned to the wilds. From the Big Horn Mountains the blizzard swept with unslackened fury, piling in drifts from five to twenty feet deep. The storm prevented his seeing any landmarks. The trail itself was covered by the drifts. Yet on he rode, as unerring as a hound on the slot.

[8] Portugee Phillips was moved by sorrow for the widow of Lieutenant Grummond, a young woman freshly out from the East, and perhaps a tenderer emotion, according to her story, "My Army Life." Mrs. Grummond later became General Carrington's second wife.

Night fell, and still the good steed breasted the snow. In the homes of civilization happy families gathered around their hearths in the light and warmth of their homes. But alone, a dot in the icy waste, Portugee Phillips was riding for the lives of the women and children at Fort Phil Kearny. Just at dawn he reached Horse Shoe station, forty miles from Laramie, and one hundred and ninety miles from Phil Kearny. He telegraphed his news to Laramie. Fortunately he did not trust the telegraph. The message never got through. After a brief rest he rode on.

Icicles formed from his beard. His hands, knees and feet were frozen. He looked more like a ghost than a man. But still, with indomitable purpose, he urged his failing horse over the trail.

It was Christmas Eve and they were holding high revel at Fort Laramie. A grand ball was in progress at "Bedlam," the officers' club. Beautiful women, garbed in silks and satins, and gallant officers, in brilliant dress uniforms, made the interior a splendid kaleidoscope of changing color. The sound of violins, the laughter of the ladies, and the gay banter of the brave men who were taking holiday from military cares, created a symphony of cheery sound.

Above this happy noise came suddenly the sharp challenge of a sentry. It was followed by the shouting of men in the fort enclosure and a rush of running steps outside, coupled with a ringing call for the officer of the day. The dancing stopped. Officers and ladies grouped themselves at doors and windows, gazing out at the snow-covered parade ground. A horse lay there, gasping its last, fallen from exhaustion. And reeling, swaying like a drunkard, a gigantic, fur-clad figure staggered toward the hall. In through the door he stumbled and stood for a moment, supporting himself on the lintel while his eyes blinked in the unaccustomed light. Then seeing the post commander, he told a story of horror which put a period to the festivities that night—the story of the Fetterman disaster.

As he gasped out his story and appeal for reinforcements, he swayed, then fell to the floor, unconscious from overexposure and exhaustion. Kind hands lifted him and carried him to a bed. Even with his rugged physique it took him weeks to recover from the terrible ordeal. To this day his ride remains unparalleled in American history.

5: THE LAST DAYS OF FORT PHIL KEARNY

THE ENEMY OF THE WHITE MAN

THE Fetterman disaster shocked the whole United States. Over night the government discovered it had a real Indian war on its hands. Four companies of infantry marched at once to Fort Phil Kearny and fresh supplies of ammunition and other stores were dispatched in response to the message Portugee Phillips had brought.[1]

Fetterman died because he disobeyed his chief, but a scapegoat was needed, and Carrington, who was not remotely to blame, was removed from his post and transferred to Fort Caspar. Colonel Wessells succeeded him. Carrington demanded a military investigation but not until twenty years later was it held. Then he was fully exonerated of any lack of soldierly discretion, courage or foresight.

The long winter dragged on. Red Cloud, the implacable enemy of the white man, stubbornly maintained his grip on the fort. He had plenty of warriors although many Sioux had retired to favorite camp grounds, such as the Crazy Woman canyon and the Powder River valley, to "hole up." There they spent the time in leisure, with dancing, feasts and other Indian merry-making, while the grim chief sat in his exposed teepee on Little Goose River, or rode with a few of his "Bad Faces" to reconnoitre the fort.

Wessells tried a winter campaign but the cold was too severe. The troops were recalled until spring came.

Red Cloud lacked the united support of his people during this trying period. He had a constant struggle to keep the Sioux interested in his "siege" of the fort. Man-Afraid-of-His-Horses, the real chief of the Ogalallas, was very jealous of Red Cloud's spectacular rise.

[1] The sequel to Portugee Phillips' ride is interesting. Records show he was paid $300 by the government for that cruel ride "and other scouting duties." But his exploit was eventually to cost him far more than the peril and suffering. The Sioux swore vengeance. Six years later they killed all his stock, depriving him of his sole property. He died in 1883 at Cheyenne, Wyoming. The government paid his widow $5,000 on her claim for Indian depredations.

He hated to play second fiddle. On June 12th he made overtures of peace to the government. At that time he told a peace commission sent out from Washington that his people wished to end the war. Then he spoiled the whole thing by asking for ammunition. It was refused. Chagrined, Man-Afraid-of-His-Horses returned to the wilderness. Red Cloud was still in the ascendancy. That chief's success in the campaign thus far had given him tremendous prestige, a prestige further enhanced by the failure of Man-Afraid-of-His-Horses.

Red Cloud continued to hector the fort throughout June and July. As August approached the Sioux planned another decisive blow, similar to the Fetterman victory. Led by High Backbone, Crazy Horse, and other famous fighters, a force of from one to three thousand warriors gathered at Red Cloud's camp. The blow was struck August 2nd. A wood-chopping detail was cutting fuel for the post, with an escort under Captain James Powell. Powell had been forced to divide his meagre detachment to take care of all the choppers. Twelve men under a sergeant were sent to the camp in the forest. Another sergeant with thirteen men escorted the wood train to and from the fort. Powell, with Lieutenant J. C. Jenness and the remaining twenty-six men, established his headquarters on an open plain about a thousand yards across.

Many Indians had been reported in the woods. Trouble was brewing and Powell made preparations. The wood haulers' wagons were made of inch boards, not able to turn a rifle bullet, but a protection against arrows. Powell had fourteen of these wagon beds dismounted and dragged into an oval corral near the tents where the soldiers slept. Across the openings at the ends stood other wagons on wheels. The supplies and ammunition were placed inside. A recent consignment of the latest type firearms—the new Springfield-Allen rapid-fire rifles—had been received. Powell's men had these guns, together with a supply of Colt revolvers and plenty of cartridges for all.

Powell's premonition of danger was speedily fulfilled. Early in the morning a daring band of young warriors swooped down on the wood-train horse herd and stampeded it. This was the opening blow.

The Indians had made elaborate plans to "eat up" the entire detachment.

WHITE MAN'S RETRIBUTION

Through the trees slipped a swarm of Sioux, most of them on foot. Only a small proportion had guns, but they were better supplied in this respect than they had been the winter before.

Wood choppers appeared ahead. The leading warriors began to shoot. Presently they saw men running across the open space to the wagon box corral. These were soldiers and choppers, chased out of the woods. Four bodies, bristling with arrows, lay among the pines, where the Sioux had caught them. But the rest reached the corral, raising the total inside to thirty-two.

The wagon box corral squatted out there in the open, silent, apparently untenanted, but with an air of menace about it. Over the top of the boxes blankets had been thrown, and between them were piled sacks of grain, ox yokes, logs and other objects. Not a movement could be seen. How many men were in there the Indians had no way of knowing. The chiefs decided to take no chances. They had plenty of warriors. It seemed sure that if they all rushed the corral at once, it ought to be easy to ride over it and kill all the white men. The cry went around to form a line at the edge of the woods.

In the little fort, Powell was coolly telling off the best shots, with two or three guns each, while the poor shots were instructed to load rifles. Nobody expected to survive the fight but they were going to make the hostiles pay for every life they took. Some of the men preferred the barricades between the wagons to the wagons themselves. One knelt behind a barrel of beans; another chose a barrel of salt. Some attached loops to their triggers so that at the last moment they could place the muzzles of their rifles at their heads and pull the triggers with their boot toes, escaping capture and torture.

By now the Sioux were ready to charge. There were some famous fighters among them. High Backbone and Crazy Horse have been mentioned. Crow King, American Horse and Big Crow were also present. Of course Red Cloud was the central figure.

A chief—probably Red Cloud himself—was seen giving the signal for the charge by whirling a blanket over his head. Whipping their ponies and yelling their war cries, the Sioux broke out of the woods and bore down on the corral at a dead run. In a charge on a fortification of any kind, there was always great rivalry among the plains Indians as to who should first touch the breastworks, as it counted coup for the warrior. The charging braves expected a volley, then silence while the defenders reloaded, permitting them to reach the corral before a second volley. But a bad thing happened.

The first volley crashed out, knocking many from their saddles. The rest kept on. But to their amazement there was no pause in the firing. A steady stream of lead poured from the wagon boxes—the new repeating rifles. On came the Sioux, howling across the plain, a wave of murder. The withering blast mowed down their best warriors, leaving the wake of the charge strewn with stricken men and horses. The sweeping front broke in two at the center, and the two wings raced around each side of the fort, pouring into the wagon beds a storm of bullets and arrows. More riders dropped, but still they grimly rode around and around the corral in a vain effort to pierce it. There was not one undefended point. From every angle the little fort spat fire and lead. The Indians grew discouraged and retreated to the woods.

The Sioux could not understand the terrible effectiveness of the white man's murderous fire. They finally seemed to have decided that the corral contained many more men than they had at first supposed to keep up such a continuous stream of bullets.

The garrison had time now to catch its breath and to check up losses. Lieutenant Jenness was dead and with him Privates Haggerty and Doyle. Others were wounded. But the survivors were still brimful of fight.

A council of Sioux chiefs was being held out of range, and on top of a near hill some of the warriors began signalling with pocket mirrors to other Indians over the ridge several miles away, telling them to come on. A different plan of attack was decided upon by the council. This time most of the warriors with guns crept up through the grass and bushes and opened a heavy fire on the corral. With their wonderful ability at concealing themselves, many of them got within close rifle range. Most of their guns were old smooth bores, but there were some new carbines, trophies of the victory over Fetterman, and a few other rifles. The old Indian weakness in marksmanship asserted itself and the shooting was all too high. The tops of the wagon boxes were riddled, but little damage was done to the defenders.

To this fire the white men responded occasionally. Now and again some warrior, growing bold, would expose himself; a rifle would crack from one of the wagon boxes; and he would crumple to the ground, an inert corpse, or else drag himself away, crippled and out of action. But for the most part the defenders were silent.

The Sioux must have concluded at last that they had killed most of the people in the corral. By this time many other Indians had arrived, summoned by the flashing mirror signals. A charge on foot was the plan.

In a huge V or wedge the Sioux ran forward, their naked bodies painted, their war bonnets fluttering, their war cries filling the air. But again the fearful blast of flame and lead burst in their faces. With the highest courage they ran forward in spite of the spray of death which kept eating out their front ranks. They came so close that the defenders said afterward that they could see the whites of their eyes. Some of the white men seized knives preparing for a last ditch hand-to-hand fight. Then suddenly the Sioux had enough. They scattered and ran for cover.

No braver fighters ever lived than those Sioux. Going up against a sustained fire which they did not understand but which left their dead scattered all over the field, the naked warriors prepared for still another charge. This time it was on horseback, the painted riders yelling challenges to each other to be the first to touch the corral. Again the explosion of flame from the wagon boxes. Again the stubborn rush in the face of death; the reeling of the line at last; and the final breaking up in flight.

It was late in the afternoon. Red Cloud and his chiefs were

through. There was, however, one more duty to perform. All around the corral lay the bodies of the slain. It was a point of honor that these bodies should be removed. A cloud of skirmishers went forward again and put the corral under a hail of lead. All the dead and wounded in easy reach were taken to the hills. Then the bravest warriors crept forward to bring out the bodies near the enclosure. Taking one end of a long rope made out of many lariats tied together, an Indian would riggle up and fasten the rope to a dead comrade's ankles. The men at the other end of the rope would drag the body back to safety, the rescuing brave returning under the cover of his shield.

While this was going on, the report of a cannon was heard, and over the hill came a line of blue uniforms. Major John E. Smith's relieving force had arrived from the fort. The rescuers could scarcely believe their eyes when the defenders crawled out of the corral as the Indians retreated. Three men were dead and three more lay wounded in the corral. Add to this the four wood choppers killed, and the white loss was seven dead and three wounded.

There is a striking disparity between the white and Indian estimates of the Sioux loss. Preposterous stories have been told in some accounts of fifteen hundred Indians having been put out of action during the battle. This is plainly ridiculous. According to some estimates there were not even fifteen hundred Indians in the battle. But equally unconvincing are some of the Indian stories. Some of the Sioux accounts say that only five or six were killed and as many wounded on their side during the fight. Indians have the habit of listing only the dead whose names they can remember. This may be the case with these estimates. But I am of the belief that they err on the side of conservatism almost as badly as the wild tales of the whites vary in the opposite direction. Captain Powell estimated one hundred and eighty killed and wounded. This, too, may be high, but it is probably closer to correct than either of the other figures. Remember that Powell was a veteran of the Civil War, and used to the appearance of a stricken field. His estimate is very likely close. The Sioux had charged in battle array and many of the white defenders were expert marksmen. No less than three charges had been broken up by the riflery of the soldiers. Under these considerations Powell's figures do not seem very far out of line.

THE END OF FORT PHIL KEARNY

The Sioux had regarded Red Cloud as invincible and the Wagon Box affair was a crippling blow to his prestige. Hundreds of warriors left his camp and went buffalo hunting. But the grim Ogalalla held to his purpose, to force the evacuation of the fort. As long as he kept his war parties around it, there was no chance for travel on the Bozeman trail. Somehow he held the rest of the Sioux together.

Winter came on again but the following spring Red Cloud's patience was rewarded. The Fetterman disaster had led the government to investigate the situation in Wyoming. In the spring of 1868 a peace commission met with the Sioux chiefs at Laramie on April 29th. The central figure was Red Cloud. His terms were definite and he never abated from them for one minute: The Bozeman trail must be closed. The government forts must be abandoned.

At last the commission agreed to all Red Cloud demanded. In consideration of a promise that the Indians would not interfere in the construction of the Northern Pacific Railroad, far south of their hunting grounds, the government ceded the entire Powder River country including the Black Hills and agreed to abandon all forts and withdraw the troops.

It was a smashing victory for Red Cloud, but he showed his distrust of the white man's word by refusing to be a party to the treaty or signing it until the troops were actually withdrawn. Then, when he had received tangible proofs that the government intended to abide by its promise, he signed, on November 6th.

In the meantime, a memorable event took place on the Piney. On a bright summer day in August, the soldiers, in full view of hundreds of their Sioux foes, hauled down the flag from the masthead of Fort Phil Kearny and marched out of the post they had built and defended at such cost of blood and suffering.

"They knew not the reason why" except that they had their

orders. Many a veteran looked with black rage at the hills which hid the dark warriors who had so long besieged them.

No sooner had the soldiers marched out of one side of the fort, than the Sioux entered at the other. Red Cloud, who had fought so long and schemed so constantly for this event, must have been there. If so, it was a moment of supreme triumph for him. How his heart must have swelled as he watched his yelling warriors apply the torch to the palisades. With what an ecstasy of pride must he have looked at the great black pillar of smoke which went rolling up to the sky, carrying with it the last vestiges of the white man—for the time at least.

6: THE GRIEVANCE OF THE CHEYENNES

CHIVINGTON'S MARCH

NORTH of old Fort Lyon stretched a rugged, barren country, dividing the plains from the mountains. Today much of it is a smiling vista of green, irrigated Colorado fields, but in November, 1864, it was a sterile waste, covered with monotonous clusters of sagebrush and soapweed.

In spite of its barrenness, the region had for many years been a favorite wintering ground of the Southern Cheyennes. That fall the big bend of Sand Creek, thirty miles north of the fort, was populous with teepees. Here were the villages of Black Kettle, White Antelope and War Bonnet. In their warm buffalo-hide lodges they defied the rigor of the elements. With a sufficiency to eat and limitless time to while away in merry-making, they lived a happy, carefree life.

The Cheyennes were a race of warriors, but now they were at peace with the world. Largely because of Mo-ke-ta-va-ta (Black Kettle), they had kept out of trouble with the white men as much as the ever-aggressive, arrogant paleface would let them.

Only the previous August the chief had written a letter to Major Colley at Fort Lyon, saying: "We received a letter from Bent wishing us to make peace. We held a council . . . All come to the conclusion to make peace with you, providing you make peace with the Kiowas, Comanches, Arapahoes and Apaches and Sioux . . . We want true news from you in return."

The Bent referred to was William Bent, who with Ceran St. Vrain had built the famous Bent's Fort, a trading post for decades, on the site later occupied by Fort Lyon. He it was who had talked to the Southern Cheyennes and induced them to come south to hunt. He it was who had married one of their women and lived with her honorably. He was the only white man the Southern Cheyennes trusted. One of his half-breed sons, George Bent, was in camp with them then, and with Edmond Guerrier, another half-breed, wrote the letter just quoted, at the dictation of Black Kettle and other chiefs.

Later Black Kettle, White Antelope and others went to Denver with Major Wynkoop and talked to Governor Evans. On their return they were told to camp on Sand Creek, where they would be under military protection as long as they kept peace. The Cheyennes had every reason to feel secure in these promises of protection. As proof of their good intentions they surrendered half their firearms to Wynkoop, keeping only enough for hunting.

The Platte and Arkansas basins had seen plenty of Indian troubles that year. The Sioux and Kiowas, aided by their allies, the Comanches, Arapahoes and some Cheyennes, scourged the wagon trails so that freight ceased for a time to move. Some helpless settlers had been killed, too. Public feeling was high against all Indians in Denver.

On the other hand the Indians had sufficient grievances of their own. There was the unprovoked attack by Lieutenant George Eayre and his men on a Cheyenne village the April before, in which a score of Indians were killed. And there were plenty of other crimes of a similar nature to be laid at the white man's door. Then there was the old sore point that the wagon trains frightened away all the game.

But the frontier cared nothing about the Indian's side of the case. It wanted the raiding stopped. And so all day on November 28th, a long trailing splotch of blue—cavalry—had moved steadily across the landscape. Toward night the troops halted. Near the head of the column rode a half-breed, his horse's reins tied to a soldier's saddle-pommel. A group of horsemen spurred up. Their leader, huge, burly, fierce-visaged, rasped out a question. The trooper saluted. It was Colonel J. M. Chivington, of the 2nd Colorado Cavalry.[1]

[1] Colonel J. M. Chivington was in civil life a Methodist preacher. He went west from Ohio where he "got religion" and entered the ministry. In 1850 he was in Colorado but later moved to Missouri, where the anti-slave controversy gave his extraordinarily belligerent nature a better chance to find the strife it en-

"The breed won't go no farther, sir," the soldier said.[2]

"Wolf, he howl," said the Indian. "Injun dog, he hear wolf, he howl too. Injun, he hear dog and listen; hear something and run off."

Hopefully he stole a glance at the white man's face—to meet there a look so fell that he shrank back. In a hard voice Chivington spoke.

"Jack," he said, "if you fool with me, and don't lead me to that camp—" he tapped his holster. The half-breed read death in his eyes.

With a sigh the prisoner again took the trail. No use to argue here. To Chivington all Indians looked alike and there was "no good Indian but a dead Indian." He knew of Black Kettle's peaceful village and he had kidnapped the half-breed, Jack Smith,[3] to lead him to the camp. Moreover, the prisoner knew Chivington's right-hand man was with him, the baleful Major Downing, who had not hesitated, as he later boasted, to wring information out of a captured Indian "by toasting his shins over a small fire."

Dazedly the guide plodded ahead. All night they marched. At daybreak of the 29th they mounted a rise and saw, stretched along a shallow, sluggish stream, the village they sought, peacefully slumbering.

A squaw in the Cheyenne camp heard the distant rumble of hoofs and cried out that a herd of buffalo was coming. The Indians rushed out and beheld the troops on the ridge. They were badly frightened.

joyed. He took part in the anti-slavery movement, first as a preacher and later as a member of Jim Lane's free-state bushwhackers. After the border war he again assumed the cloth and at the outbreak of the Civil War was presiding elder of his church in Denver.

In the first days of the war Chivington preached often to the soldiers in the barracks. His fire-eating eloquence pleased them and the upshot was that he was offered the chaplaincy in a Colorado regiment. He refused saying, "if I go with the soldiers I am going to fight." The governor gave him a major's commission instead. He soon received his colonelcy.

Like many religious fanatics Chivington appears not to have had one compunction for the deed he perpetrated at Sand Creek. In fact he gloried in it afterward, and before he set out on this expedition, he made a public speech in which he said: "Kill and scalp all [Indians] big and little; nits make lice." This quotation is contained in the sworn testimony of S. E. Brown, before the Congressional Investigating Committee which later probed—and repudiated—the whole affair.

[2] All direct quotations in this chapter are taken from J. P. Dunn's account of the incident published in 1886.

[3] Jack Smith was the son of the famous John Smith, trader, explorer and trapper, and a Cheyenne woman. His uncle was the great Cheyenne chief Yellow Horse.

In the confusion a white trader who had been sleeping in one of the lodges—pretty good proof in itself that the Indians were peaceful—came out and started toward the troops. At the same time Black Kettle ran up an American flag over his teepee, with a white flag above that. He had been told to do so to show that his camp was friendly. The Cheyennes, believing themselves under protection, and reassured by their chiefs, did not at first run. They clustered in a huddled mob in front of their lodges.

Then there was a shot, followed by two or three more. Firing became general. The trader, halfway between the camp and the troops, hesitated and stopped. A cavalryman galloped toward him but was shot out of his saddle. At that the troops charged.

It was a massacre. The Indians, bewildered and only partly armed, could not realize at first that the white men actually meant war. When they did finally understand this they fought like demons, but then it was too late.

After the first deadly volley which dropped many women and children, the Cheyennes ran up the bed of the creek. A detachment of soldiers cut off the pony herd. Some of the warriors stayed in the village to cover the retreat of the women and the children. Among these were Black Kettle and the fine old chief White Antelope, then seventy-five years old. Black Kettle saw it was useless to remain and urged White Antelope to run with him. But the old chief stood in his tracks, singing his death song, with arms folded. Presently he was shot down.

Meantime the handful of warriors who had fought in the village were all killed. Chivington was in possession of the camp.

Up the creek about three quarters of a mile the Cheyennes scooped holes in the sand for the rifle pits and made a stand. Braves, squaws and children were mixed up together. The troops were disorganized. Some lined up and shot at the Indians. The rest scattered widely. Some looted the lodges; others killed stragglers; still others with ferocity never surpassed by the Indians themselves, scalped and mutilated the dead.[4]

[4] In extenuation of this revolting circumstance, Chivington's men later said they were avenging similar mutilations practiced on white men. Contrast Chivington's attitude with that of Sibley in the Sioux War in Minnesota in 1862.

THE CHIVINGTON MASSACRE

Some of the scenes which ensued are almost unbelievable except that they were later attested by sworn statements of eye-witnesses. Women and children were killed indiscriminately. In the creek bed fight they fought side by side with the men, but in the village the noncombatants, fleeing for their lives, were slaughtered without pity.[5]

The Cheyennes battled desperately in the creek bed. The firing was at long range and try as they might, the soldiers could not dislodge them. But by noon two howitzers were brought up and began throwing shells into the position. That broke the stubborn line. The Indians fell back to a new position, leaving their dead where they lay. Chivington followed. Again with the dreaded "wagon guns" thundering, the Cheyennes retreated. This program of stand, bombard, and retreat continued all day. The soldiers drove the Indians back five miles.

At nightfall Chivington returned to the village where he camped two days while the survivors escaped. The dead Indians were left to rot where they lay.

A final cap-sheaf was added to the deed of horror when poor, cowering Jack Smith, the unwilling guide, was murdered by the soldiers. An appeal was made to Chivington to protect the poor wretch. He replied: "I have given my orders and have no further instructions to give." A short time later the half-breed was shot.

With only seven prisoners, two women and five children, Chivington returned to Denver. He had "defeated" the Cheyennes as he proved by exhibiting more than a hundred scalps in a theater between

[5] Major Anthony testified as follows before the Congressional Investigating Committee: A little baby, not more than three years old, emerged from one of the lodges after the flight of the Cheyennes from the village. Plump, brown, perfectly naked, it toddled down the pathway where the Indians had fled, crying a little, but not much, in the cold.

It was a sight which should have stirred compassion in a wolf but it stirred none in the men who were sacking the village. A soldier saw the child and fired at seventy-five yards, missing. Another dismounted and said: "Let me try the little — —," and fired, but missed also. A third, with surer aim, shot and this time the innocent crumpled up, dying.

acts of a performance. Around three hundred Indians were killed of whom about seventy-five were warriors and the rest women and children. The soldiers lost seven killed and forty-seven wounded, of whom seven afterward died.

The Cheyennes never forgot Chivington's massacre. And they avenged it bloodily in the years to follow.[6]

[6] The government repudiated Chivington's acts and paid Black Kettle's band a heavy indemnity the following year—as if indemnities could bring back murdered wives, children and husbands. In 1868 a commission appointed by Congress and consisting of Generals W. T. Sherman, Alfred H. Terry, and C. C. Augur and Messrs. S. F. Tappan, N. J. Taylor, J. B. Henderson, John B. Sanborn and others, spent seventy-two days hearing evidence on the affair. When all the testimony, pro and con, was gone into, the commission made this sweeping and damning report concerning the massacre:

"It scarcely has its parallel in the records of Indian barbarity. Fleeing women, holding up their hands and praying for mercy were shot down; infants were killed and scalped in derision; men were tortured and mutilated in a way which would put to shame the savages of interior Africa. No one will be astonished that a war ensued which cost the government $30,000,000 and carried conflagration and death to the border settlements. During the spring and summer of 1865 no less than 8,000 troops were withdrawn from the effective forces engaged against the Rebellion to meet this Indian war."

General Nelson A. Miles in his "Personal Recollections" (p. 139) characterizes the Sand Creek massacre as "perhaps the foulest and most unjustifiable crime in the annals of America."

Virtually every military authority who has ever commented on it has referred to it as a massacre, pure and simple. It was universally deplored by army leaders.

Chivington, the central character in the affair, returned to Ohio after the close of the Civil War, started a newspaper, and after two years ran for the legislature. "Sand Creek" was the watchword of his opposition and he was the object of so much execration that he finally withdrew from the race. His political ambitions shattered, he eventually left that part of the country and returned to the mountains.

7: AN ISLAND IN THE ARICKAREE

MAKING THE WHITE MAN PAY

SAND CREEK cost the Indians heavily in blood and sorrow but it cost the white man more. After the massacre a party of Cheyenne chiefs went north carrying the war pipe. There they offered it to their brothers, the Northern Cheyennes, who smoked it, and afterward to the Sioux who also smoked it. One of the Sioux chiefs who smoked the war pipe was Sitting Bull, then just coming into prominence. From that time on Sitting Bull was a more implacable foe of the white man than even Red Cloud had been.[1] The Little Big Horn had its roots in Sand Creek.

But the Cheyennes made the paleface pay far more directly than that. Early in January, 1865, a great war party composed of Cheyennes, Sioux and Arapahoes, started north from the Smoky Hill River. On the night of January 6th, they camped near Julesburg, an important point on the Overland Stage route. Close by was Fort Rankin, garrisoned by a troop of the 7th Iowa Cavalry. Early next morning a little party of Cheyennes and Sioux, seven in all, headed by Big Crow, a famous Cheyenne warrior, rode out of a ravine near the fort and charged some post employees who were working outside the stockade.

The men ran inside and the cavalry leaped to horse to chastise the rash hostiles. At top speed the troopers chased the seven Indians toward the sand hills about two miles away. Captain O'Brien hoped to catch the redskins before they reached the safety of those hills. But for some reason, try as they might, they could not catch up with their quarry, although they always seemed *almost* to overtake them. Then, just as they reached the sand hills, the crest suddenly sprouted war bonnets and lances.

It was the old trick. The seven Indians were a decoy. It was a flight for life now. O'Brien's force came within an eyelash of being

[1] See Vestal, "Sitting Bull," p. 70.

annihilated. As it was, the Indians killed a sergeant, fourteen privates, and four civilians—eighteen men—in the wild dash for the fort.

Around the stockade rode the red men, yelling and shooting. Then they plundered Julesburg. Nobody was killed in the settlement because all took refuge in the fort before the Indians got there.[2]

On January 28th the Indians again struck the stage line when they surrounded and set fire to Harlow's ranch, killed two men and carried off a woman. On the same day they raided three other places, burning buildings, setting hay on fire, looting stores and paralyzing the whole stage line for weeks.

In this raid the Cheyennes got a signal piece of vengeance. Nine men, recently discharged from the 3rd Colorado Cavalry which took part in the Sand Creek massacre, were caught by a war party. They were on their way East. The Indians killed them all. When their valises were opened, the Cheyennes found two scalps of their own people which they recognized by the hair ornaments. They were so furious that they cut the dead men literally to pieces.

In the next two weeks the allied tribes attacked and burned the Beaver Creek stage station, the Morrison ranch where seven men were killed and Mrs. Morrison and her child carried off, the Wisconsin ranch, the Washington ranch, the Lillian Springs ranch, Gittrell's ranch, Moore's ranch, and many other places. Three wagon trains were captured and looted. In a second raid on Julesburg, they burned the place to the ground while the soldiers watched helplessly from Fort Rankin, a mile away.

And so it went. Scores of white men and women paid with their lives for that Sand Creek affair. The Southern Cheyennes furnished much of the worst fighting for the troops in the Powder River campaign of 1865.

---

[2] The value of goods taken or destroyed at Julesburg was $40,000. One piece of plunder at the stage station was the strong box of the army paymaster containing thousands of dollars in greenbacks, to pay the Colorado troops. Not knowing the value of the "green paper" the Indians had a lot of fun scattering it all over the valley. Next day the paymaster had men detailed from Fort Rankin to hunt the money. They found it strewn for a mile or more, but only recovered about half of it.

THE PLATTE BRIDGE FIGHT

In the middle of that summer the Cheyennes appeared near the Platte Bridge where there was a stockade garrisoned by some Kansas cavalry. There was a skirmish near the fort. Then the Indians drew off and hid on the other side of the Platte.

A wagon train with a small military escort was coming down the river to the post and Lieutenant Caspar Collins, with a detachment, was dispatched to meet it.

Not an Indian was in sight. In fact those at the fort thought they had cleared out of the country. With no thought of immediate danger, Collins led his men across the bridge and up the flat. As if they had risen from the ground, the Cheyennes suddenly appeared, cutting the soldiers off from the bridge. Collins was fearless. He had been ordered to go to the wagon train, so he continued his march. Then a second, even larger mass of warriors rose out of a ravine on his front.

At first the young officer tried to fight his way forward. The numbers of Indians steadily increased. At last he gave the order to fall back. The Cheyennes still blocked his way to the bridge. Collins tried to cut his way through. Right into the mass of yelling savages his men rode. An arrow struck the lieutenant in the forehead and hung quivering there, but still he fought his way forward. A few yards farther he was beaten from his horse and killed.[3] Only a remnant of his command won their way through to the bridge. The rest were dead, their scalps in Cheyenne hands.

In the meantime the wagon train continued its slow journey toward the fort, ignorant of the painted death ahead. Sergeant Custard, a hard-faced old veteran, was in command. The booming of cannon when they were almost in sight of the fort was their first intimation of danger. Custard had twenty-four men. He sent five

[3] There is some evidence that Collins was tortured to death. A. J. Mokler, of Casper, Wyoming, who probably knew more about this fight than any other one man, said that the lieutenant's face had been blasted off by powder poured in his mouth and then touched off, when the body was found days later. Mr. Mokler has an interesting discussion of this affair in his book "Transition of the West."

of them, under Corporal James W. Shrader, forward to see what was going on.

Scarcely was the detail clear of the wagon train when a swarm of Indians rode out from hiding in a ravine and lashed their ponies after the soldiers. There was no chance to get back to Custard. The troopers raced for the fort. As they jumped their horses into the stream to ford it, Private James Ballew was shot from the saddle and fell into the river. His body was never recovered. The rest got across, but on the other bank Edwin Summers was killed. Corporal Shrader with Privates Bryam Swaim and Henry Smith, after two hours of alternate running and hiding in the brush of the river bottom, finally reached the fort alive.

In the meantime Custard, seeing his advance guard cut off, corralled his wagons. Many Indians came riding toward him. They were returning from killing Collins and his men. Around the train they swept in a tempest of noise while puffs of smoke spurted from the wagons. Here and there warriors fell to the ground. The Cheyennes drew back out of range.

The soldiers probably breathed more freely. A repulse like that generally meant the end of an Indian attack. But these were not ordinary Indians. They were Cheyennes, seeking still further satisfaction from the white man for Sand Creek.

A gigantic warrior, wearing a handsome war bonnet, now appeared, riding slowly around the train. He was Roman Nose, most noted of all the Cheyennes. His proper name was Sauts (The Bat), but his nose was hooked like the beak of some fierce bird of prey and the white men dubbed him "Roman Nose." His own people accepted the sobriquet and translated it into their own tongue, Woquini, or Hook Nose.

Few savages on the plains were his equal in strength or courage. He towered six feet three inches in his moccasins, and weighed two hundred and thirty pounds without a surplus ounce of flesh. In addition he was a natural leader. Roman Nose habitually took great risks in battle. He believed himself invulnerable, due to the sacred war bonnet which he always wore and which was never put on without elaborate ritual. Because of this belief he had performed so many daring exploits that he was famous throughout the frontier.

The appearance of Roman Nose at once put a different complexion on the fight. After his leisurely survey of the corral, he told his warriors to dismount. Every man with a gun—and due to the recent raids many were now so armed—crept up close to the wagons and opened a devastating fire upon them. The troopers simply melted away.

About three o'clock in the afternoon, Roman Nose stopped the shooting. Spurring forward, he rode all alone around the wagons, very close, to draw fire. Not a shot answered his challenge. Then Roman Nose dared to enter the circle itself. Every soldier was dead or badly wounded. The Cheyennes rushed in. Of course they killed all who were still living. Chivington had done the same by them.

. . . .

Because the Cheyennes and Sioux went north to carry on their warfare, the summer of 1866 was comparatively quiet in Kansas.

But in the spring of 1867 the Indians were back on the border again. General Hancock with eleven hundred men took the field in April to show the Indians "that the government is ready and able to punish them if they are hostile, although it may not . . . invite war."

His column marched and counter-marched. The Cheyennes and Sioux played will-o'-the-wisp. After four months of this, Hancock returned to Fort Harker. He had burned one empty village and killed two young Cheyennes, said to be friendly. Meanwhile the Indians were raiding far and wide and doing a tremendous amount of damage. It is impossible to enumerate all their activities.

General George Armstrong Custer, fresh from the East, had just arrived on the frontier. A dashing cavalry officer, he pursued the hostiles with great energy, but his achievements were nil. In fact they were less than that, for a promising young officer, Lieutenant Kidder, of the 2nd Cavalry, journeying with dispatches for Custer from Fort Sedgwick, was killed with his ten men and the Indian guide Red Bead. The bodies were discovered by Custer a few days later.

Late in the summer the Cheyennes wrecked a railroad train. A war party came upon the newly laid tracks of the Union Pacific somewhere east of North Platte, Nebraska. None of them had ever seen the rails before. One suggested that they put some obstruction on them and throw the train off the tracks.

A log was laid across and the Cheyennes hid. Presently a hand car, worked by two men, came into view. The men saw the Indians and pumped desperately at their handle bars to get past the danger point. When the car hit the logs it jumped the rails. The Cheyennes killed both unfortunates before they even had time to run.

But a hand car is small game when you are after a train. The Indians, encouraged by their success, prepared for a bigger exploit. After pulling out the spikes at the end of a rail, they bent the rail with levers until it was out of line. Again they lay in wait.

It was not a long wait. A glaring light appeared in the east which rapidly grew brighter. As it rushed by, the engine struck the bent rail, jumped the track and turned over on its side. Every member of the train crew was killed in the wreck except one trainman. He got off the train and ran down the track with a lantern. The Cheyennes surrounded and killed him. Next morning they plundered the train which was loaded with valuable merchandise. The Indians got their fill of loot that time.

Thus passed the year 1867. But it was tame compared to the following summer of 1868. In sixty days one hundred and seventeen settlers were slaughtered and seven women carried off into captivity. There were at least twenty-five recorded raids in that time. The Cheyennes made a desert out of western Kansas.[4]

---

[4] Following is a partial list of Indian depredations that summer, from official records which do not pretend to be complete:

Aug. 12—Solomon River settlements, 15 killed; Republican River, 2. Aug. 14—Granny Creek, 1 killed, 1 captured. Aug. 23—North Texas, 8 killed; Two Butte Creek, 3; Pond Creek, 2. Aug. 27—Ft. Lyon, 1 killed; Big Spring station, 1. Aug. 28—Kiowa station, 3 killed. Sept. 1—Lake station, 2 killed; Reed's Springs, 3; Spanish Fort, Tex., 8. Sept. 6 and 7—Colorado Territory, 25 killed. Sept. 8—Turkey Creek, 2 killed; Cimarron Crossing, 17. Sept. 9—Ft. Wallace, 6 killed. Sept. 17—Ella station, 1 killed; Fort Bascom, 1. Sept. 29—Sharp's Creek, 1 killed, 3 captured. Oct. 2—Fort Zarah and Larned, 4 killed. Oct. 4—Fort Dodge, 1 killed. Oct. 7—Purgatory Creek, 1 killed; Sand Creek, 2 captured. Oct. 14—Prairie Dog Creek, 1 killed. Oct. 15—Fisher and Yocucy Creeks, 4 killed, 1 captured. Not an Indian was killed in these affairs.

FORSYTH'S SCOUTS

Things grew so critical that General Phil Sheridan, commanding the Department of the Missouri, took the field in person. Sheridan quickly realized how futile it was to try to follow the Indians who knew the country like a book and could make their living off it, with soldiers who had to carry their own supplies, must trust to often inefficient scouts, and were otherwise handicapped.

There were plenty of good plainsmen in the frontier forts those days—men who know how to trail, shoot, and travel. To Sheridan one day Major George A. Forsyth suggested a free-lance battalion of these frontiersmen to be enlisted for scouting duty, with the hope of meeting the Indians at their own game.

Sheridan approved and authorized Forsyth to recruit the outfit. It was harder to keep the number of men down than to fill the quota of fifty. Bronzed and rugged plainsmen, aching for a chance at the redskins who had driven them from their homes, clamored for admittance. Scarcely were the lists open when they were filled—buffalo hunters, Civil War veterans, gamblers and trappers. On September 10th Forsyth rode forth with his half-hundred to scout the hostile Indian country.

It was a ridiculously tiny force, but the white man still had many lessons to learn, and every scout was filled with the sublime faith that they could whip any number of Indians they might meet.

See, then, this cock-sure handful of hard-bitten fighters, riding out of Fort Wallace that bright autumn morning. Watch them as they jingle along, Spencer seven-shooter carbines slung on their backs, holstered revolvers slapping thighs, dressed in buckskin or nondescript uniforms—the most careless, irresponsible, hard-riding, straight-shooting company of scapegraces that ever set out under the United States flag.

For two or three days they scouted westward. Then a big trail was struck and Forsyth followed it. The trail, it later developed, was made by the allied war party under Pawnee Killer—who had wiped out Kidder's command—and the Cheyenne chiefs Tall Bull and

White Horse. Roman Nose was also in this party.

Soon after the rash white scouts took their trail the Indians knew of it. The Cheyennes and Sioux later said that preparations were made nearly twenty-four hours ahead for the fight which followed.

Forsyth, hot on the trail, reached the Arickaree River. It had a wide, sandy bed with very little water meandering down the middle. A small island covered with plum brush was in the bed. On the bank of this stream the scouts camped.

As the first streaks of dawn lit the sky next morning, September 17th, a shot and a yell of "Indians!" aroused the command. With flapping blankets and shrill yelps, eight warriors rode at the horse-lines trying to stampede the animals. Seven broke away and the Indians captured them.

As if this were only a prelude, the entire horizon seemed to fill with tossing feathered head dresses on which the first rays of the sun gleamed brilliantly. In a few minutes the bottom was covered with mounted hostiles.

Pell-mell, helter-skelter, Forsyth's men rode for the low island they had noted in the middle of the stream bed. There, under the plum bushes, they began frantically to burrow out small rifle pits.

The Indians had spread out from bank to bank. One warrior, on a chestnut horse, was taken by Forsyth to be Roman Nose. Sharp Grover,[5] his chief of scouts, also thought it was the famous warrior, evidently basing his belief on the Indian's size, as he added "there isn't such another Indian on the plains." They were mistaken. Roman Nose did not appear until later in the day.

By now the Indians were ready to charge. Old plainsmen, able to distinguish the tribes by their head dresses, saw that Brulé Sioux, Arapahoes and both Northern and Southern Cheyennes were there. A black mass of squaws and children gathered on a hill overlooking the valley to watch the battle. This place is now called "Squaw Hill."

[5] Grover had lived among the Sioux (Turkey Leg's band) and married a Sioux squaw, but he did not know the Cheyennes, according to Grinnell. He was suffering from a recent wound in his back at the time of this expedition. Only a month before he, with William Comstock, another scout, had been shot while leaving a Sioux village. Comstock was killed, but Grover stood off his assailants and reached the settlements. He was later slain by a man named Moody, in a saloon brawl at Pond Creek, Kansas.

The Indians charged; the drumming of their horses' hoofs and their wild yelling rose in a wave of sound. On the island the scouts clenched their teeth as they glanced down the barrels of their rifles. But not a shot was fired. The order was to wait until the charge was within fifty yards. As it crossed that imaginary line, Forsyth uttered a single word:

"Now!"

A white cloud of smoke burst from the island. A hail of bullets whistled into the Indian ranks. And then the repeating carbines proved their worth. Instead of the usual single volley, followed by silence, the Indians rode into a continuous stream of lead. In the face of this storm their hearts forsook them. It was a repetition of the Wagon Box fight. Like an angry wave which hurls itself upon a rock and breaks upon its front, they divided on each side of the island and thundered down the river bed, to circle off to safety in the bluffs.

In spite of this the charge came near carrying home. Some of the Indian dead lay within a few feet of the rifle pits. And the red men were by no means through.

The chiefs galloped around, assembling their warriors out of rifle range. Some braves dismounted and slipped forward on foot. The prairie close to the river was level, but south of the island grew willow bushes. Behind this cover the Indians got close to the island. Firing redoubled as they exchanged shots with the scouts only a few yards away. A few Indians were killed. The rest drew off.

The scouts counted their losses. Out of fifty-one officers and men, twenty-three were dead or wounded. Among the mortally hurt were Lieutenant Beecher, second in command, who died that evening, and Dr. Moorehead, the surgeon who died three days later.[6] Forsyth himself was wounded in three places.

Like Achilles, Roman Nose had stayed out of the morning battle, and like Achilles, his absence had been keenly felt by his warriors. The day before he had destroyed the charm of his sacred war bonnet. One of the taboos connected with it was that he must not eat food taken from the pot with an iron implement. At a feast given by the

---

[6] The island was later named Beecher's Island in honor of Lieutenant Frederick W. Beecher, who died there. The fight is often called the Beecher Island fight.

Sioux, Roman Nose ate meat served by a squaw with an iron fork. Tall Bull, his friend, called his attention to the error and urged him to take purification ceremonies at once. But that very night Forsyth's command was discovered and Roman Nose had no time for the ceremonies before the battle.

He stayed out of the first charge, saying he would die if he made it. But he was such a power that the other Cheyennes kept urging him. In mid-afternoon he suddenly decided to go into the fight. Putting on the war bonnet, he mounted. With a wave of his great arm, the giant summoned his warriors. A moment later they were charging.

Forsyth's men fought this new danger desperately. At the dead run, Roman Nose thundered down upon them. Just before he reached the trenches, a shot from some bushes to one side, brought him crashing down. Jack Stilwell and two companions were hiding there. Roman Nose's followers scattered.

The place where Roman Nose fell was on the river bank. Painfully he dragged himself out of sight among the bushes. There he was found by his people and carried away. He died in the Cheyenne village that night.[7]

It will never be known how many Indians were killed at the Arickaree. Years later the Cheyennes could remember the names of only seven warriors who died, but this seems preposterous. Forsyth estimated their loss was at least one hundred.

THE JOURNEY OF STILWELL AND TRUDEAU

As evening fell, Forsyth, wounded and nearly helpless, called his men together. He pointed out their desperate situation and the fact that the nearest help was at Fort Wallace, one hundred and twenty-five miles away. Then he called for volunteers to make the journey. They had to travel on foot. All their horses were dead.

The answer surprised even Forsyth. Every man able to travel offered. Henry Trudeau, a veteran trapper, and Jack Stilwell, a nineteen-year-old boy, were chosen. At midnight they slipped out

---

[7] George Bird Grinnell, "The Fighting Cheyennes," p. 277.

into the river bed, to begin their journey. They neglected no precautions. Their boots were taken off and slung about their necks so if the Indians should see their tracks in the morning they would look like moccasin prints and so perhaps escape notice. They wrapped themselves in blankets, so that in the starlit night their silhouettes should be passed as those of Indians.

Down the river they stole. Somewhere off in the bluffs lay the Indian camp, how near they did not know. Later Forsyth's men declared they could hear the thudding of tom-toms and an occasional eery howl as some squaw expressed her mourning for a slain consort.

Hugging the bank Stilwell and Trudeau progressed several hundred yards. Then they left the river and crawled on hands and knees, taking advantage of the cover of each bit of sagebrush or soapweed. Necessarily their progress was slow. Less than two miles were covered in the five hours before dawn, when they crawled into a dry washout.

All day they sat under the blazing sun. Every moment was an agony of suspense. They did not dare to raise their heads to the level of the prairie for fear of being spied by some hawk-eyed Cheyenne. They heard firing at the island and knew that fighting was going on. The country was full of riding Indians. Now and again the thudding hoofs of a warrior's pony would pass near. Yet by some miracle no Indian came directly upon them.

Darkness fell at last and again they set out. Their progress was faster now, but they were in constant danger. Once they hid in the shadow of a rotting buffalo carcass to escape the attention of a passing war party. They made several miles that night and took refuge in the morning under a high river bank.

The next night they set out at speed. Throughout the dark hours they traveled in a bee line for Fort Wallace without seeing a hostile. At dawn they were on a flat plain without a draw in which to hide. They began to think they might now travel with safety in the daylight, but after a conference lay down in a shallow buffalo wallow, a dry mud hole where the bison had wallowed in the rainy season. A few weeds grew around the border, affording scanty cover.

It was a wise decision. Early in the morning a scouting party of

Cheyennes rode up and halted within a hundred feet of their hiding place. At almost the same moment a rattlesnake came wriggling through the grass toward them. They could have killed the snake easily but they did not dare move for fear of attracting the attention of the Indians. Even if the serpent rattled, the red men might investigate. Closer crawled the rattler, with its flat, ugly head raised menacingly and its tail already quivering slightly.

Must the crouching men choose the dreadful alternative of being bitten by the reptile or revealing themselves to their enemies? Jack Stilwell solved the dilemma. Like most plainsmen he chewed tobacco. His mouth was full of the juice at the minute. As the snake drew near, he spat a mouthful of the fluid all over its head and eyes. Surprised and vanquished by the dose, the rattler forgot its belligerent ideas and wriggled a disgusted retreat. The Cheyennes presently moved on, never dreaming of the little drama which had been enacted under their noses.

Early in the evening the scouts started again and made fine progress, but toward morning Trudeau's age began to tell and he weakened rapidly. Stilwell had to lend him the support of a shoulder. They pushed on thus. When it seemed they could progress no farther, Trudeau exclaimed: "By thunder, a road!"

And so it was—the government highway into Fort Wallace. It was not long, then, until they delivered the message which sent a strong expedition to Forsyth's relief.

In the meantime, a second pair of scouts, Pliley and Donovan, left Forsyth on the second night. These men ran into Colonel Carpenter with the 10th (colored) Cavalry. Carpenter reached Forsyth first. He found the scouts suffering terribly. For six days the Indians had stayed in the vicinity. After they left, the men were chained to the island by their wounded. For a time they ate the flesh of their dead horses. But this putrefied so that not even when covered with gunpowder could they force it down. An unlucky coyote was killed and they divided its carcass. On the sixth day Forsyth, believing all hope of rescue gone, ordered those who could travel to leave him and the wounded and get back to the settlements. But not a man stirred.

On the ninth day a sentry gave the alarm that there was another party of Indians moving in the hills. It was the last straw. The new arrivals could mean but one thing—another attack, which they could not beat off. Then a keen-eyed scout sent up a shout: "By heaven— an ambulance!"

The supposed Indians were Carpenter's relieving column. Forsyth's men were saved.[8]

[8] When Carpenter's command was returning with the remnants of the Forsyth scouts, a white teepee was noticed, standing alone in the valley. Two of the scouts rode over to it and found within the body of a dead warrior. They "identified" him as Roman Nose, and robbed him of the arms and finery which had been left with him. But years later the Cheyennes revealed the fact that the dead man was not Roman Nose, but another Cheyenne warrior named Killed-by-a-Bull, who was slain in the last charge. Roman Nose was carried away and buried after the usual custom, on a scaffold. No man knows today the place of his savage sepulcher.

8: THE CHEYENNES PAY

CUSTER'S WINTER CAMPAIGN

THE most picturesque, dashing figure in all our military history was General George Armstrong Custer. As a lieutenant fresh out of West Point he distinguished himself in the Civil War and when only twenty-six was a major general of volunteers.

Custer loved theatrical display. He emphasized his eccentricities and dramatized his personality. He wore his golden hair in long curls which fell to his shoulders and caused the Indians to call him "Long Hair." He affected the excessively wide hat, the buckskin coat and other individualized costume features which have remained a part of the Custer tradition.

He had a talent for writing. His articles in various magazines, published later in book form as "My Life on the Plains," painted a vivid picture of Indian fighting and further popularized the author.

Custer arrived on the frontier during the height of the Cheyenne war. He saw some hot campaigning and one of his first experiences was finding the bodies of Lieutenant Kidder and his ten men [1] after they were cut off and killed by Pawnee Killer's Sioux.

General Sheridan, viewing the failure of the summer campaigns, decided in the fall of 1868 that his best hope was to attack the Indians in their winter camps. His reasons for the decision were as follows:

[1] Custer's description of the incident shows the impression it made: "A sight met our gaze which even at this remote day makes my very blood curdle. Lying in irregular order, and within a very limited circle were the mangled bodies of poor Kidder and his party, yet so brutally hacked and disfigured as to be beyond recognition save as human beings. . . . Every individual . . . had been scalped and his skull broken . . . some of the bodies were lying in beds of ashes with partly burned fragments of wood near them, showing that the savages had put . . . them to death by the horrible tortures of fire. The sinews of the arms and legs had been cut away, the nose of every man hacked off . . . Each body was pierced by from twenty to fifty arrows . . . bristling in the bodies."—"My Life on the Plains," p. 77.

". . . Not less than eight hundred persons had been murdered, the Indians escaping from the troops by traveling at night when their trail could not be followed, thus gaining enough time and distance to render pursuit, in most cases, fruitless. This wholesale marauding would be maintained during the seasons when the Indian ponies could subsist upon the grass, and then in the winter, the savages would hide away, with their villages, in remote and isolated places, to live upon their plunder, glory in the scalps taken, and in the horrible debasement of unfortunate women whom they held as prisoners. The experience of many years of this character of depredations, with perfect immunity to themselves and their families, had made the Indians very bold. To disabuse their minds of the idea that they were secure from punishment, and to strike them at a period when they were helpless to move their stock and villages, a winter campaign was projected against the large bands hiding away in the Indian Territory." [2]

Custer was given the job. On November 22nd, in the midst of a bitter cold snap, with a foot of snow on the ground, he set out from Camp Supply, I. T., for the Washita River country. Two other columns, General Carr with seven troops of the 5th Cavalry, and Colonel Evans with six troops of cavalry, two companies of infantry, and four mountain howitzers, operated on each side of him as beaters. But Custer with the 7th Cavalry, was expected to do the actual fighting.

Marching south, Custer on November 26th struck the hot track of a war party returning from a raid on the Sante Fé trail. This band had killed mail carriers between Dodge and Larned, an old hunter at Dodge, and two of Sheridan's own dispatch carriers. Custer followed the track as rapidly as possible throughout the day, then decided to continue his march that night. Indian signs multiplied. Once they came upon the dying embers of a fire kindled during the day by Indian herd boys. They knew by that they were very close to the village.

Little Beaver, an Osage scout, smelled fire. He told Custer the camp was near. With the Indian, the general crept to the top of a low hill. His straining eyes made out a dark blotch on the snow—an immense pony herd. Significant noises greeted his ears. Far away dogs barked; there was the sound of a bell from the herd; once he heard the shrill wail of an Indian baby just over the hill. Custer realized he was on top of a large camp. Returning, he whispered orders to his troop commanders which sent them to their posts.

THE VILLAGE ON THE WASHITA

It will be remembered that it was Black Kettle's village which Chivington attacked on Sand Creek. Even after that black treachery Black Kettle continued to favor peace, not because he loved the white man, but because he knew the inevitable result to his tribe of continued warfare. Only a few days before Custer reached the Washita, he had talked peace with General Hazen at Fort Cobb. Now fate was for a second time to play him a scurvy trick. It was Black Kettle's village which Custer had discovered.

But Black Kettle's camp was not the only one there. Custer did not know it but all up and down the valley great encampments stretched. Kiowas, Arapahoes, Comanches, Apaches and other Cheyennes were there. It is a question if Custer would have attacked had he known the odds. There were at least two thousand warriors in that valley, although only a few hundred were in Black Kettle's camp.

Custer divided his men into four detachments. Major Joel Elliott took three troops, Captain Thompson and Captain Myers two each, and Custer retained four. The four detachments quietly surrounded the camp. Throughout the night the men shivered. At the first light in the east on the morning of November 27th, cinches were tightened and weapons examined. A bugle sounded. Custer and the 7th Cavalry rode down on the doomed village from every side.

With startled yelps the Cheyennes ran from their teepees. The charging troopers fired once; then they were among the Indians. Black Kettle and his wife were killed in front of their own lodge. Many others, both men and women, died in the village. The rest ran into the river, where they fought or tried to escape.

Red Bird Black, still living at Concho, Oklahoma, was a boy of fourteen when the fight took place. He remembers vividly the terrific cold and how the Indians, rudely awakened, ran naked except for their breech clouts into the ice-covered stream. Some of them were cut by the razor edges of the broken ice until the water ran red with their blood. Children were trampled under the hoofs of charging horses. A few brave Cheyenne men, behind the river bank, fought and fought, until all were dead, in heroic self-sacrifice, so their families might get away. An Indian woman ran out of her teepee, dragging by the arm a little white boy. Seeing escape cut off, she whipped a knife into his body. She was instantly shot dead. The identity of the slain boy was never learned.

By ten o'clock the fight seemed to be over. But to Custer's surprise, hundreds of additional warriors were seen riding up the valley. Custer was puzzled. Then a captured squaw told him there was a string of Indian villages extending ten miles down the river. From these villages men were hurrying to help Black Kettle.

Custer swung the 7th into battle line and, menacing the Indians in the hills, retreated. An officer and five men were dead, and three officers and eleven men wounded. Major Elliott and fourteen men were missing.[3] Of the Indians Black Kettle and Little Rock, chiefs, were dead. With them were killed one hundred and one Cheyennes, including many women and children. Fifty-three squaws and children were captured. Custer destroyed more than a thousand buffalo robes, five hundred pounds of lead, an equal amount of powder, four thousand arrows, all the lodges, and slaughtered seven hundred captured ponies.

THE FATE OF ELLIOTT

Although Elliott was still missing, Custer retreated to Camp Supply. Within a few days he again marched south, this time on an errand of mercy. Two white girls, a Miss White, and a Mrs. Mor-

[3] In the village later were found the dead bodies of Mrs. Blinn and her child, captured the preceding October in an attack on a wagon train at Sand Creek, Colorado, and murdered to prevent their being recaptured by the whites.

gan, a bride of a month, had been captured by the Indians in raids up the Solomon and Republican valleys the previous summer. Their capture aroused great indignation in Kansas.[4] Governor Crawford got permission from the War Department to organize the 19th Kansas Cavalry. When the regiment was formed, the militant governor resigned his office to take its colonelcy and marched with it to Camp Supply.

On December 7th, although the weather was bitter cold, Custer again took the trail toward the Washita, with this new regiment and his own. Upon their arrival at the deserted site of the village which they had destroyed they learned the fate of Major Elliott and his men.

With fourteen troopers, Elliott followed some Indian women and children down the river. There were three men with them, one of whom was the chief, Little Rock. The three warriors stopped to fight while the women and children cut across a point. Little Rock was killed during this stand. The other two escaped as did the women.

Little Rock's diversion, brief though it was, saved his people, and it was also fatal to Elliott. It gave just enough time for a big band of braves from the allied camps to get behind the white men and surround them. Every man was killed in the short fight which followed.

Custer found all but one of them in a small circle where they had fought back to back. The single exception was Seragant Major Kennedy. According to a story attributed to the Indians, Kennedy was the last survivor and an attempt was made to capture him alive. Knowing that torture was in store for him if he was taken, Kennedy pretended he was willing to surrender. He left the circle of his dead comrades and advanced toward one of the warriors with hand outstretched. The Indian approached, but Kennedy suddenly

---

[4] "The treatment of women by any Indians is usually bad, but by the plains Indians especially so. When a woman is captured by a war party, she is the common property of all of them . . . until they reach their village, when she becomes the special property of her individual captor, who may sell her or gamble her away when he likes. If she resists, she is 'staked out.' She is also beaten, mutilated, or even killed, for resistance. . . . No white woman has ever been known to escape this treatment at the hands of plains Indians."—J. P. Dunn, "Massacres of the Mountains," pp. 427–429.

plunged his saber through his body. Then the other Indians, angered, shot him dead. All of the bodies were stripped, mutilated, and shot full of arrows as was usual in such cases.[5]

Elliott's men were buried, and Custer set out again with a very good stomach for a fight. But the fighting was over for the year. Satanta and Lone Wolf, Kiowa chiefs, were met and arrested. With these as hostages the Kiowas were forced back on the reservation. Then the command went into winter quarters at Fort Cobb.

In the spring they again set out. Guided by a captive Cheyenne woman, Custer located the village where the two girls were held. It would have been easy to ride down and give the Indians a taste of lead but that would have meant the deaths of the prisoners. Diplomacy had to take the place of force. Custer flattered, promised and threatened for tedious days. Then he took the bold step of seizing three Cheyenne warriors as hostages for the safety of the girls. To sugar-coat the pill, he sent presents and promised the release of the warriors on the surrender of the captives. Next day the girls were sent to him, both mounted on a single pony.[6]

THE FRATERNITY OF WARRIORS

In a tribe whose highest ideal and aim of life was war, a society of and for warriors naturally had tremendous prestige. Such a society was the famous Dog Soldier band, which contained the fiercest and most daring of all the Cheyenne warriors in the '60's and '70's. The name is a translation of the Cheyenne name for the fraternity, the Ho-ta min-tanio. It had organizations not only among the Cheyennes, but among the Sioux, Arapaho and other plains tribes. It had its own dances, songs, ceremonial costumes and insignia, besides special medicines and taboos. Only picked warriors could belong.[7]

In the war of 1865–68 the Dog Soldiers acquired such fame in the

---

[5] Custer was accused of having needlessly abandoned Elliott and his men. This created dissension in the 7th Cavalry Regiment which continued to boil beneath the surface until after the Little Big Horn battle.

[6] Mrs. Morgan died a few years after her captivity. Miss White, however, lived to an old age. She afterward married and reared a family.

[7] There were several other warrior societies among the Cheyennes, including Fox Warriors, Flint Warriors, Lance Warriors, Coyote Warriors, and others.

frontier battles that writers of the period frequently refer to the whole Cheyenne tribe as of that name. Tall Bull, fourth of a line of chiefs of the same title, and a close friend of the famous Roman Nose, now dead, was their leader.

After Custer's campaign in the winter of 1868, many Cheyennes went back on the reservation. But the Dog Soldiers remained defiantly hostile. They had not forgotten Sand Creek and now the Washita was added to their grievances. They would have nothing of the white man's peace.

In the spring of 1869 the Dog Soldiers moved their camp to the headwaters of the Republican River. From that point they made almost daily attacks on the settlements in May and June. They killed scores of civilians, captured two women, and ran off more than five hundred head of horses and mules, thus becoming the most serious menace on the frontier. Consequently, on July 1st, General Eugene A. Carr, with five companies of the 5th Cavalry and one hundred and fifty Pawnee scouts under the famous brothers, Major Frank North and Captain Luther North, started out to find and punish the Dog Soldiers.

It was not long until the Pawnees picked up a big Indian trail on the Republican River. That very night a daring band of hostiles tried to stampede Carr's horses, but succeeded only in wounding a teamster.

Next morning the pursuit began. But Tall Bull was warned. Carr soon learned the lesson the Cheyennes always taught to pursuing soldiers. Try as hard as they might, they could not gain on the Indians. With their camp equipment, women, children, and aged, the Cheyennes could still show a clean set of heels to the best cavalry in the West.

Doggedly Carr hung on the trail. But it grew gradually dimmer as the Indians who had made it scattered. At last it divided and the scouts gathered for a conference. The trail to the right was plain; that to the left was scattered and dim. It was an ancient Indian trick. The heavy trail was obviously to be followed but the scouts advised following the other instead. Within a few miles the wisdom of this counsel was apparent. The dim trail grew heavier every hour. Before evening they were sure they were on the right track. The following day a decoy detachment, sent out under Major Royall to follow the false trail, rejoined them, reporting the track they had followed had suddenly faded away altogether.

Next day they made a sixty-five mile march in spite of the terrific heat. They were approaching White Butte Creek, which has its source in the Summit Springs. The troops were spurred by the discovery of the print of a white woman's shoe among the tracks at one of the Indian camps. About noon of July 11th, a Pawnee from Frank North's scouting party, came galloping to Carr with word that an Indian camp was located a few miles ahead. It was Tall Bull's village. He had thought himself far enough in advance of the soldiers to escape safely across the Platte. But the waters were high and he camped to let them subside.

As Carr caught up with North in midafternoon, the Pawnee scouts were unsaddling their horses. They always fought bareback and stripped of their uniforms.

THE FIGHT AT SUMMIT SPRINGS

A little farther and they came to the edge of some bluffs. At their feet was a deep valley, and in it the picturesque panorama of the Dog Soldier village. Carr ordered the "Charge" sounded. Every horse leaped forward. In a minute more they were riding through the camp, led by the Norths and their yelling Pawnees.

A white woman ran from among the teepees with the Indians shooting at her.

"Lie down!" shouted the cavalrymen, for she was in the direct line of the charge. She obeyed. Every horse leaped over her body without a hoof touching her, but she had been shot through the breast. She was Mrs. Weichell, a German immigrant captured in Kansas.

At almost the same instant another white woman was seen. Too far away to save her, the troopers watched a warrior seize her by the hair and brain her with a tomahawk. An instant later they had ridden the murderer down and killed him.[8] This woman was Mrs. Allerdice, also captured in Kansas. Her baby had been strangled by the Indians.

Then the Indians bolted. The fight was over. Carr's men had done much execution. In their brief charge they had killed fifty-two Indians and captured one hundred and seventeen more. All the teepees, arms and supplies were destroyed. Only one trooper was wounded and nobody killed, so complete was the surprise and so demoralized the Cheyennes.

Tall Bull was killed. He was cornered with a few warriors and women in a ravine by the Pawnee scouts under the North brothers. After finding protection for his wife and child behind a bank, he went to the mouth of the canyon and stabbed his horse there. Tall Bull was going to die where he stood. For several minutes the Cheyennes kept the Pawnees at bay. Then as Tall Bull raised his head above the bank for a shot, a bullet from Major Frank North's gun bored through his brain. Thirteen Indians were killed in the ravine. Tall Bull's wife and child were among the captured.[9] The body of Mrs. Allerdice was buried and Mrs. Weichell was taken back to her friends in Kansas. About $1,500 in money was found in the camp. This the soldiers and Pawnee scouts presented to the poor woman. She eventually recovered.

The Battle of Summit Springs ended active warfare for a time on the Kansas and Colorado plains. For a few months the settlers breathed more freely.

[8] This is the story told by some of the white soldiers who participated in the fight. The Cheyennes, however, say that Tall Bull killed the woman with his own hand. He did not die until later in the battle.

[9] Tall Bull's scalp, secured by the late Major Gordon W. Lillie from the Pawnees, was long to be seen at Pawnee Bill's Old Town, near Pawnee, Oklahoma. With it was the scalp of Black Kettle, which was obtained by Major Lillie from the Osages who took it in the Washita fight.

IV
The Southern Tribes Rise
1873-1874

9: THE IRRECONCILABLES

SATANTA

SMALLEST of the five nations which signed the Medicine Lodge Peace Treaty in 1867, was the Kiowa tribe. The Cheyennes, Comanches, Apaches and Arapahoes were all more numerous but there was an innate deadliness about the Kiowas which made them more dangerous, man for man, than any Indians on the plains. First and last the Kiowas probably killed more white men, considering their own numbers, than any of the other western tribes.[1] They felt the weight of the government's anger but, with ready adaptability they agreed to its demands, signed any kind of a treaty proposed—and then at the first opportunity, danced out on the war path again.

The greatest name in modern Kiowa history is that of Se-tain-te (White Bear) known to the frontier as Satanta. He was born in the atmosphere of constant danger, constant movement and constant war which was the Kiowa village of the early 1800's. In his youth he learned to hunt and fight; to ride a pony, any pony, and get out of it the last mile of service after it was ready to quit; to endure pain, hunger and adversity, without a show of emotion; and to hate all who were not Kiowas.

In his early childhood the Kiowas and Comanches smoked the pipe together and became allies, permitting his people to live south of the Arkansas River.[2] At twenty he was a graduate in the school of bloodshed and allied himself with Se-tan-gya (Satank), then in the first flush of his prominence. With him he fought and hunted, first as a subordinate, then as an equal until Satank's death in 1871.

[1] Frederick Webb Hodge, "Handbook of American Indians," Bulletin 30, Bureau of American Ethnology.
[2] This was probably about 1825.

97

Satanta rapidly won fame. No one was more fertile in strategy nor more active in warfare than he. One summer he led a harrying band of Comanches and Kiowas clear to Durango, Mexico. He constantly lurked about the base of Pawnee Rock to sweep down on unwary stage coaches and emigrant trains. His Kiowas all but destroyed traffic on the Santa Fé trail at the start of the Civil War and the irritation caused by their constant depredations was largely responsible for the Sand Creek massacre. Afterward, when the Cheyennes went to war they found able and willing allies in the Kiowas. And Satanta was ever the leading spirit.

He had high intelligence and, during the brief periods when he was not on the war path, lived amicably with the white man. He visited army posts with impunity and impudence and his manly directness and good humor made him a favorite with the officers. Satanta was a marvelous orator [3] and when he rose in council he well knew how to play on the emotions of his people. It was he, more than any other, who was responsible for the great outbreak of Kiowas and Comanches in 1874.

Although general Indian warfare ended with the destruction of Tall Bull's village in 1869, peace by no means reigned. Isolated white men were killed and scalped daily. Sometimes nobody knew

[3] He knew his power and loved to exercise it. And his sense of humor constantly impelled him to play pranks.

"Before a peace commission the old rascal grew very pathetic as he warmed to his subject. He declared he had no desire to kill white settlers or emigrants but that they ruthlessly slaughtered the buffalo (there was truth in the charge) and left their carcasses to rot on the prairie. He also said white hunters set fires which destroyed the grass and cut down the timber on stream margins to make large fires while the Indian was satisfied to cook his food with a few dead and dried limbs.

" 'Only the other day,' said he with the moving power of his voice playing at its finest, 'I picked up a little switch on the trail. It made my heart bleed to think that so small a green branch, ruthlessly torn out of the ground and thoughtlessly destroyed by some white man would in time have grown to be a stately tree for the benefit of my children and grandchildren.'

"After the pow-wow was over Satanta got a few drinks of liquor into him and his real thoughts asserted themselves.

" 'Didn't I give it to those white men?' he exulted. 'Why I drew the tears from their eyes! The switch I saw on the trail made my heart glad instead of sad for I knew there was a tenderfoot ahead because an old plainsman would have used a quirt or spurs. When we came in sight he threw away his rifle and held tightly to his hat for fear he should lose it.' "—Kansas Historical Society Reports.

who committed the murders. But on at least one occasion the Kiowas got the blame.

Satanta was a prisoner of Custer's during the winter of 1868, but the guard house had no effect on him. In the winter of 1869 he remained at Fort Dodge so long that he wore out his welcome. He loved liquor and constantly begged for it. One day he asked a stage driver for a drink. The driver was mixing a bottle of medicine to drench a sick mule. The moment he set it down, Satanta seized it and drank most of it before he drew his breath. He then started for an officer's quarters, begging for something to cure the taste in his mouth which "made his heart bad."

The officer at first refused, then succumbed to a mistaken sense of humor. He went to a closet, apparently took a swallow from a bottle containing most nauseating medicine, and placed the bottle on the shelf. Satanta watched his chance. As the officer left the room, he snatched the bottle and drained it. Even his stoical composure would not stand the strain of this jolt without breaking down. Satanta went hopping around, first on one foot, then on the other, holding his mouth and howling, while the soldiers beat their thighs and laughed until the tears ran down their faces.

But the Kiowa had the last say. Next morning he called his warriors together, crossed the Arkansas and went south to his village. Before leaving he burned all the government contractor's hay on the bank of the river opposite from the post, then went to Crooked Creek where he murdered three wood choppers—all in revenge for what he construed as an attempt to poison him at Fort Dodge.

Continuing south, he entered the Indian Territory and went on the war path. He never again returned to Fort Dodge as a friendly visitor, and in fact never conversed with a white man again—except perhaps with some victims he may have tortured—until he was taken prisoner.

In the latter part of May, 1871, the Kiowas made a bloody raid in the Red River region of Texas. Learning of their parts in the massacre, the government had both Satanta and Satank arrested. The two chiefs, with Big Tree, were sentenced to the penitentiary at Fort Richardson, Texas. Satank was a pathetic figure at the time. The old man had lost his son in Texas. On a spare horse he carried the bones with him wherever he went. After his arrest his son's bones were taken from him and he grew very gloomy. When the Indians were taken to prison, Satank rode in one wagon while Satanta and Big Tree were in another. A Caddo rode past and old Satank called: "I want to send a little message to my people. Tell them I am dead. I died the first day out of Fort Sill. My bones will be lying on the side of the road. I wish my people to gather them up and take them home."

Then he began to chant his death song. A few miles farther, he turned his back to his guards and pulled the shackles off his wrists, tearing the skin and flesh from his hands as he did so. Jerking a knife from under his blanket, he stabbed one soldier. The other jumped from the wagon. Satank seized a carbine and was trying to work the lever when he was shot twice, the second time fatally, by Sergeant J. B. Charlton, 4th Cavalry, in charge of the detail.

Satanta and Big Tree went on to Fort Richardson. Their loss was a heavy blow to the Kiowas who were quiet for two years. In the meantime the Comanches also received a stunning blow.

MCKENZIE'S VICTORY

The Quahada Comanches under Mo-wi had camped on McClellan Creek. There, on September 28th, 1872, Colonel Ranald S. McKenzie, with part of the 4th Cavalry, found them. When he came out on the wooded hills above the creek and saw the size of the village —there were two hundred and fifty lodges in it—it looked dangerous to attack. There were only two hundred and eighty-four officers and men in his command and at least five hundred warriors in that camp.

But two-to-one odds never abashed McKenzie.

"Right front into line!" he shouted. The squadrons swung into battle front. Hundreds of horses could be seen in the valley with herders frantically trying to rush them to camp so the warriors could mount.

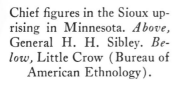

Chief figures in the Sioux uprising in Minnesota. *Above*,
General H. H. Sibley. *Below*, Little Crow (Bureau of
American Ethnology).

Refugees fleeing from the massacre area toward New Ulm, August 19, 1862. The photograph was made by Rev. Riggs during a brief rest.

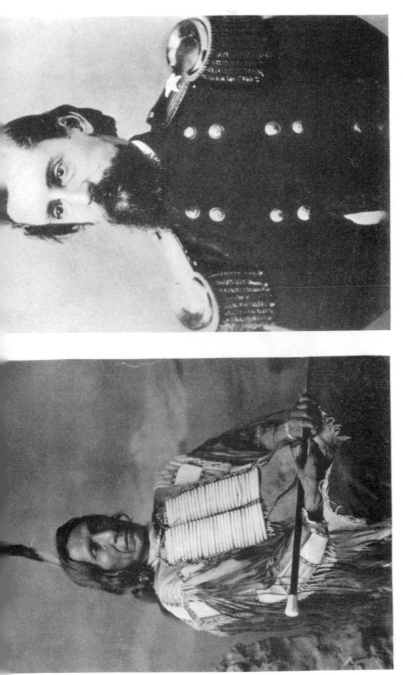

Adversaries at Fort Phil Kearny. *Left*, Red Cloud, chief of the Sioux (Bureau of American Ethnology). *Right*, General Henry B. Carrington (War Department).

Bloody Beecher's Island on the Arickaree River. This photograph, looking northwest, was made a few years after Forsyth's fight of September 17, 1868. It shows two of the surviving scouts, Chalmers Smith (*left*) and H. H. Tucker, standing approximately where Roman Nose was supposed to have fallen. Position of rifle pits is marked by the dark vegetation in foreground. The Indian charge came from the broken hills beyond the two men.

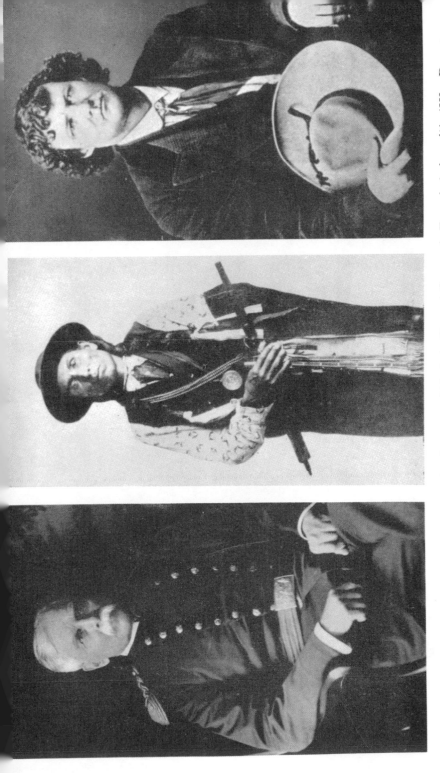

Three principals in the Beecher Island fight, Sept. 17, 1868. *Left*, General George A. Forsyth, in later life (War Department); *center*, Roman Nose (Bureau of American Ethnology); *right*, Jack Stilwell, believed to have killed Roman Nose.

Above, Officer and scout examining body of a buffalo hunter killed and scalped near Fort Dodge in the early Seventies. *Below,* A Cheyenne village on the banks of the Arkansas River. Several wagons in picture indicate these Indians are peaceful and trading with the whites.

Comanche women butchering cattle at a government beef issue during the early seventies. Man on horse, in center of trio in near background, is "talking signs" with the agency employee holding rifle.

This remarkable photograph shows a young Sioux brave actually undergoing the Sun Dance torture. Rawhide ropes, fastened to strips of flesh on his chest, extend to the center pole. Blood runs down his legs. He is dressed as for battle, carrying his shield with cover. He must dance until he frees himself by tearing out the strips of flesh on his chest. (Photograph by W. Rau, from Hutchinson's *Living Races of Mankind*, courtesy of Dodd, Mead and Company.)

Chief figures in a great tragedy. *Left,* Sitting Bull, the implacable foe of the white man. (Bureau of American Ethnology.) *Right,* General George A. Custer, who lost his own life and the lives of the men of five troops of the Seventh Cavalry, at the Little Big Horn, June 25, 1876 (War Department).

This photograph, taken on a picnic shortly before Custer's last campaign, contains the faces of eight persons killed at the Little Big Horn. *Left to right:* Lieut. James Calhoun (killed); Mr. Swett; Capt. Stephen Baker; Boston Custer, brother of the general (killed); Lieut. W. S. Edgerly, reclining; Miss Watson, with fan; Capt. Myles Keoghx (killed); Mrs. James Calhoun; Mrs. George A. Custer, in black hat; General Custer, in buckskin jacket; Dr. H. O. Paulding, on ground; Mrs. A. E. Smith; Dr. G. E. Lord (killed); Capt. T. B. Weir, seated; Lieut. W. W. Cooke (killed); Lieut. R. E. Thompson; the two Misses Wadsworth; Capt. Thomas W. Custer, the general's brother (killed); Lieut. A. E. Smith (killed). (War Department.)

On the Black Hills expedition that led to the Sioux War. General Custer is shown with a big grizzly he killed. Hunting was the general's favorite sport. Behind him, *left to right* are: Bloody Knife, Ree scout killed at the Little Big Horn; Private Noonan, Custer's orderly; and Colonel Ludlow. (War Department.)

Foes in the Nez Percé war. *Above, left,* General Nelson A. Miles, who forced Joseph's surrender (War Department). *Right,* Chief Joseph of the Nez Percés, in his later years. (Bureau of American Ethnology.) *Below,* General O. O. Howard, who pursued the Nez Percés for a thousand miles. (War Department.)

These are the warriors who survived the extermination of Dull Knife's band in early 1879, photographed on the courthouse steps at Dodge City, Kansas, where they were being tried for murder. *Left to right:* Wild Hog, George Reynolds (interpreter), Old Man, and Blacksmith. *Second row:* Frizzly Head, Left Hand, Crow and Porcupine. White man in rear is not identified.

Three irreconcilables of the plains. *Left*, Dull Knife, Cheyenne chief in the outbreak of 1878. *Center*, Little Wolf, real leader of that northward raid. *Right*, Satanta, the Kiowa scourge. (All photos by Bureau of American Ethnology.)

The Ghost dance. The Indian in the foreground is going into the trance which was characteristic of this hysterical worship. (Bureau of American Ethnology.)

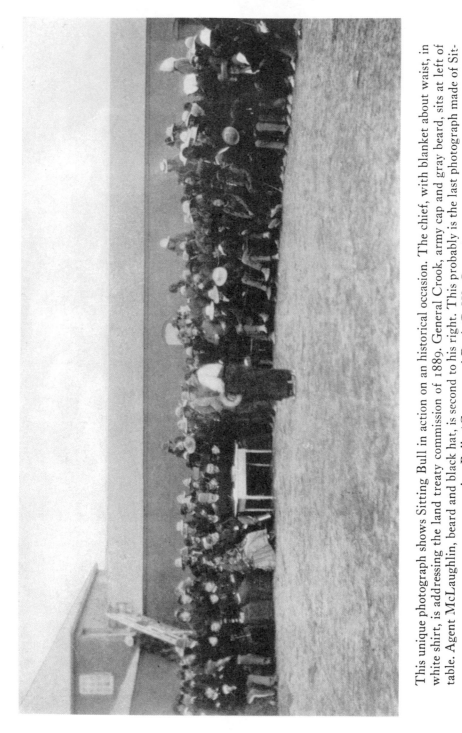

This unique photograph shows Sitting Bull in action on an historical occasion. The chief, with blanket about waist, in white shirt, is addressing the land treaty commission of 1889. General Crook, army cap and gray beard, sits at left of table. Agent McLaughlin, beard and black hat, is second to his right. This probably is the last photograph made of Sitting Bull. (Courtesy of Prof. C. W. Grace.)

"Charge!" was the next order. With guidons streaming, three troops dashed down toward the camp. The remaining troop went tearing off at a tangent, to cut off the horse herd. McKenzie knew the quickest way to whip an Indian was to dismount him.

The Comanches, taken completely by surprise, did not stay to fight. After a few volleys they bolted for the hills. One troop tried to head them off but it was too late. McKenzie lost three killed and seven wounded. Twenty-three Comanches were dead and more than a hundred captured. Their entire pony herd was in McKenzie's hands and their village burned with all its stores.

That night the Comanches showed the desperation of horse-riding Indians when deprived of their mounts. McKenzie's Tonkawa scouts had been allowed to pick the finest racing horses from the captured herd for their own. During the night the Comanches returned and, violating their usual customs, made a night attack. There was not much fighting, but the hostiles captured back all their lost ponies and the entire herd of the Tonkawas as well. It was a chagrined bunch of Indian scouts which faced McKenzie next morning, on foot, with a solitary and forlorn burro as their only remaining animal.

McKenzie returned to Fort Concho and a commission was appointed to treat with the tribes. When they met with the Kiowas, the Indians' one and only cry was "Give us back Satanta and Big Tree." Finally the government made the concession. The prisoners were to be released but not pardoned. It was a sort of parole, dependent on the good behavior of the tribe and the chiefs.

Lawrie Tatum, agent at Fort Sill, opposed very strenuously the release of Satanta. He said that "the effect on the Kiowas of the release of Satanta—a daring and treacherous chief—was like a dark rolling cloud on the western horizon." When his protests were overruled, he resigned, March 31st, 1873.

Satanta and Big Tree were brought to the guard house at Fort Sill where they were kept until the terms of their release were accepted. It was not until October 6th that Satanta walked out of his cell.

Agent Tatum spoke the truth. Two years of prison life had made a different man of Satanta. Gone was the ofttimes jovial, urbane chief. In his place was a surly, morose, defiant savage, living for one object alone—revenge. Two years of prison had aged him ten years. He seemed an old man although he was only forty-three.

At first Satanta stayed around the agency. But the old warrior was incorrigible. The Indians began to grow restless. The agents believed Satanta was the trouble maker.

Early next spring Satanta suddenly disappeared altogether. At practically the same time both the Kiowas and Comanches, with some of the Cheyennes, took the war path. Spreading over the plains, they carried death and terror over five states.[4] And Satanta was the heart and soul of the uprising.

[4] A partial list of the murders, nowhere near complete, shows 190 settlers killed. These totals are as follows: In New Mexico, 40; in Colorado, 60; Lone Wolf's raid into Texas, 7; Big Bow's raid into Texas, 4; between Camp Supply and Dodge, buffalo hunters, 5; Adobe Walls, 3; southwest from Camp Supply, buffalo hunters, 3; near Medicine Lodge and Sun City, 12; on Crooked Creek, 2; on trail north from Cheyenne Agency, 5; on Santa Fé railroad, 4; Washita and Ft. Sill Agencies, 14; Dr. Holloway's son, Cheyenne Agency, 1; killed in other raids in Texas, 30. Total 190. This list does not contain the casualties of soldiers in any of the Indian battles.

10: BEFORE THE ADOBE WALLS

THE PASSING OF THE GREAT HERD

In the spring of 1874 the lean hunters of the plains rode from their teepees in the Indian Territory day after day in vain search for the great herd of buffalo. They were Kiowas and Comanches; Cheyennes and Arapahoes; and all the lesser tribes as well; and they forgot their ancient enmities in a common dread. From the tops of the highest promontories they scanned with keen eyes the farthest horizons for the familiar dark masses which would tell them that the great herd, supplier of nearly every Indian necessity, was come at last.

But the great herd did not come to the Indian country that spring. A scattering of small herds there was, and far to the west on the Staked Plains far-riding scouts reported the presence of buffalo, but the tremendous opaque masses which the red men had known for generations, were not.

In the medicine lodges, the wizards thumped and whirled in the mazy figures of the buffalo dance. The warriors sent skyward, in ever-increasing volume, the quavering hunter's song. And still no answer came. Despair began to lay its hand on the red people of the plains.

The absence of the herds primarily meant starvation. But every portion of the bison was useful to the Indian. The skin, dressed, furnished the covering for his lodge, his robes, his bed, even the shield with which he warded off the weapons of his enemy. Buffalo hides, stretched on frames of willow withe, formed bull boats to carry the people across rivers. Saddles and halters, hair for ornaments, belts, pouches and parfleche bags—the uses for the buffalo's skin were endless.

Every part of the flesh was consumed. The hump ribs were the finest meat the plains afforded, but the Indian did not scorn the less choice portions. He ate even the intestines. Such parts of the carcass as could not be devoured on the spot were "jerked" by drying in thin strips in the sun, or put up as pemmican, to serve as reserve supplies during the long winter months. Even the dried dung of the buffalo was invaluable in the treeless plains. Pioneers still live who can tell how they gathered "buffalo chips" for hot, satisfactory fires with which to cook and warm themselves.

Food, clothing, weapons, shelter, warmth—the five great essentials—all were supplied by the buffalo. Small wonder that when the great herd failed to appear the Indians grew desperate. They blamed the white men for this failure, thinking the herds had been frightened away. The Indians were wrong. The white men had not frightened the herds—they had exterminated them.

The building of the Santa Fé, Union Pacific and other railroad lines across the plains suddenly created a new sort of a market—a market for buffalo hides and meat, which were in demand in the eastern cities. There followed the most disgraceful slaughter of animals the world has ever seen. The hide hunter set forth, pitiless, unscrupulous, absolutely fearless, and as picturesque a figure as the continent ever produced. Each hunter had his corps of skinners and his transport system. Skillful hunters could keep a force of skinners steadily busy.

The favorite weapon was the old Sharps' .50 calibre rifle, shooting 125 grains of powder and 600 grains of lead. In western parlance this weapon was known as the "Buffalo Gun," and so it is still called by the old timers. The hunters acquired an almost miraculous skill with this heavy, large-bore rifle.[1]

In doing his killing the hunter worked his way to a hiding place on top of a bluff or perhaps in one of the buffalo's own wallows. With his cartridges in his hat beside him or spread conveniently on the ground, he methodically shot the herd down, one by one. Buffalo have very dim sight and rely on their noses to warn them of danger. So far away that his scent could not be carried, the hunter killed at

---

[1] The late W. S. (Scott) Rubert of Wichita, an old plainsman, has told me of witnessing the killing of prairie chickens a long way off without breaking their skin. The hunters deliberately shot so close to their heads that the recoil of the air stunned the birds. This sounds unbelievable, but so does Billy Dixon's mile shot, and plenty of witnesses corroborated the latter.

his ease. The reports of the gun seldom frightened the quarry. Nor would they flee when one of their number was stricken. Stupidly sensing that something was wrong, they would paw the ground, bellow and snort, but remain to be killed.

It was nothing for a hunter to kill one hundred and fifty to two hundred animals in a day. And there were thousands of hunters working all the time.[2] Old timers say the shooting on a clear morning sounded like a sizable battle going on, so many rifles were at work. After the hunter came the skinners. Two skinners worked with a team of horses. A knife would split the skin down the belly and up the legs. Hitched to one edge of the hide the horses would pull it off. The hides were baled and carried to shipping points. Hams and tongues were also shipped to eastern packers. At one time there were forty thousand buffalo hides stacked in Dodge City and so rapid was the destruction that prices dwindled from four dollars and five dollars a hide to as low as a dollar.

THE OUTPOST IN THE WILDERNESS

By the Medicine Lodge Treaty of 1867, the government established the boundary line between Kansas and the Indian Territory. South of that line the Indians were to be sole masters. White men were not to hunt there and the Indians were not to cross to the north. As in so many other cases, however, the government found

[2] The following statistics show the rise and decline of the buffalo hunting industry:

Year	A.T.S.F. Hides	OTHER ROADS Hides	TOTALS Hides
1872	165,721	331,342	497,063
1873	251,443	502,886	754,329
1874	42,289	84,578	126,867
Totals	459,453	918,806	1,378,259
	Meat lbs.	Meat lbs.	Meat lbs.
1872	....	....	....
1873	1,617,600	3,235,200	4,852,800
1874	632,800	1,265,600	1,898,400
Totals	2,250,400	4,500,800	6,751,200

In 1875 the business had fallen so low that no figures were kept. The above table is from E. A. Brininstool's "Fighting Red Cloud's Warriors," by the permission of the publishers, Hunter-Trader-Trapper Co.

it could not keep this treaty. Irresponsible persons violated it and the buffalo hunters were the worst offenders.

By the fall of 1873 the buffalo were practically gone from north of the line. Then little bands of white men began stealing across and poaching in the Territory.

In the Texas Panhandle, close to where Bent Creek runs into the Canadian River, stood the ruins of an old, abandoned fort, one of the Bent and St. Vrain trading posts. Built of adobe, or mud-brick, it fell into disrepair and the rains washed the walls until they all but crumbled away. The place was known as Adobe Walls.

Because it was in the heart of a practically untouched buffalo country, a group of Dodge City men, in the spring of 1874, built a trading post and fort there. It was a simple, typical frontier post. At one corner was Myers & Leonard's log store. In another was a sod house, Hanrahan's saloon. Rath & Wright's store formed a third corner, while the fourth was the mess house, built of logs. Myers & Leonard and Rath & Wright were buffalo hide dealers of Dodge City, who helped "grub stake" the enterprise.

Their fort built, the hunters scattered to kill, bringing their hides to the Adobe Walls, constantly coming and going. For a time all went well although some of the men reported Indian signs.

Then, about the middle of June, Joe Plummer took a load of hides to the fort. When he returned to camp he found the bloody corpses of his partners, Dudley and Wallace. Both were scalped and butchered. One was pinned to the ground by a stake through his breast. Plummer almost killed a horse riding back to the Adobe Walls with the news.

Two other hunters were killed on the Salt Fork of the Red River —Cheyenne Jack Jones and Blue Billy, a German. Their camp was destroyed and all their stock run off. A big Indian camp was reported in the headwaters of the Sweetwater and the Washita. Every day saw new parties of the far-ranging hunters hurrying in to the protection of the fort.

The night of June 26th was sultry and the people at the Adobe Walls sat with open doors. Outside, the blackness of the night was only dimly lit by brilliant stars. Heat lightning played on the horizon. Horses, picketed to graze, could be heard stamping and moving about. There was another sound which the buffalo hunters, with all their experience, failed to interpret. In the timber along the creek owls hooted. The eery hooting from the woods was answered from the other side of the fort. Back and forth the owls talked, a sinister, goblin colloquy. It was noticed but the hunters thought nothing of it.

Twenty-eight men and one woman slept at Adobe Walls that night. The woman was Mrs. William Olds, wife of the restaurant man in the rear of Rath & Wright's. It was hot; the hunters spread their blankets out of doors to sleep. The stock seemed nervous. Occasionally a horse snorted or stamped. But no particular disturbance occurred until about two o'clock in the morning.

Hanrahan's saloon was a "soddy," with walls and roof of thick slabs of prairie sod, a favorite primitive building material in the early West. The slabs were laid on top of each other horizontally to form the wall. The roof was also covered with the heavy chunks. A cottonwood ridge pole, which supported the roof, proved too weak. The time it selected to break was two o'clock on that morning of June 27th. At the loud crack everybody awoke. The roof did not fall but it hung dangerously and all hands turned out to repair it. Had that ridge pole broken at any other time—say at noon, or the evening before—twenty-eight men and a woman would have been slaughtered in the Adobe Walls. It cracked just in time to awaken everybody so that there was no more sleep before dawn and thus forestalled the surprise attack the Indians had planned.

The east was pink when the repairs were completed. Billy Dixon [3] started out of the corral early to get his saddle pony. As he reached the spot where it was picketed he glanced toward the dark woods beyond. There was a movement. He strained his eyes through the morning gloom. Feathered war bonnets and painted ponies—it was a huge band of Indians.

The savages yelled as they saw themselves discovered and Dixon

[3] The biography of this remarkable plains figure is told in "The Life of Billy Dixon," by his widow, Mrs. Olive K. Dixon, of Amarillo, Texas. Mrs. Dixon is a prominent member of the Panhandle-Plains Historical Society. For many incidents in this and the next chapter I am indebted to her.

raced for life. Leaping on the back of his pony, he fired his gun and dashed for the stockade. At the shot every hunter seized his rifle. In an instant Adobe Walls was ready for defense.

THE BUFFALO HUNTERS' FIGHT

Everyone expected the Indians to follow their usual tactics— sweep around the buildings, kill anyone they found outside and run off the stock. But these warriors were on no mere horse-stealing raid. Straight as a lance thrust they drove for the buildings themselves. Plumes tossed and the vivid war paint splashed their bodies with all the colors of the spectrum. Scalps fluttered from shield rims and horses' bridles; rifles and lances waved and ornaments of bead and silver gleamed. It was a splendid, barbaric—and terrifying— sight.

Two hunters failed to make it to the enclosure. The Shadler brothers had slept in their wagon outside the stockade. The Indians caught and killed them. Into the stockade itself the red warriors charged, filling the space around the buildings in which the whites were penned. Nine hunters were in Hanrahan's saloon, where there was plenty of whiskey but very little ammunition. Eleven sure shots, well armed and well supplied with cartridges, were in Myers & Leonard's store. The remainder, six old hands, with Mrs. Olds, were in Rath & Wright's.

Straight up to the doors rode the Indians. Every glass window pane was broken by bullets. The fierce warriors hammered on the doors with butts of their rifles trying to break a way in. From the windows the hunters never for a second ceased shooting. Indians dropped fast. The wounded crawled painfully out of the stockade. Suddenly all were gone as quickly as they came.

For a time the hostiles busied themselves carrying off their dead and wounded. Then they began a long-range duel with the fort. But at this game the hunters held all the top cards. They were the finest marksmen in the world. Their huge, heavy guns carried farther than the Indian rifles. The red sharpshooters grew discouraged.

The unusual boldness of the hostiles' first charge was due to the fact that a Comanche medicine man, I-sa-tai, had convinced them that he had an infallible charm which would prevent their enemies' bullets from touching them. They rushed into the battle with full confidence and were amazed and enraged to see their warriors dropping.

During the duel the whites suffered their third casualty. Billy Tyler and Fred Leonard recklessly stepped out into the stockade to get a better shot. A Comanche bullet ripped through Tyler's lungs. Leonard dragged him indoors and he died half an hour later.

Soon after Tyler was hit the Indians made a second rush. The murderous buffalo guns shattered the charge. Then some of the boldest hostiles hid behind stacks of robes, from which they tried to pick off the white men.

At one place in the fort the ammunition question was vexing. Some of the rifles in Hanrahan's saloon were useless because there were no cartridges to fit them. A hundred feet away stood Rath & Wright's. Hanrahan's door flew open. Racing across the courtyard went two men—Billy Dixon and James Hanrahan. At their appearance the Indians opened with every rifle within range. The ground around the feet of the runners was churned and ripped by bullets. Bounding, zig-zagging, running their best, they reached the store and tumbled inside. By some miracle neither had been touched.

The purpose of the dash now appeared. Dixon and Hanrahan had come for ammunition. Rath & Wright had plenty of cartridges, but it also had the fewest defenders and the added responsibility of the only woman in the fort. The men begged Dixon to remain and help defend the building. He was known to be one of the greatest shots in the Southwest. Dixon consented. Hanrahan elected to carry back the ammunition. Filling a sack with cartridges, he waited a favorable opportunity and dashed back toward his saloon. Once more he drew the hail of bullets. But again he reached his destination safe.

About two o'clock the Indian fire slackened and at four it ceased entirely. After a time a venturesome hunter stepped out of his shelter. Others followed. The Indians were gone. In their first exploration around the stockade the hunters saw what terrible havoc had been wrought. In spite of every effort by the hostiles to carry off the dead, thirteen savages lay near the buildings, too close to be removed. Fifty-six dead horses were counted in the vicinity. There were great splashes of blood here and there in the grass. Nobody knows how many Indians were killed. The defenders estimated one hundred dead and wounded. The Indians subsequently said six Cheyennes and three Comanches were killed, a total of nine. As has been seen, however, thirteen dead bodies were found on the field after the battle.

All the horses were gone at the fort, but next day a hunter brought in some. There were still Indians in the vicinity, but Henry Lease offered to go to Dodge for help. He rode out of the fort the second night and eventually reached Dodge City safely.

Across the creek, east of Adobe Walls was a high bluff. The third afternoon following the fight a band of about fifteen Indians appeared on this bluff, gazing at the fort. They were almost a mile away, but Dixon reached for his big buffalo gun. The other hunters, among whom he had a wonderful reputation as a marksman, urged him to try a long shot. Carefully he adjusted his sights. Twice he took aim before he fired. So distant was the target that the report of the gun died completely away before there was a movement on the bluff. Everybody thought Dixon had missed. Then one of the tiny figures whirled suddenly out of his saddle. The hunter had struck his mark at nearly a mile!

The buffalo hunters were used to wonderful shooting. But they were simply dumbfounded by this exploit. The Indians scurried for cover. In a few minutes two of them crept forward and dragged their fellow to concealment. Years later a surveyor measured the distance from where Dixon fired to where the Indian was seen to fall. It was exactly 1,538 yards, just 182 yards short of a full mile. Dixon always modestly said it was a "scratch" shot. But it remains a wonder story of the West.

On the sixth day William Olds, whose wife was the only woman at the fort, accidentally killed himself by discharging his rifle while he was climbing down a ladder. His was the fourth death at the fort. Two days later the relief column from Dodge City, under Tom Nixon and Henry Lease, arrived.

11: THE ARMY TAKES THE FIELD

THE buffalo guns won a bloody victory for white hunters at the Adobe Walls, but the echoes of their thunderous reports were still to be heard on many a distant horizon. The allied tribes— Comanches, Kiowas, Cheyennes, and Arapahoes—scattered in every direction looking for revenge.

Kiowas, prowling northeast, ambushed Pat Hennessey's wagon train, freighting supplies from Wichita, Kansas, to Anadarko, Indian Territory. Every man in the train was killed. Hennessey was tortured to death.[1] Soon after a dozen men were killed by Comanches near Medicine Lodge, Kansas. Both Comanches and Kiowas raided deep into Texas. There was not a road in western Kansas, eastern Colorado, the Texas Panhandle, or the Indian Territory which was safe. About two hundred settlers were killed.

The frontier yelled for the army. General Nelson A. Miles, commanding the department, promptly marched from Fort Dodge on August 14th. Lieutenant Colonel J. W. (Black Jack) Davidson started west from Fort Sill. And Colonel Ranald S. McKenzie advanced northeast from Fort Clark. The plan was to catch the hostile bands between the three columns and thus crush them.

A cheering bit of news came to Miles on the march. Davidson and his 10th Cavalry "buffalo soldiers"[2] had fought a brisk engagement with Kiowas and Comanches at the Wichita Agency at Anadarko. The losses were slight but an important result was the capture of Satanta, regarded as the ring-leader in the uprising.

Meantime Miles had some fighting on his own hands. On the morning of August 30th Lieutenant Frank D. Baldwin, with fifty white and Delaware scouts was suddenly "jumped" by two hun-

---

[1] The present city of Hennessey, Okla., which stands near the spot where this massacre occurred, derives its name from this tragic incident.

[2] Negro soldiers. So called by the Indians because their kinky hair looked like buffalo wool.

dred hostiles as he followed a trail up the Sweetwater valley. Badly outnumbered, Baldwin's men scattered among the rocks and under-brush and held the enemy off until Major Compton and Major Biddle arrived to extricate them from their danger.

The cavalry wasted no time. Wheeling their men into line, Compton and Biddle charged. Captain A. R. Chaffee led the advance, merrily joking with his men.

"Forward!" he cried. "If any man is killed I will make him a corporal!"

The veterans rode forward laughing, scarcely noticing the bullets which came skipping about them. The Indians mounted and "skedaddled." After following them twenty-five miles over the roughest kind of country, the troops found themselves in a desert without water of any kind. Some of the men suffered so they even opened the veins in their own arms to moisten their lips with the blood.

Miles' command limped at last back to the Sweetwater. September 10th found them camped on McClellan Creek. They were short of rations. Miles' wagon train had been attacked the day before and four men killed or wounded. The general wrote a message to Camp Supply and dispatched it by a small party consisting of two celebrated scouts, Billy Dixon [3] and Amos Chapman, and four veteran 6th Cavalry troopers, commanded by Sergeant Z. T. Woodhull.

The detail, purposely small to escape notice in the hostile country, traveled unmolested for two nights, hiding by day. The second morning, however, it was discovered by a large Kiowa war party.

TWENTY-FIVE TO ONE

The Kiowas wasted no time. They charged, yelling, at the dead gallop, shooting as they came. The first volley hit four of the white men. Private George W. Smith, holding the horses, fell flat on his face, a bullet through his body. The horses stampeded with all the

---

[3] The hero of the Adobe Walls fight. He joined the army scouts after that battle. Amos Chapman was a "squaw man." He returned to live with the Cheyennes after the war and died among them in 1926.

extra ammunition. A bullet broke Chapman's leg. Private John Harrington was wounded and so was Woodhull.

Somehow, by accurate shooting, they stopped that first Indian rush. Dixon, still unhurt, looked keenly around for cover. The only depression anywhere near them was a buffalo wallow, a few inches deep and ten to twelve feet in diameter. But it was their sole hope.

"Come on, boys," the scout called. "Let's fight it out here."

Woodhull and Harrington, with Private Peter Rath, the only unwounded soldier, followed. But neither Chapman nor Smith moved.

"Come on, Amos," yelled Dixon to Chapman.

"I can't," groaned the reply. "My leg's broken."

There were at least a hundred Kiowas in sight, and every one of their rifles was kicking up the dirt around the wallow. For a few minutes the four men in it worked desperately deepening the hole with their knives.

At the first breathing spell Dixon again looked over the flat. Chapman and Smith were still there, but Chapman was painfully pulling himself along with his hands, inch by inch, toward his comrades. The sight was too much for Dixon. Heedless of warnings, he jumped up and dashed for the wounded man. Bent double to present as small a target as possible, with bullets singing in his ears, he reached Chapman untouched. At his command, Amos climbed on his back, and although Dixon was the smaller man, he carried him to the wallow in safety. As usual the Indian shooting was wretchedly poor.[4]

Dixon's exploit provoked the Kiowas to another attack. This time they swept right up to the buffalo wallow. But the veteran defenders shot deliberately, with careful aim, making every bullet count. Two of the surest rifles in Miles' army were in that wallow. The Kiowas retreated quickly to a safer distance.

[4] Chapman was quoted by General Richard I. Dodge in his "Thirty-one Years Among Our Wild Indians" as saying that he carried the body of Smith to the wallow in spite of the fact that his own leg was broken off at the ankle and the foot was dragging. This story was disproved by the testimony of the other men at the fight as well as of Dixon himself. The poor shooting of the Indians in nearly all the battles is explained by the fact that they were always so short of ammunition that they had no cartridges to spare for the target practice so essential to good marksmanship.

It was very hot. By noon every man was suffering from thirst, made more intolerable now that all were wounded, including Rath and Dixon. Yet with the utmost coolness they aimed over the rim of the wallow pulling the trigger every time an Indian came close enough for a good target. A growing clutter of dead horses and accoutrements where stricken warriors had been dragged away, showed how they had taken their toll.

Hour after hour dragged along. Under the torture of thirst some of the wounded grew delirious. But now a great black thunder cloud gathered in the southwest. The lightning began to play while the deep reverberations of the thunder gave promise of one of the violent storms which are characteristic of the prairie country. It came quickly. In blinding sheets the rain fell, blotting out the landscape, the hostile Indians, the body of poor Smith, and drenching them to the skin. But though they were wet through, the rain was welcome. The air was cooled and rivulets of water caught in the rim of the wallow to gather in a pool at the bottom. Muddy it was, and bloody too, from their own clotted wounds, but the men lay on their stomachs and drank and drank.

Ammunition was at a premium. When the rain let up somebody noticed the cartridge belt on Smith's body. The Indians had repeatedly tried to reach him but were driven away by unerring riflery. Now, their ardor cooled by the sudden drenching, they sat on the prairie out of range, holding a council while their horses grazed at the end of their lariats.

Rath went after Smith's ammunition. As he stooped to detach the cartridge belt he was surprised to see his comrade twitch. Without stopping to investigate, he lifted the still form and carried it to the buffalo wallow. Smith was still alive but with a bullet through his lungs. A few hours later he died. His comrades propped up his body so the head showed over the edge of the wallow, to make the Indians think he was still able to fight.

At nightfall Rath volunteered to go for help to Camp Supply. He and Dixon were the only ones able to move. He started east but returned in a couple of hours, unable to find the trail. He had seen no Indians. Dixon started at sun-up. He found the trail and later met a detachment of troops under Major Price whose approach had caused the Indians to withdraw. The scout led the way to the buffalo wallow where the men's wounds were dressed and Smith's body buried in the very hole where his comrades had fought for their lives.[5] Then the wounded were taken to Camp Supply and the dispatches delivered.

PALO DURO, CANYON OF DEATH

Lone Wolf, the most active of the confederated Indian leaders, stepped into Satanta's moccasins when that chief was imprisoned. He had his camp in Palo Duro Canyon, in northern Texas, a splendid base of operation from which war parties went in every direction. The canyon, a deep cleft in the flat prairie, was so naturally advantageous that there were big Cheyenne, Arapaho and Comanche camps there also.

Hoping to locate this camp, Colonel McKenzie, with his 4th Cavalry, four companies of infantry, and a detail of Seminole, Tonkawa and white scouts, marched from Fort Concho the middle of September. Blanco Canyon was supposed to be the hostile rendezvous. He reached it September 27th but no Indians were there. Disappointed, McKenzie left his heavy supply train behind and struck boldly north.

The Tule and Palo Duro Rivers lay in his path, winding through deep canyons. Indian signs indicated the hostiles might be in one or both of these valleys. With a screen of scouts and skirmishers ahead, the command was halfway to the Tule Canyon by noon of the 28th.

A sharp crackle of fire, far in advance, electrified them. "Indians!" was the exclamation on every tongue. The troops pressed forward eagerly but were disappointed. A small band of hostile scouts had exchanged some long-range shots with the advance and drawn off as the main body approached.

It was the first sight of hostile Indians. They camped that night

---

[5] On recommendation of General Miles, Congress later awarded the Congressional Medal of Honor by special vote to all five survivors of this celebrated border fight.

in the Tule Canyon, with a double guard. Just at moonrise, the expected happened. Silhouetted against the pale, star-lit sky, appeared a mass of Indians. Down toward the camp they swept. But the sentries were alert. At the first alarm shots, the troopers were ready. Two or three white-hot volleys flashed out into the gloom. There were some unearthly war whoops and the Indians drew off. But they did not leave the vicinity. All night long there was skirmishing between the outposts and prowling warriors who crept close to take pot-shots at the men near the campfires. By morning everyone was thoroughly angry and in the mood for real fighting. The Indians, however, refused to accommodate them. Having kept the troops awake all night, they drew off shortly before sunrise.[6]

After breakfast, McKenzie assigned Sergeant J. B. Charlton [7] with two Tonkawa scouts, Job and Johnson, to locate the village. It was easy to follow the Indian trail. For several miles the scouts rode rapidly; then they began to notice other trails converging with the one they were following. At last they were convinced they were almost on a great camp.

But where was it? For miles, as far as the eye could reach, the country stretched bare and level as a table. They were morally certain from the signs which multiplied at every step that they were very close to a monster Indian village. By rights, hundreds of teepees should stretch in every direction; the plain should be populous

---

[6] Just at dawn occurred a grimly humorous incident. A solitary Comanche rode into range and Henry, a Tonkawa scout, killed his horse with a lucky, long-distance shot. Thinking he had also killed the rider, the Tonkawa rode to the spot. But the Comanche was only stunned. At Henry's approach he leaped to his feet and pulled the "Tonk" out of his saddle. Then began a strange combat. Henry's rifle was in its scabbard on his horse. His blanket so encumbered him that he could not reach his revolver. The Comanche could not get a lethal weapon either but his unstrung bow was in his hand, so seizing his enemy by the hair, he began giving him the trouncing of his life. At every cut of the bow, Henry jumped about three feet in the air, and yelled at the approaching troopers, "Why you no shoot? Why you no shoot?" The soldiers were all roaring with laughter but finally someone shot the Comanche and the discomfited Henry took his scalp with great satisfaction.

[7] The same man who shot and killed Satank in 1871. To Captain R. G. Carter I am under obligations for considerable of the information concerning McKenzie's movements in this campaign. Capt. Carter's book "The Old Sergeant's Story," a compilation of the letters of Sergeant Charlton is worth the attention of any student of plains history. He is author of numerous other works on western Indian campaigns.

with grazing pony herds; a myriad flea-bitten dogs should be running hither and yon in joyous canine abandon, while their masters should be visible in scores, mounted and on foot, lazing in the shade or going about their duties.

Yet there was not a sign of life in any direction. It was creepy. The superstitious Tonkawas began to look uneasily over their shoulders as if they expected at any minute to see a full-blown camp of their enemies materialize from the air.

Quite without warning the whole mystery was explained. The scouts were forced to rein their horses to a stop. At their feet yawned one of the colossal crevices which sometimes break the monotony of the plains of North Texas. It was the Palo Duro Canyon, slashed deep into the flat face of the prairie. While Job held the horses, Charlton and Johnson crept to the edge of the abyss. With awe they gazed into its depths. Straight down, the walls dropped sheer. Halfway between the men and the bottom of the canyon soared an eagle, looking a mere speck. Far down a small stream of water trickled. Flecks of valley land were visible, with here and there dark masses of cedar trees casting gloomy shadows and making the scene almost nocturnal although the sun shone brightly on the plains above.

But something else riveted the attention of the scouts. In the valley were hundreds of grazing horses. Viewed from the immense height they looked no bigger than prairie dogs. And conical white teepees thickly dotted the banks of the stream as far down the canyon as the eye could see. They were gazing down at Lone Wolf's stronghold.

"Heap Injun!" grunted the Tonkawa in Charlton's ear.

"You bet your life, old scout, and some canyon too," whispered the sergeant as they snaked their way back to the horses.

They did the twenty-five miles back to the command in record time. McKenzie's men were in the saddle almost before the sergeant's words were out of his mouth. It was nightfall but they were spoiling for a fight. All night the troopers rode, reaching their destination just at sun-up of September 27th.

INTO THE CANYON

At their feet was the canyon, but how should they descend into it? Like hounds the scouts scattered up and down the edge. There must be some easy way down but no time to look for it now. Presently a trail was reported and McKenzie went to inspect.

It could hardly be called a trail unless by that name one can describe a crooked, zig-zag scratch in the face of the mighty cliffs down which antelope, or deer, or perhaps mountain sheep had found precarious footing to the water. But McKenzie did not hesitate.

"Mr. Thompson, take your men down and open the fight," he said.

In a moment the scouts were over the edge of the cliff, starting down the precipitous route. Down, down they went, followed by the whole command. They were descending well above the camp and they hoped to reach the bottom before the Indians were warned. They knew what the hostiles might do to them if they caught them plastered against the sides of the canyon.

Lieutenant W. A. Thompson tested every foot of the way. Sometimes the path was so narrow that the men went along with their faces to the cliff, their arms outspread and their bodies flattened against the rocky wall as they "cooned" across. For a time there was scarcely a sound. But a big body of men cannot go down a route like that without making some noise. Somebody dislodged a small boulder. Down the side of the cliff it bounded, thudding against the wall, carrying with it a miniature avalanche of dirt and gravel which gathered volume and racket as it descended.

Instantly the canyon rang with a war whoop. An Indian down the valley had heard the noise.[8] By the time the first scouts reached the bottom the hostiles were coming up the gorge to meet them. For a time it was a question whether the little group of white men could hold back the Indians long enough to permit their comrades to land.

---

[8] This man, Red Warbonnet, a Kiowa, had a herd of white horses of which he was very proud. He had gone out to look at these horses in the early morning when he heard the soldiers and gave the alarm. He was instantly shot down by the scouts.

The Kiowas took shelter behind rocks and in the thick cedar trees. The scouts were under heavy fire.

Down the canyon was a ledge, partly hidden by the tree tops, where lay half a dozen Kiowa sharpshooters. Their bullets chipped the rocks all around McKenzie's soldiers, who were in a tight place against the face of the cliff, unable to defend themselves. Two of the scouts ran toward the ledge, threw themselves on their stomachs and under a storm of bullets began a duel with the sharpshooters. White man's marksmanship won. Down from the niche pitched one warrior after another. In a short time the hole was cleaned out.

By this time the soldiers were nearly all safely down. Powder smoke made a gray cloud, giving the scene a hazy aspect. In the midst of this McKenzie could be heard shouting orders.

Along the canyon went the soldiers. The hostiles retreated. A pony herd, frightened by the uproar, charged back and forth across the bottom of the canyon, adding to the confusion. They were cornered at last in a blind gulch and kept there to the end of the fight.

It was a long way to the hostile village and the Indians were determined to hold McKenzie back until their camp could be evacuated. When sunset came, the troops were still five miles from the pass where the squaws and children were leaving the canyon. By the time the command reached it and climbed to the plain, the canyon was dark—Lone Wolf and his people had disappeared.

McKenzie returned to the gorge. Bodies of four Kiowa braves were found but they knew they had hit many more.[9] Only a hundred teepees were captured but of these they made a huge bonfire. In the morning McKenzie started back to Blanco Canyon, driving before him fourteen hundred captured horses and mules. These he killed in the Tule Valley and their bones whiten that part of the country to this day.

THE END OF THE UPRISING

The Battle of Palo Duro Canyon completely discouraged the

[9] The Comanches say that a number of women and children were killed in this fight.

Kiowas, not so much because of their losses, but because there now seemed no place they could retreat to in safety. There were still many Indians out on the Staked Plains, but hundreds surrendered.

It is extremely difficult to follow all the movements of troops and Indians in the succeeding months, so disconnected were they. Everywhere were detachments of soldiers hunting scattered bands of hostiles. There were a number of small fights but only a brief summary of this "cleaning up" phase of the campaign can be given.

Colonel Buell and the 11th Infantry destroyed a Kiowa camp on October 9th on the Salt Fork, killing one warrior and putting the rest to flight. Several hundred lodges were burned. Captain Chaffee, with Troop 1, 6th Cavalry, surprised and destroyed another Indian camp October 17th. A large Comanche village surrendered to Major G. W. Schofield at Elk Creek on October 24th. Colonel Davidson brought in ninety-one captured warriors, with three hundred women and children on October 28th. The Indians were on the run everywhere, seeking a place to hide, or some way to surrender without being shot down.

A Tennessee family named German [10] was surprised September 9th by Cheyennes. The father and mother, the eldest son and the eldest daughter were killed. The four younger girls, Catherine, 17; Sophia, 15; Julia, 10; and Adelaide, 5, were carried off as captives. The Cheyennes were from the villages of Gray Beard and Stone Calf. The two older girls went with Stone Calf's band to the Staked Plains while their sisters were taken with Gray Beard's people to McClellan Creek.

Scouts told Miles that the Indians held four white girls. He took immediate steps to recover them. Lieutenant Baldwin was given a separate command and told to find Gray Beard's village and rescue the girls. Baldwin had a troop of cavalry, a company of infantry, a howitzer and a train of wagons. He discovered the hostile village November 8th. One of the quickest fights in the war followed. Putting his infantry in the wagons and telling the teamsters to stick close to the cavalry, Baldwin charged, as the saying goes,

[10] Miles and others spelled this name "Germaine" but the correct spelling is "German." The massacre of the family occurred on the Smoky Hill River in Kansas.

"horse, foot and dragoons." Down into the village galloped the cavalry with the wagons full of infantrymen bouncing and clattering right behind. The Indians, completely baffled by the strange maneuver, did not even stop to kill their prisoners. The children were found in Gray Beard's abandoned teepee, their little bodies scarred and bruised, and half-starved. Dr. James L. Powell, the medical officer, took them to Fort Leavenworth where they were lodged with a family named Carney.

Thus two of the girls were saved, but the recovery of their sisters was more difficult. Stone Calf was far out on the Staked Plains. The girls lived lives of terror and ill-treatment. The recent reverses had made the Indians ugly. Their prisoners feared every day they would be murdered—and did not care much if they were.

But early in January Miles sent some of Stone Calf's people who had surrendered, with a message to the chief. A faithful Indian scout accompanied them, carrying a photograph of the two younger girls, taken after their recapture, with this message in the general's own hand:

"To the Misses Germaine: Your little sisters are well and in the hands of friends. Do not be discouraged. Every effort is being made for your welfare.
"NELSON A. MILES, COL., FIFTH INFANTRY."

To Stone Calf went the ultimatum that unless he surrendered the girls uninjured, Miles would hunt him down without mercy, while he would receive amnesty if he did surrender them and came in to the reservation. Stone Calf accepted the terms—he was tired of this profitless fighting. His first act was to take the sisters away from their owners of the moment and lodge them in a teepee close to his own. Late in January he surrendered at Darlington. The girls afterward identified seventy-five Indians who were involved in the murder of their family and other offenses and these were ordered arrested. The sisters were sent to Leavenworth where they joined the little girls whom they had given up as lost.[11]

Practically all the warring Indians had now surrendered. In ar-

[11] All four of the German girls were still alive at this writing (1934). All married and reared families. Two lived in California, one in Nebraska and the fourth in Kansas.

resting the men pointed out by the German girls, one resisted and tried to escape. He was shot and some of the bullets flew into the Cheyenne prison camp, causing a panic. The Indians fled to a nearby hill. In the sharp fight which followed eleven Cheyennes were killed and nineteen men of Lieutenant Colonel T. H. Neill's command were hit in trying to take the hill. Later most of the Cheyennes moved quietly to the agency and mingled among their people already there. The worst offenders were sent to St. Augustine, Florida.

Peace reigned once more in the Southwest, but there still remained to be played out the tragic sequel of the Indian war. Satanta, the Kiowa chief, was in prison for his part in the uprising. There was no proof of his guilt but he had violated his parole by leaving the reservation so he was sent to the penitentiary at Huntsville, Texas, for life. That was the end of everything for Satanta. With downcast head he entered the prison. Nothing was said but the very guards knew he would not live long. A year passed—two years —three. One day he appeared at the prison dispensary.

"My heart is bad," he said and asked for medicine. He was placed in a second story ward of the prison hospital. Shortly afterward a weird sound was heard; with many a minor chord and long-drawn wail, it descended from the air—the Kiowa death song. Then the guards saw the old warrior at the window. With one last look at the blue sky under which he had so often roamed free, Satanta folded his arms and plunged headlong. He was dashed to death on the stony ground below.

12: THE DIPLOMAT AND THE WARRIOR

CUSTER'S BLACK HILLS EXPEDITION

SCARCELY was the uprising quelled in the Indian Territory when the hard-worked soldiers of the frontier army were called to face a far more dangerous enemy a thousand miles to the north.

Frantic messages from agents in the Dakotas said that the whole Teton Sioux Nation was on the verge of an outbreak. There were more than thirty-five thousand Sioux in the country and they could muster around seven thousand fighting men. Moreover, from earliest times they had borne a reputation for ferocity and prowess. As a matter of fact, only a part of the Sioux went on the war path, but even so, the army officers were justified in looking grave at the reports.

If ever any people was goaded into war, it was the Sioux in 1876. And if United Nations Council had sat in that period, the United States would have been ruled an "aggressor nation." The Sioux war of 1876 was fought because the government could not make its own citizens abide by its treaties. For eight years after Red Cloud's campaign of 1868 there was peace of a sort, although the encroachments of the white men caused constant trouble, with frequent killings. The treaty which ended that war expressly stipulated: "The country north of the North Platte and east of the summits of the Big Horn Mountains shall be held and considered to be unceded Indian territory," and further agreed: "No white person or persons shall be permitted to settle upon or occupy any portion of the same; or without the consent of the Indians, first had and obtained, to pass through the same." The land described in this article —which closes with the agreement that the Bozeman trail and all the posts along it shall be abandoned—is the Powder River country.

At its eastern border lay the frowning Black Hills, sacred to the Sioux and among their best hunting grounds. In 1874, despite treaty stipulations, on the pretext of making a survey for military purposes, General George A. Custer, with the 7th Cavalry, was sent into the gloomy fastnesses of these hills. When he returned he broadcast the news that there was gold there. As if to reassure itself of this fact, the government sent a second expedition under Professor Jenney, which came out of the Black Hills with such indubitable proofs of gold that a stampede of prospectors followed.[1]

Now that the government had started all the trouble it tried to halt the rush of gold miners. Troops were thrown about the mountains and expeditions were sent into them to round up trespassers and bring them back. These, however, were speedily acquitted by the local civil courts. Through the lines drifted miners by hundreds, with the constant news of fresh "strikes" adding fuel to their excitement. The Black Hills were full of them. Deadwood, Custer City and a score of other mining towns sprang up. The Sioux were furious.

Red Cloud saw the handwriting on the wall and sent some of his braves to see how many buffalo were on the plains. They reported that the buffalo were few; they could not be depended upon for any length of time. Red Cloud knew he could not fight without supplies. He kept peace through the troubles which followed.

Confessing by its act its inability to keep its citizens out of the forbidden territory, the government next tried to buy the Black Hills. A commission did its best in June, 1875, to secure from the Sioux the right of mining there. The reservation part of the Indians agreed to a sale, but at prices ranging from $20,000,000 to $50,000,000. The government's offer of $6,000,000 was rejected with scorn. But the non-reservation Sioux simply refused to sell under any consideration and with deadly seriousness warned all white men to keep out. The commission returned, frustrated, to Washington.

[1] "If this fact [Jenney's expedition] does not lift the thin disguise of military necessity from the first [Custer's] expedition, one could hardly imagine what would."—Dunn, "Massacres of the Mountains," p. 587.

That fall the wild Sioux moved out into the wilderness far from the agencies. The reservation Sioux grew restless. Everyone knew war was inevitable. Two names were on every tongue—names destined to become household words—Sitting Bull and Crazy Horse.

THE LEADERS OF THE SIOUX

No man ever had a more important influence upon the destiny of the frontier than Sitting Bull, the famous Unkpapa chief. To the average reader his picturesque name conjures up a novel-inspired vision of a ferocious savage, careering over a corpse-strewn field, shaking a bloody tomahawk and suffering from a perennial thirst for human gore. A study of the great Indian's character, however, fails to justify this picture.

Sitting Bull was in all respects a remarkable man. He was a natural-born fighter and therefore had enemies all his life, not only among the white people but among his own followers. As a result there has been much traducing of his character.

It is pretty clear, however, that Sitting Bull was no coward. He was not cruel; he was not even particularly bloodthirsty. On the other hand, he was a real patriot, a great organizer and a wily politician. And he was intelligent above all his fellows for "he alone of all his people could see through the curious wiles of the white men, who were as strange and incomprehensible to the Indians as if they were men from Mars." [2]

He was a famous warrior while still in his twenties, going on his first war path at the age of fourteen. He is credited by some authorities with leading the attack on Fort Buford in 1866. Sitting Bull's now famous pictograph autobiography contains pictures showing his participation in twenty-three battles with Indians or whites, and twelve horse-taking raids. It has been charged [3] that Sitting Bull was not present at the Little Big Horn fight. But his ablest biographer, Stanley Vestal, has accumulated plenty of eye-witness evidence that he was not only there but that he fought in the front ranks.

[2] Vestal, "Sitting Bull," p. 75.
[3] Notably by Rain-in-the-Face and Major McLaughlin.

After the Miles campaign in 1877 Gall is said to have accused him of cowardice. It was an undeserved stigma. First to last, Sitting Bull's career shows not only high physical courage, but even higher moral courage. He remained the white man's enemy to the end, when everyone else had given up, even though it eventually led him to a dishonored grave.

It was not as a fighter, however, but as a diplomat and organizer that Sitting Bull rendered his chief service to the Sioux. He used his political ability to keep his people together and ready to fight. Vestal says he was elected head chief of all the Sioux bands in 1851, but the army records credit him with but small influence as late as 1875, when "he was not a chief but a head man, whose immediate following did not exceed thirty or forty lodges." [4]

In his way he was a humanitarian. He secured the release of a white woman, Fanny Kelly, in 1864. At another time he saved the life of an Assiniboine boy, whom he later adopted into his family. There are other instances of Sitting Bull's mercy.

John F. Finerty, a newspaper correspondent, who saw him in British Columbia in 1879, thus described his appearance:

"An Indian mounted on a cream-colored pony, and holding in his hand an eagle's wing which did duty as a fan, spurred in back of the chiefs and stared stolidly, for a minute or so, at me. His hair, parted in the ordinary Sioux fashion, was without a plume. His broad face, with a prominent hooked nose and wide jaws, was destitute of paint. His fierce, half-bloodshot eyes gleamed from under brows which displayed large perceptive organs, and, as he sat there on his horse, regarding me with a look which seemed blended of curiosity and insolence, I did not need to be told that he was Sitting Bull.

". . . After a little, the noted savage dismounted and led his horse partly into the shade. I noticed that he was an inch or two over medium height, broadly built, rather bow-legged I thought, and he limped slightly as though from an old wound. He sat upon the ground, and was soon engirdled by a crowd of young warriors with whom he was an especial favorite as representing the unquenchable

<hr>

[4] "Record of Engagements," p. 49.

hostility of the aboriginal savage to the hated Palefaces." [5]

So much for Sitting Bull, the most famous western Indian who ever lived and the real leader of the Sioux war of 1875–1877.

If Sitting Bull was the greatest organizer and diplomat the Sioux ever had, Crazy Horse was one of their all-time preeminent warriors.[6] One of the most tragic and heroic figures of modern history, he combined in his own character most of the virtues of his people. Crazy Horse was an enemy of all the white men but even hard-bitten Indian fighters like Crook and Miles and Bourke yielded him ungrudging admiration.

He was born in 1844 and from his boyhood up was a warrior. At the age of sixteen he had won distinction against the Gros Ventres. When the Fort Phil Kearny war broke out he was just twenty-one years old but such was his fighting ability that he was already a recognized war leader. In both the Fetterman and Wagon Box affairs he was one of the Sioux strategists and a central figure. Although an Ogalalla, he won the admiration and loyality of the Cheyennes and sometimes there were more of the latter in his camp than of his own tribe. When the trouble started in 1876 he was outstanding among the Ogalallas and rivaled only by Sitting Bull in the whole Sioux Nation. We are fortunate in having an eye-witness description of Crazy Horse, written by Captain John G. Bourke, who saw him in 1877, right after his surrender:

"I saw before me a man who looked quite young, not over thirty years old,[7] five eight inches high, lithe and sinewy, with a scar on the face. The expression of his countenance was one of quiet dignity, but morose, dogged, tenacious and melancholy. He behaved with stolidity like a man who realized that he had to give in to Fate, but would do so as sullenly as possible. While talking to Frank (Grouard) his countenance lit up with genuine pleasure, but to all others he was . . . gloomy and reserved. All Indians gave him a

---

[5] John F. Finerty, "War-path and Bivouac," p. 360.

[6] The wrong connotation is given this name in translation. Dr. Charles Eastman, a Sioux who rose to eminence in medicine and writing, says that Tashunka Witko (Crazy Horse) means an unbroken or untamed horse, rather than an "insane horse." The interpreter who first translated it boggled the job and we have the wrong sense of the word as a result.

[7] At this time he was thirty-three years old.

high reputation for courage and generosity. In advancing upon an enemy, none of his warriors were allowed to pass him. He had made hundreds of friends by his charity to the poor, as it was a point of honor with him never to keep anything for himself except weapons of war. I never heard an Indian mention his name, save in terms of respect." [8]

Crazy Horse rarely spoke in council, but when he did, his words carried weight. Generous and brave, of few words and great deeds, it is not an overstatement to say that he was to the Sioux what the great Robert E. Lee was to that other lost cause—the Confederacy.

FIRST BLOOD

By the early winter of 1875 the belief of the non-reservation Sioux that the white man would never let them alone was confirmed. Late in December runners came to all their camps, commanding them to come in to the reservations. This was an obvious impossibility. In cold weather—and the winter of '75 was one of the worst in history—no camp could be moved without serious suffering, particularly for the women, children and infirm.

Not that the Sioux had any intention of complying. When word came from General Alfred Terry to Sitting Bull, naming January 1st, 1876 as the deadline, and threatening to come looking for the Sioux if they did not obey, the chief sent a haughty reply, inviting him to come on.

"You won't need to bring any guides," he ended. "You can find me easily. I won't run away." [9]

Promptly on the expiration of the deadline the army moved. Three expeditions were to strike the Indians in early spring while their ponies were thin and it was too cold to travel. General George Crook was to march north from Fort Fetterman. General George A. Custer was to push west from Fort A. Lincoln. And General John Gibbon was to strike east from Fort Ellis. As it turned out weather conditions prevented the march of Custer and Gibbon. But Crook

---

[8] Captain John G. Bourke, "On the Border With Crook," pp. 414–415.
[9] Dunn, "Massacres of the Mountains," p. 596.

started early in March, with General Joseph J. Reynolds and ten troops of cavalry out in advance of his main body.

The weather was extremely severe, the thermometer sometimes showing forty degrees below zero, but when an Indian trail was struck in the Powder River Valley, the night of March 16, Reynolds' men pushed forward eagerly. The following dawn Frank Grouard, a scout, located a village among the cliffs along the Clear Creek branch of the Powder. They had stumbled upon the camp of Crazy Horse himself [10] and the Sioux were still asleep.

Reynolds, following the usual tactics, sent one battalion to cut off the pony herd, a second to charge the village, and a third to cut off the retreat of the Indians. As they took their positions Indian herd boys began to drive the ponies to water. The village was awakening.

One battalion ran plump into a fifteen-year-old Sioux youth. Not ten feet away he confronted their advance guard in a gully. Captain John G. Bourke leveled his revolver. The youngster "wrapped his blanket about him and stood like a statue of bronze, waiting for the fatal bullet; his features were as immobile as cut stone." But Bourke did not shoot. They wished to get closer to the village. Then the boy, knowing death would follow, suddenly uttered a war whoop. The village startled to wakefulness just as the first of the troopers thundered down into it.

It was the old story. Indians, when surprised, give way to inexplicable panics. This case was no exception. Leaping from their teepees the Sioux ran for the rocky bluffs which overlooked the valley. Some of the more resolute retreated slowly, shooting. Bullets began to thud among the troopers, killing horses and causing some confusion, but the line galloped forward.

By now the pony herd was rounded up. The Indians were afoot. Captain Egan's troop took possession of the village. So far the attack was a complete success. But the Sioux and Cheyennes recovered from their first shameful panic and Reynolds found he had caught a

[10] It has been disputed that this was Crazy Horse's village, but Grouard, the chief scout, positively said it was, and moreover yelled to Crazy Horse as the charge began. He should have known it as it was the one in which he lived for months as a friend of the chief. The Cheyennes in it are said to have been led by Two Moons.

Tartar. Crazy Horse gathered his warriors and presently they came back up the valley, occupying all the points of vantage and opening a plunging fire on the white men.

Captain Anson Mills' battalion began to set fire to the teepees and the stores. The flames, the frequent explosions of the powder kegs in the lodges and the constant zipping of the Sioux bullets made the village anything but healthy. The troopers, moreover, had discarded their heavy clothing during the charge and suffered from the cold. Four men were dead or dying; others were wounded. The Sioux were becoming more dangerous every minute. There was danger of being cut off.

Reynolds suddenly ordered a retreat and the troops withdrew so rapidly that they left their dead in the Indians' hands.[11] They retreated several miles with Crazy Horse hanging on their rear. That night as they camped, the Sioux swooped suddenly and recaptured nearly all the ponies they had lost in the attack.

Four of Reynolds' men were dead and six wounded as well as sixty-six men badly frozen. Crook came up and saved the cavalry from further punishment. He was deeply chagrined when he heard the outcome of the fight—victory for the Sioux. The aftermath of the disgraceful affair was a series of court martials and several officers resigned their commissions.

[11] There have been charges that at least one wounded man was abandoned in this retreat. If so it is almost certain that the poor wretch suffered the most horrible fate possible—death by Indian torture.

INTO THE INDIAN COUNTRY AGAIN

MARCH passed and April. It was an unseasonably late spring and the snows had only just cleared away to allow the prairie wild roses to show their buds when, on May 26th, Crook again started north over the trail he had followed when Reynolds was beaten.

Crook had wide experience and considerable prestige, due to his campaigns against the Apaches in Arizona. He had twelve hundred men, not including his pack and wagon trains. He thought he could whip any number of Indians he might meet.

Crazy Horse knew about Crook's march. Before that officer left his base he received a warning from the Sioux chief not to cross the Tongue River, on pain of being attacked.[1] But Crook marched straight to the Tongue and camped on its banks the evening of June 9th. As he did so, a sudden row of flashes lit up the tops of the bluffs across the river. The whistling of bullets sounded overhead. Crazy Horse was making good his word.

Crook was not the man to leave the gauge of battle lying. Orders began to fly. Three companies of infantry doubled forward to engage the Indians in long-range firing. Captain Anson Mills' battalion of cavalry splashed across the stream in a charge. There was not much of a fight. Having shown Crook they meant business, the Indians withdrew, content to choose a more favorable battle ground. Two soldiers were wounded. It is not known if any Indians were hurt.[2]

For four days Crook camped on the Tongue, his outposts constantly seeing Indians. On the 15th he was joined by nearly three hundred Crow and Shoshone scouts, the Crows under Alligator-Stands-Up and the Shoshones under Washakie. They were brought by Frank Grouard.

---

[1] Bourke, "On the Border With Crook," p. 296.

[2] Grinnell says the Indians who made the attack were Cheyennes from Crazy Horse's village on the Rosebud. "Fighting Cheyennes," p. 316.

Crook at once left his wagon train under a guard of infantry, mounted the rest of his foot soldiers on mules from the train, and with the scouts, these mule-riding doughboys, and his cavalry, some fourteen hundred men, crossed the Tongue early on the 16th and reached the Rosebud that evening.

Long before dawn on the 17th the troops were on the march and by eight o'clock they reached a widening of the valley where the stream ran across a level flat with high bluffs all around. At the lower end of the valley the river plunged into a gloomy gorge known as Dead Canyon. They halted in the bottoms and dismounted while the Crows and Shoshones went scurrying across the country to see what they could find.

It did not take them long to find something. Crazy Horse's scouts were watching Crook's approach and the chief was slipping up to the attack. Four Crows climbed a hill to look around. All at once they were "jumped" by four hostiles. Their sputtering shots were the first guns of the battle.

Crazy Horse's warriors came out of their canyons and rode toward where the white men were still hidden in the valley. Ahead of them streamed the Shoshones and Crows, riding for life. Rifle fire crackled. Some of the Crows were hit, but their friends carried them along.

Down the steep bluffs plunged the scouts. They raced toward Crook yelling at the top of their lungs: "Sioux! Sioux! Heap Sioux!" Then the same bluffs suddenly bristled with hostile Indians, mounted and in full war regalia. Sharp, spiteful reports cut the balmy morning air. The fight was on.

CRAZY HORSE'S ATTACK

So many Indians were in sight that Crook knew he was dealing with Crazy Horse's main force. An officer galloped to rally the demoralized scouts. The soldiers wheeled into battle line and their front plumed out in smoke. Captain Mills' battalion detached itself and charged across the valley toward a broad bluff where thick swarms of Sioux had gathered. A moment later Major Royall, on the left, was in motion also. Two pretty cavalry charges were under way at the same time, while the troops remaining in line carried on their duel with the Indians over the heads of their comrades.

With guidons streaming and horses at full speed, Mills thundered across the flat, through some marshy ground and to the foot of the bluffs, eight hundred yards away. The Sioux were shooting right in their faces, but the cavalry mounted the bluffs and drove the hostiles back a quarter of a mile to the high ground in the rear. Royall's charge was as brilliant. He quickly cleared the Indians from the bluffs in front. But as they advanced both Mills and Royall found the going harder and harder. The Indians increased in numbers every minute. Presently Mills sent a courier to Crook asking for assistance and got Captain Noyes' battalion as reinforcement. Even with this addition Mills had all he could handle.

Every man in Crook's force was now engaged. Even the mule packers were in action. Yet with everybody fighting, Crazy Horse was still in the field, undefeated.

The fight was two hours old. Fresh warriors led by Little Hawk of the Cheyennes and American Horse, had arrived. Unexpectedly the Sioux took the offensive. Major Royall's position was far advanced and badly exposed. On his extreme left was Captain Guy V. Henry's command, augmented by a cloud of Crow and Shoshone scouts.

Crazy Horse, the tactician, saw the weakness of this position. Full at its exposed flank, he sent a headlong charge of his warriors. Yelping like a pack of wolves, they rode right into the trooper line. Horses and soldiers went under as the Sioux clubbed them down. The whole mass, Indians and white men, went down the hill in a welter of dust and smoke, confusedly mixed together.

Only Captain Vroom's troop held its position, and they were speedily surrounded. Vroom might have been annihilated, but the full attention of the Sioux was not directed against him at first. His men formed a circle and drove back the first rush. By the time Crazy Horse could swing any considerable number of warriors against them, they had been rescued.

Captain Henry led the counter-charge which reached the lost troop. It cut its way through a desperately fighting mass of red men. Never had the soldiers found the Indians so willing to give blow for blow, so ready to stand up and fight, so apparently reckless of death. When Vroom was rescued, a retreat began to a less advanced position.

Hard upon the heels of the retiring troopers pressed the Sioux. War cry, rifle shot and lance thrust; scowling, painted, savage faces; tossing war bonnets; rearing, kicking ponies; mounting clouds of dust and smoke—the soldiers knew fear for the first time. But Henry, riding at the very rear, called out encouragement and his coolness steadied them. He winced once, but his face was turned toward the enemy. The troopers were too busy fighting to notice what had happened. They beat the charge off. Then the captain turned to them a countenance so ghastly that it chilled them through. A bullet had struck him full in the face, practically tearing the whole visage out under both eyes. His mangled features were covered by a great surge of blood. He was swaying with the shock. For a time he sat his horse, but the vertigo of wound sickness overcame him soon. He fell.

The Sioux instantly sensed that a leader was down. With the same valor they had displayed all afternoon they charged. Back, back they drove the troops. The ponies of their warriors plunged over the very spot where Henry lay. His end seemed certain.

But from a quarter utterly unexpected came help. The Shoshones and Crows had fought hard but futilely. The Sioux drove them back and they had been rather out of the fight for the last few minutes. Now they saw the fall of Henry as soon as their foes did.

Every old plainsman knows how the Indian warrior shows his greatest daring in rescuing dead or wounded comrades from the enemy. The scouts knew the Sioux would be on the ground about Henry in a minute, scalping him, counting "coup." Here was something they understood. With their war cries echoing from the farthest bluffs, they plunged headlong into the thick of the hostile array. Old Washakie of the Shoshones was there. So was Luishaw. Of the Crows, Alligator-Stands-Up and Plenty Coups were foremost.

Rearing, snorting horses, kicking up a dust cloud so dense the riders could hardly see—knife thrust and tomahawk blow—the Sioux ranks opened. Washakie, Alligator-Stands-Up and their warriors stood over Henry's limp body.

The hostiles fought desperately with the scouts. It created a diversion which stopped the Indian advance at its height. Royall and Vroom had time to catch their breath. Now they came back up the hill, driving Crazy Horse's warriors, reoccupying the ground held so heroically by a handful of savage scouts, and getting possession of the captain's unconscious body.

But there was no possibility of holding the position. Fighting as they went, the soldiers and their Indian allies retreated, taking the wounded officer with them. Henry subsequently recovered and eventually rose to the rank of brigadier general. The fight around his body was the fiercest mêlée of the battle. Both sides suffered severely.

DOWN DEAD CANYON

Crook believed Crazy Horse's village lay down the gloomy and precipitous canyon which ran northeast from the wide valley where they were fighting. Mills had temporarily checked the Sioux on the high ground back of the bluffs and Crook ordered him to swing his men out of the fight and take them down the gulch.

Mills' movement was unopposed by the Indians. His sudden change of front apparently caused the Sioux to draw off from the whole line and probably had much to do with saving Vroom's command.

Down the canyon trotted Mills' men, in column of twos, looking for the village which they expected to find at every turn. A clatter of hoofs behind them, a call, and Captain Nickerson and his orderly rode up—with orders to retrace their steps. It was hard to obey that order. Some of the officers, believing the Indian camp almost at hand, actually urged Mills to disobey. But Mills was a soldier; orders were orders and he complied.

Had he failed to obey that order at once, had he gone even a quarter of a mile farther, he and his men might never have come out of that canyon alive. The gorge with the significant name of Dead Canyon, was a natural trap. Only a little way from where Mills halted was a bristling obstruction of fallen trees, brush and rocks, washed up by some flood in the past. It formed a great dam across the valley, through which the waters of the river trickled and was a barrier no cavalry could have passed.

There is reason to believe that here Crazy Horse planned an ambush. With this natural abattis he could resist any attempt to move down the valley, while from the tops of the unscalable canyon walls his riflemen could deal untold damage to the horsemen below. This may be why Crazy Horse, fiercely contesting every other move, did not oppose Mills' march. A little farther and the troops would have turned the last bend. A tremendous fire from the abattis; a steady stream of lead from the canyon walls; a short, desperate struggle to get through the tangle at the Indians—then it would have been over. Another great disaster like the Custer fight would have been written.[3]

Crook's order to retreat was not based on any knowledge of this situation. He had been badly mauled and had many wounded.[4] He could not support Mills so he recalled him.

Crook camped that night on the battle field. Next day he retreated to his base of supplies. Crazy Horse was the victor. He had checked Crook, forced him to retreat and thus disposed of one more enemy.[5]

[3] Grinnell denies that such a trap was planned ("The Fighting Cheyennes," p. 317) but both Mills and Bourke ("On the Border With Crook," p. 315) speak of it. So does Finerty ("War-path and Bivouac," p. 133). I believe in the face of this testimony by men who were on the spot at the time, the theory of Crazy Horse's trap can be accepted. Grinnell visited the spot many years later.

[4] Crook lost eight killed and twenty-three wounded; the Crows had one dead and six wounded; and the Shoshones one killed and five wounded, a total of ten dead and thirty-four wounded. The Sioux loss is unknown, but the Crows secured ten scalps and the Shoshones three.

[5] Sitting Bull took part in this fight, but merely as a warrior, according to Vestal ("Sitting Bull," p. 156). Crazy Horse commanded. According to Indian testimony less than half their warriors in this fight were armed with guns. The others had to be content with bows and arrows. Under these circumstances the Sioux victory is all the more remarkable.

14: THE GREATEST VICTORY

AFTER the fight on the Rosebud, Crazy Horse and Sitting Bull moved their people across the divide into the Little Big Horn Valley. The long file of the travois-laden ponies, with their mounted escort and the huge herd of extra animals, began the trip on June 19th. At a place where the valley widened into a beautiful, smiling meadow, half a mile wide and five or six miles long, the teepees were put up. Sitting Bull looked over the ground and of course picked out the choice site for his Unkpapas, at a bend of the river, in a grove of fine trees, almost exactly in the center of the valley. A couple of small creeks ran into the river from the south. Around these the rest of the Indians camped, the Sans Arcs, Minneconjous and Ogalallas taking one, and the Brulés and Cheyennes the other.

Estimates vary as to their numbers. The Indians themselves say it was one of the greatest villages they ever got together. There must have been ten or twelve thousand people there with, say, two or three thousand warriors. Here all Sitting Bull's well-known tact, diplomacy and organizing ability were necessary. As usual where such a huge camp was located the game soon disappeared, killed off or driven away. The Indians wanted to hunt but Sitting Bull, by strenuous effort, managed to keep them together.

Toward this pleasant encampment, a famous officer and a famous body of men marched on the night of the 24th—Custer and his 7th Cavalry. Custer was under the displeasure of President Grant because of his political activities, and it was only through the intercession of Sheridan and Terry, his superiors, that he was allowed to accompany the expedition at all. Terry commanded the column to which the 7th was attached. From a temporary camp at the junction of the Powder and the Yellowstone, Major Marcus A. Reno, with part of the 7th, went scouting and returned to tell of striking a big trail on the Rosebud. This was the trail of the main

Indian camp as it moved over into the Little Big Horn.

The report confirmed Terry's belief that the Sioux were concentrated somewhere between the Rosebud and the Big Horn—probably at the Little Big Horn. He decided to move in that direction at once. To the famous 7th and its equally famous leader, Custer, he gave the post of honor—the advance. They were ordered to strike for the point where Reno had found the Indian trail. At the same time Gibbon, who had joined Terry after Crook's defeat, followed with a force equal to Custer's. Definite orders were given to Custer that if the trail led to the Little Big Horn he was to pass it and turn south long enough to let Gibbon come up to the mouth of the stream. The inference was that the two columns should then converge, catching the Indians between them. These are the instructions upon which half a century of controversy over Custer's subsequent actions have hinged. In parting, however, Terry, one of the finest officers in the army, but inexperienced in Indian fighting compared to his fiery subordinate, gave some verbal instructions which permitted Custer a far greater leeway:

"Use your own judgment, and do what you think best if you strike the trail; and whatever you do, Custer, hold on to your wounded." [1]

And so, with general instructions, but with specific permission to use his own best judgment if conditions arose to warrant it, Custer rode out for his fatal rendezvous with the foe.

He found an Indian trail half a mile wide, on the second day, and followed it twenty-eight miles up the Rosebud before he camped. His scouts reported ever-increasing Indian signs. It was apparent that the trail crossed the divide. Custer held a council of war and announced he would go over into the Little Big Horn Valley "to avoid detection by the Indians." His decision was at least a technical disobedience of his written orders. Two hours later the regiment was on the march again, stopping at two A.M. near the top when the scouts reported the pass could not be crossed at night.

Custer crossed the divide at dawn of June 25th. Shortly afterward he knew his trail was discovered. A party of packers who went

[1] Quoted from General Nelson A. Miles, "Personal Recollections," pp. 204–205.

back to pick up a box of hard-tack, dropped on the trail, saw and fired at a couple of young Sioux, killing one.[2] The other escaped to bear the news. Under the circumstances, orders or no orders, the general decided to go after the Indians and make the most of his opportunity. Had he not been smarting under what he felt was unjust censure at Washington, he might not have taken the risk. But Custer felt poignantly the need for something to win back Grant's favor. A spectacular Indian victory like the Washita would do it.

As the column topped the divide, the saw in the rays of the early sunlight a low-lying fog far down in the valley. It was the smoke of an immense Sioux village. With never a premonition of defeat, Custer made his plans to crush it. Following the usual Indian fighting tactics of the day, he divided his command into four detachments.[3] Major Benteen, with three troops, was sent far to the left to circle the southern end of the valley. Captain McDougall, with one troop, was told off to follow with the pack train. Custer and Reno continued their march together but as they reached the valley they separated, Custer going on northwest with five troops, while Reno and three troops, together with most of the Arickaree scouts, rode straight on down.

Custer was sure of victory. As he approached the valley he assumed once more the old, jaunty air he had lost since his trouble with Grant. The thought of action always served him as a stimulant and he was the jovial Custer of yore as he parted with Reno.[4]

[2] Strangely, although this occurred at eight o'clock in the morning the surviving Indian did not bring word of it to the village until after noon. By that time the troops were almost within view. In fact, Sitting Bull saw them shortly after the news was brought to him. Vestal, "Sitting Bull," p. 164.

[3] Custer has been much criticized for "dividing his force in the face of the enemy," but such criticism is unwarranted. No matter how axiomatic that rule is in ordinary war, the expedient of dividing and attacking a village from several sides had repeatedly proved successful in Indian campaigns. Chivington at Sand Creek, Reynolds at Powder River, McKenzie at McClellan Creek and Custer himself at the Washita all used these tactics.

[4] To show how confident of victory Custer was, Trumpeter John Martini, last man to see him alive, told Benteen to whom he carried dispatches that when the general saw the camp, he slapped his thigh with his hat and exclaimed: "Custer's luck! We've got them this time!"

THE VALLEY OF THE SHADOW

Down into the valley rode Reno. As his men entered the gulch of a small stream which would take them out onto the bottoms, they had a last glimpse of Custer alive. He sat his horse on a high hill. As they looked back, he snatched his hat from his head and waved it—the beloved gesture of boyish exuberance which they knew so well. A few yards farther and the bluffs shut him from view.

Reno was supposed to strike the head of the village near the mouth of the creek while Custer crossed the high ground to the right and attacked the lower end. But when Reno rode out of the defile he knew that plans had miscarried—he was not within two miles of his objective. Turning to the right he led his men at a fast trot down the valley. Indians on horseback began to appear before him. Then he saw teepees. Off toward the flats his Arickaree scouts were dash-ing forward in an attempt to drive away some Sioux ponies which were grazing there. Rifles began to flash in the woods ahead while swarms of warriors came riding toward him. Reno halted. The rippling crash of his first volley sounded. The whole valley in front was filled with a yelling mass of savages.

It was the power and might of the Sioux and Cheyenne Nations. Sitting Bull was there and so was Crazy Horse. Dull Knife, Two Moons and Little Wolf of the Cheyennes led their people. Of the Sioux, Pizi (Gall), American Horse, Hump and White Bull, Sitting Bull's daredevil nephew, were encouraging their warriors to fight. Without warning the Indians charged. As the howling, shooting horde bore down upon Reno's men the horses of two troopers became unmanageable and bolted right into the Sioux array. The hostile line simply opened and then closed, swallowing them. They were never seen again, dead or alive. At the same moment the Arickarees on the left flank gave way. Oppressed by their hereditary fear of the terrible Sioux some of the Rees did not stop running until they reached Terry's camp. Reno had to execute a rapid pivot movement until his back was against the river with both flanks resting on it. An old "ox bow" loop of the stream-bed in a point of woods formed a

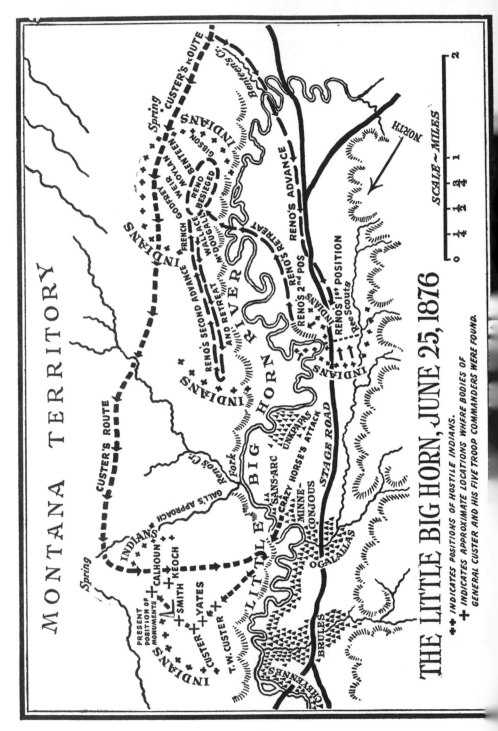

THE LITTLE BIG HORN, JUNE 25, 1876

✲✲ INDICATES POSITIONS OF HOSTILE INDIANS.
✚ INDICATES APPROXIMATE LOCATIONS WHERE BODIES OF
GENERAL CUSTER AND HIS FIVE TROOP COMMANDERS WERE FOUND.

SCALE ~ MILES

MONTANA TERRITORY

natural breastwork behind which the men took refuge.

The troopers dismounted, every fourth man holding the horses. In a solid line, at long rifle shot, the Sioux rode up and down with their chiefs galloping among them, making their dispositions. The rifles roared a crescendo of sound. With men falling left and right, Reno rode over to his senior captain, French.

"What do you think of this?" he shouted.

"I think we'd better get out of here," replied French.

Reno gave the order to mount. In the terrific noise he was not heard. Added to the concussions of gunfire were the constant whooping of the savages and the yelling of the soldiers. Some of the nearer troopers at last understood and began to mount. The others followed their example. With no attempt at order, seeking only safety, the survivors of the detachment started for the ford.

It was a rout. The Indians rode a race with the flying soldiers and death overtook many. There were deeds of heroism too. With the Sioux right on top of them, troopers reined in their horses and helped dismounted comrades to climb up behind them. Lieutenant MacIntosh was killed on the river bank. Lieutenant Hodgson's leg was broken by a bullet which killed his horse as they leaped into the river. A stirrup was thrust out by Trumpeter Henry Fisher. Hodgson seized it and was dragged to the other bank. An instant later a second bullet ended his life. Scout Charley Reynolds, Custer's right-hand man, sacrificed himself trying to hold back the savages so that his comrades might escape. And many another fell in that mad scramble across the Little Big Horn.

Struggling across, the remaining officers and men reached the bluffs on the other side. Reno had left three officers and twenty-nine men and scouts behind him in the valley, dead. Seven men were wounded seriously. And Lieutenant De Rudio and fifteen men were missing.[5] That was a total of fifty-five out of one hundred and

---

[5] Most of the missing men later rejoined Reno on the bluff. De Rudio and Thomas O'Neill, a private, hid in the bushes when their horses were shot. After almost unbelievable adventures during which they were more than once discovered by the hostiles they managed at last to cross the river and join their comrades. On one occasion they were so close to the Sioux camp they saw what they believed was the torture of some of their captured comrades.

twelve—fifty percent of the command.

Benteen came over the rise from the east. He had seen no Indians but an hour before received an urgent message from Custer, carried by Trumpeter John Martini [6] as follows:

> "Benteen. Come on. Big village. Be quick. Bring packs.
> "P.S. Bring packs."

The language of the note and the repetition of the last instructions showed that Custer was in contact with the Indians and needed ammunition. But where was Custer? Benteen and Reno were at a loss. They supposed he had struck the hostiles higher up and pursued them.

At present they were more concerned with their own fate than Custer's. Dense masses of Indians around their bluffs kept up a heavy fire. The position was poor for defense, being commanded by higher hills from which Sioux sharpshooters kept picking off men.

About three o'clock in the afternoon a strange thing happened. As if at a signal most of the savages surrounding them suddenly galloped off toward the northwest. Within a few minutes a terrific burst of firing was heard in that direction. It kept up, increasing in volume and varying little in position.

Custer was engaged at last.

WHAT HAPPENED TO CUSTER

Most of the Indians in the great village had gone to the upper end to fight Reno with no thought that they would be attacked from any other direction. Sitting Bull alone thought of that possibility and said so.[7] Some old men in the Cheyenne camp seem to have known of Custer's division and went about the circle haranguing that soldiers were coming from the lower end of the village also.[8] But the bulk of the Indians swarmed around Reno, shooting and riding.

---

[6] Martini, who died in Brooklyn in 1922, was the last to see Custer.

[7] This is the story Stanley Vestal got from relatives and friends of Sitting Bull ("Sitting Bull," p. 168). Mr. Vestal went to the Sioux themselves for his material and his book contains much information never before available to students of western history.

[8] Grinnell, "The Fighting Cheyennes," p. 336.

The situation was ideal—just made to order for Custer. But that officer had much farther to go than Reno. He had to make a circuit of nearly ten miles. Then, instead of striking the lower end of the village, he came down opposite the center at a shallow ford. By the time he appeared Reno had been beaten and driven across the stream as has been noted.

Custer's five troops were seen from the Indian camp when they reached the bluffs at the edge of the valley. There were only a few men in the village at the time—chiefly warriors who had not been on hand when the fight started, but had just come hurrying in from hunting or scouting at the sound of the battle. A charge by the troops at that moment would have completely changed the result of the battle. The Indians themselves have said that if Custer had gone through the village then, the fight would have been over.

Small things sometimes alter history. As Custer's men trotted down the slope across the river toward the ford, there was a panic among the squaws and old men in the camp. In a frightened mob they rushed away from the soldiers, out on the prairie where they huddled, helpless and scared.

Four Cheyenne warriors remained. They saw the menacing line of blue and knew the soldiers would soon be at the ford. The main body of fighting men was far up the valley fighting Reno. Those four Cheyennes turned their horses and rode across the river to fight Custer all by themselves—four against two hundred.

The names of three members of that dauntless quartet are fortunately preserved and deserve to go down in history just as surely as Horatius the Roman or Leonidas the Greek. They were Bobtail Horse, Calf and Roan Bear. The fourth man is not remembered.

As they crossed the river, two more Cheyennes, White Shield and Mad Wolf, joined them. They were both famous fighters, but Mad Wolf thought the determination of the four to fight two hundred soldiers was insane. He argued with them: "No one must charge on the soldiers now; they are too many." When he saw that Bobtail Horse and his friends had their grim faces set toward the troops, he turned off down the river with White Shield, out of the direct line of march.

The four Cheyennes kept on. Creeping behind a low ridge, they waited for the soldiers to come close. They knew they could not stop the white men's charge, but they were warriors—what little they could do must be done. If ever men looked death in the eye, unafraid, these men did.

Down the slope trotted Custer. Four or five scurrying Sioux were running before him. Seeing that Custer was headed for the ford, they swung off to one side, knowing the soldiers would not follow them. They were right; Custer did not deviate from his direct line of march.

Suddenly rifles began to crack in front of him. Bobtail Horse's tiny band had opened. A trooper was killed. The soldiers halted and dismounted. The halt was in line with good tactics. They had no way of knowing how many Indians were over that ridge. The very audacity of the challenge of that volley worked in favor of the Cheyennes. The presumption was that no mere handful would dare to oppose a force like Custer's. There must be more Indians ahead than could be seen.

But the hesitation proved fatal. While the soldiers remained on the hill, word reached Sitting Bull and Crazy Horse as they faced Reno. That was what caused the sudden change of front which had so puzzled the soldiers on the bluff.

Part of the Sioux galloped down the left bank of the river and dashed across the ford in front of the village in a smother of spray. Another big division rode up a dry coulee which ran close by the hill where Custer had halted. Still others must have gone around behind the bluffs to the east where they cut off the white men from retreat later in the battle.

Custer's men had mounted and started again for the ford when the first of the swarm of fighting Sioux, probably headed by Crazy Horse, appeared there. The soldiers began at once to retreat. But it was too late. The Indians swirled up the hill and around them. Gall was on one side; Crazy Horse on the other. And they were followed by a fighting mad horde of Sioux and Cheyennes. Pushed back by the mass of savages, Custer crossed a deep gulch and climbed a hill on the other side which looked like a good place for defense.

The line of his retreat can be traced today by the stone markers which were placed at the spots where the cluttering bodies of his men were later found.

Custer evidently thought that if he could reach the round knob on top of the hill—where the monuments now stand—he could fight off the Indians. But he never got to the top. Something stopped him when he was still a hundred yards down the slope. Very likely it was a wave of savages which came over the knob, down upon him —the Sioux who had ridden behind the bluffs to the east. Custer and many of his officers and men died there on the slope.[9]

But Custer's death was by no means the end of the fight, or rather the retreat. Headed off from the north, the survivors of his command apparently struggled southeast, at an angle of almost forty-five degrees from their former direction. The line can be clearly traced today. It headed over the ridge and down the other side, back in the direction from which Custer had originally come. Lieutenant James B. Calhoun, whose body was found almost at the end of the bloody trail far to the southeast of where Custer lay dead, was probably the last officer killed. With him were found a few straggling bodies—the last of Custer's command.

Throughout that agonizing retreat the white men fought with desperate valor. But the hill, which superficially looked like a good defensive position, proved just the opposite. Its sides were scarred by deep gullies, ideal places for Sioux riflemen to hide. And there were more of those riflemen all the time. At the beginning of the battle many of the Indians were armed only with bows and arrows but they captured a good many new Sharp's carbines from Reno's men and obtained ammunition from the saddle bags of the dead or captured horses and the cartridge belts of the dead men. To these they constantly added the arms they took from Custer's troopers as they fell.

Within an hour all the white soldiers were down. The Sioux and Cheyennes went about, looking the bodies over, giving an extra

---

[9] Their bodies were found not where the monuments are, but farther down the slope. The monuments were placed in their present location because it is superior from a view standpoint.

shot [10] in the head to those about whose condition there was any question. A few wounded survivors were clubbed to death.

The great tragedy was ended.

RENO'S FIGHT ON THE BLUFFS

To return to Reno: The noise of Custer's battle at first cheered his men, but the feeling changed to apprehension as that sinister roar rose to a climax, then hung on the air, a terrific tumult of sound. Officers and men gazed with concern toward the northwest. Instead of a sudden, sharp attack, Custer must have a real battle on his hands. More likely—they could no longer conceal it from themselves—he must be fighting for his very life.

Although most of the Indians had gone and everybody expected Reno to move to Custer's support, he remained where he was, a

[10] The theory that Custer committed suicide has been exploded. Best proof of this is that at least three Cheyennes counted coup on his body. The third of these was still living in 1940. He was Medicine Bear. The other two were the chief Two Moons, and a warrior, Harshay Horse. The Indians never counted coup on the body of a suicide. T. J. Gatchell, of Buffalo, Wyoming, who possibly knew more about the Northern Cheyennes than any other white man, asserted to me that he had proof that Custer's slayer was a Cheyenne. From the evidence of the old men who were survivors of the battle, including Medicine Bear who witnessed the actual slaying, he was convinced that either Two Moons or Harshay Horse, or both, did the actual killing of Custer. They were the first two to count coup on the general's body. Because of fear of reprisals these chief actors never admitted their part in the death of Custer during their lifetimes, except for Medicine Bear. The Cheyennes claimed that Custer was their "meat" even before the battle. They had a personal feud with him because of the Washita massacre. On the other hand, William J. Bordeaux, federal Indian interpreter of Sioux Falls, quoted Foolish Elk, a Brulé, as naming Spotted Calf, a Santee of Inkpaduta's band, as the slayer. He did not cite much evidence of a convincing nature, and it is my opinion that Gatchell's findings are correct and the Cheyennes, as they always claimed, did kill Custer. Two Moons, in his personal account to Hamlin Garland, was naturally very wary on this point, but he never denied he struck the fatal blow. Other Cheyennes, by implication, pointed to Two Moons who was a very notable fighter. As to the suicide theory, evidence in the form of a bullet hole through the head caused some persons who did not know much about it to say that Custer killed himself. But the evidence of one of the men who personally examined the body and helped in the burial of it should settle the question for all time. Uncle Dave Cummings, who died comparatively recently at Buffalo, Wyoming, was a packer under Gibbons. He was in the burial party which buried Custer. He said—and his statement is backed by other records—that Custer was shot twice, once through the body and once through the head. The body shot killed him. The head shot was merely a "coup de grâce" given after the fight was over.

bandanna handkerchief tied about his head, bewildered and indecisive. Some of the officers overstepped their authority to urge him to join Custer. But he refused to move. At length Captain Weir, with Troop D, reconnoitred down the line of bluffs without orders. At the farthest bluffs he could see, a mile and a half away, immense numbers of Indians. The firing was still heavy but he could see no soldiers. The Sioux turned toward him and he had to repulse an attack. Then Reno cautiously followed. By the time he arrived the heavy firing was over. With field glasses they could still see clouds of Indians but no troops.

There was some conjecture as to what had happened. Nobody dreamed of the real catastrophe even when they saw the Sioux coming back. Reno did not wait for them. He returned to his first position and entrenched.

The Sioux attacked without delay and there was some desperate fighting on the hill, but the white men continued to hold it. Then the savages posted themselves on the high ground and deluged the troops with bullets. In the three hours before darkness, eighteen men were killed and forty-three wounded on that bloody bluff.

Night brought a cessation of fighting. A detail of soldiers got down to water and replenished the canteens. They could hear much racket from the Indian camp [11] and were constantly annoyed by sniping from the bluffs. At dawn the battle reopened. For hours the long-range-pot-shooting continued, and the Indian rifles in some cases outranged the troopers' carbines. At nine o'clock a charge swept down the slope from the north. The hostiles almost carried the entrenchments. One daring Sioux, Long Robe, actually got within the lines and counted coup on a soldier before he was killed. But eventually the Sioux were driven back. After that they contented themselves with long-range shooting. Toward evening the whole village packed up and the Indians left the valley.

[11] Frank Grouard, one of Crook's scouts, was actually on the battle field that night. Not knowing there had been a fight, he stumbled onto some of the bodies of Custer's men in the darkness. A few minutes later he was discovered by some Indians and forced to ride for his life. This was about eleven o'clock at night. He did not know then that Reno's men were besieged on the bluff. (Joe De Barthe, "Life and Adventures of Frank Grouard," pp. 136–139.)

Another night passed. In the morning a large dust cloud was seen coming up the valley. "The Indians are returning" was the first thought, but the blue of uniforms was soon seen. They knew now why the Sioux left. Terry and Gibbon were approaching.

"What has happened to Custer?" was the question on every tongue. Terry naturally thought he was with Reno. Reno thought he had joined Terry. Gibbon went to reconnoitre the now deserted village site. Far out across the river, a mile or two to the east was Lieutenant James Bradley, his chief of scouts. A dead horse attracted Bradley's attention. Riding in that direction he saw some curious white objects which at first he could not understand. As he drew nearer, the truth burst upon him. They were the naked bodies of Custer's dead.

Bradley's hurried search discovered one hundred and ninety-seven bodies. Later nine more were found, a total of two hundred and six. Custer was found, stripped but not mutilated—not even scalped. Most of the others were butchered in some manner.

Gibbon and Terry gave what burial they were able to the dead. This was of the sketchiest nature—only three spades could be found in the entire pack train which was equipped only for rapid movements in the Indian country. The men used their tin cups, axes, canteen halves, even tin spoons and sticks, to scratch earth over the bodies.[12]

[12] Following are the losses in the Battle of the Little Big Horn:

Custer's command	Killed	
Commissioned officers	13	
Enlisted men	191	
Citizens and guides	4	
	208	

Reno's command	Killed	Wounded
Commissioned officers	3	
Enlisted men	48	52
Scouts and interpreters	6	
	57	52

Total killed, 265. Total wounded, 52. Total loss, 317.

Officers killed: Gen. George A. Custer; Captains T. W. Custer, Miles W. Keough, G. W. Yates; Lieutenants W. W. Cook, A. E. Smith, Donald MacIntosh, James Calhoun, J. E. Porter, B. H. Hodgson, J. G. Sturgis, W. Van W. Reilly, J. J. Crittenden, H. M. Harrington; Assistant Surgeons, C. E. Lord, J. M. DeWolf;

Then the expedition sadly began its trip back to the Yellowstone, carrying the wounded to where the steamboat "Far West" waited to convey them to a hospital down the river. The red man had scored his greatest triumph in history over his white enemy.

Civilians, Boston Custer (brother of the general), Armstrong Reed (Custer's nephew), Mark Kellogg, (newspaper correspondent), Charlie Reynolds (chief scout), Frank C. Mann, Isaiah Dorman (Negro interpreter), Mitch Bouyer (half-breed scout); Indian scouts, Bloody Knife, Bob Tail, Stab.

The bodies of Lieutenants Harrington, Porter and Sturgis and Dr. Lord and two enlisted men were never found. They may have been captured and tortured, although the Indians have denied they tortured anybody in this affair.

15: WANING OF THE RED STAR

THE DEATH OF AMERICAN HORSE

AFTER the Little Big Horn the Sioux scattered. Sitting Bull had held them together as long as he could—they had to hunt or starve during the coming winter. The Sioux had no further desire to fight. They had used up nearly all their ammunition beating Crook and Custer; they never had enough cartridges after the Little Big Horn fight for a major battle.[1]

A couple of trifling advantages were gained by the soldiers in July. General Wesley Merritt surprised a band of Cheyennes on the 17th, killed one young warrior, and chased them back to the reservation. At about the same time a scouting party under Lieutenant Frederick W. Sibley fought and defeated a Cheyenne war party, killing their leader, White Antelope. Otherwise the troops hunted fruitlessly through the Bad Lands for the Indians.

American Horse, one of the great old Sioux fighters, had camped on Rabbit Creek, near Slim Buttes. He was one of Crazy Horse's most trusted lieutenants and closest friends. Captain Anson Mills, escorting a wagon train to Deadwood for supplies for Crook, discovered this village by accident. His surprise attack, delivered the morning of September 8th, as usual sent the panic-stricken Indians scrambling up the bluffs which rose behind the camp site.

---

[1] Dr. Thomas S. Williamson, who lived among the Sioux for decades and knew them as few white men have ever known them is authority for this statement. In an article written March 15, 1877, he says:

"Since the fall of Custer, Sitting Bull and his associates never had enough ammunition for a regular battle, and have avoided fighting whenever it was possible. To supply their urgent needs they have captured supply trains and sometimes ranches, driving off the horses and cattle." (Minnesota Historical Society Collections, Vol. III, p. 292.)

This explains the unwillingness of the Sioux to fight pitched battles from the Custer engagement on. They did not have a chance with the well-equipped troops and they knew it. In spite of this circumstance Crazy Horse still was to offer battle at least once to Miles, a fight he might have won had it not been for Miles' hidden artillery.

But Mills penned up American Horse and four warriors, with about fifteen women and children in a cave at the end of a blind gorge. The old chief held the soldiers off nearly all day. He repulsed two charges, killed a scout, "Buffalo Chip" Charley, and a trooper, and wounded nine men, including Lieutenant Von Luettwitz, whose leg was so shattered by a bullet that it had to be amputated. Then Crook arrived, brought by an urgent message from Mills. He took charge at once.

Frank Grouard crept up under cover and told the Indians to surrender. "Come and get us!" was American Horse's scornful yell.

Crook directed a concentrated fire of two hundred rifles into the mouth of the cave. They could not silence the five Sioux rifles which fought back. Again the interpreter offered the Indians a chance to surrender. This time, after some hesitation, the squaws and children came out.

"Crazy Horse will rub you out!" American Horse taunted. Crook knew he was hoping for rescue. What was done must be done quickly.

The bombardment began again with redoubled fury. For two hours it raged. Gradually the Sioux fire dwindled, stopped altogether. Grouard crept forward again and yelled a summons to give up. A young warrior stepped into view. The offer was repeated. "Washte helo," (Very good) murmured the Indian and disappeared into the cave.

There was a brief wait. Then the youth reappeared with another brave. Between them they supported American Horse, pale with the agony of a terrible wound. He was shot through the bowels. A piece of his intestine protruded from the hole. Between his teeth was a flat piece of wood on which he bit hard to keep from showing the pain. Yet he was every inch the chief as he handed his gun to Crook.

Too late Crazy Horse and Sitting Bull came riding from their camp a few miles away, to help their friend. They retired as Crook swung into battle line, knowing American Horse was finished.

That night gallant old American Horse died, as stoically and silently as he had lived. Two other warriors and a woman and child were also dead. A handful of wretched Indians were prisoners. It was a small victory. But the white man made the most of it—his successes up to now had been so few.

MILES AND SITTING BULL

General Nelson A. Miles was summoned from the south to the Platte region and at once proposed a winter campaign. In spite of the advice of veterans of the country he went about his plans. With him were the troops who had campaigned in the Southwest in a winter when the temperature went as low as twenty-eight degrees below zero. But in this country it fell to sixty or even sixty-six below. To use his own phrase, "I equipped my command as if they were going to the arctic regions." They had abundance of woolens and fur clothing, even masks for the face—and it was well, for the winter of 1876–77 was very severe.

Sitting Bull and Crazy Horse separated to make hunting easier. Crazy Horse camped in the headwaters of the Tongue and Rosebud. Sitting Bull was north in the valley of the Big Dry. Miles set out to attack Sitting Bull.

Miles' approach was soon discovered. One night daring Indian riders attacked the soldier camp and Miles came within inches of death. They swooped down like the wind—a mere handful of them—to stampede the horses. Finding the animals too well picketed, they fired a fusillade into the camp and rode away, yelling. Two bullets whistled through the general's tent, cutting holes in the canvas a few inches above his cot, but he was not harmed.

Next morning, October 18th, Sitting Bull attacked Miles' supply train with a large force of warriors. Colonel E. S. Otis, in command of the train, formed his men as a guard on each side and ordered the wagons to keep moving. The Indians rode around and fired long-distance shots. During one of the lulls in the fighting a warrior galloped to the brow of a hill directly in the line of march but out of range, dismounted and left something, then rode away. It was a note from Sitting Bull himself. This curious missive is worth quoting. It sums up the Indian arguments and gives an idea of the imperious attitude of the great chief:

"Yellowstone.

"I want to know what you are doing travelling on this road. You scare all the buffalo away. I want to hunt in this place. I want you to turn back from here. If you don't I will fight you again. I want you to leave what you have got here and turn back from here.

"I am your friend,

"SITTING BULL.

"I mean all the rations you have got and some powder. Wish you would write me as soon as you can." [2]

Colonel Otis replied that he would go wherever he wished and if Sitting Bull wanted a fight he would have no trouble in finding it. There was some additional skirmishing but the wagon train got through.

On the 21st a group of Indians carrying a white flag approached the army lines. Most of them stopped at a distance. The flag bearer, a warrior named Long Feather, came forward to present a message from Sitting Bull, who was in the group, asking for a conference. Miles invited the chief to come within the lines, but the canny Unkpapa, no doubt remembering the fate of some other Indians who had trusted the white man, refused. He sent three emissaries instead. Nothing came of the conference.

Next day Sitting Bull again asked to talk with Miles. This time a conference was agreed upon, to be held between the lines. Sitting Bull, accompanied by six warriors and a sub-chief, White Bull, met Miles, with an officer and six troopers. They were midway between the Indian array and the soldiers.

There are varying accounts of the interview. The Indians say that Miles opened up by accusing Sitting Bull of being an enemy to the whites and scolding like an old woman. To this the chief mildly replied that he was not an enemy to the whites as long as they let him alone. There was uneasiness on the part of both leaders, each fearing treachery. They soon separated.

The following day they met again in the same place, escorted as

[2] "Big Leggins" Brughiere, a half-breed with a smattering of education, wrote the note at Sitting Bull's dictation. The document is still preserved.

before. This time both Miles and Sitting Bull quickly grew angry. Miles says in his memoirs that "Sitting Bull looked like a conqueror and spoke like one"—as indeed he had a right to do. His demands were just and reasonable from the Indian standpoint, or from any neutral standpoint, for that matter. He had fought no war of aggression and was willing to stop fighting now if the troops were withdrawn from his country and their posts abandoned. But if the chief really expected the land-grabbing white man to accede to so simple and equitable an arrangement, he soon learned his error. Miles told him such a peace was impossible; that only the unconditional surrender of the Indians would be accepted.

Then the chief flew into a towering rage, according to Miles' story. Sitting Bull looked "more like . . . a wild beast than a human being; his face assumed a ferocious expression; his jaws were closed tightly . . . and you could see his eyes glistening with the fire of savage hatred."

At last he fairly shouted his defiance: "Almighty God made me an Indian—but not an agency Indian!"

That is the story as told by Miles, one of the participants, but some of the Indians who were near have denied that Sitting Bull ever made the statement quoted.[3]

Miles and Sitting Bull rode back to their lines. Within fifteen minutes the soldiers charged. The Sioux fired the prairie but the grass was short and the flames did not hinder the cavalry which dashed right through the smoke. Sitting Bull's people fled. The troops captured their camp but the Sioux disappeared in the distance.

That autumn the soldiers twice struck Sitting Bull's band which was searching through the Bad Lands for Crazy Horse's village. But each time the chief evaded them. Pursued and hectored all the way, he at last reached the Canadian border.

There in the north, among the black pines of Canada, the Unkpapas found refuge. But Sitting Bull, scowling in the dark recesses of his teepee, took no satisfaction from that fact. He was a king without a kingdom; an emperor whose empire was broken.

[3] Vestal, "Sitting Bull," pp. 204–205.

THE AWFUL NIGHT

After the hostile Indian camp broke up, the Cheyennes went into the Powder River Valley where they made a snug camp deep in the canyon of the Crazy Woman Fork. They spent the cold months in safety and comfort there while Miles was chasing Sitting Bull to Canada, and the troops were surrounding and intimidating the friendly villages of Swift Bear and Red Cloud, who knew too much to go to war.

A Cheyenne youth, Beaver Dam traveling across the winter landscape, was seen by Arapaho government scouts, and captured November 20th. Taken to Fort Reno, he was questioned by General Ranald S. McKenzie, Crook's cavalry commander. The youth said his camp was on the Upper Powder and that Crazy Horse was on the Rosebud.

Two days later McKenzie moved his eleven hundred soldiers and scouts over to the Crazy Woman. On the morning of the 24th, he set out to seek and crush Crazy Horse's village.

It had snowed and they picked up an Indian trail. By evening the Arapaho scouts, riding far ahead, said there was a big village down the canyon. It was not Crazy Horse, but McKenzie got ready to attack anyhow. He hoped to surprise the Indians. The Cheyennes in the camp, however, had known of his proximity for some time. In fact they almost moved, and would have done so but for the obstinacy of Lost Bull, one of their chiefs, who insisted on staying where he was, to fight it out.

The ground was deep in snow and the weather was arctic. As the men worked their way through the gorge, between whose rocky sides a wild, icy mountain stream splashed its way, they began to hear ahead the sounds of an Indian camp. Drumming and singing could be heard as the Cheyennes celebrated a recent successful foray against the Shoshones in retaliation for the part Washakie and his braves had played in the Battle of the Rosebud.

Near the camp the soldiers halted. The night hours slowly passed, the village slept. Before dawn of November 25th, the ghostly blue masses of men in the canyon began a cautious advance. Just as the first rays of the sun touched the topmost crags of the canyon walls, the notes of a bugle sounded the charge. The famous brothers, Frank and Luther North, and their wild Pawnees led. Almost before the Cheyennes were awake, McKenzie's men were among the teepees.

A few warriors, caught in their lodges, died fighting. But most of the Cheyennes scurried up the sides of the canyon. Many of them had no time to dress, and were naked except for the breech clout. Undaunted, however, they rallied at the head of the gorge and their rifles were soon blazing.

Some of the Cheyennes at the upper end had time to catch up horses and mount. A few of these mounted warriors charged right at the front of the oncoming troops. It was only a bluff at a charge, to stop the soldiers long enough to let the women and children from the lower part of the village get away.

Helped by this brief check, the Indians on foot fell back rapidly and some of them, under Yellow Nose, who had distinguished him-self at the Custer fight, took up a position on a low rocky eminence which commanded the field. It was the key to the battle ground and McKenzie sent Lieutenant McKinney with his troop to capture it.

McKinney charged the knoll. Yellow Nose's braves began to shoot as fast as they could work the levers of their guns. McKinney fell. His men dropped back out of sight in a deep gulch which ran across the valley there, and three Cheyennes ran forward to "count coup" on the fallen officer.

From the knoll Yellow Nose could see the brave Little Wolf herding a big bunch of women and children to safety up a canyon which led to a pass over the cliffs. Several warriors with Little Wolf had already been knocked over by the white men's fire, but the chief stood upright at one side, directing the helpless ones up the gorge, a target for hundreds of rifles. He never left that post of greatest danger until the last of the people were safe.

Two troops of cavalry started up the gulch after the women and children. But Little Wolf had not left it unprotected. As the soldiers entered the gulch mouth, shots rang out. A trooper fell from his horse. The others drew back.

Then the cavalry dismounted and began firing volleys up the gorge. Before long a few Cheyennes jumped out of it and ran across to another cut bank. They were what was left of Little Wolf's rear guard. Nine dead Cheyenne warriors were found in that gulch after the battle. But the women escaped.

Only a few braves were now left in the valley. Five of them had been cut off on a knoll near the center of the amphitheater formed by the hills. There they kept up a grim defense but it seemed certain that they would be lost. The Cheyennes made many efforts to reach these men and save them, but all failed. Then Yellow Nose appeared on the scene. In some manner he had secured a horse, and with him were about twenty or thirty mounted warriors. All wore gorgeous war bonnets.

Yellow Nose charged toward the hill to reach his beleagured friends. Behind him came the other warriors, yelling and shooting. They made a colorful sight as they galloped hard toward where their comrades lay, hugging the rocky ground. The troops turned their guns on the charging Cheyennes. In a minute the air was full of lead. Yellow Nose raised his arm and pulled his horse back on its haunches. The whole band rode off at right angles, and swept around back to safety. The charge had been halted—but its object was accomplished. During the excitement, the men on the knoll had escaped and rejoined their friends.

Little Wolf and Dull Knife shortly had their warriors swarming along the upper ledges of the canyon where they blazed away at the troopers until their ammunition was all gone. But it was useless. McKenzie's men had the village and in spite of the bullets whining among them, they destroyed every one of the one hundred and seventy-three lodges and all ammunition and supplies. Several troopers [4] were hit but the others went stolidly about their work of destruction, which included the slaughter of the captured herd of one hundred and fifty ponies.

Night came on, bitter cold. The heroic Yellow Nose was shot

[4] McKenzie lost five killed, including Lieutenant McKinney, and twenty-five wounded. Twenty-five dead Cheyennes were left on the battle field. Others may have been killed and carried away.

through the breast. Many other warriors were dead or badly wounded. But the terrible cold was more deadly than bullets. Some of the Indians had fought naked all day. Accustomed though they were to hardship, the killing temperatures were too much for the Cheyennes, unblanketed and unprotected. Twelve babies froze to death that night and several old or sick people died. Many others were saved only by a horrible expedient. Some of the few remaining horses were slaughtered. Their bodies were disemboweled and into these bloody cavities the little children were thrust by their mothers, that the warmth and protection of the walls of flesh might save them. Some of the aged were allowed to thrust their hands and feet in and thus preserve circulation and life.

They camped six miles up the valley, without shelter, clothes or food. McKenzie retired down the gulch to rejoin Crook. Next day the Cheyennes wandered off seeking Crazy Horse. Scouts who crossed their trail later said it was red with blood and that tiny footprints showed where even little children tramped through the snow with their tortured feet bleeding.

In three days the Cheyennes reached the camp of Crazy Horse. They were not disappointed in their hope of succor. The Sioux had little, but what there was they divided with the Cheyennes. Many of them stayed right with the Sioux. But many others filed away into the snowy mountains and a few days later surrendered at an Indian agency, conquered by the ruthless elements in one week, when ten years of fighting had failed to bow their heads.

THE LAST OF THE HOSTILES

Crazy Horse's situation was desperate. With the Cheyennes gone and Sitting Bull gone, less than a third of the forces which beat Custer and Crook remained. Moreover those who did remain had very little ammunition left. In the next two months Crazy Horse played hide and seek with Miles. Poorly equipped for winter campaigning, and trailing the women and children with him, he kept the soldiers on the jump until January, when Miles finally caught up.

The general had two regiments of infantry and a couple of howitzers camouflaged under wagon bows and canvas to look like wagons. On Tongue River, January 3rd, he fought a sharp skirmish with a party of Sioux. There was another brush two days later. Crazy Horse's people were tired out. They could not pull away any longer.

On the morning of the 7th, Miles' Crow scouts captured a small party of Cheyenne women and children. These people were not Sioux, but Crazy Horse turned back to rescue them just the same. A desperate raid that night, trying to recapture the prisoners, showed Miles he was on the verge of a big fight.

Early the following morning, while the soldiers were eating breakfast in the shadow of Wolf Mountain, the battle began. Sioux appeared on the cliffs. The crackle of rifle fire stung the air. Taunts and yells of defiance from the gaunt Indians added to the noise. The situation looked bad for the troops.

But Miles had a trump card. The canvas covers were torn from the two cannon and the frosty morning air shook at the thundering reports of the guns and the screeching of the shells as they soared across the valley to explode in the Indian positions. At the first outburst from the "wagon guns," the Sioux ducked behind their rocks. Shellfire was the thing they dreaded most. It took all of Crazy Horse's leadership to keep them in the battle. Still, they kept a very annoying fire plunging down into the valley.

About the middle of the morning Major Casey was ordered to charge a high cliff where about fifty Sioux had climbed. Struggling across the snowy flats, the men fought their way up to the crags. Big Crow, a famous warrior of outstanding courage, led the Indians. During the charge, although his war bonnet was a target for every rifle in the attacking column, he ran back and forth across the front in full view, to draw the soldiers' fire and encourage his own braves. For a time he was not hit. But presently he fell. The Sioux then retreated and the troops occupied the bluff.

In the meantime the cannon had been spreading consternation wherever they turned their black muzzles. Besides, the Indians were almost out of cartridges. So taking advantage of a blinding snowstorm which began to fall, Crazy Horse drew off his people.

Miles did not capture his band at that time but on February 1st, Big Leggins Brughiere, the half-breed who wrote Sitting Bull's note to Otis, and who had deserted to the soldiers, came to the Sioux camp carrying a summons to surrender. He found the Indians camped in the snow, nearly frozen, with most of their horses dead. Two Moons and Little Chief surrendered three hundred Cheyennes on April 22nd. A few days later, Crazy Horse, discouraged and seeing the uselessness of resistance, brought his two thousand followers to Red Cloud Agency.

One hostile band remained—that of Lame Deer, a Minneconjou, who had been with Crazy Horse and refused to accompany him to the agency. Miles started after this band of bitter-enders on May 2nd. They reached and charged the village at dawn five days later. Of course there was not much of a fight. The Sioux were in no position to give battle. A soldier or two and several Indians, including one old woman, were killed; then Lame Deer waved a white rag as a flag of truce.

Everything was apparently over, but tragedy was still to follow. Lame Deer's son refused to lay down his gun. It chanced that the old woman who was killed was the youth's grandmother. He was wild with grief and rage. "I am a soldier on my own land," he kept explaining. An officer and one of the scouts rode up to him and seized his gun to disarm him. The weapon was discharged.

Nobody was hurt. But Lame Deer, hearing the report, believed he was going to be treacherously murdered. He had already laid down his rifle. Now he snatched it up and aimed a shot full at Miles. Straight back the general reared his horse. The bullet passed through the thin air where he had been a minute before and killed his orderly.

In an instant all the soldiers were shooting in retaliation. Several more Indians were killed—a needless sacrifice. A total of fourteen Sioux died in this fight, including Lame Deer and his son, Big Ankle. Four soldiers also lost their lives. The band was soon rounded up and brought to the reservation.

THE END OF A GREAT FIGHTER

The day he surrendered was the saddest in Crazy Horse's life. In the succeeding months his enemies constantly circulated rumors that he was plotting another uprising, and kept him under the suspicion and in the bad graces of the military. It is unlikely that Crazy Horse ever thought seriously of going on the war path again. He had not surrendered until it was impossible to fight longer and he knew well enough that he would be even worse equipped if he took the field now.

Crazy Horse never grew to love the white man. He simply recognized the futility of resistance. Hectored and spied on, he did his best to settle down to life as a virtual prisoner on the reservation.

The chief was still a young man and that spring he fell in love with the daughter of a half-breed interpreter, Louis Richard, at the Red Cloud Agency. The girl, three parts Sioux, reciprocated the love of the renowned warrior, and in spite of Richard's opposition, they married according to the Indian custom. For some months Crazy Horse lived peacefully and apparently happily with his bride. Then the girl sickened and the chief saw with concern that she was growing very weak.

One of the reports circulated by Crazy Horse's enemies was that he planned to murder General Crook. "Only cowards are murderers," the chief scornfully said when he was told of the rumor, and the matter dropped. But with the new stories going the rounds, Agent J. M. Lee grew "jumpy." At this critical time a further misunderstanding was caused, intentionally or unintentionally, by Frank Grouard, the interpreter.

When the Nez Percé war broke out, Crook called a council of the Sioux to enlist a group of scouts. Crazy Horse attended. He was surprised at the request. But according to Louis Bordeaux,[5] he only said: "We are tired of war; we came in for peace, but now that the

---

[5] E. A. Brininstool, "Chief Crazy Horse, His Career and Death," Nebraska History Magazine, December, 1929, pp. 15 and 38. Bordeaux was a reliable interpreter according to Dr. McGillicuddy.

Great Father asks our help we will go north and fight until there is not a Nez Percé left."

Bordeaux was not the official interpreter. Grouard was, and he rendered this speech: "We will go north and fight until not a white man is left." Whether or not the mistake was intentional [6] it threw the council into tremendous excitement. Crazy Horse, probably very much puzzled at the commotion, not understanding the error, left. Crook's attention was called to the discrepancy between the two translations, but his mind was made up that the chief meant war. Nothing could persuade him differently. From that day Crazy Horse was a marked man.

The famous Ogalalla grew more and more concerned about his wife. The girl had tuberculosis. Dr. V. T. McGillicuddy, stationed at the Spotted Tail Agency, had the confidence of Crazy Horse. As his wife failed the chief asked permission to take her to the doctor. The permission was refused. Somebody suggested he appeal to the President, the "Great Father."

"I am not hunting for any Great Father," he haughtily responded. "My father is with me, and there is no Great Father between me and the Great Spirit."

On the morning of September 4th, with a few companions and his ailing wife, he rode quietly out of Red Cloud Agency, toward Spotted Tail, in spite of orders.

Wild excitement ensued. Agency officials feared Crazy Horse more than the whole Sioux Nation. Word flew to Lieutenant W. P. Clark at Fort Robinson that the chief had broken away. It was, of course, a badly garbled account. Crazy Horse had not "broken away." He was merely taking a sick wife for medical attention. Indian police overtook him, riding slowly along beside the ailing girl. At their demand that he return with them to Red Cloud,

---

[6] Grouard had plenty of reason to fear Crazy Horse and wish him out of the way. He had long lived among the Sioux before the war, had been a personal friend of Crazy Horse's and had deserted him to scout for Crook in 1876. Grouard was a Kanaka from the Sandwich Islands. Many thought him a half-breed, but this was not the case. At the time the disputed interpretation took place, he was publicly called a liar by Bordeaux. It stands to reason that Crazy Horse, in the power of his enemies, would have made no such remark as was attributed to him by Grouard. It would be rank insanity and Crazy Horse was both sane and intelligent.

he drew himself proudly up.

"I am Crazy Horse! Do not touch me! I am not running away!" he exclaimed.

Before his glare the scouts quailed. Meekly they fell behind and accompanied him to Spotted Tail.

There Crazy Horse tried to explain that he had come merely to have his wife treated. But the rattled agent could not believe it. Here was Crazy Horse, the renowned leader of the Sioux, idol of his people. He must be gotten away and that quickly.

The chief was disappointed when told he must return to Red Cloud, yet agreed with quiet dignity. He expressed misgivings, saying he "was afraid something might happen." Those were well-grounded apprehensions.

Plans were made to imprison him. Fearing resistance, the officers in charge merely asked Crazy Horse to follow them. The Indian unsuspiciously entered the guard house. Not until the bars of the prison struck his eyes did he realize the treachery. There before him stood the grated door of a cell.

Like an animal at bay, he turned, gazing wildly about. No loophole for escape here. His war cry sounded like the scream of an eagle. A long knife flashed in his hand. Captain Kennington struck at him with a sword.

"Kill him! Kill him!" rang the shouts. The mêlée raged furiously. Alone in his last extremity, Crazy Horse fought like a cornered wolf. Everybody aimed blows at him. Little Big Man, one of his own warriors, tried to seize him. Crazy Horse slashed his arm to the bone. Three Brulés, followers of Spotted Tail who envied and hated him, grabbed him at last by the arms. It took all three to hold him. As they pinioned him, helpless, a soldier ran up behind and plunged a bayonet deep into his side.

Crazy Horse sank to the floor. The uproar was terrific. Even his enemies raged over the murder. From the nearby camp hundreds of excited warriors rushed to the scene. They were with difficulty kept from fighting.

They laid the dying chief on a counter. He grasped the hand of Agent Lee, who had protested against the tactics used, and said between labored gasps: "My friend, I don't blame you for this."

Just before the end he said:

"I was hostile to the white man. . . . We preferred hunting to a life of idleness on our reservations. . . . At times we did not get enough to eat and we were not allowed . . . to hunt. All we wanted was peace and to be left alone. Soldiers . . . in the winter . . . destroyed our villages. Then Long Hair came. . . . They say we massacred him, but he would have done the same to us. . . . Our first impulse was to escape . . . but we were so hemmed in we had to fight. After that I . . . lived in peace; but the government would not let me alone . . . I came back to Red Cloud Agency. Yet I was not allowed to remain quiet. I was tired of fighting. . . . They tried to confine me . . . and a soldier ran his bayonet into me. I have spoken." [7]

A few minutes later the listeners heard the weird sound of the Sioux death song. At last it faded away. Crazy Horse had passed to the land of his fathers.

Dark charges have been made that the whole thing was deliberately planned to "get Crazy Horse out of the way." Years later it was revealed that the government had planned to take the chief from the guard house at night, rush him to prison in the Dry Tortugas, Florida, and there keep him.

His old gray-haired father begged for the body. At daylight on the morning of September 6th, 1877, the old man and his wife followed a travois on which was lashed the body of their dead son to its final resting place on Wounded Knee Creek.

As Captain John G. Bourke, one of the officers who fought hardest against him, has said:

"Crazy Horse was one of the great soldiers of his day and generation. As the grave of Custer marked the high-water mark of Sioux supremacy in the trans-Mississippi region, so the grave of Crazy Horse marked the ebb."

[7] The full text of this remarkable death bed statement is worth reading. It may be found in Col. Homer W. Wheeler's "Buffalo Days," pp. 199–200. The portion quoted here is with the permission of the publishers, the Bobbs-Merrill Co., of Indianapolis.

16: "NEVER SELL THE BONES OF YOUR FATHER"

IN THE NEZ PERCÉ MOUNTAINS

AN OLD man lay dying in a Indian teepee high up among the hills of the Wallowa country. Outside, in the inky blackness of the night, the flat monotony of the tom-toms continued so persistently that those who sat in the ghostly circle of firelight by his pallet heard it no more than they heard the throbbing of the pulse-beats in their own ear drums. Afar in the outskirts of the shadowy village the eery wailing of the squaws rose and fell with skin-prickling quavers and minor chords. The feverish stamp and shuffle of the medicine dance, maintained by the steel-limbed Dreamer priests had sounded for a long time now.

The Indian who was gasping out his last was a great man—a father to the wild people of whom he was chief. At any time the death of Old Joseph would have been enough to plunge the Nez Percés into a frenzy of grief, but at this time it was double cause for sorrow. A great crisis faced them. The question at issue was, should they live on as a free people or as conquered prisoners of an alien race. Small wonder that the women wailed and the Dreamer priests stamped and whirled in the unending spirit dance.

The sick man's eyes were glazing fast, but presently he summoned a part of his lost vigor. A thin hand was raised from the buffalo robes. A weak voice spoke.

"Where is my son?"

A young man stepped to the old chief's side. Dead silence reigned in the lodge. This was Old Joseph's own son, In-mut-too-yah-lat-lat (Thunder-Traveling-over-the-Mountains), but history was destined to immortalize him as Chief Joseph.

Parental pride glowed in the eyes which the old chief turned upon him. This was his boy—his heir! Tall, straight as an arrow, and wonderfully handsome, he was enough to stir pride in any father's heart. The old man spoke and for a time his voice regained those sonorous qualities his tribe had loved to hear.

"My son!" he said, and affection thrilled his voice. Then began that wonderful charge to his heir, the simple oratory of which, coupled with the patriotism it expressed, have so fortunately been preserved for us: [1]

"My son, this old body is returning to my mother earth, and my spirit is going very soon to see the Great Spirit Chief. Give ear to me. When I am gone, think of your country. You are the chief of these people. They look to you to guide them. Always remember that your father never sold his country.

"You must stop your ears whenever you are asked to sign a treaty selling your home. A few years more and white men will be all around you. They have their eyes on this land. My son, never forget my dying words. This country holds your father's body. Never sell the bones of your father and mother."

The old chief sank back. Within an hour the keening of the women announced the passing of one of their tribe's greatest figures.

Young Joseph walked forth from the death lodge the hereditary leader of his people, with his father's last words resting on his soul. Those words remained the guiding spirit of his life during the strange adventures and battle-filled days which followed.

BIG TROUBLE

What kind of people were the Nez Percés? And what manner of a man was the young chief who found himself so suddenly with all the responsibility for their welfare on his shoulders?

Lewis and Clarke first met the tribe in 1805, occupying what is now Idaho and Washington. They were named from an early habit of piercing the nose for ornaments, long discarded. A peaceful hunt-

---

[1] The words are from Joseph's own story as told to Bishop William H. Hare and published in the North American Review, in 1879.

ing and fishing tribe, they were vicious fighters when aroused to war. They had shown a constant friendship for the white man, notable for half a century.[2]

When Oregon was settled, the Nez Percés ceded all their lands except the Wallowa Valley in Oregon and a large section of Idaho. Here they lived peacefully and happily until gold was found, and the gold hunters, disregarding treaties, swarmed on the reservation. At the Nez Percé protest, another treaty was offered. This time the tribe was to be moved bodily out of its home land into the Lapwai Reservation in Idaho. The Southern Nez Percés refused to sign. They have never signed to this day.

The death of Old Joseph left at their head an Indian who approaches nearer to Cooper's famous Indian heroes than any modern red man. Young Joseph was little known except as a handsome young man and a fine hunter. He had never seen a shot fired in anger. Yet such were his natural qualities that before he finished he taught the best soldiers in the United States Army lessons in tactics.

Joseph was fortunate in that the Sioux war on the plains kept the army too busy to bother with the Nez Percés for three years after his father's death. By that time his people had grown to know and trust him. In 1877 the Sioux were beaten, and General O. O. Howard, a fine officer and a sincere friend to the Indian, was ordered to round up the non-agency Nez Percés and put them on the reservation.

Howard called a council with Chief Joseph and his head men at Fort Lapwai. Joseph did not attend. He sent his younger brother Ollicut, a fine, dashing youth, and five other chiefs. Howard insisted that Joseph come and he finally did so. The council lasted all day. Joseph astonished Howard with his dexterous intellectual fencing. Here is a sample of it:

"If we ever owned the land we own it still, for we never sold it. In treaty councils the commissioners have claimed that our country

---

[2] The Nez Percé boast was that no member of the tribe had ever taken the life of a white man in fifty years. It could not be said that no white man had ever killed a Nez Percé.

has been sold to the government. Suppose a white man should come to me and say, 'Joseph, I like your horses, and I want to buy them.' I say to him, 'No, my horses suit me, I will not sell them.' Then he goes to some neighbor and says to him, 'Joseph has some good horses. I want to buy them but he refuses to sell.' My neighbor answers, 'Pay me the money and I will sell you the horses.' The white man returns to me and says, 'Joseph, I have bought your horses and you must let me have them.' If we sold our lands to the government, that was the way they were bought."

The logic was all on Joseph's side. Howard's patience became frayed. He got into an argument with Too-hul-hul-sote, a Dreamer priest,[3] and had him arrested. Joseph, Ollicut, White Bird, Hush-hush-cute and Looking Glass left the council at once. The Nez Percés were indignant over the arrest of their high priest. Joseph had difficulty in keeping them quiet.

Five days later, to secure Too-hul's release, Joseph unwillingly promised to go on the reservation. His intentions were honest. He thought he was doing the best thing for his people. But while he was preparing to move them, they took affairs out of his hands.

Among the young warriors were three who wanted blood atonement for past wrongs. One was the son of a man who had been killed by a drunken white. The others were two who had been tied up and whipped by another white. This trio rode out from the camp on June 13th, 1877, and killed an old ranchman named Devine on the Salmon River. Next morning they killed three more whites and in the afternoon a fourth. Then they rode back to the Nez Percé camp, waving their scalps and yelling for war. The blood-thirst of the young braves was aroused. Seventeen of them joined the three. They rode back to the Salmon Valley. Harry Mason, the man who had whipped the two warriors, was living there. The Indians killed him as if he had been a rabid wolf. Seven more persons in the vicinity died also. Next morning the Nez Percés attacked Cottonwood House, a ranch, killed three, wounded two more so badly that they died, and hurt others. In two or three days the Nez Percés had

---

[3] The Nez Percés were advocates of the Smohalla religion, a quasi-Christian native belief similar to the later Ghost Dance religion.

taken the lives of eighteen white persons.

Joseph was away at the time. When he returned he found his people in a fighting mood. Already plans were made to send war parties in every direction. Joseph protested. In vain. Either he must go with his people or leave them. The young chieftain must have muttered something equivalent to Stephen Decatur's famous toast, as he made up his mind to stay with his tribe.

WHITE BIRD CANYON

As has been said, Joseph had no war experience. Nobody knew his capacity as a soldier, but they were to find it out without delay. As the first messengers reached Fort Lapwai with news of the Salmon Valley massacre, General Howard sent two troops of the 1st Cavalry under Captains Perry and Trimble to protect the settlers and punish the Indians. Nobody expected much fighting. The Indians had always been peaceful. Two days brought Perry to the deep canyon of White Bird Creek, eighty miles away.

It chanced that the Nez Percés were camped in that very canyon. The White Bird runs through mountainous country, cutting a deep gorge. It is slightly timbered and opens widely into the Salmon River valley. Perry with his one hundred men moved down the canyon looking for hostiles. The village was hidden among the buttes and ravines at the mouth of the gorge, and Nez Percé scouts discovered Perry miles up the canyon. Joseph took command in his first battle as though he were the veteran of a hundred engagements.

He had about two hundred warriors which he divided into two groups. Part of them under White Bird, hid in the brush to one side of the canyon. The others lined the buttes at the opening into the valley.

No West Pointer could have set a neater trap. Perry blundered right into it. Lieutenant Theller with eight troopers rode somewhat in advance of Perry's and Trimble's commands. The buttes ahead suddenly became alive with Indians. The sharp roll of rifle fire broke out. A yelling body of mounted Nez Percés charged across the valley at the startled soldiers. Theller had to run. Then Perry and Trimble galloped up and wheeled into line beside him. The troops formed a line clear across the valley. On the extreme left, on a high bluff, Perry's scouts ensconced themselves where they could make their marksmanship felt.

The firing was heavy for a few minutes. Battle smoke began to fill the valley. Under the close shooting of the soldiers, several Nez Percés were hit. The rest fell back. Perry thought he had the fight won.

At this moment White Bird dealt his blow. A blast of fire which knocked over several troopers was the first warning of the flank movement. The howling Nez Percés charged and drove the sharpshooters from their bluff. Trimble was driven back, but Sergeant McCarthy and six men were left behind. They fought off the hostiles until Trimble charged again and brought them off. Two more men were killed. The rearward movement became a retreat.

Up the canyon streamed the soldiers, swiftly becoming panic-stricken. Perry was badly whipped. Leaving gallant Theller with sixteen troopers as a rear guard, he turned his efforts to extricating his command. Grimly Theller held back the rushes of Joseph's victory-mad warriors, until the last of his comrades crossed the top of the divide. Then he followed.

But this remnant was not to escape. Joseph swooped like a hawk. Fighting to the end, Theller and his men, to the last trooper, were killed. The rest of Perry's command was chased clear to Graingeville. It was a stunning disaster. Theller and thirty-six men were dead. The Indian loss was slight as they fought almost entirely from cover.

That evening the Nez Percés moved across the Salmon, forestalling Howard's prompt march with three hundred men. Arriving at the river the general found Joseph placed where he could retreat in any direction or oppose a crossing as he chose.

"No general could have chosen a safer position or one more likely to puzzle and obstruct a foe," was Howard's admiring comment.

The leaders, red and white, sat down on opposite sides of the turbulent stream, to watch each other.

17: ACROSS THE MOUNTAINS

THE FIGHT ON THE CLEARWATER

IT WAS war to the hilt now, without hope of mercy to the vanquished —and Joseph had only two hundred warriors. Seven hundred soldiers were mustered against him, with more coming.

All day he watched Howard across the river. At noon the general dispatched Major Whipple with two troops of cavalry to intercept Looking Glass' band of Nez Percés which was marching to join Joseph.

It was what the chief was looking for. He pulled his people away after dark, descended the heights and was after Whipple like a cat after a mouse. That officer, sparring with Looking Glass, learned to his dismay that Joseph was almost on top of him. Just in time he threw up defenses at the Cottonwood. The Nez Percés surrounded him. They cut up two scouting forces, killing Lieutenant Rains and eleven men.

It took Howard twenty-four hours to untangle himself from the mountains. When, by forced marches, he followed Joseph to the Cottonwood, the Indians were gone. Looking Glass' reinforcements raised Joseph's fighting total to two hundred and fifty—and incidentally increased his baggage train and noncombatant list in proportion. Joseph was encumbered with four hundred and fifty women, children and aged, and a herd of two thousand ponies. But that did not discourage him.

Like a grim old bulldog Howard hung on the Nez Percé trail. At last, seeing he could not evade pursuit, Joseph deliberately chose a battle field and waited to meet his foe. On the banks of the Clearwater River, far south of the reservation, he threw up rude breastworks. Howard's scouts crept up on the morning of July 10th and drew shots from the Indians. Then the main force came up. The first spattering of shots grew into a steady roar. Joseph was badly outnumbered but he handled his small force with consummate skill.

The general later admitted that only the arrival of reinforcements prevented the loss of his supply train. Joseph almost turned Howard's right with a flank movement. There was some violent hand-to-hand fighting. The chief led repeated charges, but the troops managed to hold their ground.

Night fell. The Nez Percés held the only spring and they also controlled the river banks—so the soldiers slept thirsty. At dawn the battle reopened fiercely. The Nez Percés showed the same fighting qualities and deadly marksmanship.[1] But Howard's artillery, a howitzer and two Gatling guns, had at last arrived. The big guns drove Joseph's men back from their trenches. Major Marcus P. Miller led a charge through the Nez Percé left, then crossed the ravine and took Joseph in the rear.

A critical moment. But Joseph called a handful of warriors and threw himself so fiercely at Miller that the troops were driven back. Then he turned on Howard and held him off until he could get his people safely away. There was not one false move. He withdrew in masterly manner and retreated slowly northward. Thirteen soldiers were dead and twenty-seven wounded. The Nez Percé loss was larger, twenty-three dead and forty-six wounded—chiefly because of artillery fire. Joseph had lost no honors.

At Kamiah Falls, Joseph and his chiefs sat in council. Should they stay and fight? Or should they leave their country and try to reach safety elsewhere? Joseph decided on the latter course. The wrench it gave him is shown by his own words:

"I said in my heart that I would give up my country. I would give up my father's grave. I would give up everything rather than have the blood of my people on my hands. . . . I love that land more than all the world. A man who would not love his father's grave is worse than a wild animal." [2]

That was a momentous decision. It involved a retreat of two thousand miles with certainty of pursuit. It meant hard fighting and

---

[1] "The Indian fire was terribly accurate and very fatal, the proportion of wounded to killed being about two to one"—Major C. E. S. Wood.

[2] Joseph's personal narrative, North American Review, 1879.

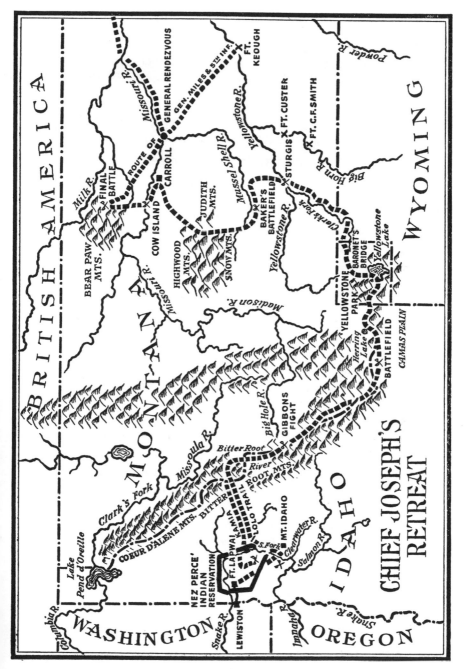

CHIEF JOSEPH'S RETREAT

harder marching. But once they reached the haven of rest, Canada, it meant safety. The only alternative was surrender.

THE LO-LO TRAIL

His decision made, Joseph, like Napoleon, called his fighting men before him and made a short, stirring speech.

"Some of you tried to say once that I was afraid of the whites," he ended. "Stay with me now and you shall get your bellies well filled with fighting." [3]

The Nez Percés rallied around their leader in wild enthusiasm. Rifles, knives, spears were tossed on high. They were ready.

Like Moses of old, Joseph struck into the unknown and barren country, with his flocks and herds, his women and children, his old and weak. But, unlike Moses, he had no Almighty to swallow up the pursuing hosts in an ocean. Joseph had to stand off pursuit by his own unaided effort. Leaving a small rear guard which delayed Howard for a day at Weippe, he started up the Lo-lo Pass.

The Lo-lo trail crosses the Montana mountains at one of their most inaccessible points. It is admittedly one of the most difficult trails in America. With jagged rocks, fallen timber, shoulders hanging over dizzy abysses, torrents and seemingly impassable forests, its natural difficulties were complicated by extremely nasty weather. It rained practically all the time. Every foot of the trail was slippery. So great was the difficulty of crossing this pass, that the troops, unencumbered by camp baggage, averaged a scant sixteen miles a day. Joseph's people with their women, children, herds and camp luggage, pulled steadily away from them.

At the pass which led down to the plains from the Coeur d'Alenes, they found a hastily constructed fort, held by Captain C. C. Rawn and about sixty men. Rawn had been told to stop those Nez Percés. Outnumbered, he bravely prepared to do his best. But he was dealing with a great strategist.

When Rawn refused to let him pass even though he promised to commit no depredations, Joseph made a noisy feint in front of the

---

[3] From Major C. E. S. Wood's article "Chief Joseph the Nez Percé" in the Century Magazine, 1884, copyright by the Century Co. Major Wood got his information about this incident from one of Joseph's warriors.

fort, then quietly led his people through some hitherto unknown mountain trails, around the fort and down into the Bitter Root Valley. The doughty captain retreated hastily to Fort Missoula.

Joseph religiously kept his promise to commit no depredations. The Indians were peaceful, and they amicably traded with the whites in the little towns they passed, buying rifles, food and cartridges. When the military afterward protested, these frontiersmen replied that the Nez Percés had always been good Indians and they could see no reason for fighting them.

Howard was clear out of the picture for a time. But from Helena, General John Gibbon was straining every nerve to cut the Nez Percés off. The Indians, after their friendly treatment in the valley, supposed the war was over. They camped peacefully, their teepees pitched on a little meadow by the Big Hole River. Willows and underbrush choked the sides of the stream. The high ground was covered with trees. On this unsuspecting village, Gibbon with two hundred men made a stealthy advance, just as day broke on August 9th.

THE BATTLE OF BIG HOLE

A Nez Percé boy, out to look at the horses, saw the moving shadows fording the river in the first gray light. His wild war whoop ended all concealment. Thrashing through the willows, the soldiers swept the camp. The Nez Percés dove into the bushes of the bank and the trees beyond, naked and carrying only their arms and ammunition. Gibbon had captured the village.

But he did not get to keep it long. Joseph had his men in hand in a few minutes. Here and there his chiefs—Ollicut, White Bird, Too-hul-hul-sote, and Looking Glass—were busy rallying their warriors. Back came the Indians; the thickets and woods were full of them. The soldiers heard the chiefs exhorting their braves.

"Why are we retreating?" shouted White Bird. "Since the world was made, brave men have fought for their women and children! Fight! Shoot them down! We can shoot as well as any of these soldiers!" [4]

[4] Quoted from "The Battle of the Big Hole" by G. O. Shields.

Captain Logan's troop penetrated farthest. Now it was beset by a pack of human wolves. A tall Indian leaped at Logan and both fired. The Indian fell dead. From nearby a woman—his sister—sprang forward, tore the still smoking revolver from his dead hand, and shot Logan through the head. Instances of this kind of hand-to-hand fighting were many. The white men were pushed back with heavy losses. During the charge Tap-sis-il and Wal-lit-ze, two of the three youths whose massacre had caused the war, were killed.

Joseph posted sharpshooters in the heights overlooking the valley. These braves, the best Indian marksmen on the continent, deliberately picked off the officers. Gibbon was one of the first to be wounded. Lieutenant Coolidge was shot through both thighs and Lieutenant Woodruff was hit. In spite of his pain, Gibbon formed his men in two lines, back to back, and sent them charging through the woods in opposite directions. The Nez Percés hurled both lines back.

A detachment led by Lieutenant James Bradley [5] was cut off. Bradley was killed. Only by very hard fighting did a few survivors reach Gibbon. The troops could no longer stay where they were and the general ordered a retreat. Carrying their wounded, they went back up the hill to a little rise. As they left the camp the Nez Percés took possession.

The soldiers faced a new difficulty. A height above was occupied by the Indians. Gibbon's men now had to carry the place by assault.

From behind rocks and trees the warriors fought fiercely. One, with a few large rocks piled in front of him, fired through a loophole and picked off man after man, secure from the many shots aimed at him from short range. At last a veteran soldier, an expert marksman, sent a bullet into the loophole which struck the rock on one side, glanced and entered the Indian's eye, passing out of the back of his head—a perfect carom shot.

Meantime the Nez Percés swarmed to attack Gibbon's knoll. His men dug rifle pits with their trowel bayonets and settled down to the grimmest defense of their lives. All day the destructive Indian

---

[5] Lieutenant Bradley was the officer who discovered the dead bodies of Custer's men after the Battle of the Little Big Horn.

rifles snarled and snapped. Lieutenant English was killed and Captain Williams was wounded twice. Many of the men were hit. Every officer used a rifle now, to augment the fire. Gibbon, despite his wound, handled a hunting rifle with deadly aim.

Gibbon had a howitzer, which had fallen behind during the march. Now its gun squad tried to bring the gun to him. But Joseph had tasted artillery fire at the Clearwater. Thirty mounted Nez Percés burst out of the woods and charged. The gunners had time to fire their piece twice. Then the white men fled. The Indians dismounted the howitzer so it was of no further use in the fight. The same thirty horsemen also captured a packload of two thousand rounds of ammunition.

Late in the afternoon the Nez Percés set fire to the grass. For a time it looked as if the flames would drive Gibbon out. But luckily for him the wind changed, the blaze faltered and died.

As darkness fell the Indians withdrew. Volunteers, covered by a firing party, managed to crawl to the river and fill their canteens. A dead horse formed the soldiers' food. They did not dare build a fire for fear of sharpshooters, so had to eat the horse raw.

During the night Joseph struck his teepees, packed his baggage and moved his people down the valley. A few warriors stayed in the vicinity the next day. Gibbon's crippled command could not pursue. By the night of the 10th the last Nez Percé left and when the 11th dawned there was not an Indian in the country.

Joseph had won again. He had lost eighty-nine dead of whom fifty were women and children. There were twenty-nine soldiers killed and forty wounded. Joseph's faithful lieutenant, Looking Glass, was among the fallen. Looking Glass' daughter and two of Joseph's wives were also killed.

It was a thankful Gibbon who saw Howard's advance guards pushing down the valley next day. He knew exactly now how Reno had felt that fatal day on the Little Big Horn, months before, when Gibbon was the rescuer.

18: "FROM WHERE THE SUN NOW STANDS"

SOUTHWARD, ever southward went the Indians. Joseph was getting farther away from the Canadian border with every step but there were to be no more surprises. Nez Percé scouts hung far back on the trail, keeping constant watch on Howard's movements. At last the chief reached his farthest south. Not one step more would he be driven. It was northward or die.

Joseph's scouts brought word that a detachment of soldiers—under Lieutenant Bacon—had been sent away to occupy a pass ahead. This fitted exactly with his plans. On the night of August 20th forty warriors, riding in column of fours, entered Howard's camp. Their formation was so unusual for Indians that they were mistaken in the dark for Bacon's returning force. They were inside the picket lines before the alarm was given.

Among the tents the Nez Percés worked with perfect coordination. Some shot at the soldiers who rushed out of their sleeping places; the rest went to the picket lines and tried to stampede the horses. They got the pack mules loose but the horses were too well tethered.

When things got too hot, the audacious forty rode out of the camp with Howard's troopers in close pursuit. It was a race for a while. Then spurts of flame sprang out from rocks on three sides of a wide ravine into which the Indians had led the cavalry. They were in a cul-de-sac—it was sure death to remain.

Out of those jaws of death they galloped—all but Captain Norwood's troop. Cut off, they found a strong position and by sheer cold courage held off the Nez Percés until Howard could return and rescue them. Then the whole command retreated. The night had saved them from being cut to pieces as the Indians could not see to shoot accurately. One man was killed, and seven, including Lieutenant H. M. Benson, were wounded.

The Camas Meadows fight stopped Howard's pursuit. He was without a pack train and with a sizable hospital list. He had to sit down and wait for supplies from Virginia City.

Joseph was free to go where he chose. He moved leisurely eastward through Thatcher's Pass—which had been vacated by Bacon—and into Yellowstone Park. Here two parties of tourists were surprised and captured. The men fought and were killed or wounded. Two women were captured but were released unharmed.[1]

Crossing the park, Joseph burned Baronet's bridge over Clarke Fork of the Yellowstone and turned north. By this time practically every body of troops in Montana was on the move. Lieutenant Gilbert's two troops of cavalry crossed the Nez Percé trail, but such was this tribe's reputation that Gilbert retreated, and at such speed that he failed to make a junction with Howard and finally arrived at Fort Ellis.

The 7th Cavalry tried to trap Joseph in the Yellowstone Valley but the chief laughed at them and slipped through a dense forest northward. Not until next day did Colonel Sturgis learn he had been tricked. He gave chase. With his fresh horses he overtook the Nez Percés at Canyon Creek, on September 13th.

It was a short but very hot battle. Joseph had posted his rear guard to hold back the cavalry while the women and camp equipment escaped. As the 7th galloped after the main body of Indians, seen a mile down the stream, a sudden rattling fire broke out from the ridges on each side. Two saddles were emptied and all thoughts of catching up with the noncombatants departed.

Sturgis dismounted his men and sent them swarming up the slopes. Less than a hundred warriors were there to oppose three hundred and fifty troopers. One by one the 7th drove the Nez Percés from their positions. By night Joseph was again in retreat. But Sturgis, with his wounded to care for, could not pursue.

The Indians lost twenty-one braves killed and wounded in the fight. Sturgis had three dead and twelve wounded, including the veteran Captain French. The most serious loss the Nez Percés suf-

[1] J. P. Dunn says this is the only authentic case on record where white women captured by Indians escaped outrage. "Massacres of the Mountains," p. 427.

fered was the capture of their herd of nine hundred ponies by the Crow scouts.

MILES AGAIN

Westward and northward rode the Nez Percés. Behind, exhausted or crippled, were three strong bodies of soldiers, each outnumbering them, but beaten and out of the fight. Howard, Gibbon and Sturgis were disposed of, but a new enemy loomed ahead. The enormous advantage of railroad and telegraph was working for the white man.

General Miles, with his famous 5th Infantry and five troops of cavalry, two guns and a supply train, was marching at an angle calculated to cut off the Indian retreat. Joseph, through his peerless scouts, knew every movement of the enemies in his vicinity. But he had no way of knowing distant movements, so was ignorant of Miles' approach.

Past the Snow Mountains and straight toward his long-sought goal he drove his Spartan people at a killing pace. Some instinct told him every minute was precious. At the ford of the Missouri he found a little fort on Cow Island, garrisoned by twelve men. Joseph could easily have destroyed the place. But he contented himself with a single attack in which three of the defenders were killed. During this attack he got his women and children across the river; then he burned all the freight at the station and went on.

On the Missouri River he halted just long enough to brush aside the weak force of Major Ilges, a troop of cavalry and thirty-six civilians. Far ahead loomed the Bear Paw Mountains, with Canada and safety only thirty miles beyond. Could the Nez Percés make it? On and on they marched, with ponies dropping at every mile along their agonized path. Human flesh and blood could not endure the strain. They reached the mountains, but there for a time they halted. That halt was necessary but fatal. One brief day's journey would have taken them to the border. But the people were unspeakably weary. Joseph's humanity caused him to relax his iron purpose —he seemed so very near the goal. The cup, poised to his lips, was dashed to the ground. The prize, almost won, was snatched away.

Miles rode to cross the Indian trail. He had fresh troops, fresh horses, fresh scouts. And he was fresh to the fray and knew the mistakes of his predecessors. In the dead of night he crept up on Joseph's camp, pitched on the northward slope of the mountains, where he could almost see his destination.

Morning of October 3rd dawned, cold and stormy. With the first light came the opening shot of the final battle. The Indian camp was in a cup-shaped ravine overlooked by high cliffs and bluffs. What sickening despair must have been Joseph's as he saw the troops galloping toward him, spreading out like a mammoth fan. No chance to escape here. The Nez Percé knew his time had come. He was outnumbered four to one. Everything favored the soldiers.

On charged the cavalry, converging from three sides. Captain Hale's troop led. A sudden level sheet of fire cut his men down. Posted on the bluffs, the Nez Percés made every shot count. In two minutes half the troop was hit. By the time the supporting companies under Captains Moylan and Godfrey arrived, Hale's men were almost wiped out. The Nez Percé wolf was at bay at last, but he was going to make his end memorable.

Godfrey and Moylan rode to the right, to the rear of Hale, their horses leaping over the bodies of his fallen. A shot killed Godfrey's horse and he was stunned in the fall. Moylan was hit at almost the same moment. When the soldiers reached him Hale was the only captain left in the battalion.

With a trail of dead and wounded behind them, Hale's men dismounted on the ground which was too steep for their horses and slippery with the blood of their comrades, and began the last stage of their charge on foot. Godfrey revived from his fall and took the head of his men only to be shot down. Lieutenant Biddle dropped with a bullet between his eyes. Under that storm of lead the troopers wilted like autumn leaves. But the survivors kept on.

Up, up they climbed. Over boulders and through underbrush, to come to hand grips with their red foes. Fifty feet remained—thirty-five. And every foot, almost, won by the life of a comrade. Only twenty feet remained to the crest of the bluff and then—

a choking gasp. The gallant leader was down—brave, chivalrous Hale, joking in the face of danger—instantly killed.

One officer was left now. All the rest lay somewhere on that bloody slope. Lieutenant Eckestrom led on. The men clenched their teeth, gripped their carbines, and using fingernails as well as toes, made the last grim climb into the very muzzles of the heated Nez Percé rifles.

It was madness. But it was splendid. The impossible was accomplished. The men tumbled over the top of the bluff—the hill was theirs.

But at what a cost. Fifty-three were killed or wounded out of the one hundred and fifteen who began the charge. Hale's troop lost more than sixty percent of its strength.

Meanwhile Joseph, cool-headed, seeing everything, set at naught the charge by withdrawing his men at just the right time. The Indians retreated to the ridges behind the camp. But the 5th and the other cavalry had gotten into action. The Indians were surrounded.

THE SURRENDER

Miles found he had an old wolf instead of a stag at bay. But he was not the man to halt for that. The 5th charged directly into the teeth of the Nez Percé fire. Their first lines were mowed down and they reeled back. But not until they had almost captured Joseph himself.

The rush cut the camp in two. The chief was cut off with about seventy of his people, including White Bird. He could have escaped but he put his ten-year-old daughter on a pony, told White Bird to lead her to safety, and turned his own horse to the main camp.

"With a prayer in my mouth to the Great Spirit Chief who rules above, I dashed unarmed through the lines of soldiers," he said afterward. Bullets cut his clothes; his horse was shot; but he was unhurt. At the door of his lodge was his brave wife. "Here's your gun. Fight!" she said. And he turned to meet the foe.

White Bird's group got across the hills to eventual safety. Two days later they joined Sitting Bull's Sioux in Saskatchewan.

But the fight still raged in the Bear Paws. The cavalry attacked repeatedly. They were beaten back by the deadly Nez Percé rifles. Ollicut was killed. It was like a stab in the heart to Joseph. Between the brothers was the deep affection sometimes seen in men of noble natures. The dash and ardor of Ollicut had turned many a critical situation. After the youth died the heart seemed to go out of Joseph.

When night fell Miles called his troops into besieging lines. Joseph's position was too strong to be taken by direct assault. The white man had two other expedients—artillery and hunger. Next morning the guns were brought up. All day the shells shattered in the Indian lines. All should have been killed, but when a troop of cavalry began a cautious advance, it was driven fiercely back.

That evening General Howard with a few aides, rode into Miles' camp. He had learned that Joseph was at last cornered and, leaving his wearied men behind, rode fast to be "in at the kill."

Early the following morning a white flag was raised by the Indians. The long fight was over. Miles, who had lost a fifth of his force and dreaded the possibility of Sitting Bull's coming down at his back, saw that white banner with a sigh of relief.

At sunset Joseph gave himself up. With him were five of his warriors. The chief was riding, his body bent forward, his head bowed, his hands clasped over the saddle horn. The five with him walked, their faces earnest as they looked at him. Miles and Howard waited on a little hill. As he reached them, Joseph dismounted and handed Miles his rifle, butt first, in token of surrender.

Then he spoke. And the speech remains one of the most pathetic and beautiful Indian utterances ever recorded:

"Tell General Howard that I know his heart. What he told me before—I have it in my heart. I am tired of fighting. Our chiefs are killed. Looking Glass is dead. Too-hul-hul-sote is dead. The old men are all dead. It is the young men who say 'yes' and 'no' (that is, vote in council). He who led the young men (Joseph could not bear to utter the name of his slain brother Ollicut) is dead. It is cold and we have no blankets. The little children are freezing to death. My people—some of them—have run away into the hills, and have no blankets, no food. No one knows where they are (he referred to

White Bird's detachment which contained his daughter). Perhaps they are freezing to death. I want to have time to look for my children and see how many of them I can find; maybe I shall find them all among the dead. Hear me, my chiefs, my heart is sick and sad. From where the sun now stands, I will fight no more, forever!"

It was the end. Joseph, who never commanded more than three hundred warriors, had opposed five thousand soldiers, besides hundreds of civilians. He had actually met in battle two thousand troops. Of these he had killed or wounded two hundred and sixty-six. His own loss, including women and children, had been two hundred and thirty-nine killed and wounded. He had defeated the best soldiers of the nation again and again; had marched at least two thousand miles through enemy country without a supply train and carrying his noncombatants; and had come within thirty miles of complete success, in spite of his tremendous handicaps. The history of warfare hardly shows a parallel to this campaign.

The captured Nez Percés, eighty-seven warriors and two hundred and fifty-four women and children, were sent to a reservation in the Indian Territory. Years later, through the influence of General Miles, they were moved to a reservation near their former home, where they resumed the peaceful trend of their lives. And Joseph, adopting the white man's ways in education and industry, lived out his years, and finally died, honored by red man and white.[2]

---

[2] The losses in the Battle of the Bear Paw Mountains were as follows: The troops suffered twenty-four killed, including Captain O. Hale and Lieutenant J. W. Biddle; and forty-two wounded, including Captains Moylan and Godfrey and Lieutenants Baird and Romeyn—a total of sixty-six officers and men. The Indians lost seventeen killed and forty wounded. "Record of Engagements," p. 74.

19: WITHOUT BENEFIT OF MILITARY

THE STAKED PLAINS

THE Battle of Adobe Walls, in which a handful of buffalo hunters beat a large body of Kiowa, Cheyenne and Comanche warriors in June, 1874, has been widely celebrated. But the Staked Plains War, a bona fide campaign, conducted without the benefit of military assistance or sanction, against the Comanches in 1877, by a party of those same buffalo hunters, has scarcely been noticed.[1] Yet the Staked Plains War, culminating in the Battle of Pocket Canyon, was far the most daring of the two and its results were more important, since it broke the warlike power of the fierce Comanches.

The feud between the buffalo hunters and the Indians was of long standing. The hunters had practically exterminated the great buffalo herds and the red men bitterly resented this wanton slaughter of their chief source of food. There was no love lost between the two groups.

By the summer of 1876 the buffalo had been so killed off that only in the Texas Panhandle could they be found in sufficient numbers to make hide hunting profitable. The hunters therefore moved to that section. With them went the traders. Charles Rath of the Dodge City firm of Rath & Wright, whose trading stores had been on every buffalo hunting frontier, established a post on Double Mountain Creek, a tributary of the Brazos.

Far to the east lay the Comanche reservation. The Indians were

---

[1] For incidents, names and much of the information in this and the next chapter I am indebted to John R. Cook's valuable little book "The Border and the Buffalo." Use of these facts is made by the kind permission of the copyright owners, Mrs. Alice V. Schmidt, of Houston, Texas, and Charles A. Maddux, of Los Angeles.

supposed to be peaceful, but the Comanches had not really felt the brunt of the 1874 war, and many of them were still unconvinced of the white man's power. Besides, the government was slow with its rations. And constant reports came to them of the continued extermination of the buffalo—their buffalo—in the west, contrary to the promises made to them. They grew very restless.

The Comanches were one of the great fighting tribes of the plains. General Richard I. Dodge called them "the most cunning, the most mischievously artful of all the United States Indians." For two centuries they carried on a constant war against Mexico. Their warriors were as familiar with the passes of Chihuahua as with their own Red River country. When Texas became independent, the Comanches extended their hatred to the Texans, and long distinguished between "Texans" and "Americans" with whom they were friendly.[2]

It is not strange that this warlike tribe should chafe under conditions as they existed, nor that, late in December, 1876, a band of Comanches numbering one hundred and seventy warriors, under Black Horse (Tu-ukumah) with their families, should leave Fort Sill and head toward the Staked Plains. Two troops of cavalry pursued them but lost their trail when a heavy snow came unexpectedly. That winter Black Horse's band camped in Thompson's Canyon, an opening in the escarpment of the Staked Plains. It was an ideal location, with plentiful game, protection from the elements, and far enough from the nearest buffalo hunters' camps so that nobody suspected the Indians' presence.

BEGINNING OF HOSTILITIES

In the latter part of February, 1877, a few of the young Co-

---

[2] One of the Comanches' most celebrated exploits was the sacking of Parker's Fort in northern Texas. The Comanches, led by Peta Nokoni (The Wanderer), captured the fort and killed nearly everybody in it. Among the prisoners were two children, one a little girl named Cynthia Ann Parker, granddaughter of Elder John Parker, in whose honor the fort and later the city were named. The girl was thirteen years old. Peta Nokoni later married her. She bore him three children before she was recaptured by the whites. Her eldest son was the famous Quanah Parker, who took his surname, by Comanche custom, from his mother. This chief at last became head chief of all the Comanches, and the town of Quanah, Texas, is named after him.

manche braves went on the prowl and came on some outlying hunters' camps close at hand.

John F. Cook and Rankin Moore, camped with the Benson outfit south of the Red River, were the first to see the enemy. A solitary Indian sneaked up on Cook and tried to shoot him from ambush. He missed and escaped, but not until he had dodged a perfect spray of bullets from Cook and Moore.

The incident disturbed the buffalo hunters. They remembered Adobe Walls. Warnings were sent around. Late that evening came a report that Marshall Soule [3] whose camp was near the escarpment had been killed. On the same day the camp of Bill Devins was raided. Although his men escaped with their lives and their weapons, the Indians captured all their ammunition and supplies.

That was February 22nd, Washington's Birthday. Rath's store on Double Mountain Creek was the natural gathering place of the hunters, and thither they went as fast as they were warned. A tall, raw-boned Texan, Pat Garrett by name, was largely responsible for carrying the word of warning, riding scores of miles to tell outlying camps of their danger. It was this same Pat Garrett, who later as sheriff of Lincoln County, New Mexico, was to put an end to the career of the notorious outlaw, Billy the Kid.

Nearly three hundred hunters gathered at Rath's and a council of war was held. It was voted first to send a party of eighteen volunteers to Soule's camp, to see if he was really dead. The party made the trip and found the scalped and mutilated body of the hunter. They buried him and returned to the post.

Rath's bartender was Limpy Jim Smith. He was an ex-road agent from Montana, had escaped from that country just ahead of the vigilantes who broke up the Plummer gang, and carried a bullet in his leg to his dying day. But he was a man of nerve and courage. He proposed that the hunters organize. At the proposal one Tom Lumpkins cried out that "he hadn't lost any Injuns and didn't propose to hunt any." The remark brought sharp words between Lumpkins and Smith which culminated a month later in a gun fight

[3] Or Sewell. The hunters were not very sure how they spelled their own names. The spelling in the text is that of the army records.

and the death of Lumpkins.

Most of the hunters favored the sending of a punitive expedition against the Comanches. If anybody had the nerve to suggest an appeal to the army, he was laughed to scorn. The buffalo hunters knew how to handle this case themselves. Forty-five volunteered to go, which was considered a sufficient number.

Among the hunters was Big Hank Campbell, an old Indian fighter. He had been one of the leaders in the Sappa Creek massacre in 1875, when a band of Cheyennes was wiped out by buffalo hunters and soldiers in northern Kansas. He was elected commander. Limpy Jim Smith was also elected one of the leaders. The third was Joe Freed.

The expedition set out the next day. Thirty hunters were mounted. Fifteen went on foot to guard the wagons which carried two hundred and fifty rounds of ammunition for every man, besides bar lead, powder, primers and reloading outfits. They had with them José, an English-speaking Mexican, who had scouted for General McKenzie in 1874 and knew the country thoroughly. Ben Jackson as quartermaster, issued grain, and Shorty Woodson, tallest, slimmest man on the range, a former druggist, took charge of the medicine supply. The roster was kept by Powder Face Hudson, with guards detailed in rotation. Most of the men had been soldiers in either the Union or Confederate armies. The whole thing was handled in thoroughly military fashion.

All told, it was one of the best-equipped and outfitted expeditions ever to go against the Indians, army expeditions included. The men carried their long-range, heavy calibre Sharp's buffalo guns, with which, by continuous practice they had become wonderful judges of distance and could shoot extremely accurately by raising the muzzle, without adjusting the rear graduated sights.

Just before they started, another bunch of hunters came in from Godey's camp. There were fifteen or twenty of them and they carried in one badly wounded man, Spotted Jack, while two or three others were slightly wounded. There were only three horses among them. This was the story they told:

The previous day, while camped on their way to Rath's rendezvous, a band of Comanches, headed by Black Horse himself, had stampeded their entire horse herd, except for three animals. Badly outnumbered—they had counted sixty hostile war bonnets—they opened fire. The buffalo guns did good execution. A couple of Comanches turned flip-flops in the sun as the ounce slugs hit them, and the rest took to cover.

Most of that day, completely surrounded, they fought against odds of more than three to one. Every once in a while they could hear the heavy report of a buffalo gun, whose dull roar formed a contrast to the sharper cracks of the Winchesters most of the Indians carried. This meant the party was the same which had killed Soule and carried off his gun.

In the afternoon Moccasin Jim, one of the hunters, "got a bead" on the Comanche who was using Soule's gun and "drilled him." The Indian crumpled up. Another Comanche snaked through the bushes and got the gun. It was soon busy again.

The hunters were certain they killed at least three of the Comanches, probably more. Three or more of their own number were wounded by this time. Old Godey finally rose and said: "Well, boys, this is no place to be tonight. Let's go back."

In spite of the redoubled fire of the Indians, the stark hunters arose, walked down the trail, and leaving the Comanches behind, joined their fellows at Rath's.

20: THE BATTLE OF POCKET CANYON

ON THE INDIAN TRAIL

MARSHALL SOULE had been universally respected and liked by the buffalo hunters. John R. Cook, one of them, later wrote:

"My mind wandered back to the lonely apology of a grave (Soule's). He was an educated man, a native of Pennsylvania. He was a man who possessed a useful fund of information. He was not obtrusive, but was courteous and polite; respected others' opinions even when he differed from them. He was not a professed Christian, but believed in the observance of the Golden Rule. . . . Why should he have been taken when such men as Hurricane Bill, Dutch Henry, Squaw Johnny and some others that I had in mind, could roam those prairies, disregarding law and morality, with a price placed on some of their heads?"

The expedition started at last. At the edge of the Staked Plains on the escarpment, they had great difficulty in getting their wagons to the top. This was finally done by passing along its base until they reached a narrow, winding, steep incline, where by doubling their teams they finally reached the upper level.

Here they found an Indian trail, dim it is true, but still a trail. Congratulating themselves on their luck, they started in pursuit. It seems almost incredible to think that this handful of men were actually gleeful as they took the trail of an Indian band containing many times their number of warriors, to carry war to their vastly superior foe. But the buffalo hunters, each a hair's-breadth shot with his heavy rifle, each endowed with a reckless disregard for his own life, were probably, man-for-man, among the most formidable individuals who ever trod this continent.

The whole day was spent ferreting out the dim trail. That night they came upon traces of a camp, where they found two burned teepees. This meant two men had died, and they thus were able to determine the extent of the damage done by Godey's outfit.

At midafternoon the next day, José, riding ahead with Cook and Louie Keyes, located the hostile camp. Back they went to warn the hunters. That night the audacious white men made their camp within two or three miles of the Indian village, in a gorge which hid their wagons and horses.

As camp was being made, José saw an Indian cross the canyon and ride the back trail. If he discovered their track the Comanches would break camp at once and be "hard to catch." To stop him was vital.

Louie Keyes was a half-breed Cherokee. He now daubed his cheeks with red paint and snaked out to intercept the rider. On came the Comanche. Suddenly a rifle rang out. The Indian whirled out of his saddle. The shot had not been fired by Keyes but by an Englishman, a member of poor Soule's outfit. The Indian got up and started to run, zig-zagging. It was useless for him to attempt to escape. The hunters killed him and hid his body among the tall reeds near a water hole.

Hank Campbell now gave his simple orders. The wagons and camp outfit were to be left where they were. Three fighting divisions were named. Campbell commanded half the mounted men; Limpy Jim the other half; and Joe Freed the dismounted men. Old Man Godey with Cook and José were to scout the Indians. Smith's men were to charge through the village and run off the pony herd. Then the hunters expected, with supreme self-confidence, to exterminate the whole Comanche outfit, although they were admonished by Campbell not to kill any women or children "if they could help it."

Darkness came and the three scouts, their horses' hoofs muffled with grain sacks, started up the canyon. By lighting a match under a blanket, they were able from time to time to examine the trail. It was perilous in the extreme and nerves were keyed to high tension. The whir of a disturbed bird, a stumble or an involuntary cough or sneeze might mean their deaths. Near morning they discovered the camp. Cook rode back to bring the hunters.

THE FIGHT IN THE CANYON

Broad daylight on March 18th. The three divisions of hunters, approximately fifteen men each, stopped at the head of the pocket canyon where the Comanche village stood. There Campbell arranged the two mounted platoons about two hundred yards apart, with the "infantry" between. Everything was ready.

"All right!" shouted Campbell.

"Go for them!" yelled Limpy Jim, the ex-road agent.

Forward swept the hunters. There were many stalwart fighters in their line. John Cook, a veteran Indian scout; Joe Jackson, an ex-Confederate soldier; Squirrel-eye, another ex-rebel; Lee Grimes, taciturn and dour; Louie Keyes the Cherokee, now beginning his war chant—they were a formidable group. As they began to move Keyes uttered a war whoop and Squirrel-eye gave the old rebel yell. Then, shouting like mad, the hunters charged.

Indian teepees came into view. The Comanches were seen running out to a low hill from which they began shooting rapidly at about two hundred yards. It was death to continue into the teeth of that fire. Hank Campbell, riding like a crazy man, headed the hunters and yelled at them to fall back to the canyon. Before they could obey, Joe Jackson flopped from his saddle and Lee Grimes was down, his horse shot under him and his wrist broken.

Devins and Cook leaped from their horses and ran to Jackson, whom they began dragging to a place of safety. A sharp cry from Devins, and he dropped his hold. A Comanche bullet had shattered his arm.

"For God's sake," gasped the wounded Jackson, "lie down or they'll get you all!" Grimes crept up and the four men, three of them hurt, listened to death whispering above them.

Hank Campbell's men, down in the draw, did not see the new menace slipping up on them. They were so much interested in the fight on their front that the band of more than one hundred warriors, creeping up the gorge toward them on the north, escaped their attention. But Cook and the wounded hunters, forced to lie out in their exposed situation, saw them. Their sudden shooting revealed the move. Campbell's men turned their rifles and the Comanches retreated, dragging six of their number with them.

Cook, Devins and Grimes crawled down from their perilous location, taking the helpless Jackson with them. All chance of capturing the Comanche herd was gone and for the first time the buffalo hunters were beginning to respect the fighting ability of their adversaries.

Now the Comanches mounted and swept about the white men in a wide circle. The latter scattered to places of advantage. Part of them faced clear around to meet the attack from the rear. Whooping and yelling, the Indians flashed across one draw opening after another, the hunters' rifles shooting like mad. Several horses went down. A warrior, his pony shot out from under him, ran for a ravine. He had thirty yards to go and the heavy slugs from the buffalo guns ripped the sod all around him. All at once he was flat on the ground. The hunters turned their rifles elsewhere.

Grizzled Hank Campbell and Limpy Jim Smith held a conference. Then Campbell spoke:

"Boys, we must leave this place. Smith will take horses and wounded men down the side ravine to the long water hole. The rest of us will crawl to that crest and fire at the camp until Joe Freed can get his foot men out of the mess they are in."

The whole aspect of the fight had changed. Instead of a joyful campaign of annihilation, it had become a grim struggle for life with the odds heavily in favor of death. Campbell's sharpshooters crept to the crest. About four hundred yards away was the Comanche camp in plain view with a big bunch of horses behind it; among the teepees fifty or sixty ponies with travois were being loaded by the squaws. Off to the left was a tall pole with a red flag flying from it —some Indian signal. To the right was an Indian working his looking glass to flash messages to his comrades. Campbell's hunters fired a couple of long-distance volleys at the camp. Then, like a swarm of bees, a fusillade of bullets buzzed over their own heads.

"Let the camp alone and comb the grass at the crest this side of it," ordered Campbell. From end to end that crest was swept with bullets, about three hundred rounds being fired at it. Then the shooting at the camp began again, the cool hunters, with their tobacco quids in their cheeks, deliberately picking special targets to shoot at.

THE ESCAPE OF THE COMANCHES

By this time Joe Freed and his men had returned to the main body. Poor José, the Mexican scout, was shot through the shoulder but wore a grin on his face. José told them they had picked a hornet's nest indeed. Instead of seventy-five or a hundred Comanches there were nearly three hundred warriors fighting them. Another camp was just around the bend of the canyon with a big band of Plains (Lipan) Apaches, allied with the Comanches for years.[1]

But Campbell, the indomitable Scot, merely laughed. "Mebbe we've bit off more than we can chew," was his only comment.

The Indian fire suddenly died down. Something was up. Black smoke sprang up and advanced down the draw. The Indians had set the prairie grass ablaze.

Right behind the smoke dashed a daring young warrior, wearing a magnificent war bonnet and riding a speedy white horse. Directly across their front he rode, drawing the fire of half the men, some of whom shot the second or third time before the running horse fell. Then under the fusillade from the crest the daring brave quickly crumpled up and was still.

Far down the draw, waving their lances and uttering the demoniac Comanche scream, which once heard is never forgotten, came a band of Indians. They halted at long rifle range. Their purpose was to draw attention from the camp where the real attack was being prepared, but they failed to catch the hunters off their guard.

Suddenly through the grass smoke of the upper draw came a magnificent, swooping rush of the Comanches. The smoke screened their movements until they broke through it. Then the full roar of

---

[1] Some of these Apaches were later shown to be Mescaleros from the Victorio band in northern Mexico.

the buffalo guns crashed out. Many warriors went down. The Indians drew off.

The wounded white men were calling for water now, and during the lull which followed the charge through the smoke screen, Ben Jackson, brother of the wounded Joe, and Cook volunteered to get some water from a hole, fifty yards away. With their comrades shooting over their heads to keep down the Indian fire, they crawled to the spring and came back with their boots filled with the precious liquid. "Shorty," the druggist, had bound up the wounds and given each wounded man a big drink of fourth-proof whiskey.

It was noted that the Indians had disappeared. Cautiously scouts advanced to their first position. Then came the surprise. The wily Comanches had tricked them. The whole camp was gone. The Indians had escaped.

The buffalo hunters did not try to pursue. They were burdened by wounded, but more than that they were devoutly thankful to be alive after their attack. They craved no further experiences of the kind. Poor Jackson was in particularly bad shape. The bullet which had struck him in the groin was from Soule's buffalo gun, which the Indians used throughout the fight. Jackson lived until he got to camp but died a little later.

Weeks later they found out the extent of the damage they had done. Captain P. L. Lee, with a troop of the 10th Cavalry, rounded up the Comanches near Lake Quemado, after a brief fight in which he killed four of them. Both Black Horse and his wife were among the dead he reported.[2] The Indians were very ready to surrender.

Lee learned that the hunters had killed thirty-one Indians in the fight, mortally wounded four more, and seriously wounded twenty-two. Fifteen pack horses were killed in the camp during the battle. Lee also found out something else: the Soule gun was a hoodoo to the Comanches. Everyone who used it had been killed or wounded.

[2] This report was in error. Black Horse, also known as Pako-Riah (Colt) and Ta-Peka (Sun Rays) lived for many years afterward and died at Cache, Oklahoma, about 1900. The leader killed at Lake Quemado was Ek-a-wak-a-ne (Red Young Man), who was not a chief, but is remembered by the old Comanches as an extremely fearless and reckless warrior who absolutely refused to surrender and never went on the reservation.

The first Indian who used it was killed, the second badly wounded. Then Black Horse's son took it and he too died with the gun in his hands. Five Feathers used it until near the close of the fight when he, too, was killed. After that the Indians would not use it. They left it wrapped in a blanket with the two scalp locks they had taken from Soule's head. It was found by Lee's men.

The Comanches never went on the war path after that campaign. It was planned, carried out and fought by buffalo hunters, but it could not have been more effective had it been executed by the best trained of soldiers.

VIII
The Odyssey of the Cheyennes
1878

21: LITTLE WOLF'S RAID

THE FAITH OF THE WHITE MAN

Two years had passed since McKenzie wiped out Dull Knife's village in the Crazy Woman canyon. Not long after that the Cheyennes surrendered—as fine a body of Indians as the continent contained.

"Tsi-tsis-tsa" [1] they called themselves, which means "*The* People" with a large, black accent-mark over "The." Proud, well-dressed, handsome, fearless, famed for their horses, the beauty of their women and the prowess of their warriors, such were the Northern Cheyennes when they surrendered in the spring of 1877.

One would scarcely have recognized them as the same people two years later. September 8, 1878, found them famished and dying of fever in the Indian Territory, nearly a thousand miles south, penned on a reservation so unhealthy that their extinction was only a matter of time. The white man had promised them a reservation on their northern plains, with supplies, protection and other rewards for making peace. Thus had the white man kept his faith.

Almost without arms, almost horseless, squalid, in rags, with the ribs of their children standing out, and with patched teepees, the Tsi-tsis-tsa begged to be allowed to return to their own country. Little Wolf, tall, high-shouldered, gaunt with fever, spoke for his people, every word carrying intense meaning. The agent, look-ing at his pock-marked face, with its tremendous breadth through

---

[1] The Bureau of American Ethnology gives another spelling as Dzi-tsii-tsa. Literally "Our People" or "The People." The word Cheyenne is from the Sioux "Sha-hi-yena" or "Shai-ena," meaning "people of alien speech," and is the French corruption. The word has no relation to the French "Chien," meaning dog, as has been claimed by Custer and others.

the cheek bones and its lines of chiselled granite, may very well have remembered that here was the greatest warrior in the Cheyenne Nation.

It was Little Wolf who, in 1857, refused to give up his horse which was claimed by some white man. They offered to pay him a "reward" for "finding" the animal, but the Cheyenne, already a famous man, coldly refused. There followed the treacherous arrest of a Cheyenne and the killing of another near the Platte Bridge. That was the genesis of the Cheyenne troubles with the white men.[2]

Little Wolf was one of the ten warriors chosen to decoy Fetterman's command into the trap near Fort Phil Kearny in 1866. Eighty-one men died as that trap closed.

He fought at the Rosebud and the Little Big Horn. In the attack by McKenzie on Dull Knife's village in 1876, it was Little Wolf who led the helpless women and children to a place of safety and stood on a high rock while the bullets sprayed around him until every one was hidden. And it was he who led the Cheyennes later when they desperately tried to recapture their camp.

Many other brave deeds were attributed to this man. The agent may well have listened with more respect than he showed.

"Why did you send for me?" asked Little Wolf.

"Three of your young men have run off. Now I want you to give me ten of your young men to hold here as prisoners until I get back the three that have gone," replied the agent. Wild Hog and Crow, who had come with Little Wolf, stirred uneasily as they heard this insane request. They knew before it was spoken what the answer would be.

"I will not do what you ask," said Little Wolf. "If you follow those three men, you cannot find them. Three men traveling over the country can hide so that they cannot be found. You never could get them back and you would always keep my men in prison."

---

[2] It was a matter of principle with Little Wolf. Four horses had been lost and three picked up by the Cheyennes. The white owners claimed the three and identified one of Little Wolf's string as the fourth. This particular animal had been in his possession for a long time and they had no claim on it. Hence his refusal, in spite of threats, to give it up.

It was simple justice. Why should ten young Cheyennes be imprisoned because three others had grown home sick and started back to their own country in the north? Little Wolf did not blame them.

"If you do not give me these men, I will cut off your rations," threatened the agent.

As Little Wolf bleakly continued to refuse the ten hostages, the agent grew more and more insistent. At last the chief turned away. As he did so, he shook hands with the agent and the army officers present. There was something in his cold manner which made them stare. Then out of a clear sky, the Indian hurled this ultimatum:

"I am going to my camp. I don't wish the ground about this agency to be made bloody, so listen: I am going to leave here. I am going to my north country. If you are going to send soldiers after me, let me get a little distance from the agency. I do not want to see blood spilt about it. If you want a fight, I will fight you and we can make the ground bloody at that place." [3]

There was no dispute with his decision when he announced it to his people in their camp, about twenty miles above on the Canadian River. Every Cheyenne knew that in two years their fighting men had been reduced in numbers from two hundred and thirty-five to seventy-nine, and their women and children in proportion. It was time to fight, and fight hard. With silent speed the ragged teepees were struck. The few thin ponies were gathered in, the worn belongings loaded on travois, all as quietly as if by shadows. The littlest child knew better than to whimper. By dawn the Cheyennes were on the march—a march which will always live as a tradition of the West.

Five great military barriers were opposed to their northward flight. Along the Santa Fé trail were General Pope's forces. General Crook lay along the Union Pacific in Nebraska. The banks of the Niobrara were watched by General Bradley. A fourth line stretched east from the Black Hills; and a fifth, under General Gibbon, guarded the Yellowstone. Thirteen thousand soldiers, with addi-

---

[3] The man who interpreted this conversation, Ed Guerrier, was still living in Oklahoma up to within the last few years. This conversation is quoted by Grinnell. "Fighting Cheyennes," pp. 387–88.

tional thousands of civilians, cowboys, miners, and ranchers; forts, artillery, railroads and the telegraph were pitted against the tiny handful of starving Indians.

THE RAID ACROSS KANSAS

Little Wolf's first necessities were mounts and arms. To get them he scattered his foragers over a thirty-mile front. Here and there they swooped down upon herds of horses in corrals and pastures; here and there they picked up guns or ammunition. Before they crossed the Kansas border they were well supplied with horses and fairly well with rifles.

Their escape was discovered early the following day. Telegraph keys rattled; troops were mustered; the war jig was on. A hard-riding troop of cavalry caught up with the Indians on the Little Medicine Lodge River. Little Wolf rode out alone to meet and talk with them. He exchanged a few words with an Arapaho interpreter, when the soldiers began shooting at him. The chief rode back to his lines under fire and the fight began. It was a long-range battle. Nobody was killed. The troops retreated and the Cheyennes went on.

Two nights later they were again overtaken near the Cimarron River. This time the Indians were ready. They built some fortifications on a hill. The soldiers advanced on foot. When they were close, the Cheyennes gave them a volley which hit several men and drove the rest back. Three soldiers were killed. No Cheyenne was hit.

They were unmolested the next day. That was the last time the troops overtook the Indians. Henceforth the Cheyennes fought—many, many times—but their battles from that hour were with foes on their front, not in the rear. No cavalry could keep the killing pace they set, sometimes seventy miles a day.

The Indians traveled most of the time at a steady lope. Far in front and on each side rode their scouts, nosing here, listening there, prowling and searching, alert, wild, seeking news of danger for their people. Sometimes these scouts were miles from the main body. The women and children and the camp travois kept bunched well together. Dull Knife was the nominal chief of the band, but the grim Little Wolf was the real leader.

They crossed the Kansas border, eluded a detachment from Larned and turned west toward Dodge City. As they rode, they gobbled up the ranches, killing a few cowmen and hunters who tried to fight, and taking every horse, gun and cartridge.

Colonel William H. Lewis and two hundred and fifty men waited at Fort Dodge for word of the Indians. Before he knew it, they were past him and gone. Some Cheyenne scouts were seen within four miles of Dodge City on the evening of the 19th. The following morning, just before daybreak, a shadowy mass which drifted across the prairie like smoke in the vagueness of the night, reached the Arkansas River. It was the main Cheyenne body. A few miles west lay the little cattle town of Pierceville, but not a soul in the sleeping hamlet knew it, as the Indians, traveling at the steady Cheyenne lope, rode down to the river, splashed across, and disappeared into the dim distance.

Next morning Lewis learned that Little Wolf's people had crossed. Taking an angle calculated to cut off the fugitives, he rode after them. The Cheyennes stopped for a day or so to rest on the Punished Woman Fork of the Smoky Hill. There Lewis' scouts located them about five o'clock on the evening of the 28th. The cavalry, vastly superior in numbers, charged at once. In an angry clatter the Cheyenne rifles spoke in the dusk. Lewis spun out of his saddle. Three more of his men dropped. The charge halted. There was a cloud of dust and the Indians were gone. Lewis was dead.

Straight north Little Wolf rode while the soldiers bore the colonel's body back to Fort Dodge. The Cheyennes had one great, vital need—horses, ever more horses. When they found them they ruthlessly took them. If the white owners fought, they were killed. But the Indians never went out of their way to kill white men—except once.

On the night of September 29th the band crossed the North Fork of the Solomon River. They had just had the sharp fight with

Lewis. Troops were flocking behind in great numbers. At such a time it would seem that the Indians should have made all speed out of Kansas. But they had one inviolable law. "An eye for an eye, a tooth for a tooth," the Old Testament teaching, was also the red man's teaching.

Three years before, April 23, 1875, a company of soldiers under Lieutenant A. Henely, and some buffalo hunters led by Hank Campbell,[4] surrounded Bull Hump's village of Cheyennes, some seventy men, women and children, camped on Sappa Creek in northwestern Kansas. The Indians had taken some horses from nearby ranchers and looted the hunters' camp. In the fight which followed, twenty-seven were cut off from their main body which escaped. When the smoke cleared away, twenty-two of them were dead, including Bull Hump. Only two soldiers were killed.

The Cheyennes neared Sappa Creek on the morning of September 30th. With a single mind they turned aside and visited a terrible vengeance upon the place. Down on the peaceful community which had sprung up in the intervening years, they swept like a whirlwind. The white men had given Bull Hump's people no chance, and the Cheyennes gave the white people no chance. Women screamed, guns thudded, and tumbling clouds of smoke rose from burning homes.

When the Indians rode on they left eighteen corpses behind to pay for the lives of the Cheyennes taken three years before.[5] Thus far they had taken forty white lives and lost less than ten braves. But they were approaching the Union Pacific Railroad and Crook. It was wise to take precautions. In small parties, scattered over a wide front, they slipped across the Kansas line into Nebraska.

[4] This was the redoubtable Hank Campbell who later commanded the buffalo hunters in the Staked Plains war against the Comanches in 1877.

[5] The following were killed on Sappa Creek: William Laing, John Laing, Freeman Laing, William Laing, Jr., J. D. Smith, Frederick Hamper, E. P. Humphrey, John Humphrey, Moses Abernathy, John C. Hutson, George F. Walters, Marcellus Felt, Ed Miskelley, Ferdinand Westphaled and son, Mr. Wright, Mr. Lull and Mr. Irwin.

H. D. Colvin and his brave wife barricaded their cabin and successfully defended their lives. The Cheyennes left the settlement a smoking ruin. No women were killed but some were outraged it is claimed. This was the only deliberate massacre on the whole journey.

The pace was beginning to tell. Some of the weaker ones in the tribe died under the awful strain of the march. The constant skirmishing had reduced the number of warriors until there were hardly enough left for scouting. Each day's journey was shorter now. But at last the Cheyennes crossed the South Platte and entered the comparative safety of the Niobrara Hills.

Here the leaders disagreed at last. Dull Knife, old and beloved, wanted to wait and rest. Little Wolf, hard and fierce, insisted on continuing the march. Their arguments were characteristic.

"This is our own country. Nothing bad ever happened to us here. Let us rest. The soldiers will leave us alone, for lo, we are in our own land," said Dull Knife with the simplicity of a child.

"You can go that way if you wish, but I intend to work my way up into the Powder River country. I think it would be better for us all if the party were not divided," responded Little Wolf.[6]

The upshot was that the band divided. During the night Dull Knife's retainers moved their teepees a few yards away from Little Wolf's. We have no record of the words that passed between the two chiefs in parting, but between these men was a deep affection and respect.

Next morning Little Wolf's band was gone.

[6] This incident and conversation were given to George Bird Grinnell years later by Little Wolf himself. "Fighting Cheyennes," p. 395.

22: DULL KNIFE'S LAST FIGHT

CAPTURED

DULL KNIFE hoped the white men would leave him alone. Like a child trying to reassure himself, he went about the camp next day saying: "Now we have reached our own ground, and from this time forth we will no more fight any white people." On almost the last horse able to trot, a messenger rode to Red Cloud's camp, while the rest of the Cheyennes scattered to avoid discovery. A few days later they reassembled to hear the answer to their message. It fell like lead on their hearts. Red Cloud's sad reply to their plea for protection was that it was hopeless to resist the President's will. The time had come to meet the white man face to face with no chance of escape.

That was a piteous assemblage. In rags, nearly out of ammunition, with scarcely a single horse, suffering from cold, they were in no condition to resist. And they were mostly old men and women.

Colonel J. B. Johnson, with two troops of the 3rd Cavalry, discovered them in the sand hills on October 23rd, and received Dull Knife's surrender. The soldiers were astonished at the plight of the fugitives. A few stalwart warriors were there, including Wild Hog, a young chief, and Buffalo Hump, Dull Knife's own son. There was a scattering of young women. But haggard, old men, ancient withered squaws, a few thin-faced little children—these constituted the bulk of the "capture."

"There can be no resistance here, surely," thought the soldiers. They were mistaken. Dull Knife and his chiefs talked to Johnson and told him they would rather die than return to the Indian Territory. They wished to go to the Sioux Agency. Two days later they were told they must go to Fort Robinson. This was toward the hated southland and the Indians grew bleak and sullen as they listened.

A heavy snowstorm set in. The Cheyennes were told to camp in the brush along the deep valley of Chadron Creek, while the soldiers retired to the upper levels. That night, in the bitter cold, old men and women worked through the dark hours digging rifle pits in the bushes. In the morning the soldiers saw a fight looming. Persuasion was vain. Only when two pieces of artillery came up did the Indians submit.

Again Dull Knife's people, weaker than ever, were prisoners. Sullenly they marched to Fort Robinson. They had been searched for arms, but in some manner managed to retain five guns and about eleven revolvers, with some ammunition. During the search the men were deprived of their firearms but allowed to keep their bows. The women were not searched. One of them later said that throughout the search she had a carbine hanging down her back. Other guns were taken to pieces and concealed by the squaws and children—a piece of stock on this one, a lock there, a barrel yonder. Some of the children wore springs and locks as ornaments around their necks, where they were not noticed. When they reached the fort they were confined in long wooden barracks. The first thing they did was to reassemble the guns and pistols and hide them under the floors of the prison.

Winter came down with extreme rigor. One day Dull Knife was told that the Interior Department had ordered him and his people sent back to the Indian Territory. Surprised and angered, he refused to obey. After that the Indians' small measure of liberty was taken away and guards were set over them in the barracks.

In December a group of Sioux chiefs was brought over to talk with them. Red Cloud, American Horse the Second, Red Dog and No Flesh sat in the council which was also attended by army officers, including Captains Wessells and Vroom. Red Cloud counselled submission. He reminded the Cheyennes of his friendship but called attention to the power of the government, and to the fact that snow was on the ground, ponies thin, and resistance madness.

"So listen to Red Cloud, your old friend, and do without complaint what the Great Father tells you," he concluded.[1]

---

[1] The description and quotations from this council are from E. B. Bronson's book "Reminiscences of a Ranchman."

Then Dull Knife, the grand old leader, stepped forth. His sixty-odd years seemed to slip from him. Grim-faced, he looked every inch the chief in spite of his shabby blanket and worn canvas moccasins. His speech was terse but eloquent:

"All we ask is to be allowed to live, and live in peace. . . . We bowed to the will of the Great Father and went south. . . . There we found a Cheyenne cannot live. . . . So we came home. Better it was, we thought, to die fighting than to perish of sickness."

Turning to Wessells he pleaded that his people be allowed to remain in their northern home.

"Tell the Great Father if he tries to send us back we will butcher each other with our knives rather than go!" he concluded.

Silent as graven images sat the Cheyennes, except that the powerful figure of Buffalo Hump, the chief's son, unable to restrain his feelings, arose and paced the floor behind the council circle, hate burning in his eyes.

Captain Wessells could only promise to send the message to the Great Father. That was all. The fruitless council adjourned.

TREACHERY

With the 1st of January a blizzard covered the ground deep with snow and sent the mercury far below zero. It was weather for staying close indoors. Yet on January 5th Wessells received as a reply to his message containing Dull Knife's plea, a peremptory order to march the captives, without delay and with proper escort, to Fort Reno, far to the south, over the same trail they had traveled with such pain coming north.

Wessells saw the terrible mistake. The swivel-chair bureaucrats in the Indian Department could not. But duty was duty. He had the three chiefs, Dull Knife, Wild Hog and Crow, brought to him and explained the order. Dead silence greated his words. Only the wild beast glare in their eyes told the suppressed passion which was making infernos of their hearts. It took Dull Knife minutes to control himself so he could speak with a steady voice. His reply, quiet and cold, was:

"It is death to us. If the Great Father wishes us to die—very well. We will die where we are. If necessary by our own hands."

But Wessells could only obey orders. He gave his ultimatum: Unless they agreed, he would cut off all their fuel, food and water. In stony silence the chiefs heard their sentence; then went back to their people.

• • • • • • • • •

Days passed—five days of bitter cold and hunger in the wooden barracks where shivered the half-clad Cheyennes. Day and night their despairing death songs sounded, with even the little children joining their weak treble voices in the chants. The Indians had made up their minds to die of cold and hunger rather than submit.

At last, on January 9th, Wessells sent again for the chiefs. But this time the people would not let Dull Knife go. Strong Left Hand took his place.

For an hour the Cheyennes paced the floor of their barracks, straining their ears. Then they heard a sudden wild, desperate war whoop. It was Wild Hog's voice and it told its own story. Strong Left Hand ran in. The two others had been seized and put in irons. Wild Hog had defied Wessells. And he had stabbed and all but killed a guard before he was overpowered. That wild, ringing cry was his warning and farewell to his people.

From the prison barracks rose the answering yells of the Cheyenne men, the cries of women and even the shrieks of little children.

Doors and windows were barricaded. From under the floor were taken the five rifles and the revolvers which had been smuggled in. Floors and iron stoves were broken up to make clubs. Every man who had a gun gave his knife to another who had no weapon. The Cheyennes expected an immediate attack, but none came. The night of January 10th came on, still and frightfully cold.

Just as the last tremulous notes of "Taps" sounded, a shot rang from the barracks, startlingly clear and sharp. A sentry pitched forward in the snow. Three more shots in a rapid rat-tat-tat. Two more guards were down. Then from the doors and windows of the barracks poured the heroic last fragment of the Dull Knife band.

Starved, despairing, they nevertheless acted with coolness and clear judgment. The dead sentries, Corporal Pulver and Privates Hulz and Tommeny, were stripped of their arms. While the few braves with guns formed a rear guard, the Indians ran out of the fort and started across the snow-clad plain.

Out of the barracks poured the troops, half-clad but shooting. Under the heavy fire the gallant Cheyenne rear guard melted fast. But the main body was well on its way to the hills, where a high, precipitous divide separated Soldier Creek from White River, three miles from the fort.

That was a forlorn hope if ever there was one. Within the first half mile of the awful running fight, more than half the Cheyenne fighting men were shot. But as the warriors fell, their weapons were seized by half-grown boys, tottering old men, even women. Often the advance guard of the soldiers and the rear guard of the Indians fought hand-to-hand. The women fell as thickly as the men.

A mile from the fort the troops, many of them badly frozen, were called back to get their clothing and horses. Across the frozen river and up the steep hill toiled the Indians. The cavalry caught up again as the ascent was being made. At the foot of the bluffs the shattered rear guard drew up for a last resistance. The cavalry charged. Back it was hurled. Dull Knife's daughter, known as the "Princess," fighting in the front rank, was killed. So were several others. But the precious minutes gained allowed the rest of the people to climb the cliff.

Further pursuit ended for the night. On the way back to the fort the soldiers marked the line of retreat by the huddled bodies in the snow. Buffalo Hump, the chief's son, was one of the dead.[2]

[2] His dying gesture was splendid. "He lay on his back with arms extended and face upturned. In his right hand he held a small knife, a knife worn by years and years of use from the useful proportions of a butcher knife until the blade was no more than a quarter of an inch wide at the hilt, a knife descended to domestic use by the squaws as an awl for sewing moccasins, and yet, the only weapon this magnificent fighter could command in this, his last fight for freedom! As I sat . . . believing him dead . . . he rose to a sitting posture and aimed a fierce blow at my leg with his knife. Instinctively . . . I jerked my pistol, but . . . he fell back and lay still . . . dead. So died Buffalo Hump, a warrior capable, with half a chance, of making martial history worthy even of his doughty old father."—E. B. Bronson, "Reminiscences of a Ranchman."

As the soldiers returned to their warm quarters, the surviving Cheyennes struggled on through the bitter night. For seventeen miles they traveled without a halt. Even well-fed, well-clothed troops would have considered it a wonderful march under the circumstances. Yet it was made by women, children, old men and wounded men, half-clad and weak from five days' starvation.

The limit of even a Cheyenne's endurance finally came. They camped back of a knoll and prepared an ambush—fighters to the very last. In the morning Captain Vroom's pursuing troop stumbled right into the trap. The spiteful crackle of fire emptied three saddles. The cavalry retreated, dismounted and surrounded the knoll. All that day they fought a long-range battle. As night fell the troops built decoy fires around the knoll and marched back to the warmth of the fort.

But Dull Knife's scouts were not "decoyed." They laughed grimly at the white man's transparent trickery and walked over the decoy fires to continue their retreat.

THE FINISH

Thirty-seven Cheyennes were dead and fifty-two, mostly wounded, captured by the night of January 10th. Next day the remnant was brought to bay in a difficult position to attack, far up Soldier Creek. During the fighting that day a troop horse was killed. At night the Indians sneaked out and from the carcass of that horse the poor wretches got the first mouthfuls of food they had eaten in seven days. The troops withdrew, so taking what little flesh was left on the dead horse, the Cheyennes slipped away for six miles more and entrenched themselves in the bluffs, dogged and defiant.[3]

[3] During the second day's pursuit the troops ran into unexpected opposition. A single old man, unable to keep up longer because of frozen feet, remained behind with a loaded carbine to do what he could as a rear guard of one. As the soldiers came up he opened fire. Sixty men concentrated their rifles upon him. But the old Cheyenne continued to shoot his carbine as long as he could. Toward the last he was seen to fire three times with his left hand, resting the barrel of his gun along the edge of the washout where he lay, his right arm hanging useless. Then he dropped lifeless in the washout. He had been hit five times, the bullet which killed him passing through the top of his head. Corporal Everett was killed and a private wounded by this old man before they got him.

Wessells brought a twelve-pounder Napoleon gun from the fort that day. It arrived at noon and all afternoon its sullen boom was the dominant sound in the snowy wastes. Forty rounds of shell were thrown into the Cheyenne position. The Indians could not reply. Yet Wessells failed to dislodge them. Flattening themselves in the shallow depressions they dug in the frozen ground, they endured as well as they could the concussions of the bursting shells.

Toward evening Wessells sent James Rowland, an interpreter, close to the lines, to tell them to surrender. Here was something the Cheyennes could reach with their guns. Rowland was glad to get back to his own lines with his life. No surrender yet.

Wessells was growing worried. The Indians were working toward the cattle country where they could find food and horses. He doubled the guard around their position. But on the morning of the 14th the Cheyennes were gone as usual. Somehow they had slipped through the cordon once more and gone up Hat Creek.

It is wearisome to repeat the details. For six days it continued. Day after day the Cheyennes fought. Night after night they used their matchless skill to slip away from the encircling lines of soldiers. Each day their numbers grew smaller.

The inevitable came at last. The Cheyennes made their last stand in the Hat Creek Bluffs, forty-four miles southwest of Fort Robinson, on the morning of January 21st, 1879. Worn out, most of them wounded, practically all suffering from frozen hands and feet, they lay in a washout, shoulder-deep, on the edge of the bluffs.

A last summons to surrender. It was answered by three scattering shots from the washout. Those three shots were the last cartridges the Cheyennes had. Forward rushed the soldiers, up to the very edge of the washout. Not a shot was fired by the Indians. Into the huddled mass the troops poured a single crashing blast of flame. Without waiting to see the execution done, they leaped back to reload.

And now they saw a strange, uncanny apparition. Over the edge of the washout clambered three awful figures. Smeared with blood they were, their starvation-pinched features looking like living skulls. One carried an empty pistol. Two had worn knives. Tottering on their weak limbs, they poised for a moment on the edge of the grave of their people—the last three warriors of the unconquer able Cheyennes. Then with quavering war cries they madly charged, right into the muzzles of three hundred rifles.

With a shattering roar the fire leaped from those muzzles. The three warriors collapsed, literally shot to bits. They were the last fighters of their people. The Odyssey of the Cheyennes was ended.

WHAT HAPPENED AFTERWARD

The washout was heaped with bloody bodies, twenty-two dead and nine desperately wounded. All but six of the Indians who had fled the fort were accounted for, and one of them was Dull Knife himself. As fate would have it, the old chief had become separated from his people and did not even have the satisfaction of dying with them. With five others he found refuge in the teepees of the Sioux, were he lived, embittered, brooding, hating the white man with his last breath.

But what of Little Wolf and his half of the tribe?

They went north after leaving Dull Knife. Near Fort Robinson they carried out a bold coup. A mile from the fort was the cavalry remount depot. One night Little Wolf led his raiders right un- der the muzzles of the cannon in the fort. There was a flurry of shooting; two ranchers were killed and another wounded. The Indians, without a warrior lost, rode away with horses for the whole band.

The cavalry mounted in hot haste and pursued for hours that night. Morning found them near Crow Butte where they found the vestiges of an Indian camp—but the Indians were gone. The trail was plain, but what cavalry could follow its makers?

In the wilderness of Montana, far from the settlements, the Cheyennes spent the winter. Spring came and on March 25th, Little Wolf met Lieutenant W. P. Clark—"White Hat" to the Indians whom he had always befriended.

"I have prayed to God that I might find my friend Little Wolf," said Clark. "And now I have done so." Sincere joy was in his voice.

The Indians knew White Hat would allow no massacre of their women and children.

"It is well; we will go with you wherever you say," replied Little Wolf.

This part of the Cheyennes, with few exceptions, was allowed to remain in the north. There Little Wolf and his warriors, enlisting as scouts, did valuable work for the government in helping to run down the few outlaw bands of hostile Sioux who, in spite of the peace made by their chiefs, still remained on the war path.

23: THE MEEKER MASSACRE

MOUNTAIN FIGHTERS

FROM the time the first white trappers entered the Rocky Mountains, the Utes were known by them—and respected. Those early mountain men knew the Utes for natural warriors, great wanderers, and "bad medicine" generally speaking.

By preference they made the high ranges their home. But they often went hundreds of miles out of their way, into strange country, for the sheer joy of fighting with the plains Indians. Thus, the reports of the Indian Service from 1862 to 1865 are full of references to the trouble given to settlers by Utes traveling through the passes near Denver and Pueblo, in their raids against the Cheyennes and Arapahoes, and the return raids against the Utes by those tribes. A large war party of Arapahoes in 1859 camped in the heart of what is today Denver. They left their women and children there and crossed the mountains to steal horses from the Utes. Shortly they came pell-mell back over the mountains, with the Utes close behind. The whites in Denver feared that the fierce warriors from back of the ranges might seek reprisals on them for allowing the Arapahoes to camp there. In 1863, a Ute war party ran off a herd of Cheyenne ponies under the noses of their owners, and within the sight of Fort Lyon, Colorado.

These incidents are mentioned merely to show what manner of warriors these Utes were. Surprisingly, outside of occasional fights with the early trappers and miners, they avoided warfare with the white men, even when the latter began coming in increasing numbers, elbowing the Indians for room in their own domain.

The Utes signed a peace treaty in 1859. During the next few decades they suffered the usual fate of Indians. They were shunted around here and there, each time the white man discovered that their latest habitation was valuable.

All this the Utes bore with great patience. Ouray, their chief, knew they must remain friendly. He was an Indian of exceptional wisdom and force of character. His name signified "The Arrow" and he was all that the name implies—keen, straight, direct and swift. Over the Utes he had tremendous influence. He was recognized as head chief by the Uncomphagre, White River, Uintah and other Ute bands, but not by the Cimarron or Southern Utes, whose chief was the great Ignacio.

Placer miners had long dug for gold in the mountains. But one day in the northwestern part of Colorado, deep in Ute territory, a peculiar heavy substance resembling clay was found, and an enterprising miner, annoyed by its clogging of his rockers, had it analyzed. It was carbonate of lead, rich in silver. Followed the famous Leadville mining excitement, which filled the mountains with prospectors. The rush was a typical mining stampede. Every little stream was defiled; every mountain canyon, no matter how inaccessible and wild, soon had it claims staked out. The country was ruined for game.

The Utes naturally viewed the horde of earth-grubbing white men with horror and alarm. The boundaries of their country were recognized by government treaty. Yet these men invaded with impunity those boundaries. The powder was all set for an explosion.

Horace Greeley, of the New York Tribune, was patron of a colony in Colorado named after him—Greeley. The leader of this colony was N. C. Meeker, an honest, upright man, but overbearing and arrogant. Meeker used his influence with Greeley to get the appointment as agent for the White River Utes in 1878. He had his own ideas about handling Indians and his first act of office was highhanded. He arbitrarily moved the agency to Powell's Valley, on the White River, fifteen miles below the old location, over the protests of every Ute on the reservation. The Indians used the valley as a winter camp, and the presence of the agency buildings ruined it for hunting.

Old Utes still remember "Nick" as they called the agent. "He was always mad. I think he was sick in his head," is the way Samson Rabbit,[1] a brother-in-law of Colorow, one of the chiefs, describes him. This was the impression his aggressive, dictatorial attitude gave to all the Indians. His erratic actions puzzled them. "We never knew what to do. He was mad all the time."

When the agency was moved, Meeker took his next step. "I shall . . . cut every Indian down to the bare starvation point if he will not work," he wrote Senator Teller soon after he assumed office. One thing which prevented any great interest in work among the Utes was their love of horse racing. They had a race track in the valley. Meeker ordered the building of a school house in such a way that it ruined this track.

Next the agent quarreled with his Indians over the question of their sending their children to school. According to Rabbit, he summoned Colorow, Douglas and Matagoras, chiefs of the White River Utes, and demanded that they send their youngsters to his school. The Utes were still savages, in the "hunting stage." They were suspicious of this white man's device. "They did not know what it would do to their children." Moreover the school, because of its location, was an object of execration. The chiefs were evasive. "Too hot now. In about a month it will be cooler," they said. This was about September 1st.

Meeker flew into a rage, according to the Indian account, and threatened to call the soldiers. That alarmed the Utes. Meeker took it that they agreed to his proposition. But several days passed and still no children came. He sent for the military this time and some soldiers came and talked with the chiefs. Just who these soldiers were, the old Utes do not know, but they were probably from Fort Fred Steele. The talk accomplished nothing. The troops admonished the Indians and went back to the post.

Seven days passed. Meeker ordered the valley ploughed for cultivation. Again the Utes protested, but as usual the agent re-

[1] Samson Rabbit, about eighty-five, in 1934, lived at that time near Durango, Colorado. His brother, Buckskin Charlie, was the chief at the Southern Utes. His sister married Colorow, one of the leaders in the Meeker uprising. He was a young man in his early twenties when the trouble took place.

fused to listen. As the ploughing began, some Indians appeared with their guns. A shot was fired. Rabbit claims the "farmer" (the ploughman) fired with his six-shooter, but Meeker reported that one of the Indians fired from ambush. At any rate, the ploughing stopped.

By this time the feeling against the agent was murderous. A half-breed named Johnson got into an argument with him. They fought. Meeker was badly thrashed and thrown out of his own house. What authority he may ever have had was completely destroyed. He telegraphed to Fort Fred Steele for help.

At the receipt of the message, Major T. T. Thornburgh, with three troops of cavalry and a company of infantry, about one hundred and fifty men, left the fort, just north of the Wyoming border, and marched rapidly south. Close to the reservation line he was met by a party of five Utes, who protested against his entering the reservation. The Indians were deadly serious. Thornburgh replied that he must go on, but suggested that he would not go to the agency direct, camping near it instead. The Utes disappeared.

At this critical time, Ouray was somewhere in the mountains hunting deer. He was the only one who could have averted the coming tragedy. Rabbit says that the five chiefs after their talk with Thornburgh, dived into the bush and went straight to the Ute camp. There they held a council and the Utes voted to stop Thornburgh from going to the agency. The Indians were "not mad." This is reiterated over and over again. Evidently their decision was perfectly dispassionate and was gone about in the most methodical manner.

THE BATTLE OF RED CANYON

The road which Thornburgh took passed through a deep canyon known as Red Canyon. Its sides are covered thickly with scrub oak and along the ridge on one wall runs an ancient Indian trail. Here Colorow and Jack arranged their warriors, in the shrubbery and behind the boulders. The reason given by Rabbit is that the trail runs through tall bushes. Most of the Indians had no guns. "They had to hide near the road so their arrows would reach."

Thornburgh's command started into Red Canyon. Captain Payne's troop led, with Captain Lawson following, and Lieutenant Paddock, with the wagons, in the rear. But for an accident the whole command would have been wiped out. The wagons were hard to bring over the mountain road and Lieutenant Paddock had fallen back about half a mile. Up the canyon a scout saw a movement and reported Indians. Thornburgh halted and Lieutenant Cherry's advance guard pushed forward to reconnoitre.

The sudden chatter of many guns and a sleet of arrows sent the advance riding hard for their supports. The hills ahead were alive with Indians. Thornburgh threw his cavalry into battle line and signalled Paddock to stop and park his wagons.

Through the rocks and bushes the Utes began to slip, concealing themselves so skillfully that the troops could hardly see them, and keeping up a constant shower of bullets and arrows. From the flanks came the cry that the Indians were stealing around behind. Thornburgh had to retreat at once if he ever hoped to get to the wagons.

"Fall back!" came the order. The troopers executed the dangerous movement with veteran precision, in spite of the galling fire from the bush. But just as it was completed, the gallant Thornburgh was hit by a Ute bullet. He fell from his horse on the bank of the Milk River, and throughout the days of fighting which followed his men could clearly see his body from their defenses. After his fall the troopers managed to reach the wagons. The fight was already raging there.[2]

The Utes were quick to take advantage of the natural features of the battle field. The wagon corral was wretchedly situated, its only advantage being that it was close to the river. Ridges commanded it on three sides. One of these was too far away to be of much use to the Indians but they occupied points of vantage on the other two. From these points the keen-eyed Ute marksmen, trained

[2] The Ute strategy had been pretty. Colonel E. V. Sumner in his article "Besieged by the Utes," Century Magazine, 1891, copyright by the Century Co., says that at the beginning of the battle the Indians had less than half as many men as Thornburgh, or about seventy-five warriors. Rabbit agrees with this estimate, saying there were less than one hundred. With this small force they gave the troops a bad lacing. Undoubtedly Jack and Colorow received reinforcements later.

deer hunters all, kept a deadly fire on the corral. If a soldier so much as exposed an arm he was likely to feel a bullet.

Now the Indians fired the grass and sagebrush on the valley floor and creeping up under the smoke, poured in a murderous volley. But there was no charge. The Utes lay concealed, picking off the horses and occasionally a man. By nightfall not five horses were standing. As the sun set, Captain Payne of the 5th Cavalry, the senior officer now, called for volunteers to carry a message for help. Out of the several who offered, a wiry, hard-riding Irish trooper named Murphy was chosen. At pitch dark he led one of the few unwounded horses cautiously down the valley for a mile. Then he mounted and rode for his life.

AT THE AGENCY

All the afternoon while Thornburgh's men fought in Red Canyon, Meeker, twenty-five miles away, sat in ignorance that a battle was going on. An Indian runner loped in with news of the fight for the other Indians, but not one word was breathed to the whites. Meeker fatuously supposed the trouble was over. He placidly prepared a letter to Thornburgh, saying "Things are peaceable." As he wrote, the man to whom the words were addressed lay dead.

Wilmer Eskridge started to Thornburg with the letter. Two Utes, Antelope and Ebenezer, accompanied him. Barely out of sight of the agency, two miles down the road, they killed Eskridge and hurried back.

Utterly unsuspecting any danger, the agency people went about their daily tasks. Dinner was over and Mrs. Meeker and her daughter Josie washed the dishes, while Mrs. Price, wife of the post trader, did the week's washing outside. Shadduck Price, her husband, and a youth named Frank Dresser, were throwing dirt from a wagon on the roof of a new building, on top of which Art Thompson spread the dirt and tramped it down. Meeker and Bill Post, the carpenter, were taking an inventory in a warehouse. The others were at their usual duties.

The return of Antelope and Ebenezer was a signal. There are conflicting accounts of what followed. According to the white account, obtained from the three women who were the only survivors, twenty Indians, led by Douglas, left their teepees and ran toward the buildings, shooting and yelling. Rabbit, however, says the shooting was started by the white men who realized suddenly that things were going wrong. Whoever started it, it seems pretty clear that the Indians intended to clean out the white people in the agency. Price and Thompson were killed at the first volley. Just when Meeker met his fate is not known. Frank Dresser was shot through the leg but ran for the agency house.

Mrs. Price entered first and handed the youth her husband's gun. He was all fight. With the gun barrel he smashed out a window pane and killed Johnson's brother. Mrs. Meeker and Josie, crazed with fright, ran in. Dresser, in agony from his wound, was the only man in the house. He knew the place would soon be afire, so led a dash to the adobe milk house, near at hand. They reached it safely and remained there until nearly sundown. All that time the shooting continued. Some of the agency men had obtained weapons and were fighting. Just who these last survivors were, will never be known. After a time the firing ceased.

The Utes looted the buildings. As they emptied them of all goods they set them afire. Smoke from the main agency house poured into the milk house in strangling clouds. They had to run for the timber.

At the first step the Utes were after them. Dresser was shot down and Mrs. Meeker slightly wounded. The bounding Indians overtook and seized the women. Mrs. Price was fearful they would be burned. "No burn white squaw; heap like-um," grinned the Indians. Mrs. Price's captor was Ahu-u-tu-pu-wit, a small, ugly Indian. Josie fell to the lot of Persune. Douglas tried to take her away, but Persune threatened to fight for her. Douglas was finally contented with the ownership of Mrs. Meeker. The three women were held as captives until October 23rd, when their release was obtained.

24: OURAY'S PEACE

BESIEGED BY THE UTES

Up in Red Canyon, Thornburgh's men, their leader dead, still lay surrounded by the Utes. The night of September 30th was black but the wounded were begging for water. Some men volunteered to crawl down to the river and fill the canteens. Fire from the opposite bank drove them back. Again the men crawled down, this time covered by riflemen. A duel in the dark followed, the soldiers shooting at the flashes of the Indian guns while their comrades filled the receptacles. The whole party got back safely with the precious canteens full.

As daylight came, the sniping from the surrounding heights began again. Not an Indian was in sight. There would be a puff of smoke. When a soldier returned the shot, his foe was usually yards away behind another boulder or bush.[1] Payne had to conserve his ammunition so he ordered his men to reply only occasionally—just enough to prevent open attack. During the long hot day the remaining horses were killed and some of the men hit. Among the dead were Lieutenant Paddock and Surgeon Grimes.[2]

So exhausted were the men that evening that many of them fell asleep at the breastworks. Payne and Lawson held a council of war. Had Murphy gotten through? Was help coming? What had happened at the agency? A check showed they had lost thirteen killed and forty-three wounded, more than forty percent of the command.

As October 2nd dawned clear and bright, the sharpshooters in

[1] The Utes who were killed were nearly all shot through the top of the head, according to Rabbit. This was because they protected themselves so well behind boulders that only a few inches of their skulls were exposed at any time, and that only when they were firing.

[2] An incident occurred during the day which almost ended several lives. A horse, frantic with wounds, furiously thrashed about and finally fell into the pit where the wounded were kept. A quick-witted trooper shot the animal dead and nobody was injured.

the hills again began their pot-shooting. But shortly after sunrise the welcome sound of galloping hoofs was heard down the valley. There were some shots and a cheer, a troop of the 9th (colored) Cavalry came riding in. Captain Dodge, in command, brought the cheering news that Murphy had gotten through. More help was coming.

Undaunted by the reinforcements, the Utes fought doggedly on. Very soon the horses of the Negro troopers joined those of their white comrades in limbo. The new arrivals dug their elbows into the dirt and settled down to the siege.

But help was really on the way. General Wesley Merritt was coming from Fort Russell with four troops of cavalry and a company of infantry in wagons. At Rawlins he was joined by four more companies of "charioteers" as the cavalry called the wagon-riding doughboys. All day October 2nd they rode and all the following night. At dawn of the 3rd they came upon the hideous sight of a civilian train, massacred to a man. A little way farther, and with glad rejoicings, they reached the entrenchments.

If anybody expected to see the Utes run at the arrival of Merritt's overwhelming force, he soon saw his error. The Indians were hard to scare. One Ute, from his eyrie, shouted in broken English: "More horses, more shoot-um!"

Merritt's skirmishers went out. The first volley from the infantry rolled like a clap of thunder through the mountains. But the Ute fire never slackened. Merritt's men were tired and he decided to let them rest before beginning the assault on those hill tops.

He never had to charge the hills. Shortly after noon, a white flag waved. A few minutes later a white man came toward the soldiers from the Indian lines. He proved to be Joseph Brady, a miller at Los Pinos, accompanied by a friendly Indian. He carried a letter to the Utes from Ouray, who, far away on his hunt, had heard of the outbreak and now sternly ordered them to desist. Even at a distance Ouray's influence was potent. The Utes slipped away. The war was ended.[3]

---

[3] Rabbit insists that Ouray arrived at the scene of the battle in person after riding all day across the mountains, but sent his emissaries to talk to the soldiers instead

GATHERING UP THE WRECKAGE

The wounded were taken from the "fort," now stinking from the putrefying bodies of dead men and horses. The dead were buried, thirteen of them. There were forty-three wounded. The Indian loss was unknown at the time. The military later claimed that thirty-seven were killed.[4] Samson Rabbit, however, says only six bodies were brought from the battle field by the Utes. The latter count is probably the nearer correct, since the Utes fought entirely from cover.

Merritt moved to the White River Agency on the 11th. All along the road were evidences of the massacre. The body of Carl Goldstein, a freighting contractor, was found in a gully six miles from the agency. Nearby was the corpse of Julius Moore, his team-ster, hacked and mutilated. Farther along, in a deserted mine, lay Henry Dresser, of the agency, dead. He was unmutilated and evidently crawled into the hole to die after being mortally wounded. Two miles from the agency was the murdered Eskridge, stripped and scalped. Then came the agency itself—and what a scene of desolation it presented.

Blackened heaps of ashes alone showed where the agency build-ings had stood. Around the yard was strewn the débris of articles looted from the storehouses. Here and there were the bodies of the agency men. Meeker was found a hundred yards from the ashes of his home. The top of his head had been beaten in. His mouth was stretched to a horrible width by a barrel stave driven into it. His body was slashed and disfigured and around his neck was a log chain by which he had been dragged. Frank Dresser, a bullet through his heart and another through his leg, was found in a nearby field. George Eaton's body was partly devoured by dogs or wolves. The corpses of Thompson, Price and others, were gathered and buried.

There was nothing more to be done here. Merritt turned his

---

of going himself, for fear of being shot while he tried to negotiate with them. The military had no record of the presence of Ouray.

[4] "Record of Engagements," p. 91.

attention to recovering the women prisoners. During the negotiations word came that Lieutenant W. B. Weir and Scout Humme had been killed in a brush with Utes October 20th, as a detachment was reconnoitring twenty miles from the White River. The Utes said this attack was provoked by Humme who shot at several peaceful Indians.

In the end the release of the three agency women was brought about largely through Susan, wife of one of the chiefs, and a sister of Ouray. Susan had been rescued from captivity among the Arapahoes by the whites several years before. She felt under obligations and boldly harangued the warriors until she convinced them the women should be released. General Charles Adams, special agent for the Indian Department, risked his life during these negotiations by going boldly to the Ute camp.

The captives were brought to Merritt on the night of October 23rd. Then the commission on Indian affairs held a fruitless session. No direct testimony could be brought against any but the ringleaders of the uprising and those involved in the captivity of the women. The hearings dragged on for days.[5] Then suddenly came word of the death of Ouray, the great chief, the peacemaker, the white man's steadfast friend.

It was like a closing curtain. The Northern Utes were moved to the Uintah reservation in Utah. The Southern Utes were allotted reservations in the Animas and Florida valleys of southern Colorado. Four or five of the chief offenders were punished by being sent to Leavenworth penitentiary. Among these were Persune, Douglas, Johnson, Ahu-u-tu-pu-wit, Colorow and Matagoras. The latter came back after two years in prison with his mind gone—"stir

[5] A strange complication arose after the Utes voted to release the captive women. Persune, the young warrior who had captured Josie Meeker, fell in love with her. Although most Indians scorn to show such a weakness as interest in a particular way toward a woman, this brave forsook all tradition. He implored the girl to stay with him; made all sorts of extravagant promises, such as that she should never have to work, and that he would give her all his possessions; and wept in quite un-Indian way when she refused. Persune was inconsolable after her departure. He always considered her his squaw, so much so that when she died some years later in Washington, D.C., where she was employed in the Treasury office, the other Indians thought he should have painted his face black and gone into mourning for her as a man would ordinarily mourn for a dead wife.

simple" to use a modern slang phrase. He was killed, according to Rabbit's account, a few months later by two Utes who were afraid he might, in his crazed condition, harm someone.

25: THE GHOST DANCERS

SITTING BULL RETURNS

MUCH water, historically speaking, passed under the bridge in the decade between 1880 and 1890. In the Southwestern deserts, the long and bloody war with the Apaches was fought to a conclusion. Cochise, Victorio, Nana and Geronimo had taken turns raiding and burning or leading the troops in fruitless chases through Arizona and New Mexico, until finally the Apaches were pursued across the line and run to earth deep in Mexico itself. There were some troubles in the mountains, notably the Bannack and Sheepeater wars of Idaho. The plains themselves, although the major Indian wars were ended, were far from peaceful. Small bands of Sioux continued to defy the government, to attack small parties of white men, and to run off the stock and commit other depredations.[1]

Sitting Bull continued to live with several hundred of his Sioux north of the Canadian border. He got along well with the "Red Coats," as he called the British, and was respected by them. During his entire residence in Canada, from May, 1877, to July, 1881, his band was charged with only one depredation, the theft of one hundred horses from some neighboring Canadian Indians. Sitting Bull restored the horses to their owners and severely punished the guilty braves when he was notified of the affair by the mounted police.

In spite of his exemplary record, he was suspected by the United

---

[1] In the two years 1880 to 1881, the War Department records show ten troop movements after Indian war parties, with nine skirmishes, four soldiers or scouts killed, fifteen hostile Indians killed and the surrender of one thousand, seven hundred and seventy-nine Sioux in Montana and the Dakotas. The last figure includes Sitting Bull's large following which surrendered at Fort Buford in 1881.

States of stirring up the trouble which kept detachments on the move pursuing vagrant bands of irresponsible Sioux. The Dominion officers also were anxious to get rid of their unbidden guests. At last, after negotiations were opened by "Fish" Allison, a scout and interpreter, and Major Walsh, of the Dominion police, Sitting Bull was persuaded by a French trader, Louis LeGare, to return to the United States. His surrender was at Fort Buford, Montana, July 19th, 1881. For two years he was a virtual prisoner at Fort Randall, but in 1883 was allowed to return to his old home near the Standing Rock Agency, where Major William McLaughlin was agent.

The old chief remained bitter. So an attempt was made to "break" him by recognizing other Indians as chiefs. It did not work. In 1883, shortly after his arrival at Standing Rock, a commission appeared to try to induce the Indians to take up agriculture. Sitting Bull arose to speak. The chairman tried to put him in his place, as the saying is, by telling him that he was no longer a chief, but a common Indian with no rank, and therefore had no right to speak.

Sitting Bull merely waved his hand. Every Indian got up and left the room. The commission realized it could "recognize" whomever it wished. But the Sioux still recognized Sitting Bull. At the next sitting, the old chief's remarks were listened to at great length and with marked respect.[2]

When General Crook and another commission came in the summer of 1889 to try to buy a big block of Sioux land for a song, Sitting Bull stopped the whole negotiation for a time. Agent McLaughlin, however, finally managed to get most of the Indians to sign it and the deal went through. That was the first time the Sioux went against the wishes of Sitting Bull. His power was waning.

THE BEGINNING OF THE CRAZE

In the winter of 1889 a new spirit possessed the Sioux. For the first time in years they looked with hope to the future. There lot was no easier to bear. Dishonesty on the part of many Indian agents; cheating of the red man right and left; and white crooks acquiring

[2] Vestal, "Sitting Bull," p. 247.

fortunes by thefts for which they were never punished—these all continued as before. But the Indians were seized with a strange religious fervor.

Far to the west the Ogalallas had heard that an Indian Messiah had arisen. The news spread like wildfire. Not only the Sioux but practically every other tribe in the West caught the inspiration. It was similar to scores of the religious crazes which break out from time to time among more civilized people. But to the Indian, prostrate under the heel of the white conqueror, it was doubly significant, because it held out a hope to him of freedom from oppression —divine help in his extremity.

It is a weird circumstance that the last hope and belief of the unfortunate red race was founded upon the doctrines of the Christian religion which it had fought for more than three hundred years, from the Atlantic coast to the Pacific.

Harassed, not knowing which way to turn, the Indians hearkened to the words which had been ceaselessly poured into their ears by white missionaries. They had heard of the second coming of Christ, how He would return to His own people; that the meek and lowly, the downtrodden and oppressed would be exalted and redeemed. They had also been taught that the generations gone before would be restored to life; and that evil would be banished from the world. But it was a strange, bizarre interpretation which the red man put upon these teachings.

As the rumor of the Messiah grew among the despairing Indians, a great religious revival appeared among them. No "protracted meeting" of the white man ever approached it for awful sincerity of conviction. Night by night, day by day, the ceaseless throb of the tom-toms echoed from every Indian camp in Montana and Wyoming, Nebraska and the Dakotas, Texas and Oklahoma.

The strange, half-Christian, half-savage belief spread silently and swiftly. Almost overnight it was flourishing, full-blown. The Messiah was coming, they said. He had come once to save the white race but they had despised and killed Him. Now He rejected them and would come to destroy the whites and save His red children. All who believed in Him were to wear a peculiar kind of dress and to practice the Ghost Dance as often and as long as they could. The Ghost Dance, in common with many Indian dances, notably the Sun Dance, was a test of endurance.[3] It was believed that if anybody died of exhaustion during this dance he would be taken directly to the Messiah and enjoy the company of those who had gone before.

Word was brought by the Arapahoes in the fall of 1889 that the Messiah's camp could be found near Walker Lake, Nevada. The news aroused to concert pitch the religious fervor of the Sioux. Two of their trusted warriors were elected emissaries to the holy one, representing two great divisions of the Dakota Nation. One of them, Kicking Bear, was an Ogalalla. The other, Short Bull, was an Unkpapa.

Knowing little English and with only vague directions of rumor to guide them, the two men started west, and traveled until they reached the Shoshone country—lands in which their people had not traveled without bloodshed in the memory of tradition. But now, in the shadow of the new common interest, they were received with honor, feasted and sent on their way with new directions. They took train to the country of the Paiutes. And now they entered lands so far distant that the farthest wanderings of their forefathers had never carried them thither. Among tall mountains, with lovely lakes and forests interspersed with burning deserts, again they found welcome and new tidings which set their feet southward. Everywhere as they progressed they met Indians who bore tidings that the Messiah had actually come. Finally they reached their destination. They saw the Messiah himself.

THE MESSIAH

His name was Wovoka, but he had lived for a time in his youth with a white family named Wilson, and the whites in the vicinity

---

[3] Mrs. J. A. Finley, wife of the post trader at Pine Ridge, described a Ghost Dance participated in by 480 Indians, which lasted from Friday noon until Sunday at sundown. During that time none of the dancers touched food or water. Scores succumbed to exhaustion or the trances typical of the dance. Seven or eight died as a result of another dance held near Wounded Knee.

of Walker's Lake, Nevada, knew him as Jack Wilson. He was unknown and insignificant up to the time of his great vision. When the Sioux visited him, he was about thirty-five years old. He was a full-blooded Paiute, affecting white man's clothing and distinguished by tattoo marks on both wrists. He had never been out of Mason Valley in which he was born and spoke only Paiute, except for a smattering of English.

Wovoka's great "revelation" occurred about two years before he talked to Short Bull and Kicking Bear. At that time the "sun died" (an eclipse) and he went into a trance, being taken to the other world. He said he saw God, together with all those who had died before, engaged in their favorite occupations, all happy, and all young. After these things were shown to him, he said, God told him to return to his people, "tell them they must be good and love one another, have no quarreling, and live in peace with the whites; that they must put away all the old practices that savored of war; that if they faithfully obeyed his instructions they would at last be reunited with their friends in the other world." He was then given the dance which he was commanded to give in turn to his people.[4]

This was the man whom the emissaries met. He received them with cordiality but severe formality. The prophet proclaimed that the Messiah promise had been fulfilled. He said that they were only a few of many who had come to hear the words of truth.[5] Then he announced that he was about to move eastward, when there would be driven before him vast herds of wild horses, buffalo, deer, and elk, and as he came the dead Indians would rise and join the living. Finally, he taught them various mystic rites unknown to them and charged them to go before him and announce his coming.

Kicking Bear and Short Bull returned to their homes after a

---

[4] James Mooney, 14th Annual Report of the Bureau of American Ethnology, 1892–93, personal description of Wovoka whom he saw and interviewed, pp. 771–72.

[5] Porcupine, a Cheyenne, made a similar pilgrimage shortly before the Sioux. He told Lieutenant Robertson of the 1st Cavalry that fifteen or sixteen tribes were at the council at Walker Lake which he attended. Among those he named were Cheyennes, Arapahoes, Gros Ventres, Utes, Navajos, Bannacks, Shoshones, Crows and others who left before he came. The mention of these widely scattered tribes shows how far the belief had spread.

journey of more than two thousand miles among strange peoples. At a great council the emissaries expounded the story of the Messiah's coming. It was received with profound rejoicing.

Thus far the Messiah craze had been purely a religious mania. "The Ghost Dance was entirely Christian—except for the difference in rituals." [6] But it needed only a spark to convert it into a roaring explosion of slaughter. That spark was furnished by a green "tenderfoot" agent, R. F. Royer, at Pine Ridge.

Alarmed by the growth of the religion and the reports, prejudiced and untrustworthy, that the Indians were on the "verge of a big outbreak," Royer wired for troops. They reached Pine Ridge October 19th, 1890. Thousands of Indians immediately took to the Bad Lands. Overnight the newspapers of the nation began printing the Ghost Dance on their front pages. Settlers in the Sioux country deserted their homes and fled to the cities.

Sitting Bull stayed quietly at his home on the Grand River. He was credited all over the country with being the high priest of the new religion, but it seems that he took little, if any part in it. Major McLaughlin, at Standing Rock, gave out a statement that there was no danger from his Indians. Still the name "Sitting Bull" was a name of menace. The attention of the whole United States was fixed on the great Unkpapa's movements.

Thanksgiving Day dawned ominously. The government sought to quiet the Indians by an issue of beef at Pine Ridge. But Plenty Bear, a friendly Sioux brought word that in the camp of Big Foot on the Cheyenne River, there were three hundred and sixty-four lodges, or more than two thousand Indians, and others were coming in every hour. Agent Royer [7] was scared silly.

General Miles, still in command of the department, had to do something. He resolved on a two-fold plan: To arrest Sitting Bull; and to disarm the rest of the Indians.

[6] Vestal, "Sitting Bull," p. 279.
[7] The Sioux called him Lakota Kokipa-Koshla, or "Young-Man-Afraid-of-the-Indians," which is eloquent testimony to their opinion of him.

26: THE LAST INDIAN BATTLE

BUFFALO BILL CODY, the circus man, came to Fort Yates, November 28th, with an order to "capture" Sitting Bull. Cody and Sitting Bull were friends. The chief had been an attraction in Buffalo Bill's wild west show one year. Now Cody proposed to take him a wagon load of presents and induce him to come in and surrender of his own free will.

McLaughlin opposed the move on the ground that the weather was too pleasant, giving the Indians an advantage if conflict developed. He recommended a delay, saying he would attend to Sitting Bull and the other Indians as soon as cold weather arrived. Cody's order was countermanded.

But McLaughlin's hand was forced. Short Bull, near Pine Ridge, claimed to have received a revelation that because of white interference the Messiah was speeding up his coming. Sitting Bull was interested. On December 12th he asked for a pass from Standing Rock to Pine Ridge.

The request may have been perfectly innocent. The fact that he asked for a pass instead of slipping away without permission, lends color to that theory. But Agent McLaughlin thought that Sitting Bull was about to go to the "hostiles." The same day Miles ordered Sitting Bull's arrest.[1]

McLaughlin had built up a fine body of Indian police. Couriers that night notified all of these Sioux policemen to assemble at Sitting Bull's village on the Grand River. Loyally they responded. Some of them rode forty miles at night to be at the rendezvous on time. Captain E. G. Fechet, with one hundred men and a Hotchkiss gun

---

[1] Charges have been made that there was an understanding between the agent, the officers of the Indian police, and the military that Sitting Bull should be "put out of the way." The New York Herald, December 17th, 1890, said so in plain words. The charge was also asserted on the floor of the United States Senate. Miles and other officers with the expedition, strenuously denied these charges.

marched from Fort Yates, arriving near the village at daybreak of December 15th.

The sun was not yet up when the Indian police, led by Lieutenant Bull Head and Sergeants Shave Head and Red Tomahawk, surrounded Sitting Bull's cabin. Bull Head and a small squad entered. The old chief was asleep on the floor. He was aroused and told to get into his clothes.

Although he complied, wrath blazed in the old man's eyes. Here was an indignity which he could ill brook. Like any common felon he was hustled out of the house, with Bull Head and Shave Head on each side of him and Red Tomahawk behind.

By this time Sitting Bull's warriors were swarming about like angry hornets. Winchesters were in evidence everywhere. Cries of anger, threats, and taunts filled the air. The women began wailing.

Suddenly Sitting Bull's voice was heard above the tumult.

"I am not going!" he shouted. Then he began giving directions for his own rescue. A war whoop screeched out. From close at hand a rifle crashed and Bull Head collapsed, shot by Sitting Bull's friend, Catch-the-Bear. As he fell, Bull Head turned and shot his prisoner through the body. Two more shots rangs out close together. Red Tomahawk had fired into the chief's back. Sitting Bull pitched into a huddled heap. Either of the bullets in his body would have killed him.

On that frosty morning air a sudden cachinnation of rifle shots rose. Everybody was firing. Shave Head dropped, hit by a bullet from Strikes-the-Kettle's gun. Several more police went down. Surrounded, they fought like tigers and beat back the furious Unkpapas. Sitting Bull's cabin door stood open. It was the only refuge and they ran toward it, carrying their dead and wounded. In the house they found Crowfoot, Sitting Bull's seventeen-year-old son, cowering. They killed him without mercy.

Captain Fechet galloped up. His Hotchkiss gun took a hand and began spraying death. At first the shells fell close to the police. But Fechet altered his range. The hostiles caught the full impact.

Their chief was dead and Sitting Bull's people scattered across the river.

Four police were dead. Two more were dying and two others were wounded. Besides Sitting Bull, eight Unkpapa warriors were killed, including Catch-the-Bear, Jumping Bull, the chief's adopted brother, and his son Crowfoot.

The dead police were buried in a common grave at Standing Rock. Sitting Bull's body, the head smashed in by the angry police after the fight, was dumped into a wagon and carried to the agency, where it also was buried—in quicklime.

So passed Sitting Bull. At his hour of glory he was a figure of almost epic splendor. In his death he bequeathed to his people a legend of grandeur, and to the world the spectacle of one more man who chose death rather than submission.

WOUNDED KNEE

Sitting Bull was dead. Now came the more difficult of Miles' two measures—the disarming of the hostiles.

At news of the chief's death the whole Sioux Nation became tense. Within three days after the killing on Grand River, there were two fights on or near Cheyenne River, where Big Foot's village stood. On the other hand many of the Indians returned to their agencies. For example, a thousand Ogalallas returned to Pine Ridge on October 18th. Six days later, Hump's band, numbering two hundred and twenty-four, gave up at Fort Bennett.

But there was still one big band at large—Big Foot's village on the Cheyenne. The remnants of Sitting Bull's people had joined that chief.

Colonel E. V. Sumner of the 8th Cavalry, tried diplomacy and talked with Big Foot. The chief said he wanted to be friendly. In proof of this three hundred and thirty-three of his people surrendered on December 21st. Then orders came to arrest the chief. That order stopped the movement toward peace.

Big Foot's band fled to the Bad Lands on the night of December

22nd. Nearly three thousand troops began at once to close in on them. On December 28th Major Whiteside of the 7th Cavalry, found the village on Wounded Knee Creek and called upon the Indians to surrender.

Big Foot tried to parley.

"We want peace," he said. "I am sick and my people—"

"I will not parley with you," said Whiteside. "You must surrender or fight. Which shall it be?"

"We surrender," answered Big Foot. Then he said something which tells a story of the despair and perplexity of the Sioux: "We would have done it before, if we had known where to find you."

That afternoon the whole band of about two hundred and fifty men, women and children, was marched to the 7th Cavalry camp down the creek. The Indians camped near the tents of the soldiers.

Next morning, December 29th, Colonel J. W. Forsyth, commanding the 7th, formed his five hundred men around the Indian village, with four Hotchkiss guns trained on the Sioux. Then he ordered the prisoners disarmed. Big Foot's statement the day before that he was sick was no exaggeration. He lay in his tent suffering from pneumonia.

The braves, sullen and uncomprehending, failed to obey the orders of Whiteside as quickly as he believed they should. Only a few rifles were given up. The major grew irritated. At last, after consulting with Forsyth, he brought the cavalry closer, formed them into a hollow square, and sent squads into the teepees to look for weapons.

Into the lodges strode the soldiers, shouldering their way in, driving forth the women and children, throwing over beds and other camp furniture, intensifying the mounting anger of the watching warriors. A medicine man, Yellow Bird, began haranguing the Indians, calling out that the ghost shirts nearly all of them wore were bullet proof and urging them to resist. A trooper grabbed the edge of a warrior's blanket to jerk it away. Yellow Bird stopped and tossed a hundful of dust into the air. Sharply a rifle shot rang out.

It was what the 7th Cavalry was waiting for. For fourteen years they had wanted to wipe out the Custer disaster in blood. This was too good a chance to miss.[2] Right into the crowd of sitting and standing warriors, many of them so close to the muzzles of the carbines that they could nearly touch them, the soldiers discharged a shattering volley. Nearly half the warriors in Big Foot's band were killed or wounded by that first discharge.

Like wildcats the survivors leaped to their feet and threw themselves against the cordon. Most of them were unarmed, but they seized knives, clubs, anything to fight with. They were outnumbered nearly four to one, and far more than in arms, yet they charged right at the throats of the troopers with desperate bravery. The squaws and even children took part. Captain Wallace fell with a wound in his leg. Before he could rise, he was clubbed to death by a swarm of Indian women.

The Hotchkiss guns went into action. Rapid-fire shells burst among the Sioux with terrible execution. Within a few minutes the field was strewn with the bodies of dead and wounded Indians. A handful broke through and fled in wild panic down a deep ravine. The blood-mad soldiers pursued, and the Hotchkiss guns never ceased to hurl their shells into the helpless, fugitive crowd. This was massacre in all its horror.[3]

The bodies of some of the women and children were found two and three miles away, where they had been pursued and killed by the human bloodhounds.

The killing was over by nine o'clock although some parties of soldiers still hunted fugitives in the hills. Twenty-nine whites were dead and thirty-three wounded. The Indian loss will never be

---

[2] General Miles brought charges against Forsyth for his conduct of this affair, mentioning specifically the circumstance of the slaughter of women and children three miles from the scene of the engagement. Forsyth was, however, exonerated by the Secretary of War, Redfield Proctor.

[3] The attitude of the 7th Cavalry is reflected in a conversation between a scout and an unnamed officer of that body right after the fight. This officer said, "with much gluttonous thought in his voice: 'Now we have avenged Custer's death,' and this scout said to him: 'Yes but you had every chance to fight for your lives that day; these poor Indian people did not have that opportunity to protect and fight for themselves.' " This quotation is taken from the statement of the Rev. C. S. Cook, a half-breed clergyman of the Episcopal Church, which was made before the Secretary of the Interior, and members of the Indian Bureau, at Washington, D.C., February 7th, 1891.

known. A blizzard set in that night and it was three days before the soldiers returned from Pine Ridge where they had taken their prisoners and wounded. How many helpless Indians, shot and unable to move, perished in the cold, it is impossible to guess, but there must have been many. Two or three little children were even found alive, protected through those three bitter days and nights by the bodies of their dead mothers.

By the time the soldiers returned to the scene, the bodies of many of the Sioux had been carried away by their relatives. But plenty of corpses still remained. The burial party reported sixty-four men and boys, forty-four women, and eighteen young children, or one hundred and twenty-six. General Miles, in his final report, however, says that not less than two hundred were killed. Among the dead was Big Foot, who was found lying in front of his tent.

Dr. Charles Eastman, who visited the battle field after the blizzard, before the burial of the bodies, thus describes it:

"It was a terrible and horrible sight to see the women and children lying in groups, dead. Some of the young girls wrapped their heads in their shawls and buried their faces in their hands. I suppose they did that so they would not see the soldiers come up to shoot them. At one place there were two little children, one about a year old, the other about three, lying on their faces, dead, and about thirty yards away from them a woman lay on her face, dead. These were away from the camp about an eighth of a mile. In front of the tents, which were in a semi-circle, lay dead most of the men. . . . This was where the Indians were ordered to hold a council with the soldiers."

AFTER THE MASSACRE

The guns of Wounded Knee could be clearly heard at Pine Ridge, nine miles away as the crow flies. There was intense excitement among the Indians at the agency as they heard the distant roar of firing and knew a fight was going on. Many of the warriors jumped on their ponies and rode to the scene, but the soldiers forced them back. Then a big body of Indians appeared on the ridge several hundred yards to the west of the agency and began to shoot at it. General Brooke ordered the Indian police to reply. They doubled past the agency school, and lay in line along the fence, their faces inscrutably calm, shooting at the Sioux who were now thick on top of the ridge.

The attacking Indians were not Ogalallas, but Brulés, led by Two Strike, Kicking Bear and Short Bull. After losing a man or two, they withdrew.

The situation was extremely grave. The troops had several skirmishes in the succeeding days. The very day after the massacre the Sioux almost trapped Forsyth and his men who were saved only by the prompt arrival of the 9th (colored) Cavalry.

By January 5th, 1891, the general situation was about this: Of the twenty-five thousand Sioux Indians on the northern reservations, twenty-one thousand, five hundred, were living in peace, while only thirty-five hundred were out. Of this number, less than one thousand were warriors. With the constant arrival of more troops, Miles now had eight thousand soldiers in the theater of war. It was the largest force ever assembled in one place to fight Indians.

But even with this army the outlook grew daily graver. All night the signal fires twinkled on the horizon and through the days constant puffs of smoke, dotting the air over practically every high bluff or ridge, showed where the Indians were telling each other of the movements of troops and other information.

Skirmishing continued constantly. Yet day after day passed and the great battle was postponed. On January 7th, Lieutenant Edward H. Casey, with a company of Cheyenne scouts, tried to pacify a band of Sioux. He was shot and killed by Plenty Horses, a Brulé.[4]

Miles worked day and night to avert the explosion. He counted on the sensible Indians, by now disillusioned of the miraculous powers of their Messiah priests, to bring the people to peace.

Slowly his soldiers pressed the great body of hostiles on three

---

[4] An interesting after-act of the war was the trial of Plenty Horses for the murder of Casey. On May 28th, 1891, Federal Judge Shiras peremptorily stopped the proceedings and ordered the jury to bring in a verdict of "not guilty." He held that a state of war existed between the whites and the Sioux and that under the laws of war Plenty Horses was justified in killing an enemy officer.

sides, moving them toward the Pine Ridge Agency, where it was planned to disarm and keep them. The Indians, sullen and restless, traveled slowly and grudgingly. At any moment an unfortunate act might have precipitated a general battle. But fortune was with Miles as it had been so many times before. In two days, during which he moved the hostiles thirty miles, the general scarcely slept.

Within sight of the agency, the Indians halted and said they would go no farther. Double guards walked in the army lines that night. Miles and his officers, tense, watchful, gazed toward the red flicker of the Sioux campfires.

The moon rose. Suddenly rifles began to speak. Furious yelling broke out among the teepees. Every soldier snatched his gun, convinced that the battle had come at last. But nothing happened. The noise ceased. Dawn came peacefully.

Next morning the extraordinary occurrence was explained. True to Miles' surmise, the calm element in the Sioux camp had at last convinced the others that to fight would be suicide. Despairing, enraged, heart-sick, the bitter-enders sought wildly for something on which they could vent their pent-up feelings. They rushed out with their rifles and ran amuck, shooting down their own dogs and horses.

It was relief of a sort. Next day the thousands of recent hostiles, eagle feathers fluttering, paint and beadwork gleaming, rode sullenly to the agency and camped. Thirty years of war was ended.

.   .   .   .

A few years ago, unnoticed in his squalid hut, died Wovoka, the Indian Messiah. Without honor even in his own tribe, his death created not a ripple in the land his influence once dominated. His body was buried in a sandy grave on the shores of Walker Lake.

No thumping drums, no spirit song accompanied his passing. Symbol of the red man's last hope, once worshipped by fanatical thousands, the news of his demise, on October 4th, 1932, served only to recall a troubled day in the West—the final, tragic stand of the retreating red man; the swan song of his race.

The Ghost Dance was dead long before its prophet.

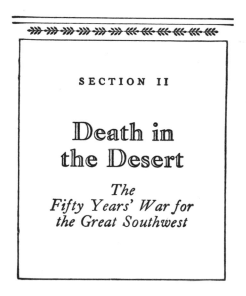

SECTION II

Death in the Desert

The Fifty Years' War for the Great Southwest

CONTENTS FOR SECTION II

I.
THE PURGING OF SANTA RITA DEL COBRE
1822–1840

II.
BLOOD IN THE PUEBLO
1846

III.
AN EYE FOR AN EYE
1846–1862

IV.
EXTERMINATION
1862–1871

V.
THE WAR IN THE LAVA BEDS
1871–1873

VI.
NAN-TAN LUPAN
1871–1876

VII.
THE HUNTING OF VICTORIO
1877–1880

VIII.
WARRIORS WITHOUT LEADERS
1880–1883

IX.
THE GERONIMO WAR
1883–1886

ILLUSTRATIONS IN SECTION II

MAPS

I
The Purging of Santa Rita del Cobre
1822-1840

1: AT THE COPPER MINES

THE WEAKNESS OF JUAN JOSÉ

To THE Apaches, the Copper Mines of Santa Rita del Cobre had been for years an abomination and a menace. The mines were situated in the southwestern corner of what is now New Mexico, the very heart of the Apache country; and that Mexican miners should be permitted to live and work there, without harm or hindrance, ate like a canker into the heart of every warrior.[1] Moreover, the miners were driving their shafts into what had been for generations the Council Rocks of the tribe.

It was a supreme tribute to the power of Juan José, chief of the Mimbreño Apaches,[2] that the settlement of squalid adobe houses and the tiny *presidio*, had not long before this been pulled to pieces. To ask the lean desert destroyers to withhold their hands from the sleek Mexicans, was to ask lobo wolves to refrain from worrying a flock of sheep. Yet such was the prestige of Juan José that Santa Rita, its three-cornered fort with the squat, turret-shaped towers looking over the jumble of *casas* scattered without plan about the wide, dusty *plaza*, existed for years with never a thought of death to disturb it.

Little pot-bellied Mexican children played in the dirt. Broad-hipped *casadas* shrilled to each other from house to house. In the

---

[1] "The Mexican government . . . held that the Indians had no rights, as original possessors of the land, which it was in any manner bound to respect, and to this policy is due the unceasing war which has been waged by this brave people (the Apaches) against the Mexicans."—Vincent Colyer's Report to the Board of Indian Commissioners, 1871 (p. 5).

[2] The Mimbreño Apaches at this period ranged from the east side of the Rio Grande in New Mexico, to the Verde River in Arizona. Prior to the Santa Rita massacre they were one of the most numerous branches of the Apache people.

evenings men slouched across the *plaza* or lounged in lighted door-ways. With night came the tinkle of guitar strings as youths sere-naded their *señoritas* in the dusk.

Strange sights, strange sounds, strange odors for Apacheria. Yet Juan José, the fat and lazy, kept his people in leash when their every instinct maddened them with the desire to kill.

The chief's own degeneration was to blame for his complaisance. In his youth he had been an Apache of Apaches. None had been al-lowed to surpass him in the long, dangerous raids down into Sonora and Chihuahua, as the Indians waged their bitter, unending war with the Mexicans. But age and much booty had taken away the rancour of his nature, so that he grew broad of back and loved no longer the feel of a straining pony beneath him, nor the hunger of the war path and its hot triumph.

In 1822 there came to Juan José the envoys of that wealthy Span-ish grandee, Don Francisco Manuel Elguea of Chihuahua, with pro-posals for a treaty of permission to work the copper mountain which Don Elguea had puurchased from its discoverer, Colonel Carrisco. The latter had found the great lode in 1804, but it was worthless to him since the Apaches would not permit him to remove the ore. Don Elguea was a different man. He well knew how to appeal to one like Juan José. The offers of cloth, of weapons and horses, were clinched by a present of strangely shaped casks of ardent spirits. Juan José, drunk by that time, gave permission to establish a settle-ment and work the mines.

There were, to be sure, some restrictions. The Mexicans were not to leave the settlement without permission. Even then they must agree to follow only two specified trails back to Mexico in their activities, one toward Chihuahua and the other toward Sonora. Yet, although they meticulously observed these restrictions, anyone could see that the Mexicans grew daily in numbers at Santa Rita del Cobre. Women came, among them young *señoritas*, who swung their hips with their peculiar, insinuating walk, causing the eyes of the Mim-breño warriors to glow as they watched them.

Still Juan José forbade hostility. And his word was yet law to the

Mimbreños. Even though he no longer rode, they remembered that he owned the strange magic of reading the thick-writing. A *padre,* hoping to win him to the priesthood and thus obtain a foothold in the wild tribe, had trained him in his youth. But Juan José was too truly an Apache to linger long with the gentle teachings of the Cross. He returned to his people and used his learning to intercept messengers and read dispatches, thus forestalling by lightning escape or well-planned ambush, the military movements against him.

So long had he been successful as a leader in war, that now, although his warriors' hands itched for the bow and spear as they watched the great *conductas* with their pack mules wind their way periodically south, they remained quiet. While Juan José was chief, Santa Rita was safe.

It is not to be supposed that all of the Mimbreños submitted tamely to such a condition. Perhaps more than half of them broke away and established their camp at Ojo Caliente (Warm Springs), about eighteen miles east of the Copper Mines. This division came to be known as the Warm Springs Indians, as distinguished from the Copper Mines Indians who remained with Juan José.

While Juan José, on the heights above Santa Rita, looked down on the miners at work, the Warm Springs Apaches maintained the old ways of the tribe. Under the bitter leadership of Cuchillo Negro (Black Knife) they continued the great, killing raids deep into old Mexico, bringing back ponies and plunder and captives. The Warm Springs Indians kept the lean Apache look. The Copper Mines Indians were grown fat with their chief. They learned to go among the adobe houses of Santa Rita village, to beg for food or *mescal,* occasionally to sell furs, and to acquire habits and manners which were looked upon askance by the elders of the tribe. Many now spoke Spanish. The younger squaws began to swing their hips like the *señoritas.* And the youths adopted the insolent Mexican swagger.

It was high time for a change. The Copper Mines had now run fifteen years—this was in 1837. Many of the warriors were beginning to look beyond Juan José at another figure—Mangus Colorado, who was of Cuchillo Negro's mind, but of Juan José's camp.

MANGUS COLORADO

In many ways Mangus Colorado had focussed the eyes of the people upon himself. He was that anomaly among the Apaches, a giant. Six feet, six or seven inches tall he stood in his moccasins.[3] Yet his legs, vastly bowed, were scarcely longer than those of an ordinary man. All of the great difference was made up by his tremendous torso. His head was great in proportion, huge enough to fill a cask, the eyes deep sunk and very bright, lips wide and thin as a knife slash, and a vulture's beak of a nose curving down to meet the rocky up-jut of his chin. Among a people who averaged below the usual height and size, his mightiness had no parallel.

His strength was that of two or three men. Two Apache squaws were already in his lodge, but he captured a beautiful Mexican girl and added her to his household. This was contrary to custom, under which he should either have killed her or turned her over to his wives as a slave. But Mangus Colorado made his own customs. In the face of tribal disapproval he established the foreigner as an equal with his other women. It was, to them, a slap in the face. Apache law gave both his wives the right to appeal to their relatives. Mangus Colorado was challenged by a brother of each to the terrible Apache duel—naked, with knives as weapons and death to the vanquished. He accepted. And before all the people the great Apache bull slew both his challengers. After that nobody, least of all his wives, dared question his right to bring anybody he desired to his lodge.[4]

Mangus Colorado signifies (in defective Spanish) "Red Sleeves." One story is that he won his name by leading the band of Apaches which followed for weeks the Sylvester Pattie party of American trappers as they worked down the San Pedro River in the spring of 1825, finally running off their horses. The white men concealed their furs and went to the Copper Mines for help. Then the Apaches

[3] There is dispute as to his exact height. John C. Cremony ("Life Among the Apaches," p. 48) says "about six feet." Lieutenant Cave C. Couts ("Diary of a March to California") says six feet, two inches. Other authorities say, however, that he was taller than either of these estimates. Charles F. Lummis ("Land of Poco Tiempo," p. 161) gives his height as six feet, six inches.

[4] This incident is vouched for by Cremony ("Life Among the Apaches," pp. 47–48).

robbed them of their entire catch. In the loot, so the story goes, was a red flannel shirt which Mangus donned and thus obtained his name. Whether or not this be true, it is certain that in 1837, when he was about forty years old, he was the most talked about of all the Copper Mines Indians.

He was a friend of Cuchillo Negro, the Warm Springs leader, a sullen, vicious Apache, much esteemed among his people for his craft and burning hate. The two of them saw eye to eye in the matter of Santa Rita del Cobre. Either would gladly have led an attack on the place. But had not the government of Chihuahua taken a hand, the opportunity to slake their Apache hatred for the Mexicans would possibly never have come.

Rendered desperate by Apache incursions which never left them in peace and which their soldiers seemed powerless to stop, the *junta* of Chihuahua promulgated, in 1837, the *"Proyecto de Guerra,"* or project for war. It was a barbarous law, a law conceived by men who despaired of ever meeting the Apache menace by any civilized means. It was a last-ditch law, dictated by the fear which death from the north had engendered in every Mexican heart. The state agreed to pay a sum equivalent to one hundred dollars for the scalp of every Apache warrior brought to the capital; fifty dollars for the scalp of each squaw; and twenty-five dollars for the scalp of each child. Sonora already had such a law.[5]

Here was a peerless opportunity for the unscrupulous. And it carried in it the seeds of bitter hatred which the Apaches were eventually to bear for every member of the white race. Up to this time the Apache hostility had been directed at the Mexicans with whom they had a feud for generations. There were only a few white men in the country, trappers or traders, and toward these the Indians had a more or less friendly attitude. Beyond occasional petty thievery along the trap lines, or, as in the case of the Pattie party, the stealing of horses, there was remarkably little hostility shown toward the whites. Among the trappers in the country at the time was one James Johnson. Not much is known of this man, save that

---

[5] As late as 1866, Grant County, Arizona, offered a bounty of two hundred and fifty dollars each for Apache scalps.

he was driven by an all-encompassing greed for gold. There is some dispute as to whether he was an American or an Englishman.[6] No matter; he was of the *Pinda Lick-o-yi*, the White Eyes,[7] and generations were to suffer because of him.

With a mind less scrupulous even than the Mexicans, Johnson plotted a wholesale slaughter which should put scalp-collecting into the realm of big business. With his partner, a man named Gleason, he enlisted to his project a party of Missouri trappers, led by one Eames. The whole band went to Santa Rita, where an additional bounty was offered by the owners of the mines, an inducement for Johnson to commit his crime there.

Letters of introduction from Chihuahua authorities and from the company officials obtained full cooperation for Johnson at the mines. The plan was simplicity itself. A great feast was held to which the Apaches were invited. Such an invitation was an immediate lodestone to the glutton Juan José. At his eager acceptance, the Copper Mines Indians agreed to come almost en masse. Numbers of squaws and children from the more remote Warm Springs village also rode over to attend.

The Mexicans lived up to their promises of hospitality. Roast steers, *soccoro* mush, and *mescal* were served in abundance. The Indians gorged themselves, with the huge-paunched Juan José showing his people the way.

In the middle of the feast, laborers carried out bags of *soccoro* meal—corn grist—and heaped them in the *plaza*. To one side was a screening of branches and sacking. Here lounged Johnson and most of his men.

Best proof that the Apaches were thoroughly drunk is contained in the fact that none of them investigated the screen. That was not Apache. Had anyone taken the trouble to look, he would have seen something which would have sent him screaming an alarm to his people.

[6] Cremony calls Johnson an Englishman. Wilson says he was an American.

[7] The word "Paleface" was unknown among the Apaches. Their generic name for members of the white race was *Pinda Lick-o-yi*, "White Eyes," and seems to have referred to their blue or light gray eyes which looked white in comparison to the Apaches' own black orbs.

Behind the branches squatted the ugly bulk of a howitzer, loaded to the muzzle with bullets, nails, pieces of chain, slugs and stones. It was trained directly upon the pile of *soccoro*.[8]

THE MASSACRE

And now the *alcalde* came forward with an oily invitation to the Apaches to help themselves to the *soccoro* as a free gift from the people of Santa Rita. Not dreaming of treachery, the squaws and children gathered around the pile in a laughing, chattering mob. Now was Johnson's time. When the crowd was thickest about the bags, he touched his lighted *cigarro* to the vent hole of the gun.

The screen of branches and sacking was burst asunder by the shattering blast of the howitzer. Right into the thick of the unsuspecting Indians hurtled a devil's collection of missiles. It mowed a swath as clean as if a giant scythe had slashed through the heart of the crowd.

At the roar of the gun, the trappers, led by Johnson, and the Mexican soldiers from the *presidio*, leaped forward to finish the slaughter. Muskets thudded and knives and sabres flashed and sank home. In wildest panic, bewildered, terror-stricken, the Apaches fled in every direction. Only the swiftest-footed escaped. The ground was heaped with corpses, foul with blood.[9]

As the surviving Indians stampeded into their own village, they began to count their losses. Juan José did not appear. He was dead. How naturally the tribe now turned to Mangus Colorado. He had escaped death by some miracle and they looked to him for leadership in the crisis. The Apache giant was ready for the responsibility.

Mangus Colorado was forty and he had spent his manhood preparing himself for this moment. He had studied the Mimbreño warriors. On the heels of the greatest disaster his people had ever known, or soon thereafter, he named a group of warriors to positions of responsibility under him, who were afterward to be known as the

[8] Accounts differ as to the type of gun used. Cremony says it was a six-pounder, Wilson a blunderbuss, Dunn a howitzer. Whatever it was, all agree on the results which followed.

[9] According to Cremony ("Life Among the Apaches," p. 31) four hundred Apaches lost their lives in this massacre.

most redoubtable in the history of the Apache Nation. Delgadito (The Slender), Poncé, El Chico, Pedro Azul, Coletto Amarillo (Yellow Tail), Cuchillo Negro, and last, but not least, the warrior who was to go down in history as Victorio, were selected to serve as sub-chiefs under Mangus Colorado.

It was to be a holy war of vengeance. For the first time in fifteen years the Mimbreños were together. The Red Sleeves abandoned the old Copper Mines camp and took his people to their kindred at the Warm Springs. Thenceforth all were known as Warm Springs Indians.

Meantime, like ripples of a pool into which a pebble is thrown, the lines of Apache fighters moved swiftly outward. There were several parties of American trappers in the country. The Indians knew where to find every one. Santa Rita was the main objective, but meanwhile the Apaches could whet the edge of their appetite for blood atonement upon these white men outside the village.

Two trapping parties were on the Gila River. One, composed of twenty-two men led by Charles Kemp, was forty miles downstream from the mines. Another, of only three trappers, headed by Benjamin D. Wilson, was even closer to the Mimbreño headquarters.

In the gray of a dawn the Apaches opened fire on the Kemp party. Surprised, caught in a deep ravine with high walls all around and commanding it, the white men died under the Mimbreño arrows. Not one survived. Particularly careful to take every rifle and all ammunition, the Apaches looted the camp. Then they passed on and the buzzards dropped down into the gorge.

Forty miles up the river, Benjamin Wilson and his two companions camped. Silent shadows slipped around their tent and the Americans found themselves suddenly caught and bound. It was Mangus Colorado again. Wilson's story of what followed is extant in the form of a manuscript.[10]

Mangus Colorado tried to preserve their lives. But his people demanded the trappers. At last the chief brought about a compro-

[10] Quoted by Frank C. Lockwood in his "Pioneer Days in Arizona," pp. 155-157.

mise; two of the Americans should die; the other be released.[11] To the teepee where the three prisoners were confined, he went. Wilson was the lucky man who was given his freedom.[12] His companions died horribly, hanging head down over a slow fire.

Mangus Colorado had struck two blows. It was now time to consider Santa Rita itself. Like wolves the Apaches turned toward the Copper Mines.

[11] This is Wilson's story and it is certain that he did survive while his companions were killed. But the writer is at a loss to explain why Mangus Colorado had this sudden softness of heart. There is something behind his sparing Wilson's life. Perhaps even this early Mangus Colorado was beginning his long effort to conciliate the white man.

[12] Wilson, in the final stages of exhaustion, eventually reached Santa Fé. He recovered his health and lived to become noted as a rancher, merchant, Indian agent, state senator in California and later the first mayor of Los Angeles.

2: APACHE RETRIBUTION

Sun-baked and hot the village of Santa Rita del Cobre lay athwart the landscape as if a giant hand had cast a fistful of adobe blocks haphazardly. Above loomed the summit of the Needle [1] from which the Mexicans were wont to watch for the *conductas* bringing pack trains loaded with provisions and mail from Sonora or Chihuahua. Within the town, huddled close to the walls of the ugly little *presidio*, the usual activities went forward. Miners, shop-keepers, a few *ricos* and perhaps a *padre* or two, strolled in the narrow, crooked streets. The throng of children still tumbled underfoot and kept up an indescribable babel of sound, while their mothers looked on proudly from their various occupations.

Yet there was definable about the place an air of uneasy expectancy—a feeling which a close observer might have identified as dread. Now and again, wandering toward the *plaza*, the eye of a citizen might have gazed at a long, low ridge of fresh earth beyond the limits of the village. It was not strange if he crossed himself as he gazed.

It was a place of ill omen, that ridge of new-turned earth. Beneath lay the bodies of many Apaches, mostly women and children, massacred in the *plaza*, victims of the gold lust of the American trappers, Johnson, Gleason, Eames and their followers. The scalps had been torn from the heads of the murdered Indians, to be taken to Chihuahua for the bounty there offered.

Not a single Indian now squatted in the sun of the *plaza*. None lounged in the shade of the adobe shops. Yet the people of Santa Rita del Cobre derived small comfort from the circumstance. Had they known the Apaches as the Apaches knew them, they would have sweated with something even more poignant than the sick dread of the silence which now oppressed them. At this very moment the vil-

[1] Now called the Kneeling Nun.

lage was under the surveillance of Apache eyes, focussed telescopically upon the place, observing every movement in it. The watch had been maintained unceasingly by the Mimbreños since the hour of the massacre. Not a man left his home, not a movement was made, which was not seen. And yet no glimpse of an Indian was ever caught by any inhabitant of the town.

Forty or fifty miles away in the Gila valley, lay the hacked and mutilated bodies of twenty-two American trappers. Thirty miles further up-stream, the corpses of two more still hung, head down from the trees, their skulls burst open over the black ashes of fires now dead.

This, so far, was Apache vengeance. But bigger game was afoot. The great, hulking shadow of Mangus Colorado visited the Apache observation posts at night. Nothing less than the destruction of the settlement of Santa Rita itself would satisfy the chief.

Far to the south the Apaches met a *conducta* in a mountain pass. The soldiers guarding it knew little of Apaches. They entered the valley trustingly . . . like little children. . . .

At the counting of the loot that night the Mimbreño chiefs enumerated many rifles and great store of powder and ball; much cloth, *soccoro* and horses and mules to gladden the heart. It has been a rich *conducta* carrying supplies for the Copper Mines. None remained alive of the pack train and its guards. The Apaches had finished them all—some of them quickly, in the heat of the fight; others slowly, with ingenious devices to prolong life and bring out the finality of agony in dying, while voices made their plaint from the dark valley in which little groups of Indians squatted about prostrate figures.

Later another, smaller *conducta*, on its way north from Janos, was similarly cut off by the Mimbreños. Nothing of this was known at Santa Rita. But as the days lengthened, the people began to realize that the time for the coming of the *conductas* was long past and their supplies were so low that, if the *conductas* were much longer delayed, starvation faced them. In the fifteen years during which the mines had been operated, the *conductas* had come with such regularity that the miners grew to count upon them absolutely. Long ago the practice of keeping stores for possible emergencies had been given up. Santa Rita lived very much from hand to mouth.

Still time passed. Work at the mines ceased altogether. The miners wandered uneasily about the village. Children wailed with hunger in the adobe *casas*. The Santa Ritans began the habit of toiling up the steep slope of the Needle, to gaze anxiously south from palm-shaded eyes, for signs of the dust cloud which would herald the coming of help. But the horizon remained bleakly bare.

Johnson, Eames and the rest of the Americans grew tired of the monotony and struck out from the village toward the Chiricahua Mountains on the west. These men the Apaches attacked and almost exterminated. Johnson, the arch-plotter, was one of the few who escaped. Even of this attack Santa Rita knew nothing.

All this activity and tragedy around them had occurred with no intimation to the people. There was nothing tangible for them to lay their hands or minds to. It was clearly apparent, however, that things had reached a stage where it was no longer possible to remain at Santa Rita. The *alcalde* and the commandant of the few soldiers of the *presidio* sat long at night, with their heads together.

One day they called the people into the *plaza* and announced to them that, as a last resort, a heavily armed force of men, strong enough to hold its own in case of an Indian attack, would ride south to find the missing *conductas*. At once protests arose. It was urged that such a force would take practically all the armed men in the settlement; that those who stayed behind would be defenseless. There was only one alternative. The whole population of some three or four hundred men, women and children, was ordered to prepare to travel.

THE DEATH FLIGHT

And so the desert witnessed a pitiful hegira. Out of Santa Rita del Cobre filed the long, motley caravan. Every kind of a vehicle obtainable was there, loaded with belongings of the people. Few of them understood what actually awaited them on a march such as the one upon which they were embarking. They tried to take along their most precious possessions, sacrificing speed with useless treasures, adding weight to the burdens. Even wheelbarrows from the

mines were requisitioned. Mules and burros staggered under towering packs. And many of the men and even women and children
walked with their shoulders bent beneath heavy bundles.

Leaving their little homes, which would presently become the
abode of pack-rats and coyotes, they commenced the long trek southward. It is not likely that the women wept much at the departure
from Santa Rita. Apprehension sat too heavily upon all of them.

One day—two days—they traveled. Their path presently became a tragic *via dolorosa*, strewn with bundles, broken vehicles,
dead animals—and, with growing frequency, graves, particularly
little graves, with tiny crosses stuck hastily into the heaped-up sand.

So far they were not molested by the Apaches. The crags on either
side of the trail appeared deserted. Not a sign of life could be seen
in the yellow-gray waste. But although they knew it not, every foot
of their way was paced by unseen human wolves whose eyes did not
miss a movement the fleeing Santa Ritans made.

It is not known just when or how fate overtook them. Probably
it was upon the third or fourth day. The reader can picture for himself what happened: Without warning, without preliminary, from
the sides of a narrow pass, arrows and bullets whizzed. Men died
and with them women and little children. Those who escaped the
missiles struggled desperately forward out of the gorge. The
wounded were abandoned where they fell. Presently the surviving
Mexicans heard behind them the outcries of these deserted ones,
under the expert hands of Apache torturers.

Ahead was another narrow canyon and the Santa Ritans knew too
well what awaited them between its jaws. Yet the gantlet must be
run. Men clenched their teeth and gripped their muskets; women
wailed and clung to their children as the train plunged into the
gorge. Again the blighting sleet of death from the walls above:
stricken people and animals in the canyon. No time to stop and help
them now. The soldiers tried to fight back, but how can one fight
when he cannot see his enemy? The remnants at last escaped from
the gulch. Behind was repeated again the dolorous sound of Apache
death being brought to the wounded.

All this is only a conception of what took place. There is no detailed account. But this we know: Harried, pursued, never permitted to rest, the three or four hundred souls who left Santa Rita were almost wiped out. Scarcely half a dozen ever reached Janos, the first settlement to the south. The bleaching skeletons of all the rest sprawled on the road between.

Thus Mangus Colorado took payment for the treachery of Johnson and his *soccoro* bags.

.   .   .   .

Once more the Mimbreños pitched their camp on the high ridge overlooking the valley of the Copper Mines. They were one people now, with Mangus Colorado their recognized chief. Under him served at least two of the authentic blood of chiefs—Poncé, nephew of Juan José, and Cuchillo Negro—yet both were content and proud to be his lieutenants.

War was the accustomed state of the Apaches and the whole people breathed more freely, more cleanly, now that they were in their element again. Mangus Colorado did not propose to lose the white heat of this new spirit. He began again the raids into Mexico. And he spent his brief leisure between forays in numerous acts of policy, designed to knit the surrounding tribes to him. Born to him by the Mexican girl for whom he had fought the double duel, were three comely daughters. These he presented to Cochise, chief of the Chiricahuas; to Hash-kai-la, of the Coyoteros; and to Ku-tu-hala, of the White Mountains, thus drawing the three groups to him.

It was a time of fulfillment for the Mimbreños. In the years which followed the purging of Santa Rita del Cobre, no Mexican dared enter the borders of Apacheria. The Indians, on the other hand, raided often and far into Mexican territory, and Sonora, Chihuahua and Durango were loud with wailings because of the *ranchos* burned, men slain, and women and children carried away.

Beside their Warm Springs, or near the Council Rocks, the Mimbreños feasted after raiding, and planned new exploits. All men looked to Mangus Colorado for leadership. Those were good times for the Apaches.

But a change was coming, and that soon.

3: THE MASSACRE AT TAOS

PEOPLE OF THE PUEBLO

Rose-brown in the glory of the New Mexican sunlight, Taos Pueblo crouched in its surrounding amphitheater of mountains—crouched like a beast gathering for its spring. Within eye-shot of whoever stood upon its higher *azoteas* was the town of San Fernando de Taos, the village of white men and Mexicans which lay a short ride to the westward.

Tomasito, the war chief of the Pueblos, could remember when San Fernando de Taos had been a sleepy Spanish town with never an *Americano* in it. Those were the days before the trappers began to filter down from the high Rockies; before the Bents and Ceran St. Vrain established their residences in Taos; before Broken Hand Fitzpatrick and Kit Carson, with their train of strenuous, hard-bitten mountain men, had converted the picturesque village into a white man's outpost.

The Pueblos had never grown used to the white men and their highhanded ways. The half-humorous contempt, with which the *Americanos* treated them, was resented. And now, in the dying months of the year 1846, conditions had changed even more for Taos Pueblo.

The annexation of Texas by the lusty new republic of the United States in December, 1845, together with many other causes in which the people of the Pueblos were not in the remotest way interested or concerned, brought about war between the power of the north and Mexico, which was formally declared in May, 1846. By April an army was moving across the plains, and down through the mountains toward New Mexico. Don Manuel Armijo, the showy governor of New Mexico, issued a bombastic proclamation, and gathered an army, but when he met General Stephen W. Kearny, and his Missourians and Tennesseeans, "half hoss, half alligator," the Mexican soldiers melted away and the glittering governor himself led the flight out of the territory. Thus it came about that on August 19th, 1846, Kearny occupied Santa Fé, the capital of New Mexico, raised the flag of the United States over the governor's palace, and proclaimed the country a possession of his government by right of conquest.

It did not seem to occur to the American commander or any of his officers that the Taos Indians might be a factor to be considered in governing the new-won territory. For centuries they had been known to be peaceful. When the Spaniard first crossed the deserts, he found the Pueblos there, already civilized, hard-working and prosperous. At that time they occupied seventy-six towns [1] which were scattered over an area hundreds of miles in extent. The largest of these, and the most notable for its location, with the single exception of cliff-perched Acoma, was Taos, which was also the most northerly of all the Indian cities.

The Spanish were struck with wonder at the progress which the Pueblo Indians had made up the ladder of civilization. Five-story Taos Pueblo, for example, was three stories higher than the houses to which the Dons were accustomed in their own lands. And the Pueblo irrigation systems showed skill even superior, in their way, to the buildings. Some of these great aqueducts have been traced for as much as fifty miles, and their design is so perfect that modern engineers have been unable to gain an inch a mile in fall over these masterpieces of antiquity.[2]

Every Pueblo Indian was a combined farmer and trader. He was

---

[1] Now reduced in number to thirty-six.

[2] Several of these old canal beds have been used to advantage by modern irrigation ditch builders. In one case, the Mormon settlement of Mesa, Arizona, saved thousands of dollars by employing an ancient aqueduct which curved around a volcanic knoll for three miles, at one point being chiseled twenty to thirty feet deep into the solid rock for several hundred feet. Through this remarkable system of irrigation the Pueblos were able always to keep the spectre of starvation away; even to acquire a surplus of food for barter. (See F. W. Hodge, "Handbook of American Indians," p. 621.)

a hunter and warrior last of all. In the latter respect, the Pueblo was America's first pacifist. He believed, however, in preparedness—for defensive warfare. His communal houses were primarily fortifications and his very life depended upon their impregnability. For hungry killers came out of the desert and sat slavering outside the walls as they sensed the richness of the Pueblo possessions. Ordinarily these killers—Apaches, Utes, Comanches, or Navajos—when they had traded their meat and furs for blankets and grain, returned to their wilds. But sometimes they made a savage effort to carry the place and thus possess its wealth without having to barter.

None of the pueblos was superior to Taos as a fortress city. Built of native adobe, and tinted the gorgeous titian shade which, once seen, is never forgotten, its two large community buildings had long laughed at any threat from the neighboring tribes. Their first stories had no doors or windows looking outward. Their roofs could be reached only by ladder over the outer wall. Upper stories receded in succeeding terraces, giving pyramidal shape to the whole.[3]

At nightfall, or whenever danger threatened, the ladders were drawn up. Sentries patrolled the walls. If attacked, the whole manpower of the pueblo, and the women also, swarmed to the defense. Small wonder that the Comanches and the Navajos, when they prowled through the mountains, gave Taos Pueblo wide berth.

THE CONSPIRACY

The yoke of Spain had been accepted by Taos with comparative meekness. Even in the furious outbreaks in which their brethren of the south once or twice indulged, bringing death to hundreds of Spanish settlers, the Taos people figured slightly, if at all.[4]

[3] The present-day Taos Pueblo is but little changed from the structure of 1846. Tourists who have seen it can gain a clear picture of the scenes here described. In one respect the pueblo is different. Modern day Taos has windows and doors in its first story, since the need for safety from savage tribes has passed.

[4] The Pueblo revolt of 1680 was one of the bloodiest which ever occurred on the North American continent. On August 10th of that year, the Indians, goaded to desperation, broke out, killed a score or more Catholic priests who had served them devotedly as missionaries, and slaughtered more than four hundred Spanish colonists. The revolt was put down by Diego de Vargas, in 1692, when he reconquered New Mexico, twelve years after the Spaniards were driven out. Taos was isolated and took a minor part in the revolt.

But this was a different day. After Kearny swept the Mexican army out of northern New Mexico, he consolidated the territory, then moved on toward Chihuahua and California. Everything in his wake seemed peaceful. The Mexican residents of the country apparently had accepted the inevitable. The Pueblo Indians showed small concern in the change of overlords.

Troops occupied all the more important cities, including Taos village, and Charles Bent, a resident of Taos, was appointed the first governor of the new territory. Bent was one of the famous brothers who built Bent's Fort on the Arkansas River, and with St. Vrain controlled the fur traffic of the southern plains. He had a Mexican wife. His neighbors at Taos included men like the noted Kit Carson, Judge Beaubien, St. Vrain and others. He was liked and respected by everybody.

But while all moved so smoothly on the surface, an internal volcano seethed in New Mexico, and the smouldering flames had reached the *kivas* of the Indians. There had been secret councils at Taos Pueblo. Tomasito had presided at conclaves where others than Indians spoke.

The truth was that the Mexicans hated their conquerors. And with Kearny barely started on his march south, a plot was already hatching to overthrow the government of the *Americanos*. Colonel Diego Archuleta and Tomás Ortiz, the arch-conspirators, knew well the fury of the Indians when aroused, and one of their first steps was to enlist the support of those at Taos. In this they received the help of the mission priests, whom the red people trusted and believed. With the *entrée* gained for them by these priests, the conspirators laid optimistic plans and promises before the Taos Indians.

As had been said, the Pueblos had accepted the change in rule over New Mexico with much indifference. But Ortiz and Archuleta told them that the *Americanos* were pitifully weak, unable to defend themselves; and that, if revolt was successful, the plunder would be rich. The council agreed to take part in the insurrection.

The Mexican leaders of the revolt showed their usual incompetence. Plans miscarried; delay followed delay. The outbreak was first set for December 19th. The church bells were to ring, and, at the signal, the conspirators were to go to the *plaza* of Taos, seize the artillery parked there, and kill every American in the village. But the irresolute leaders changed their minds. They postponed the date until Christmas Eve, to take advantage of the celebrations all over the city which they felt would make the time more propitious for their coup. This time the plot was exposed. A mulatto girl, who had married one of the disbanded soldiers of Armijo, the former New Mexican governor, heard of the plan and hurried with it to Colonel Sterling Price at Santa Fé, three days before the time set. At Price's orders several of the ring-leaders were arrested. Ortiz and Archuleta fled to Mexico. Early in January Governor Bent proclaimed the suppression of the revolt and enjoined the people to be loyal to the government. It was hoped the trouble was over.

But the Pueblo Indians were less vacillating in their temper than their Mexican friends. The conspirators were gone but the organization they had built was still present, awaiting only something to put it into action. That something occurred January 19th, 1847.

Three Taos Indians had been arrested for stealing and were locked up in the Taos jail. On the morning of the 19th a rabble of men from the pueblo marched into the town, crowded in an ugly, restless mob in front of the prison, and demanded the release of their tribesmen. Stephen Lee, an American, was sheriff. One look at the scowling faces around him, and he moved to comply. But before he could do so, the *prefect*, a Mexican named Cornelio Vigil, appeared. Vigil was both tactless and pompous. He loudly forbade Lee to obey the Indians. Then he began to insult and abuse them.

It was as if a taut cord snapped. Like snarling dogs the Pueblos leaped at Vigil, hurled him to the ground, literally cut him to pieces. All in an instant they were mad with the fury of killing. The prefect's voice was heard, momentarily, calling upon all the saints for succor, then was stilled as a Taos knife slipped through his throat and the choking blood stopped further sound.

Stephen Lee fled. But the Indians were after him as soon as they released the prisoners in the jail. They "treed" him on his own house-top and shot him down as if he were a catamount in a pine.

James W. Leal, the circuit attorney, blundered into the mob. Him they scalped alive, then dragged him shrieking through the streets, pricking him with their lances until at last he died. Narcissé, the young son of Judge Beaubien, and his companion, Pablo Harvimean, were found in an outhouse and ruthlessly killed. Judge Beaubien himself would have shared their fate had he not, the day before, gone to Santa Fé on business. All through the village groups of Indians hunted Americans out of their hiding places and mercilessly slew them.

And now came the climax. With their blood at fever heat, the Indians gathered around the house of Governor Bent, who was home from Santa Fé for a brief visit with his family. He was still in bed when the mob gathered. His terrified wife called to him, telling him of the gathering danger outside. Then, frantic with fear, she rushed in with his pistol, imploring him to fight, to make his assailants pay, even if he must die in the end. He could easily have killed several of them, but he refused.

"I will not kill any of them—for your sake," he said. "At present, my death is all these people want." [5]

He meant that if he allowed himself to be killed without resistance, the mob might be satisfied, but if he fought they would massacre everybody in the house.

By this time the Indians, aided by Mexicans, had chopped and broken a hole through the roof. They poured into the room. Governor Bent made the appeal to them which he knew would be futile, calling to their minds the many favors he had done for them in the past. They laughed in his face.

An arrow flashed into his body—another—another. As the governor tottered, a bullet tore through him. He fell, and Tomasito stepped forward with a pistol and blew his brains out.

Mrs. Bent and the family were spared, but the Indians scalped Charles Bent as he lay twitching in his death struggles on his own bedroom floor. The scalp was nailed to a board with brass-headed tacks and, shouting and dancing, the whole wild mob roared down the street, carrying the ghastly trophy at its head, like a bloody banner of insurrection.

[5] Dunn, "Massacres of the Mountains," p. 62.

4: TURLEY'S MILL

SIMEON TURLEY was a character unique even in a land and time of unique characters. An ex-trapper, he had found his way into New Mexico by way of the fur trade, met there a bright-eyed *señorita*, married her and settled down.

On the banks of the Arroyo Hondo he built a grist mill and a distillery, where he produced more than his share of the famous "Taos Lightning," a fiery whiskey made from the native wheat, much in demand among trappers, traders and wild Indians because of its potency.

The years passed and prosperity came to Turley. His *rancho* in 1847 included numerous substantial buildings such as granaries, stables and offices, as well as the mill, distillery and his home, all arranged in a hollow square with a large front gate and a small postern gate, leading to the corral enclosed within. Here Turley lived in feudal happiness. His door was always open to the wayfarer; his table groaned with the luxuries of the country and guests were ever welcome to it. He was never known to refuse a request for financial or other assistance. Well did he merit the esteem in which his neighbors held him.

The morning of January 19th, 1847, Simeon Turley, at peace with the world and entertaining a half-dozen or more of his friends who had "dropped in" for a meal or two and copious draughts of the fiery Taos Lightning, received ominous information. A rider sped by, halting just long enough to drop word that the Taos Indians had broken out, had raged through the streets of Taos Village killing every American they met, and had murdered and scalped the governor of New Mexico himself—Charles Bent.

Turley's face was grave as he heard this news, but so friendly were his relations with the natives that it did not occur to him that he might himself be in danger. But there were with him eight men who never took anything for granted. Not for nothing had those trappers fought Indians and grizzlies through the Rockies and shared a thousand adventures.

"Better bar them gates," was their laconic recommendation. To please his guests, Turley did so. The trappers lounged about, loose-jointed and deliberate. One took his hickory cleaning rod and ran an oiled rag down the polished barrel of his rifle. Another whetted his hunting knife to razor keenness on the sole of his moccasin. They did not appear apprehensive but they seemed watchful, as men who expect momentous events.

Loud yells down the valley sent the men to the windows. Armed with guns, bows and lances, a mob of Pueblo Indians and Mexicans could be seen coming toward the mill. It was the same crowd which had murdered Bent and other Americans at Taos that morning.

A white flag broke out at the head of the on-marching Indians. Shortly a small group came forward to negotiate with Turley.

"Have you anybody in there beside yourself?" they demanded.

"Yes," said Turley. "There are eight *Americanos* here."

"Señor Turley, you are a friend of the Indians and of the *Nuevo Mejicanos*," was the next remark. "We do not wish to shed your blood. But every other American in the valley must die. Surrender these men with you and you will be spared."

That was a hard choice which Turley faced. If he surrendered the trappers, he and his family and property would be safe. He did not hesitate.

"I will never surrender my house or my men," he growled. "If you want them, you'll have to come and get them." [1]

[1] Perhaps his refusal was due in part to his distrust of the offers made. On that very day two American trappers, Markhead and William Harwood, were treacherously murdered after they trusted to peaceful offers of a similar nature. Not dreaming of danger, they permitted the Indians and Mexicans to disarm them, under assurance of safe conduct to Taos. As soon as they started a Mexican rode up behind Harwood and shot him. "I'm finished, Markhead," the trapper cried as he fell. Markhead, one of the most famous mountain men, the hero of a hundred hair's-breadth escapes, saw that his time had come. He made no attempt to resist or escape, but sat his horse until he was shot several times in the back and killed. Both were scalped and horribly mutilated. This occurred on the Rio Colorado. The same day eight other Americans were ambushed, captured and murdered near Mora. These included L. L. Waldo, Benjamin Prewitt, Romulus Culver, Louis Cabana, one Noyes and three others.

Events moved rapidly after that. At Turley's refusal, the Indians, with wild yells, scattered and took to cover in the cedar and piñon brush, and the rocks which covered the hills on each side of the narrow valley. White smoke wreaths began to curl up from the shrubbery. Like a rattle of hail the first volley of bullets thudded into the sides and roofs of the buildings. From that moment to the end of the bloody episode there was scarcely a second when the leaden balls were not smacking into the house, seeking every cranny and crack and loophole, a constant danger to the men inside.

The defenders knew exactly what they were about. No greenhorns these. Every man had been through many a "scrimmage." Shifting their quids in their jaws, they moved deliberately to points of vantage. The windows were blocked with sacks of grain and chunks of wood, leaving only narrow apertures through which the trappers aimed their long rifles. Whenever a gun spoke from Turley's mill, it generally carried death to an enemy.

TO THE FINISH

Through the whole day the fight continued—tumultuous, noisy and harmless on one side; slow and deadly on the other. Now and then a besieging Indian or Mexican fell bleeding among his bushes or rocks. By night several had been killed or wounded, while Turley's men had not yet suffered a scratch. The trappers knew they were scoring by the sight of the Mexicans down the valley carrying away the wounded.[2]

Darkness came and with it a new peril—the enemy might attack under the cover of night. Sentinels watched but the veteran mountain men wasted no lead in the gloom. Inside Turley's house they discussed the chances of escape, ran bullets, cut patches. With Turley were Albert Tarbush, William Hatfield, Louis Tolque, Peter Roberts, Joseph Marshall, John Albert, Austin and one other whose name is not recorded. All knew their chances of escape were

[2] The exact loss of the attackers in this fight was never ascertained. Benjamin M. Reed ("Illustrated History of New Mexico," p. 447) says five Indians were killed. He does not attempt to state how many Mexicans lost their lives and makes no mention of the number of wounded. The losses must, however, have been heavy.

almost nonexistent. But there was no sign of fear as they prepared in the morning to resume the fight.

During the night the attacking party, which had originally numbered about five hundred, had grown greatly. They spent the dark hours shooting at the Turley house. Some time that night a few of them sneaked through the gloom and reached the stables in the square. One of these adjoined the main building in which Turley and his men were barricaded. Here the Indians tried their best to break through the wall. Of adobe reinforced by logs, it however resisted them so well that they gave up the effort.

All at once it seemed very desirable to the Indians in the shed that they get back to their friends. To do so they had to cross a wide stretch of open ground in order to reach the far side of the enclosure. Several had already dashed to safety when the trappers noticed them. The very next man who made the attempt was a Taos chief. A rifle rang from one of the loopholes and the chief, "drilled plumb center," dropped dead in almost the exact middle of the area.

It was an instinct with most Indian tribes to try to rescue the bodies of the fallen. As the chief dropped, one of his braves ran out and tried to drag the corpse to shelter. Again the rifle spoke. The second Pueblo crumpled across the body of the first. Surely the fate of these two should have warned the others. But with brave, though foolhardy resolution, the Pueblos tried and tried to get that body. A second rescuer, followed by a third, added their bleeding forms to the heap in the corral. And now three Indians, with courage worthy of the highest admiration, rushed out together. One took the chief's legs, another his head and the third his body. Lifting together, they had started toward safety when three puffs of blue smoke sprang out from Turley's house, and all three collapsed in a pile.

As the bloody wreck fell, a single, concerted yell of rage rose from the attackers. An instant later the heaviest volley they had so far discharged, blazed at the house. For the first time two of the trappers were hit. One, shot through the loins, suffered excruciating agony. He was carried to the still house and laid on the grain in one of the bins, the softest bed which could be found for him. Both wounded men died soon.

The shooting lulled. Only seven defenders were left and their ammunition was running low. The Indians and Mexicans had lost heavily. Both sides rested.

Shortly after noon the attack began again. The Americans, unruffled and calm, watched with keen eyes for any exposure of their enemies and made every shot tell. In spite of this the besiegers succeeded in setting fire to the mill. It blazed up in a shower of sparks and smoke. This new danger was met only by the greatest effort on the part of Turley and his men, but they succeeded in quenching the flames before they spread to the rest of the structure.

While the trappers were busy with the blaze, the Indians occupied all the out buildings on the other side of the corral. There they vented their anger in typical Indian fashion by slaughtering Turley's hogs and sheep. Fires kept breaking out in different parts of the defenses.[3] It was increasingly apparent that the place could not be held another twelve hours.

Turley called a second council of war. The trappers voted to wait until night. Then each was to make his escape as he could. Darkness fell at last. Suddenly the wild trapper yell rang out. Together they charged forth, long rifles cracking. John Albert and a companion rushed through the little postern gate, firing their guns right into the faces of the enemy, then leaped forward with clubbed rifles. As his comrade was beaten down, Albert threw himself under the fence. There he lay in the darkness, listening to the other trapper's screams as they clubbed and stabbed him to death. The Indians thought Albert had escaped and made no search for him. Later he found a chance to get clear away, reached the mountains and eventually a rendezvous of his friends near the present site of Pueblo, Colorado.[4] Two others also escaped and got to Santa Fé.

[3] The Pueblos were probably using fire arrows, although the chronicle does not say so.

[4] It is to this circumstance that we owe the preservation of the story of the defense of Turley's Mill. George Frederick Ruxton was at the rendezvous when Albert reached it. He heard the story from Albert's own lips and later included it in his book, "Wild Life in the Rocky Mountains," pp. 135–145.

The crowning tragedy befell Simeon Turley himself. Having risked and lost for his friends, he broke through the cordon. He reached the mountains and was hiding when he saw approaching a Mexican he had known for years. Turley stepped out from his hiding place and asked for help. He offered his valuable watch for the use of the Mexican's horse, although the animal was not worth half as much. The Mexican refused, pretended pity, and rode away, promising to bring help. As fast as his horse could carry him he galloped to the mill and told the Indians where Turley hid. A little later they found him and mercilessly killed him.

5: THE STORMING OF TAOS PUEBLO

It must have been a "morning after" feeling with which the Taos Indians surveyed the results of their orgy of bloodshed and looting. A few days of retrospection showed them that the outbreak would have most dire consequences. In the first place, although they were gorgeously successful at Taos, things grew more difficult for them every hour after that. Turley's Mill was a bitter lesson. Considering their losses they may well have felt the results hardly justified.

Then they learned, with disquieting suddenness, that their Mexican allies were already regretting their part in the revolt. Word of the massacre at Taos reached Price at Santa Fé on the 20th, brought by Charles Towne, one of two Americans who escaped from the slaughter. Sterling Price was a man of prompt action. Within three days he had concentrated his troops at Santa Fé and was on the march northward. A second expedition under Captain Isaac R. Hendley started from Las Vegas at about the same time, but was driven back from Mora, in a sharp fight in which Hendley was killed. Captain Morin revenged him on February 1st, when he returned to the town, attacked it, and destroyed everything in it.

While this was going on, Price's force marched rapidly toward Taos. The American army included a battery of four 12-pound howitzers, three hundred and fifty-three infantry and—in many respects the most formidable of all—a company of "calvalry," sixty-five mounted men led by the redoubtable Ceran St. Vrain. These cavalrymen doubtless had a motley look. But they were more to be dreaded, man-for-man, than any other body of fighters in the whole American force. They called themselves "the Avengers." They were led by a mountain man whose dearest friend was the murdered Governor Bent. And in their muster roll were many other mountain men, long, lean, buckskin clad, whose fine instinct for killing had been whetted by the death of some comrade or friend at Taos, Mora, the Rio Colorado or Turley's Mill.

With growing dread the Taos Indians heard of Price's approach. He met the Mexicans at La Cañada on January 24th, 1847. They outnumbered him three to one, but he routed them with a brief cannonade and a sharp charge. Four days later he was joined, at Luceros, by Captain Burgwin and his company of United States dragoons.

Next day after receiving this accession to his forces, Price reached a canyon leading to the village of Embudo, where he found six hundred and fifty of the enemy posted along both sides of the gorge. But Burgwin's dragoons took one side and St. Vrain's "Avengers" the other, and the Mexicans were chased out with a whoop. Pablo Chaves, one of the leaders in the uprising, was killed in the short battle.

So, after twice beating and scattering the Mexicans, Price reached Taos, on the afternoon of February 3rd. It was the day of reckoning. The Taos Indians, deserted by most of their quondam friends, faced the white men alone.

Taos Pueblo consisted then, as now, of two large buildings, both several stories high, flanked by a church and some smaller structures, such as stables and granaries. The sparkling waters of Taos Creek splashed and bubbled between the main structures. The whole was at that time surrounded by a high wall of adobe brick and pickets. It was the larger northern pueblo which the Indians selected in which to make their final stand.

There were, of course, no doors or windows in the pueblo's first story. Ladders gave the only way up and these had been withdrawn. The church, also of thick adobe construction, had been adapted for defense by piercing its walls with loopholes. Part of the Indians were inside of this structure. All in all the Pueblos presented a formidable appearance as Price deployed his army before them.

So confident were the Indians that they wasted some energy and breath in shrill yells of defiance. But Price went into action at once. Lieutenant Dyer, commanding the battery of artillery, was ordered up with his howitzers. The guns were unlimbered, and for two hours they bombarded the west side of the old church, but its thick adobe walls swallowed up the cannon balls in their spongy mass and refused to breach. Evening was approaching. The troops were exhausted by their long march. Price decided to withdraw to the town, to rest.

As his soldiers drew away from before the pueblo, the Indians thought they were retreating. Loud were the taunts and jeers they sent after the Americans.

THE PUNISHMENT OF THE PUEBLOS

With some consternation they saw the troops returning next morning and realized they had been mistaken in supposing that Price was in retreat the previous evening.

The American leader made his dispositions carefully this time. He placed Burgwin's veteran dragoons, with two of the howitzers, west of the pueblo. St. Vrain and his "Avengers," their hard jaws grimly closed, sat their horses on the east, to prevent the escape of any fugitives to the mountains. The infantry formed north of the pueblo with the remaining guns in front of them.

With thunderous reports and white clouds of smoke, the first shots of the artillery were fired at 9 o'clock that morning of February 4th. For two hours the dull, shattering booming of the heavy guns echoed from mountain to mountain. Then Price, at 11 o'clock, ordered a charge. It was an old-fashioned military charge, with ranks dressed, officers waving flashing swords in front, drums rolling and fifes squeaking. Captains Aubrey and Barber, and Lieutenant Broon stepped forward gallantly at the head of the infantry. At the same time Captains Burgwin and McMillin surged forward from the west with their heavy dragoons.

Instantly the Indians in the pueblo and church opened a furious fire. The charging infantry and the dragoons alike made for the church, whose high, bluff walls offered shelter from the galling fusillade from the pueblo. There the whole contingent took refuge, safe for the time being under the western walls, since the loopholes above were so cut that the guns of the defenders could not be depressed sufficiently to shoot men immediately below them.

The soldiers were busy. Some of them, with axes, began an attack on the thick wall. Others hastily constructed a makeshift ladder and, climbing to the roof, set it on fire. Holes were presently chopped through the church walls and through these the men tossed lighted shells by hand into the interior, the projectiles bursting murderously inside.

The church door faced the corral, and the pueblo to the east. Captain Burgwin decided that if he could batter down that door, he could more quickly win the fight. Calling to his men, the reckless young officer clambered over the adobe wall of the enclosure and tried to beat down the door. A number of the dragoons joined him. But the move was both foolish and fatal. What Burgwin had done placed his detachment at the mercy of the Indians behind them in the pueblo. A storm of bullets and arrows beat on the troops. Burgwin reeled with a bullet in him, then fell. Several other soldiers were hit. The Indian shooting was wickedly deadly at this point. It did not take the troops long to realize that. Carrying their wounded, the survivors tumbled over the fence again and ran to the safety of the church wall. The attempt to batter down the door had been a costly failure.[1]

Meanwhile Price had sent the big guns up to within sixty yards of the church, where by shooting at places already breached by the axes of the soldiers, a gaping hole was blasted at last. Through this the troops crowded. They found the church full of smoke from the burning roof and the bursting shells. Gasping for air they groped forward. But the enemy was gone. The defenders had scuttled out of the east side as the soldiers entered the west.

Part of the Indians, fleeing from the church, attempted to reach the main pueblo. But the rest ran for the mountains—a tragic decision. For there, grim and deadly, waited St. Vrain and his "Avengers."

[1] Burgwin was shot, not by a Pueblo, but by a Delaware Indian known on the frontier as "Big Negro" who was trapping in the country at the time and espoused the cause of the Taos insurrectionists. He escaped after the fight, to the Cheyennes. This warrior killed five Americans in the corral before the church door. His wife, Pin Dassa, a Mexican woman, stood on top of the pueblo and loaded guns for her husband throughout the fight.

Now rose the long trapper yell and the mountain men rode down their foes. In vain the wretched Pueblos doubled and dodged and tried to hide. With his own hand St. Vrain shot down Jesus Tafoya, a Mexican who had been one of the chief factors in bringing the Taos Pueblos into the revolt. Tafoya was wearing the coat and shirt of the dead Governor Bent when he was killed. Later, seeing an Indian lying by the roadside apparently dead, St. Vrain dismounted to examine him. Only shamming, the savage leaped up and grappled with the leader of the mountain men. The Indian was a powerful athlete; the chief of "the Avengers" was slight and growing old. It might have meant St. Vrain's death had not another famous trapper, Uncle Dick Wooton, ridden up behind and brained the warrior with a tomahawk. Out of fifty-three or -four fugitives who left the church and tried to reach the mountains, fifty-one were killed.

Night fell and hostilities ceased. Price quartered his troops in the church and other buildings west of the pueblo, prepared to resume battle in the morning. But the Pueblos had more than enough. They saw now how they had been duped by the Mexicans. Already they had lost one hundred and fifty killed out of six hundred and fifty persons in the pueblo, to say nothing of the wounded. At dawn the Taos Indians, men and women, came out bearing white flags and crucifixes, and on their knees begged for mercy. Price granted it. But he spared them only on condition that they surrender the chief Tomasito and a number of other leaders, to stand trial for the murder of Governor Bent.

In the following weeks a grim tribunal sat in Taos Village. On the bench was flint-faced old Judge Beaubien, whose son had been killed by the Indians. Among the witnesses against the prisoners were the widow of Governor Bent and the wife of Kit Carson, who had witnessed the governor's death.

With unmoved countenance Tomasito heard these women point him out as the slayer of Bent. He did not intend to hang for the deed. Nor did he. Before the date of the execution, Tomasito made a break for freedom and was shot to death by the guards.

It is not likely that the Indians had much chance with the carefully hand-picked jury which included only Americans and New Mexicans whose sentiments were well known and "safe." [2] On February 9th, six of them, found guilty of the murders in Taos, were hanged from the same gallows, in the presence of the army and the people. It was the final act in the tragic drama. Never again did the Pueblo Indians deviate from the strict path of peace and loyalty to the United States government.

[2] Illustrating the attitude taken toward the prisoners is the case of Juror Baptiste Brown, a trapper by trade, and a French-Canadian. Juror Brown slept through most of the proceedings, but as soon as the jury room was reached, and without consulting the rest of the veniremen, shouted: "Hang them all! They may not be guilty now, but they soon will be!" (Colonel Henry Inman, "The Old Santa Fé Trail," p. 136.)

6: THE COMING OF THE *PINDA LICK-O-YI*

APACHERIA AGAIN

EVEN before the Taos Indians made their one wild bid for independence from the white man in northern New Mexico, uneasy word of the American invasion reached the Apaches in the southern part of the territory. Mangus Colorado received the news perhaps by messenger from his ally Gian-na-tah (Always Ready), chief of the Mescalero Apaches to the east of the Mimbreño country. The word was that the Mexicans had fought the white men from the other side of the plains and had been beaten. And the soldiers of the victorious *Pinda Lick-o-yi*, the White Eyes, were marching upon Apacheria.

Such news must sorely have troubled the Mimbreño chief. Not that he was surprised at the defeat of the Mexicans; his own warriors had whipped them so often that his respect for them had long departed. But Mangus Colorado had tested the mettle of the American trappers and miners and found them of tougher fibre than the Mexicans. The White Eyes, for example, were not given to panics. Even when taken by surprise, their movements had a surety and a deliberate, deadly purpose.

Apache scouts paralleled the column of General Kearny every foot of the way after he reached southern New Mexico in the autumn of 1846. Marching rapidly from his almost bloodless conquest of Santa Fé, with California as his objective, the American general stopped briefly at the Copper Mines. He was met by Mangus Colorado and some of his chiefs near the mines, at San Lucia Springs.

The Apaches thoroughly approved of the American war on the

279

Mexicans. One of the chiefs spoke thus: "You have taken New Mexico and will soon take California; go, then, take Chihuahua, Durango, Sonora. We will help you . . . the Mexicans are rascals; we hate and kill them all." [1] Greatly to the relief of the Indians, Kearny moved on after buying from them some mules and horses. The first American invasion ended bloodlessly.

But not for long were the Apaches unmolested. The great tide of empire was about to move west. On February 9th, 1848, James W. Marshall, overseer of a grist mill in California, found a glittering stone in the mill race. It was a gold nugget, as he instantly knew. The mill belonged to Captain John A. Sutter, and was situated on the American River, an affluent of the Sacramento. Sutter and Marshall tried to hush up the matter, but to keep such news from spreading was impossible. By May, 1848, the whole nation knew that gold had been found in fabulous quantities in California.

At once began the strange, hysterical stampede known as the "California Gold Rush." Cold, heat, hunger, and every imaginable peril failed to stop it. Trampling their way westward, the gold seekers thrust out of their road or slaughtered the Indians who lived in the country. Almost overnight life changed for the aborigines. They found themselves in the path of a crazed typhoon of humanity, charging desperately west, deaf to every consideration except the desire to get to the coast to dig gold—gold—gold.[2]

Inevitably the Indians fought back. They began to attack the wagon trains, and bloody tales come down to us from those days when the emigrants fought for their lives on the way to California across the desert country.[3]

---

[1] J. P. Dunn, "Massacres of the Mountains," p. 365.

[2] "What effect did this discovery (of gold in California) have on the Indians? It was fraught with greater evil for them than any other one event in the history of America, except the discovery of America itself." (*Ibid.*, p. 125.)

[3] The famous Oatman massacre, which has received so much attention from writers of Southwestern history, was typical. The Oatman family was attacked by a band of nineteen Tonto Apaches, as it was crossing the Gila at what is now known as Oatman Flat, April 18th, 1854. The father and mother, two daughters and one son, were killed. The other son, Lorenzo, was left for dead. With the loot from the wagons and the two surviving Oatman girls, Olive and Mary Ann, the Apaches slunk way. Lorenzo was rescued by friendly Pima Indians. Nursed back to health, he began a search for his sisters. It was five years before he once more saw his sister

The California Gold Rush did not at first directly affect the Mimbreños. Their country was out of the line of travel. But after the Guadalupe-Hidalgo Treaty closed the Mexican War, the work of surveying the Mexican-United States border began, and in 1851 J. R. Bartlett, at the head of the American Surveying Commission, reached Santa Rita.

The arrival of the surveyors, with their strong military guard and large retinue, was a complete surprise to at least one redoubtable Mimbreño chief. Cuchillo Negro, seeing a lone white man riding through the country, ambushed him in a little grove of trees. The rider, all unconscious of peril, came into the net spread for him, and suddenly found himself surrounded by a score of Apaches, as deadly as so many rattlesnakes coiled to strike.[4]

The lone white rider was Captain John C. Cremony, interpreter for the Bartlett expedition. He had every reason to be frightened out of his wits, but he acted calmly, if instantaneously. Jerking his revolver from its holster, he sank his spurs into his horse's flanks, causing the animal to bound forward right beside the Indian whom Cremony took to be chief. The captain's judgment was unerring. Cuchillo Negro found himself looking down the barrel of the officer's pistol. At his signal, knowing death was near him, the warriors stopped their stealthy, circling approach. An astonishing colloquy followed.

Surrounded by Apaches, and preserving his existence only as long as he kept Cuchillo Negro under the muzzle of his pistol, Cremony had the temerity to jeer at the chief because he had been so lax in his watchfulness as to allow a party of white men to enter his country without knowing it. He told the Mimbreño that he was the forerunner of a large body of Americans. The Apache replied that Cremony lied; that, if there were many with him, he would never have wandered thus foolishly through the Mimbreño country alone. But

Olive. The other girl, Mary Ann, died of hardships and exposure. Olive's strange and fascinating story of captivity among the Indians has been the subject of many books and articles.

[4] Cuchillo Negro was not on the war path but hunting. That made little difference to him, however. It was too good an opportunity to overlook. An Apache, particularly this one, could change at any time, on a moment's notice, from a peaceful hunter to a warrior.

presently the glint of many rifle barrels showed through the trees, and the doughty captain allowed his *vis-à-vis* to slink away.

Bartlett's party camped near the ruins of Santa Rita. The commissioner was visited shortly by Mangus Colorado himself. The chief told Bartlett he had been following the commission several days: that the Apaches had been near the white encampments throughout the journey. The Indians were uneasy, fearing the Americans had come to stay. Bartlett assured them he was there only temporarily. For a time things went along peacefully. But that ended as might have been expected.

WHITE LAW AGAINST APACHE LAW

Taking advantage of the presence of the Bartlett party, three Mexican traders came to the Copper Mines, as they would otherwise never have dared to do, bringing with them a beautiful fifteen-year-old Mexican girl named Inez Gonzales. She had been captured by the Pinal Apaches and later sold to these traders. The Mexicans were taking her to Santa Fé, probably to sell her or keep her for immoral purposes, the usual fate of such slaves. Bartlett interfered and released her, restoring her to her relatives a few weeks later.[5]

Without emotion the Apaches watched this little drama. But a few days later it came directly home to them. Two Mexican boys, Savero Aredia, thirteen years old, and José Trinfan, eleven, were prisoners in the Indian camp. They saw the rescue of Inez and decided to take advantage of the same opportunity.

One evening they darted into Cremony's tent, begging for his protection. The captain heard their story and took them to Bartlett. Almost on his heels came the Apache chiefs to demand the return of their property. Mangus Colorado, in person, headed the delegation and was its chief spokesman. He outlined the position of his people as follows:

---

[5] The sequel to the fair Inez's adventures is interesting: "Inez was returned to her parents by the commissioner when he arrived in Santa Cruz. She subsequently became the mistress of Captain Gomez, who commanded the troops in northern Sonora. He married her at the death of his wife, and after his death, Inez married the *alcalde* of Santa Cruz, her social standing not having been at all affected by her romantic adventures."—Dunn, "Massacres of the Mountains," p. 366.

"You came into our country. You were well received. Your lives, your property, your animals were safe. You passed by ones, by twos, by threes through our country. You went and came in peace. Your strayed animals were always brought home to you again. Our wives, our women and children came here and visited your houses. We were friends—we were brothers! Believing this, we came among you and brought our captives, relying on it that we were brothers and that you would feel as we feel. We concealed nothing. We came not secretly nor in the night. We came in open day, and before your faces, and showed our captives to you. We believed your assurances of friendship, and we trusted them. *Why did you take our captives from us?"* [6]

Bartlett was in an awkward position from the standpoint of logic. At the very moment there were millions of Negro slaves in the South. He did his best to explain the attitude of the United States on slavery—as practiced by somebody else. Finally, in desperation, he offered to pay for the captives. The reply was surprising:

"The brave who owns these captives does not want to sell. He has had one of these boys six years. He grew up under him. His heart strings are bound around him. He is as a son in his old age. . . . Money cannot buy affection. His heart cannot be sold. He taught him to string the bow and wield the lance. He loves the boy and cannot sell him."

The boys, apparently, were being adopted into the tribe, a common practice among the Indians of that time and section. But there was nothing Bartlett could do about it. The United States had bound all its officers, by the Treaty of Guadalupe-Hidalgo, to release all Mexican slaves and stop the traffic in them. At last he prevailed upon the Apaches to accept about two hundred dollars' worth of trade goods for the boys. The Indians departed in ill humor, but still remained non-hostile.

Once more things moved serenely. Mangus Colorado, with some three hundred Mimbreño warriors and their families, camped on a rise four miles from Santa Rita. Delgadito, with another band, was

[6] These conversations are quoted verbatim by Cremony. ("Life Among the Apaches," pp. 62–66.)

at the Warm Springs. Four hundred Navajos moved down presently and established a village in the Gila Valley, twenty-eight miles from the Copper Mines. Still the white men of the boundary commission, in twos or threes, hunted or carried on their various errands, moving through the Indian country without molestation.

A climactic incident occurred July 6th. Jesus Lopez, a Mexican laborer employed by the commission, causelessly shot an Apache warrior during a petty argument. Many Indians were in the camp at the time, including Mangus Colorado himself. As the Mexican's shot sounded, they ran out and mounted their ponies, riding wildly away in panic. Too well they remembered the massacre by Johnson at this same place. Bartlett placed the murderer under arrest and sent word to the Apaches that he had done so.

The chiefs cautiously reappeared. As soon as they saw that Bartlett was sincere in his friendly position, they demanded the murderer's life. The commissioner, hampered by law, could not summarily execute the man, guilty as Lopez was. Bartlett could only promise a trial in Santa Fé and an execution there. But that did not coincide with Apache ideas.

"This is all very good," said Poncé. "The Apaches know the Americans are their friends. . . . They know that the Americans do not speak with two tongues. . . . They know that you will do what you say. But the Apaches will not be satisfied to *hear* that the murderer has been punished in Santa Fé. They want to *see* him punished here, at the Copper Mines, where the band of the dead brave may see him put to death—where all the Apaches may see him put to death." [7]

Bartlett made a counter-proposal that he keep the murderer in chains and make him work, giving the money he earned to the family of the slain man.

"Money will not satisfy an Apache for the blood of a brave," exclaimed Poncé with scorn. He could not understand such reasoning at all. Did the White Eye think one could purchase honor with gold? Or bribe an Apache to forego his vengeance? Poncé simply could not follow the reasoning.

[7] Cremony, "Life Among the Apaches," pp. 68–69.

In the end, Bartlett had to refuse the Indians' demands. Every face was sullen as the Apaches left camp. Within a few days horses and mules began to disappear from the commission's herd, so fast that within a month nearly two hundred were gone.

Proof that the Mimbreños were guilty of stealing the animals came when Delgadito was seen leading one of the raiding bands. The Americans did not retaliate. There was, indeed, no time for it. The commission had to move on about its business.

Almost afoot Bartlett's party went on its way. And to Mangus Colorado and his chiefs, there could be but one reason for the departure: they believed they had driven the White Eyes away.

7: THE WAY OF THE WHITE MAN

MANGUS COLORADO IS FLOGGED

DURING the stay of the United States Boundary Commission at Santa Rita that summer of 1851, gold was discovered at Piños Altos, northwest of the Copper Mines. Men at once flocked thither and began to work the diggings. By the time Bartlett moved on, there was a settlement of one hundred and forty miners, and they remained behind, fully confident of their ability to maintain themselves even in the heart of the Apache country.

Their presence was a cause of keenest anxiety to the Apaches, particularly Mangus Colorado. The Red Sleeves had succeeded beyond all expectations in removing the Bartlett party, using—from an Apache viewpoint—most pacific means. He now turned his diplomatic talents to removing the miners.

By long hours of observation from cover, he became convinced of a puzzling truth. The strange white men labored and sweated among the sizzling rocks for nothing more important or usable than the yellow metal which the White Eyes called gold and which the Mexicans knew as *oro*. Since getting gold was their sole desire, his reasoning ran, the best way to induce them to leave the Apache country would be to show them where there was more gold than at Piños Altos.

It was good reasoning, but Mangus Colorado failed to count upon the suspiciousness of the White Eyes. Pursuing his plan, he one day ventured near the mining camp and spoke to one of the miners. He had a smattering of Spanish and perhaps the miner knew a little Apache. At any rate he succeeded in making the white man understand that if he would accompany Mangus Colorado, he would be shown where there was much *oro* to be found—far more than could be scratched out of the rocks at Piños Altos.

The miner had no intention of trusting himself alone with this fierce savage. He put the Indian off with an excuse. Later, Mangus

Colorado, still working under his great idea, approached a second miner with the same proposition.

It is quite probable that the Mimbreño was telling the truth. There was much gold in the section and it would not be strange that he knew where some of it was. But no Piños Altos miner would believe that an Apache would take so much interest in him, unless for the purpose of luring him out of the reach of friends and murdering him. And that idea stuck in their minds in spite of Mangus Colorado's patient, oft-reiterated explanation that he only wanted them to leave Piños Altos and go peacefully to the country of the Mexicans.

After a time one of the miners, probably drunk, suggested that they tie the chief up and whip him. It sounded like a capital idea; it appealed to the brutal frontier sense of humor. One kept the Apache in conversation. Others sneaked behind him. All at once a dozen men leaped on him. In spite of his bull strength he was borne to the ground.

Rawhide cords were lashed about the great wrists. The straining arms were spread-eagled on a tree and a brawny miner rolled up his sleeves as he picked up a blacksnake whip . . .

There is no record that Mangus Colorado winced or uttered a sound while the lash bit deeper and deeper into his flesh, cutting the skin of his back to ghastly ribbons, bringing the blood in streaming rivulets to trickle down his legs. He was no longer young, but an Apache knew how to bear agony without a sign. They finished at last. Then they released him and jeered at him as he staggered out of camp.

They could not have made a greater mistake. Better for the whole white population of the Southwest would it have been had they finished by killing him. Mangus Colorado stumbled forth from the Piños Altos settlement a changed man. In spite of Johnson's massacre at Santa Rita; in spite of Bartlett and the Mexican murderer; in spite of a score of other causes for action, he had tried to remain friendly with the White Eyes. But that whipping changed all that. He never forgot it. Deeper than the wounds on his lacerated back were the wounds in his heart. It was the greatest insult that could be inflicted even on an ordinary Indian. And Mangus Colorado was a great chief. He devoted the rest of his life to avenging his shame.

Thereafter Mangus Colorado wore a shirt to conceal the puckered weals. And each day he sought with savage concentration to wipe out the dishonor in blood. Never before had the Apaches seen a chief so single-purposed in destruction. Never before had they seen one who raided so incessantly, harrying the settlements in New Mexico and Arizona and even going out into the plains of Texas in search of ease for his scarred back. The White Eyes and Mexicans who died slowly, lingering out their mortal hours in agony under the Apache torment, were many.[1] And even more were those who died quickly, in the heat of a rush, with lances running red.

THE AFFRONT TO COCHISE

Among all the Apache chiefs, Cochise, the snake-like Chiricahua, was closest to Mangus Colorado's heart. The Chiricahua Apaches lived to the west of the Mimbreños and shared with them the grazing lands between the Warm Springs and the Chiricahua Mountains, a broad stretch of fine pasture unequalled in all of Apacheria. They were war partners of old with the Mimbreños and, in the old, good days before the *Pinda Lick-o-yi* descended on the desert country like grasshoppers for numbers and like lobo wolves for grimness, had shared often with Mangus Colorado's people in the fierce, bloody raids down into Mexico.

Mangus Colorado had bound to him by diplomacy or fear all of the great Apache leaders. There was Gian-na-tah, who led the Mescaleros in the flat, bitter alkali, east country, and Piah, of the White Mountains, who dwelt to the northwest, and Hash-kai-la of the Coyoteros, whose land stretched north toward the cold Navajo

[1] The following from Cremony ("Life Among the Apaches," p. 267) is a good description of a typical piece of Mangus Colorado's work: A party of Mexicans having been captured, "each man was seized, bound to the wheel of a wagon, head downward, about eighteen inches from the ground, a fire made under them and their brains roasted from their heads. The women and children were carried off captive. . . . As I was the first to pass through Cooke's Canyon after this affair, the full horror of the torture was rendered terribly distinct. The bursted heads, the agonized contortions of the facial muscles among the dead, and the terrible destiny certain to attend the living . . . were horribly depicted in my mind."

plateaus, and others. These men waited on Mangus Colorado's word. But to Cochise only did the Red Sleeves give his friendship. The great Mimbreño's comeliest daughter, offspring of the Mexican *señorita* for whom he had fought a double duel, was given to Cochise for wife. Often the two blew a cloud together in council.

At first Cochise hung back from warring against the White Eyes, although he had always been willing to foray into Mexico. But one day a thing occurred which made him as eager as was ever Mangus Colorado himself for the blood of the invaders.

Living on the Sonoita River was an Irishman named Johnny Ward [2] with his Mexican mistress and her son. The woman had been a prisoner among the Apaches and the boy was born while she was thus a captive, the father being an Apache warrior. After her rescue with the child, Ward gave her a home in his ranch shack.

One October day, in 1860, while the Irishman was away, a raiding band of Apaches rode up to the house, plundered it, and drove off a herd of cattle. They also carried away the child.[3] Ward returned to find the destruction wrought, and rode a horse "into the ground" to reach Fort Buchanan, twelve miles away, and get help.

Sixty men were promptly dispatched by the commandant of the post, Colonel Pitcairn Morrison, with orders to search for the missing cattle and child. Lieutenant George N. Bascom, fresh out of West Point, with all of a newly created shavetail's cockiness, commanded the detachment.

Through the heart of the Chiricahua Mountains slashes the deep and narrow Apache Pass, up which went the stage road. Best proof of the peacefulness of the Chiricahuas at this time is the fact that the stage line was in operation, without molestation, through the middle of their range. About halfway up the pass was a stone stage station. The station keeper, a man named Wallace, was one of Cochise's friends and had contracted with the chief and his people to supply the wood for the station. To better furnish this wood, the Chiricahuas camped near, at some springs about six hundred yards away.

[2] The name is also given as Wadsworth.

[3] This boy grew up among the Apaches. He is believed to be Mickey Free, who later became an interpreter and scout for the United States Army during the Geronimo days.

Bascom knew of the peaceful camp at the springs and headed straight that way. When he arrived with his troops, Wallace offered to go to Cochise's village and tell him why they had come. Presently the chief himself, accompanied by several of his people, came to Bascom's camp. The lieutenant was sure the missing cattle were in Cochise's village—on what evidence nobody knows. He opened his negotiations by ordering the chief to surrender the cattle and child, threatening him with military punishment unless he did so. Cochise seemed at a loss to know what cattle or what child Bascom meant. As for the soldier's threat, he treated that as a joke at first—he could not believe that the officer was serious in such an absurd declaration.[4]

Bascom was short tempered and grew furious. So sure was he that Cochise's band was guilty that he made a move which was dangerous, impolitic, even fatal. He ordered the arrest of Cochise and all his warriors, in spite of the fact that they had come into his camp under a flag of truce, and announced his intention of holding them as hostages for the return of the cattle and the boy.

Now for the first time Cochise realized that the officer was in earnest. The whole complexion of the affair changed from the jocular to the deadly serious.

Arrest Cochise? Not while he was able to fight. A war whoop like a panther's scream burst from his lips, and like a panther he leaped for freedom. So instantaneous was his charge that the ranks of the soldiers failed to hold him. Right through them he dashed, with part of his warriors at his heels. A volley fired after him wounded him, but did not disable him. Five of the slowest braves were seized by the soldiers and imprisoned.

Wounded though he was, Cochise ran like a deer up the slope with the bullets spatting around him. His people rallied. A ragged volley broke out from the heights. Bascom began to realize that he had a serious situation on his hands. Heavier and heavier grew the Apache fire. Several soldiers were hit. The rest dove behind the rails of the mail corral from which they fought off the Indians until dark.

[4] Brigadier General B. J. D. Irwin, writing of this incident in "The Infantry Journal," April, 1928, says that Cochise "scoffed at the idea of force being brought there to compel obedience on his part." This is perfect proof of Cochise's failure to understand Bascom's attitude.

Late that night the Overland Mail coach from California struggled up to the corral. One horse had been left dead on the trail behind, the driver's leg was shattered by a bullet, and a passenger was shot through the chest. Apaches had attacked it down the pass. By a miracle the plucky driver succeeded in cutting the dead horse loose and getting the rest of the frightened animals to pull the stage up the pass. That was the last Overland coach to traverse Apache Pass in many long months.

There were several wounded men in the corral by this time. As night fell, a daring soldier volunteered to attempt to reach Fort Buchanan, which lay to the westward, with a message for help. He led a mule over the steep hillside of the canyon wall after dark, and actually succeeded in reaching the mail station at Dragoon Springs, from which he rode in safety to the post with news of Bascom's peril.

REPRISAL

Early next morning an Indian woman, who had been held prisoner overnight, was freed and told to inform Cochise that the hostages held by the troops were to be taken to Fort Buchanan. A few minutes later the chief himself appeared with a white flag—the protection of which he still seemed to trust—and asked for a conference. Accompanied by two soldiers and the stage employees, Wallace, Jordon and Lyons, Bascom went forward. The stage men could not believe that Cochise had really turned hostile. They knew him so well that they went along voluntarily to mediate. But it was a different Cochise they found. Gone was the friendly, quiet, affable Indian. In his place was a savage with a flint-rock face and a burning heart. Their friendly pleadings fell on deaf ears.

Suddenly a lookout on the roof of the station house signalled that some Indians were hiding in a ravine close behind Cochise. Bascom smelled treachery and began a retreat. At the movement the hidden Apaches leaped out and dashed forward to surround the party. Rifles crackled. Several bullets cut the young lieutenant's clothing, but he was unwounded. Wallace and his two companions had mingled with Cochise's party. They were seized and dragged away.

While this was taking place, Cochise's imprisoned warriors in the soldiers' camp made a bold attempt to escape. One slashed a slit in the tent which held them, and led the dash. But the guard was alert. A bullet laid one ducking, buck-jumping fugitive low. Another was knocked down and horribly transfixed to the ground by a bayonet. The rest were overpowered and bound.

Bascom and his two soldiers had reached the corral safely. The situation was desperate. There had been a heavy snowfall and all the nearer snow was gathered and melted to water the men and horses. But it lasted only a few hours. The springs were six hundred yards away. By the third day the stock was going crazy for water. Bascom divided the herd and sent a part to the springs, holding the rest at the corral. As the horses approached the springs, the Apaches pounced down upon them. There was a sharp roll of rifle fire and the guard fell back, carrying several wounded. The horses were in the hands of the Indians.

But help was on the way. When the first news reached Fort Buchanan, Captain B. J. D. Irwin volunteered to lead fifteen men to Bascom's relief. Colonel Morrison sent a courier to Fort Breckenridge, a hundred miles northwest, asking for two troops of cavalry to be sent to Apache Pass. Irwin started at once on his ride toward Bascom. As his small detachment approached the pass, it ran into a handful of Indians driving off some cattle. There was a sharp brush, the soldiers captured the cattle and took three warriors prisoners. Then they resumed their journey.

That night Cochise placed a cloud of braves at each end of the pass. A small train of five wagons, whose teamsters knew nothing of the sudden hostility of the Chiricahuas, blundered into the hands of the Apaches. Next day, when Irwin passed the place, he found the wagons burned and plundered. Lashed to their wheels were the charred remains of eight human bodies—the first victims of Cochise's reprisal. And the Indians had carried off into the mountains three prisoners from the same train, who were to be found later.

A stroke of uncanny good luck saved Irwin's party from the same ambush. After the herd of horses was captured from Bascom, part of Cochise's warriors drove the animals down the pass and out on the west side of the mountains. While they were running them toward the level country, the Indians saw a company of infantry on the march, changing station from Fort Breckenridge to Fort Bliss. The troops did not see the Indians, but the warriors followed the command, thinking it might be marching to the east side of the pass to attack Cochise from the rear. In doing so, they left the western entrance open for a few hours. During that brief period Irwin entered the pass, marched up it and reached Bascom with his reinforcements and the three Indian prisoners.

Stories vary as to what next took place. One account says that Cochise brought his trembling captives—the three stage attendants and the three men from the captured wagon train—to a place in full sight of the white camp and called out that he would exchange them for the warriors held in Bascom's camp. This is not mentioned in Irwin's story. In any case no exchange was made. A little later the two troops of cavalry arrived from Fort Breckenridge and Cochise withdrew to the high peaks.

Next day the soldiers left the pass. As they marched down it they noticed a flock of buzzards circling in the heights some distance to the right of the trail. Scouts were sent to investigate. At their approach more of the obscene birds flopped heavily up among the trees. And now the horrid feast upon which they had been gorging was seen. There were the remains of the six unfortunates Cochise had captured—Wallace, Lyons, Jordon and the wagon train men—tortured to death and left for the vultures.

Bascom and Irwin, at the insistence of the latter, immediately executed six of their prisoners on the same spot and left them hanging there for Cochise to cut down.[5] One of the Apaches hanged was the

[5] "It was then and there that it was determined to execute an equal number of Indian warriors confined at the mail station. The silly fabrication that a game of chance decided their fate is as absurd and groundless as the ridiculous assertion that I objected to their execution and wanted to take them to the post of Fort Buchanan. So far from having remonstrated against their merited punishment, it was I who suggested their summary execution, man for man. On Bascom's expressing reluctance to resort to the extreme measure proposed, I urged my right to dispose of the lives of the three prisoners captured by me, after which he then acceded to the retal-

warrior who had been stabbed in the stomach by a bayonet when he attempted to escape. In spite of the terrible nature of his wound, he was forced to walk a mile and a half to his place of execution.

The old Mosaic law had been obeyed. An eye had been demanded for an eye, and a tooth for a tooth. It was war to the knife now between Cochise and the white man. The Apaches never really ceased fighting for a quarter of a century after that. Thousands of lives and an inestimable amount of property were destroyed because of the treachery toward Mangus Colorado and Cochise.

---

iatory proposition and agreed that those prisoners and three of the hostages taken by him should be brought there and executed, which after full and deliberate consideration was accordingly done. . . . The punishment was an extreme mode of reprisal but was demanded and justified by the persistent acts of treachery and the atrocious cruelties perpetrated by the most cowardly tribe of savages infesting the territory." —General B. J. D. Irwin's article, "The Apache Pass Fight," in the April, 1928, issue of "The Infantry Journal."

This article, written by General Irwin in 1887, was published posthumously. The general's contention that the hanging of the six prisoners was "merited punishment" is hard to follow. None of the six had anything to do with torturing the six white men. Three of them were imprisoned when they came to Bascom's camp under a flag of truce. The other three were captured out on the desert, in the fight over the stolen cattle. The names of four of the Apaches killed by Bascom and Irwin were later given by the Apaches as Sanza, Kla-de-tahe, Niyo-kahe and Gopi.

8: MANGUS COLORADO EVENS THE SCORE

WHEN Beauregard's guns opened their thunderous bombardment of Fort Sumter, April 12th, 1861, they loosed consequences so far-reaching that people even so remote as the white frontiersmen of Arizona and New Mexico, and the Indians who lived in those territories, were affected.

Soon after the Civil War began the North was forced to abandon practically all the forts in Arizona and New Mexico. The Apaches took instant advantage of the circumstance. Believing they had driven the soldiers away, Mangus Colorado and Cochise, with the enthusiastic cooperation of all the other Apache leaders, systematically laid waste to the whole Southwest. The mines were abandoned, even the large workings at Tubac, and cities were deserted, until practically the only settlement remaining in Arizona was Tucson, whose population was reduced to two hundred persons living in daily fear of their lives. The Indians made a smoking desert out of a country as large as all of New England with New York State included.

The Confederacy was quick to invade southern New Mexico. A small army of Texans followed hard upon the heels of the retreating Union troops and occupied Fort Davis, in Texas, Fort Stanton, in New Mexico, and other posts. Fort Davis, built on Limpia Creek, Texas, in 1854, as a safeguard for the Chihuahua trail, had always led a hectic existence. When Lieutenant Colonel Washington Sewell first came with his detachment of four hundred men to establish the fort, he had to fight his way into camp through an Apache ambush. Throughout its existence thereafter the fort was a constant center of seething trouble.

The Mescalero Apaches,[1] in whose country the fort was estab-

---

[1] The Mescalero Apaches ranged between the Rio Grande and the Pecos in New Mexico, and extended their country into the Staked Plains and southward into Coahuila, Mexico. (F. W. Hodge, "Handbook of American Indians," p. 846.)

lished, always resented its presence. Their chief was the famous Palanquito, but he died the year after Fort Davis was built, and his son, Gian-na-tah, known also to the Mexicans as Cadéte (Volunteer), succeeded him. There were numerous sub-chiefs, such as old Nicolás, notable for their energy and singleness of purpose when it came to slaughter. In the twenty years following its establishment, Fort Davis was attacked more often than any other post in the United States.[2]

Fort Davis was garrisoned by six companies of the 8th United States Infantry when the Civil War opened. Most of the officers of the regiment joined the South, and the enlisted men were forced to surrender to the 2nd Texas Confederate Mounted Rifles under Colonel John R. Baylor.[3]

The Mescalero country was now occupied by Confederates in gray instead of United States troops in blue, but the color of their uniforms failed to exempt them from the common hatred for all white men which the Apaches felt. Gian-na-tah and his warriors killed every White Eye they met. The Texans found themselves in a hornets' nest. The Mescaleros literally wiped out the settlements along the Rio Bonita. Then they turned their attention with bloody effect to those along the Rio Grande. In large war parties the Apaches prowled through the Big Bend country of Texas. The white ranchers learned to look with what philosophy they could upon the loss of their livestock, and the deaths of their families or friends.[4] The whole region was depopulated.

Within six miles of Fort Davis was the beautiful ranch of Don Manuel Musquiz, a wealthy Spaniard. Like most ranchers of his

[2] C. G. Raht, "Romance of Davis Mountains," p. 137.

[3] Colonel Baylor was later named governor of Arizona by President Jefferson Davis of the Confederate States of America and became a storm center when he made the initial suggestion of an "Extermination Policy" against all Apaches, a suggestion which lost him his position.

[4] To show the strange equanimity with which Indian depredations were viewed, the following quotation is given from a business letter, written by Pat Murphy, a storekeeper at Fort Davis, to John W. Spencer, at Presidio del Norte, December 29th, 1861. In the last paragraph, thrown in as if it were a matter of little interest or an ordinary event, is this statement: "Night before last, the Indians came to my corral and drove off a number of my cattle. A party of thirty-three men pursued them yesterday, hot on the trail, and I hope will be successful. Yours, P. Murphy."

day, he had a number of peons, and these, with his family, made up a little settlement of approximately twenty persons. Because of the number of people at the ranch and its proximity to the fort, it was deemed safe from attack. But soon after the arrival of the Texas troops, while Don Manuel was on a business trip to Presidio del Norte, a large Mescalero war party, led by old Nicolás, swooped down, killed three of Don Manuel's men, and drove off every one of his fat cattle.

Colonel Baylor ordered Lieutenant May, a dashing young Texan, to pursue. May had twelve mounted riflemen and four civilians with him. Nobody knew the size of the Mescalero raiding party [5] so a messenger rode to Fort Stockton for reinforcements.

Hot on the plain trail left by the large herd of cattle, galloped May and his men. The track led toward Mitre Peak, ten miles northwest of the present Alpine, Texas, then south toward Cathedral Peak, where it plunged down a canyon leading to the Rio Grande. Eager for distinction, the young lieutenant perhaps failed to read correctly from the signs the odds against him. But it is more likely that the wily Nicolás purposely kept his main body of warriors to one side of the cattle trail where the number of their ponies' tracks would not be noticed.

After a day's ride May caught up with the Apaches. As he spurred down the canyon he caught sight of a small band of Indians, perhaps a dozen or so, fleeing ahead. The men cheered and whipped their horses in pursuit. No attempt to fight was made by the red men, who seemed concerned only with escape. Closer and closer drew the Texans. They seemed about to catch the Apaches, but they could not quite close the last gap.

Then the roar of a volley from above awakened shattering echoes. White smoke fluffed out from the cliffs high on either side. Arrows glinted in the sunlight. Too late the white men saw that they were in a cunning trap laid by old Nicolás. The Indians they had

[5] Raht ("Romance of the Davis Mountains," p. 146) says there were two hundred and fifty warriors in this party, but I question whether such a number could have made a raid that close to the fort without being detected. Only one man survived after May's fight, a Mexican guide, and he probably estimated the number of Apaches through the eyes of fear.

been pursuing were a decoy. Before May's men could turn, their retreat was cut off by a swarm of vicious Mescaleros.

There, in the bottom of the gorge, ringed around by deadly enemies, the Texans fought it out, game to the last man. And one by one they died.

Only a Mexican guide escaped. As soon as the fight started this man dismounted and hid among the rocks. He found a cave in the canyon wall and lay in it for a night and a day. The Indians knew he was in the vicinity and hunted for him, but the saints were good. The Apaches failed to find him.

Next day Nicolás and his braves gave up the search for the Mexican and moved leisurely on with their booty. The guide walked to Presidio del Norte with news of the tragedy.

PIÑOS ALTOS AGAIN

Thus continued the war all over the desert country. The Chihuahua trail was abandoned. Only the settlements of Presidio and El Paso remained in the Big Bend area. Presently conditions became even more tense for the few whites, because the Confederate troops were withdrawn for the fighting to the north. The Apaches roamed free, literal masters of all they surveyed.

They even carried out their long ambition of sacking Fort Davis. Nicolás again was the leader in this raid. There were eight persons in the post at the time, a stage agent named Diedrick Dutchover, four Americans, a Mexican woman and her two children. These took refuge on the flat roof of one of the adobe houses which had a small parapet around it. The Indians, not knowing of their presence, never thought of climbing to the roof of that particular house, and for two days as they looted the place and destroyed the post buildings, the eight persons crouched behind the low wall which alone hid them from their enemies. During this entire time the refugees existed on a sack of flour and two barrels of water. The third night, after the Indians left, Dutchover, the woman and her children, and three of the Americans began the ninety-two mile journey to Presidio on foot. The other American, too sick to move, was left behind and died at the fort. But the rest of the party eventually reached safety.

All this time Mangus Colorado and his Mimbreños, aided by the Chiricahuas, Mogollons and Tonto Apaches, were indefatigably active, interspersing their constant destruction in the United States with frequent raids deep into Mexico.

Once the Red Sleeves paid his compliments to the Piños Altos mines, strong as they were. With two hundred warriors he suddenly descended upon the settlement early on the morning of September 27th, 1861. Had he struck twenty-four hours sooner, he might have carried the place, but, on the night before the attack, Captain Martin, with a detachment of Arizona Guards, arrived at the mines. The Apaches were outnumbered and after several hours fighting, drew off. As they retreated they attacked a government wagon train, coming out from Piños Altos toward the Mimbres River, and besieged it for fourteen hours. But the appearance of troops saved it.

These two checks were about the only ones suffered by the Apaches during the year, but since they touched his dearest hate, they disappointed Mangus Colorado bitterly. The Red Sleeves felt it was time now to extirpate the blot at Piños Altos. Too long had the miners scratched at the rocks in the valley. It was a plague spot in Apacheria. Mangus Colorado's great back smarted all over again every time he neared the place. Only the rubbing out of the settlement would bring easement to his scars.

The chief understood the serious nature of his task. The White Eyes at Piños Altos differed from the Mexicans at Santa Rita. Every Apache knew this. They had studied the habits of the miners at length and with deliberation. Above all they were interested in the white men's great efficiency with the rifles without which they never moved. It was well known that these men were very difficult to kill; and that even in dying they thought of only one thing—to take with them as many of their enemies as possible into the land of shadows.

So Mangus Colorado, considering the numbers of his own warriors, sent to his friend Cochise for help. But Cochise's word was that he could not come. He had troubles of his own.

Forgetting his own present problem, Mangus Colorado, with two hundred fighters at his back, rode to learn what was wrong with the Chiricahua. He found Cochise high in the fastnesses of his mountains, watching a towering dust cloud far out in the desert to the west. Instantly the Red Sleeves understood. And when he learned that the approaching dust cloud was made by many white soldiers, Mangus Colorado settled back on his haunches like a great beast. He would stay and have dealings with these white men.

And then, unexpectedly as come most of the desired things of life, the huge Mimbreño had his chance to scotch the Piños Altos miners after all. Word that a party of fourteen miners was rambling across the country toward Apache Pass was brought to him by his scouts. At that moment the Mimbreños were waiting in that very cleft through the Chiricahua Mountains, for the soldiers advancing from the opposite direction.

The Red Sleeves knew that the keen eyes of the hardrock men would be doubly sharpened when passing through such a patent Indian stronghold as the pass, and that to bring about their deaths would be costly to his people unless some unusual stratagem was employed. He was equal to the occasion.

Out on the plain, two miles from the foot of the mountains, was a ragged gully which ran right across the flats, cutting the trail to the pass. Here Mangus Colorado placed a party of warriors, instead of planting the ambush in the pass itself. The gulch could not be seen unless one came right upon it. From in front the entire terrain appeared open and unobstructed.

On came the miners. Suddenly the earth seemed to open before them. Half the party was downed by the first Apache volley. The rest fought with despairing bravery. But one swooping rush wiped out all of them.

The fourteen bodies, mutilated, pin-cushioned with arrows, were left where they lay, to be found days later by Captain Cremony's command, a bloody record on the ledger that Mangus Colorado had evened his long account with Piños Altos.

9: THE FIGHT IN APACHE PASS

THE detail of the miners having been attended to, Mangus Colorado turned with Cochise to meet the advance of the soldiers from the west.

Nobody knows exactly how many warriors the two chiefs commanded. Cremony's estimate was seven hundred [1] but that is probably extremely generous. There is no record, so far as the writer can find, of any Apache force of seven hundred braves ever being assembled for battle. The Chiricahuas may have been able to muster, at an outside figure, three hundred warriors. If to this number is added the two hundred Mimbreños brought by Mangus Colorado, the total of five hundred is still probably somewhat greater than the number of Indians actually in the battle.

It was the advance guard of General J. H. Carleton's California Volunteers, marching east to fight for the Union in the Civil War, which was creating the dust cloud out to the west. Captain Thomas Roberts, 1st California Infantry, was in command of the force, which included three companies of infantry, a troop of cavalry under the Apaches' old acquaintance, Captain John C. Cremony, formerly of the Bartlett Boundary Commission, and two howitzers—a total of about three hundred men and two cannon.

Roberts apparently never thought of danger, although he should have known that the way through the Apache Pass had long been closed to the stage route. He blundered into the canyon with his infantry, the howitzers, and a few troopers, as if he were marching through his own peaceful California hills. Without any particular precautions in the way of flankers or scouts, the command began the steep ascent of the pass, heading toward the springs and the abandoned stage station at the top of the divide. Two-thirds of the way up, the dread Apache yell echoed from canyon wall to canyon

---

[1] "Life Among the Apaches," p. 161.

wall, and from both sides of the battlemented gorge, bullets and arrows rained down among the troops.

Roberts' position was impossible. His command was strung along, route marching, with no semblance of fighting formation. Well-nigh unassailable rocks, high up the mountain sides, were occupied by the Indians. The soldiers fought back courageously enough, but Roberts' order came just in time to save them from being cut to pieces. Back out of the pass they tumbled. The triumphant yells of the Apaches followed them.

The first attempt to go through the mountains had been repulsed, but not for long. Far up the pass lay the springs, the only available water supply. The Californians had to reach them or die of thirst. They had marched forty miles that day under the Arizona sun, over an alkaline desert, with their throats parched and their eyes blinded by the dust fog. It was forward or perish.

Bringing up his two howitzers, Roberts sent the infantry into the pass once more. This time they were in battle order. With the Apaches fighting like wild-cats, the Californians pushed forward until they reached the abandoned stage station [2] but the springs were still six hundred yards farther on.

Here the advance stopped. Mangus Colorado knew the importance of holding the water supply. On two steep peaks which commanded the springs, one to the east and the other to the south, he had posted strong parties of warriors. Rocks were piled for breastworks on the summits by the Apaches. There was no way to return effectively their fire from below. The soldiers were completely worn out by their long march and the hard fight.

It was a critical situation. The springs had to be carried. Roberts still had one trump card and now he played it. At his order, the howitzers were brought up. There was some bungling at first. One of the guns was so badly handled that it was overturned right under the heights where it was exposed to enemy riflery. The gunners scurried away from it.

---

[2] This was the very spot where Cochise was arrested the year before and where Bascom had his fight with the Apaches. Not a mile and a half away was the place where the six white men were tortured to death and the six Indians hung in retaliation.

Sergeant Mitchell, of the cavalry, and six of his men, ran forward under the Apache fire, righted the howitzer and brought it back down the hill to a position where it could be used. By some miracle nobody was wounded in performing this exploit.

And now the heavy reports of the cannon echoed ear-splittingly up and down the cliffs. For the first time the Apaches faced shell fire. To their astonishment and alarm, the missiles which landed among them exploded when they struck, scattering fragments in every direction, and adding the shock of their terrific detonations to the fear of death.

The artillery was too much. After a few minutes of shelling, the Indians began to retreat over the mountains. Roberts found himself in possession of the springs, where, preparing for a still harder fight in the morning, he camped that night.

THE EXPLOIT OF PRIVATE JOHN TEAL

No one can predict what might have happened in Apache Pass the second day of the fight, had not an incident during the night changed the whole aspect of affairs.

Roberts, believing that some of the most dangerous fighting was still ahead, and expecting even fiercer resistance from the Indians in the morning, sent messengers back to Cremony, who was following with the supply train, warning him to protect himself. Then he inspected his camp, stationed sentries, and prepared for the morrow.

Early next morning the Californians' bugles sounded, and the men examined their weapons and grimly surveyed the heights before them. Presently the advance began. Indians were seen on the distant cliffs, but when the howitzers wheeled into action and sent a shell or two screeching in that direction, the red men disappeared. Roberts went on through the pass without further molestation. The Apache resistance had ended.

What happened between sunset and sunrise to change the Mimbreños and Chiricahuas from fighting warriors to fugitives? It is a story of the courage of a single man, coupled with strange good fortune—the kind of an incident upon which history often turns.

As we have seen, Roberts sent messengers back to warn Cremony the evening before. The small detachment of cavalry, led by Sergeants Mitchell and Maynard, was assigned to the perilous duty of going back down the pass.

Scarcely had these messengers left the command, when Mangus Colorado's scouts informed him of it. The chief wanted to cut off such messages, hoping to destroy Roberts' men in the morning, and fearing the coming of reinforcements. With fifty or more of his best-mounted warriors, he rode in pursuit.

The Apaches, some of whom had splendid horses, gained ground and after a time it became a running fight. Sergeant Maynard's right arm was shattered by a rifle ball. Two horses were killed, but the riders were pulled up behind their comrades and the flight continued.

Private John Teal's horse was lagging. He had fallen behind the main body two hundred yards or so, in spite of his rider's whip and spur. A dozen of the Indians on swiftest ponies had gained ground so that Teal was forced off toward the left, riding south at an angle with the line of his companions' flight. An Apache bullet brought his mount to the ground, shot through the body. The trooper was afoot, surrounded by his enemies. So completely outnumbered were Mitchell's men, that they were forced to ride on, leaving Teal to his fate.

There was no thought of escape in the soldier's mind. He only hoped to kill at least one Apache before they finished him. Crouching behind the carcass of his horse, he began shooting with his carbine, one of the newly issued breech-loaders. Because he could keep up a much more rapid fire than the old muzzle-loaders were capable of, the Apaches were disconcerted, and at first did not close in upon him.

Around him they galloped, at fairly long range, shooting and yelling. Their leader was a giant. Teal knew from his every movement that he was a chief of consequence, although he did not dream that it was the dreaded Mangus Colorado himself. He aimed at the giant with all possible care, however, and pulled the trigger.

To his delight, the huge warrior fell out of his saddle. The Apaches instantly seemed to lose interest in the fight. It had grown dark and Teal could hear the exclamations as the Indians gathered about their leader. After a time he could "hear their voices growing fainter in the distance," as he subsequently reported to Cremony.

For a long time Teal waited where he was. The Indians were certainly gone. He arose at last. It was eight miles to Cremony's camp, but the trooper was a thrifty soul. He took the saddle and bridle from his dead horse and walked the entire distance, carrying them. Not an Indian was seen on the way.[8]

.   .   .   .

The panic of the Apaches at the wounding of their leader proved his high standing. No man stood higher. It was Mangus Colorado himself who received Teal's bullet in his body.

With wonderful care the warriors hurried south, carrying the chief, across the mountains and into Mexico. Fifty miles or so to the south of Santa Rita was the Presidio del Janos, a fortified post, with a village near by. Indifferent to the presence of the Mexican soldiers at the fort, the Mimbreños bore their leader right into the town. Their dark figures occupied the streets. Mexican women and children cowered behind closed doors as they peered out in frightened awe at the harsh faces of the desert destroyers. A Mexican doctor was known to live in Janos. Straight to his door the Indians carried the great, limp body of their chief.

"You make Indian well," said the spokesman. "He no die, everybody live. He die, everybody in Janos die, too."

It is probable that no physician ever went about the practice of medicine with greater care than did this one. Upon his skill depended not only the life of the patient, but his own life and the lives of his family and all the people of Janos as well. Fortunately the rawhide constitution of the sufferer was in his favor. The bullet was extracted, the wound bound up, and great care lavished upon Mangus Colorado.

[8] Private John Teal's own story of this affair, and the events which succeeded it may be found in detail in Cremony's "Life Among the Apaches," pp. 158–160.

He lived.

After a time he was well enough to leave the *presidio*. But it was too late then to prevent the white man from passing through the mountains. Without Mangus Colorado the Apaches were nothing. And that is why on the second day of his advance through Apache Pass, Captain Roberts found it easy, without fighting, to do what he had been unable to do with the hardest kind of battling the day before.

IV
Extermination
1862-1871

10: THE END OF MANGUS COLORADO

NORTHERN *versus* SOUTHERN ETHICS

APACHE tactics, which swept Arizona and New Mexico bare of civilized life during the early days of the Civil War, aroused bitterness in Union and Confederate officers alike. As they fought each other they found time to wish that the Indians would let them alone, and later they devoted their energies to fighting the desert nomads.

Independently both Confederate and Union leaders suggested a policy of extermination toward their common enemies. Late in 1862, Colonel John R. Baylor, appointed by Jefferson Davis governor of Arizona for the Confederacy, proposed that every Apache man, wherever found, should be killed on sight, and the women and children sold into slavery. This proposal was promptly and emphatically disapproved by President Davis, and an explanation demanded of its author.

In an attempt to justify his recommendation, Baylor wrote on December 29th to General J. B. Magruder, commanding the Confederate district of Texas, New Mexico and Arizona. He cited past cruelties of the Indians, their depredations and their untamable nature. He even included, as a ghastly exhibit, the scalp of a Miss Jackson, which had been taken by the Indians, and asked that it be sent to the President.

"Arizona has been kept in poverty by Indian depredations," he wrote. "Not a cow, sheep, or horse can be raised there now except by being herded day and night. As the Indians there live almost exclusively by stealing, depredations are a daily occurrence, and the people are kept poor from want of protection. Treaty after treaty has been made and broken, and the general belief among the people is that extermination of the grown Indians and making slaves of the children is the only remedy. This system has been practiced in New Mexico. There is not a family of wealth in that country but has Indian slaves derived from that source. In fact so popular is this system of civilizing the Indian that there have been several efforts made to pass a law in the New Mexican legislature, making all Indians slaves for life. It is a knowledge of this custom among the people of Arizona that to some extent induced me to give the order that has been the cause of complaint against me."

This letter, forwarded by Magruder to Jefferson Davis, was given by him to his secretary, J. A. Seddon, with the curt note:

"This letter requires attention. It is an avowal of an infamous crime and the assertion of what should not be true in relation to troops in Texas, &c. (Signed) J. D." [1]

Shortly afterward, G. W. Randolph, Secretary of War, ordered Magruder to revoke Baylor's authority to raise troops for the Confederacy. The order was put into effect at once. Thus the Confederacy's high command dealt with the first attempt at an "Extermination Policy."

The North, however, was not so meticulous. Soon after General Carleton took over the command of the Southwest from General E. R. S. Canby, he instituted the very policy of extermination which the South had refused to sanction. There was no disapproval from Washington as there had been from Richmond.

[1] Other cogent arguments for this method of "civilizing" the Indians are contained in the following letter, written by M. H. McWillie, delegate to the Confederate Congress from Arizona, to President Davis, January 10th, 1863:

"With further reference to that clause in his (Baylor's) order directing the women and children to be sold into slavery, I can only say that it has been the unvarying custom of the country from the time of the Spanish colonists to the present day; and I cannot recollect a single instance wherein Indian captives have ever been set free by the people of that country. In Mexico the long-continued practice has acquired the force of law. The usage was recognized and guaranteed by a treaty between the United States and Mexico. From this custom originated the peonage system of New Spain and Mexico and that admixture of European and Indian races which for nearly three centuries has been slowly but gradually absorbing and civilizing the once powerful aboriginal tribes of Spanish America. Captive Indian women and children are reckoned in the same caste as peons, perform similar duties and are treated with moderation and humanity. This state of servitude, it would naturally seem, is infinitely preferable to the only other alternative of having them perish of starvation and exposure among the mountains and deserts." To his credit be it said, President Davis saw no more value to McWillie's arguments than those of Baylor.

With Colonel Kit Carson to help him, Carleton began a relentless war against the Apaches. Fort Stanton, recaptured by the Union, was Colonel Carson's post. He had five companies of New Mexican volunteers and instructions to campaign against the Mescalero Apaches and the Navajos. Captain William McCleave, with two California companies, was sent to hunt Indians toward the south, while Captain Roberts, the hero of the Apache Pass fight, marched with two more companies on a different route. The orders of command were the same: *"The men are to be slain whenever and wherever they can be found. The women and children may be taken prisoners, but, of course, they are not to be killed."*

The results of the extermination campaign were at first indecisive. The troops attacked a few Apache *rancherias*, burned a few *jacales*. There was some fighting of a haphazard character. Riding along a dry washout, a small detachment of soldiers would hear a spiteful volley, and a few of them would be down. Usually that would be the extent of it. By the time the troops were ready to return the fire, they would only see the dirty breech clouts of the Apaches fluttering among the rocks high up the mountain side and know there was no chance to overtake them. Sometimes there was a real battle. Then the carbines whanged, the bullets kicked up little puffs of dust and ricocheted, and now and again a tawny warrior, dressed in his soiled white garments, flopped and kicked among the scrabble. But most of the time it ended in flight—weary plodding through the burning sand; Apaches popping up from God knew where, blazing away, and then disappearing to God knew where again.

It was long before the extermination policy yielded its first-fruits.

DEATH COMES TO THE RED SLEEVES

Now the sands were running low for Mangus Colorado. He was more than seventy years old—very long for an Apache warrior to live—and age had taken from him some of his hardness. His giant size, his cunning, above all his implacable hatred distilled out of that day when he was spread-eagled and flogged by the miners at Piños Altos, had given him a prestige unequalled among his people. But he began to wish for peace in his old age.

The Red Sleeves had made a vast contribution to the history of his race. Cremony, who knew him better than any other white man, wrote of him: "He was the greatest and most talented Apache of the Nineteenth Century. . . . His sagacious counsels partook more of the character of wide and enlarged statesmanship than those of any other Indian of modern times. . . . He found means to collect and keep together, for weeks at a time, large bodies of savages, such as none of his predecessors could assemble and feed . . . and taught them to comprehend the value of unity and collective strength. . . . Take him all in all, he exercised influence never equalled by any savage of our time." [2]

It was his old age and his eagerness for something which in his prime he would have scorned—peace with the White Eyes—which was Mangus Colorado's undoing. Early in January, 1863, Captain Joseph Walker, with a party of prospectors, was in central Arizona, looking for gold. This was in line with Carleton's policy, which was to encourage miners to come into the country so that the government would be forced to send additional troops to protect them, thus gradually crushing the Indians out.

While camping near Fort McLean, Walker's party learned that Mangus Colorado was not far away with a portion of his Mimbreños. At the same time that this information was received, Captain E. D. Shirland, with a company of Californians, came into Walker's bivouac. Calling the officer to one side, the prospector suggested a plan to take the Mimbreño chief prisoner—a plan which would have made a Judas blush. Shirland, however, was no Judas. He agreed promptly and without blushing.

Word that the *nan-tan* (chief) of the soldiers wished to see him was carried to the Red Sleeves by a Mexican. The great Apache eagerly accepted the invitation.[3] He was ready for a treaty.

---

[2] "Life Among the Apaches," pp. 176–177.

[3] This is according to the story of Geronimo who was a young warrior in the Mimbreño camp at the time. If it be true it shows a great change in the chief's

Very soon he was on his way, accompanied by about fifteen warriors. He left his people over their own protest. There were many misgivings as he rode away. But Mangus Colorado believed he was doing the best thing for his band.

Riding up the trail, he saw a white man, Jack Swilling, a member of the Walker party, standing ahead of him and motioning for a conference. The gimlet eyes of the old Mimbreño must have detected the rustlings in the bushes where Shirland's troops crouched in hiding, but he showed no sign of fear or suspicion as he went forward to talk with Swilling.

They conversed in Spanish. Then Mangus Colorado turned and spoke to his warriors in the Apache tongue, telling them to go back to their camp. Obediently they turned and trotted away down the trail.

Now the huge Indian came on into the camp alone with Swilling. He did so in good faith. He came of his own free will and alone. He believed he was protected by a truce, and that he would have a chance to discuss terms of peace with Shirland in safety.

Quickly he learned his mistake. When he was inescapably within the toils of the ambush, the concealed soldiers rose and surrounded him. As Mangus Colorado proceeded to Walker's camp, he was a prisoner and knew it.

That was the afternoon of January 17th, 1863. As soon as he heard the news that the Apache leader had been captured, Colonel J. R. West, in command at Fort McLean, rode to Walker's camp to see the prisoner. He arrived after dark. It was chilly and there was a big fire. Beside this Mangus Colorado had calmly stretched his huge form, wrapped in his blanket.

West walked up to the lounging giant and surveyed him from head to foot as he lay there. Then he ordered two guards with fixed bayonets to stand watch over the Apache. Before he left the campfire for his own tent, he inspected the two guards, Privates James Collyer and George Mead, and then gave them their final instructions for the night.

---

spirit. A few years before, that Mexican messenger would have been bound on an ant hill to die in agony.

"Men," he rasped, "that old murderer has got away from every soldier command and has left a trail of blood five hundred miles on the old stage line. I want him dead or alive tomorrow morning; do you understand? *I want him dead.*" [4]

He tramped away. The soldiers glanced at each other, then at the prostrate prisoner. One of them began to stir the embers of the fire with his bayonet. Presently he allowed the point of the bayonet to remain in a bed of glowing coals. Now and then he took it out and looked at it.

Mangus Colorado, apparently dozing by the fire, seemed not to see the action. It is not probable, however, that any movement of the soldier escaped him. He must have clearly divined the guard's purpose.

When the bayonet became white hot, the soldier thrust it suddenly into the Apache's leg. Mangus Colorado leaped up. The reports of both the soldiers' rifles rang out simultaneously.

The Red Sleeves fell in a great, sprawling heap. Collyer and Mead came closer and emptied their revolvers into him.

By the time the sergeant of the guard arrived, the chief was dead.[5]

---

[4] This conversation was quoted by Clark B. Stocking, a California soldier, who was present and heard it. Frank C. Lockwood cites it. ("Pioneer Days in Arizona," p. 159.)

[5] In his report, Colonel West said that he left the old Indian under a guard to make sure that he should not escape and that he was killed at midnight "while trying to get away." A disgusting detail is that the dead man's head was severed from his body by a surgeon and the brain taken out and weighed. The head measured larger than that of Daniel Webster and the brain was of corresponding weight. The skull is said now to be in the Smithsonian Institution in Washington, D.C. We should hesitate long before we criticize the Indians for mutilating dead enemies.

11: MURDER BY WHOLESALE

THE murder of Mangus Colorado gave new impetus to Carleton's campaign of extermination. Presently the dogged persistence of his troops began to obtain results. Within two days of the Red Sleeves' death, Captain William McCleave fought the Mimbreños near Piños Altos and killed eleven of them. On January 20th, 1863, Captain Shirland, who had received credit for capturing Mangus Colorado, surprised an Indian *ranchería* and killed nine Apaches besides wounding many more.

McCleave, now a major, with seventy-nine men, took the trail of a band of Indians which had run off the post herd of horses from Fort West. After he had exhausted his men and practically worn out his horses, he reached Canyon del Perro (Dog Canyon), on March 27th, 1863. There he was suddenly rewarded. Quite to his own surprise, he located a *ranchería*, charged and completely destroyed it and killed twenty-five Indians. Only one soldier was wounded. Later the Apaches attacked McCleave's column, wounding Lieutenant French and one private soldier. The troops charged up both sides of the canyon, driving away the Indians and killing three.[1]

The Apaches were completely routed. A few days later this band appeared at Fort Stanton and begged for peace. They were Mescaleros and at their head was Gian-na-tah himself. To Colonel Carson the chief said:

"You are stronger than we. We have fought you so long as we had rifles and powder; but your weapons are better than ours. Give us weapons and turn us loose, we will fight you again; but we are worn out; we have no more heart; we have no provisions, no means

---

[1] The following from the military report of this battle gives an interesting sidelight: "As an illustration of the way in which our men are able to beat the Indians at their own game in fighting, Corporal Charles E. Ellis crept up to a rock behind which an Apache was hidden. When he got to this place, he coughed. As the Apache raised his head, he (Ellis) shot him."

to live; your troops are everywhere; our springs and water holes are either occupied or overlooked by your young men. You have driven us from our last and best stronghold and we have no more heart. Do with us as it may seem good to you, but do not forget that we are men and braves." [2]

A warrior speaking to a warrior. Carson had his orders, direct from Carleton: "The men are to be slain, whenever and wherever found. The women and children may be taken prisoners . . ." But the old scout and trapper had lived too long among the Indians. He was unable to look upon them as wild animals. To him they were human, and he took them under his protection. They were sent to a newly created reservation at the Bosque Redondo, on the Pecos River, in eastern New Mexico, and placed under the control of Captain Cremony, who also understood Indians. For a time the Mescaleros ceased to be a troublesome factor.

But there were other Apaches. Captain Walker's prospecting party, which had trapped Mangus Colorado, went on to interior Arizona where Pauline Weaver had discovered gold placers, and there the prospectors found large gold fields, which brought a rush of people into the country. Although this was the invasion of lands which had immemorially belonged to the Apaches, Carleton had no scruples against ejecting the red owners in favor of white interlopers.

He proposed to the Mexican governors of both Sonora and Chihuahua, that they cooperate in running down and killing all the Apaches in their joint provinces. The general further enlisted as scouts the miners in the gold and silver districts, and the friendly Pima, Maricopa and Papago Indians, all hereditary enemies of the Apaches.

Then began a huge man-hunt in Apacheria, with orders always the same: "Kill every Indian man capable of bearing arms and capture the women and children." From every direction moved the hunters, the military and civilian forces of two great nations. It is impossible to give even a list of encounters which took place. Six pages of fine type were required to enumerate them in the General Orders for 1865. The figures show that three hundred and sixty-three In-

[2] Dunn, "Massacres of the Mountains," pp. 383–384.

dians were killed and one hundred and forty wounded; seven soldiers killed and twenty-five wounded; eighteen civilians killed and
thirteen wounded. Much livestock was recaptured from the Indians.

And how were these results achieved? An example, the famous
"Pinal Treaty" will show:

Colonel King S. Woolsey, aide to the governor of Arizona, started
with a party of thirty Americans and fourteen Pima and Maricopa
Indians, from the Pima villages on January 24th, 1864, to hunt for
some livestock which had been stolen, supposedly by the hostile Indians. About sixty miles northeast of the villages, Woolsey's party
saw smoke signals dotting upward from a mesa, and a little later
observed Indians on the eminence.

Colonel Woolsey believed in subtleties. He devised a scheme on
the spot by which he could avoid fighting and yet carry out General
Carleton's wishes. One of the Pima scouts was sent forward to tell
the Apaches, who proved to be Pinal Coyoteros, that the white man
wanted to make peace with them and invited them to his camp.

Led by their chief, Par-a-mucka, a harsh-faced savage, the Apaches
accepted the invitation and thirty-five of them came in. Par-a-mucka
loftily demanded a place to sit. Woolsey silently handed him a
folded blanket.

The colonel addressed the Indians through an interpreter, telling
them that he would make a treaty with them and give them certifi-
cates of good conduct which no white man would ever question.

By this time Woolsey's followers had gathered closely about the
sitting Apaches. The colonel himself gave the signal. Whipping out
his pistol, he shot Par-a-mucka dead. In an instant every white man
was shooting. Part of the Indians got away, some of them wounded.
But nineteen bodies remained behind, mute witnesses to the depend-
ability of the white man's promises.

THE AFFAIR AT CAMP GRANT

A little to the east of where Woolsey "signed" his treaty on the
dead bodies of his conferees, another drama was taking place. The
Aravaipa Apaches, under their chief, Eskimo-tzin, had been harried

from one end of their country to another. Eskimo-tzin himself, a rim-rock Apache, had a gall-bitter hatred for everything white.

Throughout the dreadful 'Sixties when Carleton's Indian-hunters pursued his people up and down the desert, Eskimo-tzin had managed to keep clear of the troops. He watched Carleton bring the Mescaleros under control and then subjugate the Navajos. Kit Carson performed the last-named feat. He marched with four hundred men through the depths of the Canyon de Chelly, the stronghold of the Navajos in northeast Arizona. He did not find much resistance. The soldiers laid waste the peach orchards and the corn fields they found, rounded up the sheep and cattle, destroyed the villages and killed a score of Navajos. Then the Indians sued for peace and Carson sent them down to the Bosque Redondo, where they were to remain until 1878 when they were removed to their present reservation. Exit the Navajos from the arena of history.

Much time passed and the pressure of the army on the Apaches grew more severe each month. One by one Eskimo-tzin's sub-chiefs were killed. At last he himself saw that there was no longer any hope.

It was February, 1870, when five old Aravaipa squaws crept into Camp Grant and timidly asked to see a little child who had been captured from their band on the Salt River months before. The permission was granted. The old women received such good treatment that they returned to their people with gifts and with glowing descriptions of the white man's generosity. Even Eskimo-tzin was impressed. Perhaps, after all, he had not been well informed about the *Americanos*.

Presently, through the same squaws, Lieutenant Royal E. Whitman, in command at Camp Grant, began negotiations with the chief, the result of which was that the Aravaipa leader surrendered. By March 11th, more than three hundred Indians, among them the most dangerous of the Apaches, had come in to Camp Grant and were living there in peace.

Lieutenant Whitman understood Indians far better than most of his military associates and took deep interest in his wards. He found them terribly poverty-stricken, many being nearly naked and almost starved. Wisely humane, the officer looked about for some way to employ them, and hit upon a plan which was later used with much success at other posts—he set them to cutting hay for the fort, using their knives and bringing it in on their backs, and being paid for it at the rate of a few cents for each fifty pounds they delivered.

It was almost pitiful to see the joy of the Apaches at having something to do. They worked with a zest which within little more than two months produced nearly three hundred thousand pounds of hay, all of it cut with butcher knives and carried in on the Indians' backs. Under Whitman's policy the numbers of Apaches at Camp Grant gradually increased, until they totalled five hundred and ten.

Then, on April 1st, Captain Stanwood arrived at the post and took command. He approved of Whitman's methods, but he had been ordered to make a long scout through the southern part of Arizona, and for this he needed nearly all the soldiers at Camp Grant. Almost immediately he departed, leaving Whitman only fifty men to garrison the post.

Arizona in those days possessed some of the most precious scoundrels in the whole world. Driven out of California by the Vigilantes and flocking wherever mining camps promised easy pickings, a shifty population of gamblers, "road agents," [3] cattle "rustlers," [4] and loafers hung in a cloud about every lively town in the Territory. Tucson at this time was infested by some of the worst of these, and news that the bulk of the soldiers had left Camp Grant reached their ears almost at once. Within four days a mob of Americans, Mexicans and Papago Indians started toward the post with the expressed determination of killing the Apaches camped there.

Captain Penn, at Fort Lowell, discovered the plot, and sent a warning to Whitman. But the messenger arrived too late. Whitman received the word on April 30th, and immediately sent instructions to the Apaches to come in closer to the post—they were then camped about five miles away. His messenger was back in an hour. The Apache camp was a mass of burning ruins, he reported to Whit-

[3] "Road agent" was the expressive western expression which included highway robbers of all types, particularly those which made a specialty of "standing up" stage coaches from mining towns for the gold shipments carried by them.
[4] "Rustlers" were cattle or horse thieves.

man, and there were no living Indians in it, while the ground was strewn with dead and mutilated women and children.

AN APACHE OBJECT LESSON

To see his months of patient work brought to nothing was a terrible shock to the officer who had done so much for these people. He at once dispatched the post surgeon, Dr. C. E. Briesly, with a guard of twenty men, to see what could be done.

The surgeon, as he approached the camp site, could see the smoke from the burning dwellings. Then horrid scenes began to unfold themselves. Here and there, scattered about in the contortions of death, were the bodies of twenty-one women and children. Some were shot. Others were stabbed and their brains beaten out with stones. Two at least of the squaws had been first ravished, then killed. At one point an infant only ten months old was discovered, shot twice and one of its legs nearly hacked off from its tiny body.

"There was little for me to do," Dr. Briesly wrote in his report. "The work had been too thoroughly done."

The scene was deserted except for the dead; the mob from Tucson had departed, on the way back to the saloons and gambling houses which had spawned it.

Next morning Whitman sent a burial party to the place, and the work of interring the slaughtered unfortunates began.

"I thought the act of caring for their dead would be evidence to them of our sympathy at least," said the lieutenant sadly, "and the conjecture proved correct for while at the work many of them came to the spot and indulged in their expressions of grief, too wild and terrible to be described. That evening they began coming in from all directions, singly and in small parties, so changed in forty-eight hours as to hardly be recognizable, during which time they had neither eaten nor slept." [5]

Two wounded women were found and taken to the post. When the totals were summed up, it was discovered that eighty-five persons had been killed, of whom only eight were men. Twenty-nine

[5] Lieutenant Whitman's statement in Vincent Colyer's report, p. 32.

children had been carried away into slavery. "Get them back for us; our little boys will grow up slaves, and our little girls," pleaded the Indians concerning the kidnaped children. "Our dead you cannot bring back to life but those that are living we gave to you and we look to you to get them back." [6]

Lieutenant Whitman did what he could. Two of the twenty-nine abducted children escaped and five were later recovered from Arizonans. But the other twenty-two were all sold into slavery in Mexico and were never again seen by their families.

And what of Eskimo-tzin? His eyes had been fully opened. As a climax to his woes, he and some of his people were shot at by troops on June 8th, under the mistaken notion that they were hostile. He fled to the mountains with the remnants of his band, crazed with grief, since he had lost two wives and five children in the massacre.

During this flight an incident occurred which has been much and often quoted as proof of the lack of all human feelings in an Apache. But let the reader consider the background and then judge of the question for himself: A few miles out from Camp Grant, there dwelt an elderly trapper named Charles McKenny, who had often befriended Eskimo-tzin. For many years they had known each other, and even before his surrender, the Aravaipa chief had frequently been a guest at the white man's cabin. The trapper remained the one white friend Eskimo-tzin possessed.

On the day that he fled from the troops following the massacre, the Apaches' line of flight took the chief right past his friend's dwelling place. He stopped on the way and ate a meal with the trapper. When he had finished, he coldly raised his rifle and shot the white man dead. Then he continued his journey.

Years later he was asked by Sam Bowman, assistant chief of scouts under General George Crook, why he had performed such an extraordinary act of treachery. His reply gives one food for thought:

"I did it to teach my people that there must be no friendship between them and the white men. Anyone can kill an enemy, but it takes a strong man to kill a friend."

The Romans lauded Brutus who sent his sons, whom he loved, to

[6] *Ibid.*, p. 33.

the execution block to uphold the Roman law, because he thus set the example of placing Rome above all human considerations. Eskimo-tzin's act was not unlike that of Brutus in its final analysis. By it he cut himself off from all communication with the white man, and, as he believed, taught his people a lesson.

Not long afterward he was captured again. For three years he worked hard in chains, before he was freed on the order of General O. O. Howard.[7]

And so the war of extermination progressed. But while many Apaches were killed, and for a time their activity decreased, it became more and more evident as time passed that the complete extermination of the Indians would take too long and was too expensive to be practical.

Life burned too deep in the Apache's body.

[7] Misfortune followed Eskimo-tzin to the last. By General Howard's order he and the seven or eight families remaining in his band were given a small piece of supposedly worthless land at San Carlos.

There he was visited in 1873 by Lieutenant Britton Davis, who commented on the great progress the Indians had made. At that time they had adobe houses, fenced fields, farm implements, good teams and cows. They dressed like Mexicans and resembled a prosperous Mexican community. Davis dined with Eskimo-tzin and particularly praised the cleanliness of the dining table and the excellence of the meal.

At this time all seemed well. Eskimo-tzin had apparently solved the problem of following the white man's road, but appearances often deceive. Somebody discovered, under this apparently worthless land, a vein of coal. Then a reservation lawyer found that the lines of the reservation had been inaccurately surveyed and finally it was proved that the farms of Eskimo-tzin were south of the reservation line.

And so the robbery of the red man progressed. Eskimo-tzin was removed from his farm, and his friends from their homes. All fixed improvements were turned over to white settlers, while the despairing Indians were marched to another dreary waste.

Shortly after this Eskimo-tzin died. His spirit could not survive this last blow.

V

The War in the Lava Beds
1871-1873

12: WHEN THE MODOCS REBELLED

RED MASSACRE AND WHITE DUPLICITY

WHILE the troops in Arizona and New Mexico were fighting out their never-ending war with the Apaches, another episode was taking place far to the west, which for two years or more took the attention of the nation from the Southwestern theater and focussed it on truly spectacular events in northern California.

The first settlers who drove their high-pooped covered wagons over famed South Pass into Oregon found there a beautiful, tree-covered, smiling country, and also some of the deadliest enemies on the continent. These were the Modocs, a unique people, hunters and fishers, but primarily warriors. In one respect they resembled the Arabs of North Africa. They were fierce and predatory slave-drivers,[1] periodically raiding down into the desert regions of California and Nevada, where dwelt the miserable and degenerate

[1] The slave traffic was so well organized in Oregon that it was recognized by the Hudson's Bay Company and even encouraged. The price of a slave ranged from five to fifteen blankets, according to Slocum, with the women valued higher than the men. If a slave died within six months of his purchase, the seller returned half the purchase price to the buyer. These slaves did menial work such as cutting wood, fishing, and digging camas roots for food. Employees of the Hudson's Bay Company generally owned two or three of these slaves each, which saved the company from employing an additional large number of workers in its operations. One chief, Casino, of the Klickitat tribe, was followed by a retinue of at least one hundred slaves wherever he moved. The fate of the slaves was often terrible. According to Hodge ("Handbook of American Indians," p. 598), they were often killed and buried under the corner posts of their huge houses by the Tlingits, while among the Makahs a chief's favorite slaves were buried with him when he died. Their masters had the power of life and death over them and sometimes killed them outright in moments of passion. Slaves could not hold property or have part in ceremonials. They married other slaves, or, occasionally when a free Indian married a slave woman, their children did not have the full rights of free people. Among the Tlingits at one time, one-third of the population was slaves. Not even Africa equals this record.

Digger Indians. Sweeping out on the wastes, they rounded up the helpless natives, marched them north and sold them to the wealthy tribes such as the Klickitats, Tlingits and Haidas.

This haughty, fiercely independent tribe resented immediately the calm assumption of the white man that the beautiful land was his. Aided by their former enemies, the Umpquas, the Rogue River Indians, the Klamaths and the Pitt River Indians, they fought the paleface from the beginning. As early as July 14th, 1834, the Umpquas attacked a party of fourteen men sent to the coast by the trading firm of Smith, Jackson and Sublette and headed by the famous Jedediah Smith himself. Eleven of the trappers were killed. Smith and two others escaped and finally found refuge at the Hudson's Bay Company post of Fort Vancouver.[2] The following year the Rogue Rivers slew four out of a party of eight led by Daniel Miller, wounding the others. Frémont's Third Expedition was attacked by the Klamaths at Klamath Lake, in August, 1845. The Indians crept into camp and killed three men before Kit Carson's wilderness-trained ears heard their silent movements, warning him to leap to his feet and give the alarm which saved the rest of his party.

There were many other attacks. Major Phil Kearny fought a short campaign with the allied tribes in 1851, defeating them and taking about thirty prisoners. Shortly afterward the Rogue Rivers signed a peace treaty, which, however, was never ratified by the United States Senate.

In the meantime the other tribes in the section kept on fighting. The war was climaxed in August, 1852. Led by their chief, Old Schonchin, the Modocs attacked an emigrant train containing thirty-three persons and massacred everybody in it. A volunteer company of Californians under Captain Ben Wright, and one of Oregonians under Captain Ross, marched into the Modoc country. They saved another train from annihilation, by beating the Modocs off after they had surrounded the wagons for several hours. A dozen or more warriors were killed in this fight, in which eighteen white men lost their lives.

After that, with Ben Wright at the head of the combined forces,

[2] Leroy R. Hafen and W. J. Ghent, "Broken Hand," pp. 67–68.

the volunteers scoured the country, trying to catch and punish the Indians. They found they had undertaken a task which they could hardly complete. For three months the Modocs played hide-and-seek with Wright and his men, and the white men were always "it." At last Wright fell back upon treachery to accomplish what he could not accomplish by open warfare.

That November he sent a captured squaw to summon the Modocs to a feast, after which they were to talk peace. The Indians attended the council in good faith. They did not know that the food placed before them was poisoned with strychnine. Wright and his men watched the meat, but for some reason the poison did not take effect.[3] Finally, the Californian grew impatient. Drawing his revolver, he shot twice, killing two of his Indian guests. At the signal every white man opened fire. Thirty-six more Indians fell. Only ten escaped. And that murder was committed under the sacred symbol, a flag of truce.

As it chanced, Old Schonchin, due to illness, had not been able to attend the council. One of the ten who escaped was Schonchin John, his younger brother, who was destined to play an important part later in the Modoc War of the 'Seventies.

Whatever we may think of Wright's act [4] it broke the power of the Modocs. They never again were a threatening factor to settlement. By 1871 they were little more than a band of mendicants in their own land. They had been reduced to only a fraction of their former numbers. They were living in southern Oregon, on a miserable reservation, hectored and abused by the Klamaths, over whom they had formerly lorded it, and despised by the white settlers

---

[3] "Some say that the squaw got an inkling of what was going on and informed the warriors, who thereupon refused to eat. Others say that they ate, but the poison did not operate; that Wright used to swear afterwards over the way he had been imposed upon by the druggist."—Dunn, "Massacres of the Mountains," p. 193.

[4] Wright's treachery, of course, should be condemned by every right-thinking person. But, as was the case when Colonel J. M. Chivington perpetrated his massacre of the Cheyennes at Sand Creek in 1864, the people of the section were so wrought up over the Indian troubles that they made him a popular hero. He was given a great ovation at Yreka, when he returned to California, and the California Legislature paid the volunteers for their services. Wright was given a position as an Indian agent. But retribution finally overtook him. Four years later when the Rogue Rivers again went on the war path, they killed him in his own agency.

around them.

Yet in proof of the fact that the meanest of men can stand only so much and will then fight like tigers, these same ragged tramps gave the United States its most costly war, from the standpoint of losses and expense, when the number of enemies is considered.

AT LOST RIVER

When their treaty, signed in 1864, was not ratified for six years, the Modocs reached the end of their endurance. Grim Old Schonchin complained to Agent A. B. Meacham and the agent, a good friend to the Indians, consented to their removal to a new reservation in the Sprague River Valley. But conditions failed to improve. So tormented were the Modocs by white and Indian neighbors that they could not harvest the crops and were on the verge of starvation. The agent consented to another move.

But a new power had arisen among the Modocs. Kientpoos, known to the whites as Captain Jack, refused to go on the new reservation. There was a display of power by the government and Old Schonchin, with the bulk of the tribe, submitted. Captain Jack, however, with his small group of bitter-enders, moved thirty miles up the Lost River to their old home near Tule Lake.

Their arrival was the signal for a general outcry from the settlers in the vicinity who visioned an immediate massacre. So much pressure was brought to bear that the situation came to the attention of the commander of the department, General E. R. S. Canby.[5]

Canby was a sincere friend to the red man. He had repeatedly forestalled moves against the Modocs, because he knew they were

---

[5] "Brigadier-General Edward R. S. Canby . . . began his career as a cadet at West Point in . . . 1835 . . . continuously served thirty-eight years, passing through all the grades to major general of volunteers and brigadier general of the regular army. He served . . . with marked distinction in the Florida and Mexican Wars, and the outbreak of the Civil War found him on duty in New Mexico, where . . . he remained in command and defended the country successfully. . . . Afterward, transferred east, he had the honor to capture Mobile. Since the close of the Civil War he had been repeatedly chosen for special command by reason of his superior knowledge of law and civil government, his known fidelity . . . and his chivalrous devotion to his profession, in which his success was perfect."—General Orders issued to the Army at the announcement of Canby's death, April 14th, 1873.

How the broncho (wild) Apaches lived. This is a hostile camp, photographed while negotiations were under way for the surrender of the Indians. The negotiations in this instance failed and the Indians broke out again on the war trail. (N. H. Rose Collection.)

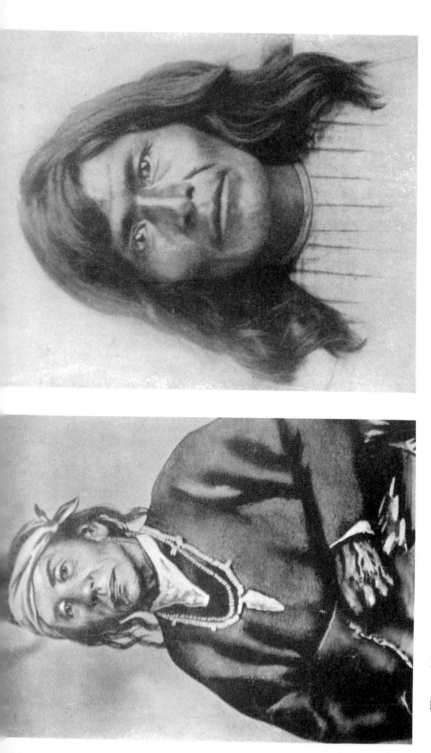

Two celebrated Apache chiefs. *Left*, Cochise, the famous Chiricahua, ally of Mangus Colorado. (N. H. Rose Collection.) *Right*, Victorio, Mangus Colorado's chief lieutenant, and next to him the greatest war leader the Apaches had. Of Mangus Colorado himself there is no authentic photograph. (War Department.)

These are the two pueblos at Taos. *Above,* the north pueblo, which was the scene of Price's battle, Feb. 3 and 4, 1847. *Below,* the smaller south pueblo across the creek, which was deserted as the Indians massed in the larger structure.

A quintet of Apache notables. *Left to right*: Geronimo, last of the great chiefs; Ulzana, who made the raid of 1885; Nana, successor to Victorio, who made the raid of 1881 (with cane); Chihuahua, brother of Ulzana; and Loco, who fought Forsyth at Horse Shoe Canyon in 1882. The photograph was taken after the surrender of the Geronimo band.

The children of Geronimo's hostile Apache band, photographed in 1886. In foreground is a little white boy, Santiago McKinn, who was held captive by the Apaches for many months. At extreme left is a little Negro boy, also a captive when this band surrendered. (N. H. Rose Collection.)

Old Fort Apache, in the White Mountains of Arizona, as it looked in 1880, when it was a focus of military operations against the warring Apaches. Flagpole marks headquarters building, on bank of deep cut White River. (War Department.)

A trio of desert fighters. *Left*, Colonel John R. Baylor, of the Confederate army, who first advocated the policy of exterminating all Apaches. (N. H. Rose Collection.) *Center*, Lieut. Charles B. Gatewood, who persuaded Geronimo to surrender. (War Department.) *Right*, General Adna R. Chaffee, who as a captain defeated the White Mountain Apaches at Chevelon's Fork crossing. (War Department.)

The central figures in the Modoc war. *Left*, Captain Jack, the Modoc chief. (N. H. Rose Collection.) *Center*, General E. R. S. Canby, treacherously killed during peace negotiations. (War Department.) *Right*, Hooker Jim, leader of the extremist element of the Modocs. (N. H. Rose Collection.)

The two great desert adversaries. *Above,* Geronimo, the lifelong antagonist of the white men. This picture was taken when he was an old man, after his Florida captivity. (Bureau of American Ethnology.) *Below,* General George Crook, who campaigned for years against the Apaches. (War Department.)

Three notable frontiersmen of the Southwest. *Above, left,* Tom Horn, chief scout under Captain Emmett Crawford, who was wounded when Crawford was killed. Horn was later executed for murder during the Wyoming cattle war. (War Department.) *Above, right,* Sergeant John Smith, Sixth Cavalry, who killed an Apache medicine man with an axe in the Cibicu fight, Aug. 30, 1881. (N. H. Rose Collection). *Below,* John P. Clum, the able agent to the Apaches. (N. H. Rose Collection.)

A group of Apache scouts who served well during the campaigns
against Geronimo. Seated in center is Al Sieber, chief of scouts in
the Department of Arizona. The white man standing behind is an
official from Washington who "dressed up" for the occasion. (War
Department.)

Above, In the days of captivity. Apache squaws, as prisoners of war, receiving rations issued at Fort Sill, Oklahoma. *Below,* Judge H. C. McComas and his family. Judge and Mrs. McComas were murdered by Chato's raiding Apaches between Silver City and Leitendorf, March 28, 1883. (N. H. Rose Collection.)

Above, left, Chato, Apache chief who chose to go to prison rather than betray his people. *Right,* Captain Emmett Crawford, killed by Mexican irregulars Jan. 11, 1886 when he had almost captured Geronimo. *Below,* General H. W. Lawton, who as a captain led the "Flying Column" after the renegades. (All photos by War Department.)

Geronimo and his warriors. Geronimo stands in the center. The photograph was made just before the conference with General Crook, March 27, 1886. These Indians, still hostile, and deadly as so many rattlesnakes, were observing only a temporary truce at the moment. (N. H. Rose Collection.)

These are Crawford's scouts, the Indians who went with him to hunt Geronimo. Photograph was taken just after their return from Mexico, following the death of their leader. Lieutenant Maus was in command. (N. H. Rose Collection.)

The momentous conference between Geronimo and Crook, in Canyon de los Embudos, Sonora, March 27, 1886. The following can be identified, *left to right*: Lieut. Faison; Capt. Roberts; Nachite (top of head seen above hats of Faison and Roberts); Geronimo (facing camera, wearing turban); Coyetano (hidden behind Geronimo); Concepcion; Nana (beside Geronimo); Tom Blair (by horse in background); Noche (sergeant of scouts); Lieut. Maus; three interpreters, José Maria Yashez, Antonio Besias, and José Montoya; H. W. Only (above interpreters); Capt. John G. Bourke; General Crook (in sun helmet); Charley Roberts. Apache warriors in background are of Geronimo's band, but not identified. (War Department.)

badly treated. He tried once more on this occasion to smooth matters out. But this time he failed. A new agent, F. B. Odeneal, now held the reins. The friction grew until it culminated in a formal request from Odeneal to Major John Green of the 1st Cavalry, commanding Fort Klamath, to put the Modocs on their reservation, "peaceably if you can, forcibly if you must." On the night of November 28th, 1872, Captain James Jackson, with twenty-eight soldiers and ten civilian volunteers, marched silently to the Modoc camp on Lost River.

Two years before Captain Jack had killed a Klamath medicine man. The chief's daughter was ill, and he, passionately fond of his children, summoned the medicine man to attend her. The shaman was highly renowned among his own people but in spite of his most solemn incantations, the girl died. Captain Jack showed little emotion when he was told she was dead. But he went into his hut, came out with his rifle, and without a word of explanation, shot the medicine man dead.

Captain Jackson was authorized to arrest the Modoc leader on a charge of murder based on this incident. Of course the murder charge was only a pretext and all the Indians knew it.

Jackson reached the Modoc village shortly after dawn of November 29th. The Indians were camped on both sides of the river, the larger band on the near side, and the rest, headed by Curley Headed Doctor and Hooker Jim, just opposite. Jackson approached the larger camp, while the ten civilians crossed the river and headed for the smaller one. The Indians came out of their huts and listened with astonishment to the white commander's order to surrender. Captain Jack remained inside his lodge.

Surprised though they were, the Modocs were not ready to comply. Among them was a particularly ferocious-looking savage called Scarface Charley. His had been a sad and bitter experience with the whites. With his own eyes he had witnessed the lynching of his father.

Lieutenant F. A. Boutelle, with a squad of men, started toward the Indians at Jackson's order. With a harsh cry, Scarface Charley threw his rifle to his shoulder and fired. The soldiers halted, then returned a scattering volley. The Modoc War was on.

At Scarface Charley's shot, Captain Jack stepped out of his door for the first time, and calmly took command. Almost at the same moment the civilians across the river opened fire on Hooker Jim's village.

Short, sharp and fierce was the battle. Captain Jack had only fourteen warriors, who were hampered by the presence of their women and children. Hooker Jim had even fewer. But on his side of the river, the ten civilians were badly beaten. Three of them were killed and another wounded. The survivors were driven for refuge to Crawley's ranch which was near. On the opposite side of the river, Jackson's troops fired volley after volley into the smoke of the Modocs' guns, hitting several women and children. Sergeant Harris was killed in the fight and seven enlisted men wounded.

The Modocs retreated. With eight of his twenty-eight men disabled, Jackson could not pursue. He also retreated, ferried his wounded over to Crawley's ranch, and sent for help.

•   •   •   •   •   •   •   •   •

Near Tule Lake, in northern California, exists a peculiar geological freak, known as the Lava Beds. Some time during remote ages, a volcanic eruption spread hot lava over an area about fifty square miles in extent. The formation which resulted is thus described by Captain Lydecker of the United States Engineers, who surveyed and mapped it:

"The beds present the appearance on first view of an immense sagebrush plain, with no obstructions to easy movement in any direction. A closer examination, however, develops the fact that the plain is broken at irregular intervals by sections of low, rocky ridges. The ridges are not isolated, but occur in groups, and form a perfect network of obstructions, admirably adapted to a defense by an active enemy; they seldom rise to a height of ten feet above the bed, and are, as a rule, split open at the top, thus giving continuous cover along their crests."

To these Lava Beds, one of the most perfect natural fortifications to be found in the whole American continent, Captain Jack led his people. His band molested nobody on its march. Hooker Jim's people, who went in a separate division, killed every male settler they met—seventeen in all—but even they harmed no women.

In the northern end of the congealed mass of lava, near Tule Lake itself, the Indians established their camp in what are now known as the Modoc Caves. Captain Jack was soon joined by Hooker Jim and his braves, together with other warriors who came in, raising the Modoc leader's fighting force to fifty.

Meanwhile Lieutenant Colonel Frank Wheaton marched for the Lava Beds. He found the Modocs in a natural fort, every inch of which they knew so well that they could traverse it blindfolded without being seen at any time by watchers from outside. Wheaton camped his four hundred soldiers and a battery of howitzers at the edge of the Lava Beds. The men were all well armed and equipped, eager to attack and confident of victory.

The Modocs were equally confident. They boasted they could hold off a thousand soldiers. The boast was shouted to the white men when they arrived at the Lava Beds. It was laughed at then, but events proved it literally true.

WHEATON'S DEFEAT

Cold and foggy dawned the morning of January 17th. Wheaton believed that with the fog to mask his movements he would have little difficulty in brushing the Indians out of their stronghold. He ordered three companies of troops to attack. "If the Modocs will only make good their boast to whip a thousand soldiers all will be satisfied," he had written airily two days before.

Joyous at the prospect of action, the soldiers started out across the slag heaps. A stunning surprise awaited them there. As they entered the Lava Beds, they were met by a sudden deadly fire, which left numbers of them crumpled among the rocks. Forward they went, but it was no brisk charge such as they had anticipated. The razor edges of the volcanic rocks, tortured into weird whorls and gullies by the long-dead fires from the bowels of the earth, hampered them so that they moved forward at a bare walk. All day they fought. They scrambled over seemingly impassable crevasses. They shot blindly and saw their comrades struck down at their sides by a continuous withering fire which came from they knew not where. The fog, upon which Wheaton had counted to hide their movements, proved the Modocs' best friend. Throughout the whole long day the soldiers never saw an Indian.

Forward they still stumbled. Their shoes were slashed to ribbons by the sharp needles under their feet. Occasionally they saw a puff of smoke, but when, after half an hour's creeping on bleeding knees, they reached the place, the Modoc whose rifle had spoken there was gone. Bullets whined constantly about their ears. They lost and lost, without wounding a single enemy. The long day dragged its course. At evening Wheaton ordered them to withdraw.

The men were utterly exhausted. They had lost thirty-nine, nine of them dead. The wounded were carried out of the Lava Beds but it was impossible to move the dead. Even the unwounded were cut and bleeding from the diabolic rocks. Practically a fourth of the battalion which began the battle was on the casualty list. Included in this number were three wounded officers, Captain Perry and Lieutenants Kyle and Roberts.

The Modocs had made good their boast, but Wheaton was not through. All the more he was determined to drive those Modocs out of the Lava Beds at any cost. A message was sent for reinforcements and his changed opinion and new respect for his enemy was revealed in the report he made with his request for help:

"In the opinion of any experienced officer of regulars or volunteers, one thousand men would be required to dislodge them from their almost impregnable position, and it must be done deliberately with a full use of mortars."

What a compliment was that report to the tattered handful of Indians with their muzzle-loading rifles and their few revolvers. It brought General Canby down to take command in person. As has been said, Canby's sense of fairness was never limited by the color of a man's skin. He knew that the poor, hectored handful of humanity now besieged had been shamefully treated and his first thought was that things might be adjusted peaceably.

A suspension of hostilities was ordered by the general on January 30th, to permit a peace commission to treat with the Indians. Nothing came of it. The Indians refused to meet where they would be in the power of the whites—they remembered too well the lesson

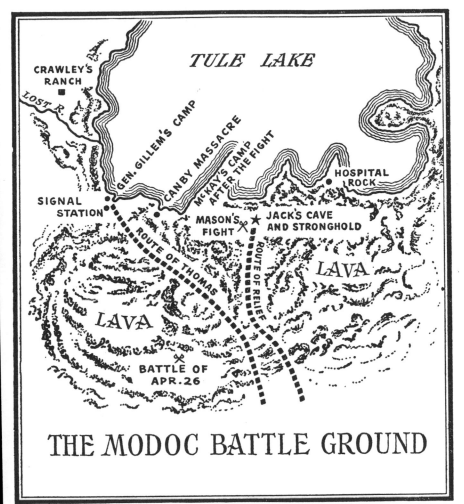

THE MODOC BATTLE GROUND

Ben Wright had taught them. The whites were equally cautious about going into the power of the Indians. So February passed without results.

In the meantime reinforcements had been brought up until between one thousand and twelve hundred troops were camped at the edge of the Lava Beds. Canby made one last effort for peace. He changed the personnel of the peace commission which had been composed of men not trusted by the Modocs, and included in it the following: Judge Roseborough, Reverend Eleazer Thomas, L. S. Dyer, and A. B. Meacham, the former agent of the Modocs. To this group the general added himself.

Negotiations dragged. Captain Jack showed a desire for peace. He sent a letter by his sister Mary to the commission on March 6th in which he said:

"I am very sad. I want peace quick or let the soldiers come and make haste and fight. . . . Let everything be wiped out, washed out, and let there be no more blood. I have got a bad heart about these murders. . . . I want the soldiers to go away . . ." [6]

Canby knew that with the civil authorities to satisfy he could not accede to the request of the chief that the troops be moved away, until the leaders of Hooker Jim's band,—Curley Headed Doctor, Bogus Charley, Shacknasty Jim, and Hooker Jim—were surrendered to stand trial for their murders of settlers while on the march to the Lava Beds.

In the Indian camp an evil leaven was working. The proscribed leaders, of course, wished the war to continue. Well they knew that their shrift would be short if they surrendered. Captain Jack, who thus far had waged a war which was well within the limits of civilized rules, was torn between conflicting desires. His people demanded that he continue to fight. Yet he knew that peace was best for them. As the debate raged, tense scenes were enacted in the Lava Beds.[7] Finally the chief gave in. And when he submitted to the wishes of his tribe, he seemed to decide that he would stop at nothing.

General Canby was invited to enter the Lava Beds with his peace commission—unarmed of course—to treat with the Indians. Canby knew his danger, but resolved to risk it. On March 10th he and the commission entered the Lava Beds, to deal with Captain Jack and the Modocs in their stronghold.

---

[6] Dunn, "Massacres of the Mountains," p. 562.

[7] It is said that Captain Jack's warriors finally put a woman's shawl on the chief and told him he was nothing but a squaw. This insult, coupled with his inability to agree upon anything with the commissioners, broke down his resolution. He threw the shawl to the ground and told his tormenters that if they wanted war they should have it—and he, Kientpoos, would not be the one to ask for peace.

GENERAL CANBY'S MURDER

REPEATEDLY the peace commission appointed to treat with the Modoc Indians in the Lava Beds had been warned by well-wishing friends, that it stood in peril of death. Knowing that the warnings were not based on fancy, the members of the body nevertheless braved the danger to do their duty by the government and by the poor, desperate, badly advised savages who were cornered like wild beasts in the stony wastes.

On the morning that it started on its perilous mission, the treaty group contained the following persons:

General E. R. S. Canby, commander of the department and a proved friend of the Indians; Reverend Eleazer Thomas, a Methodist Episcopal minister who had devoted his life to them; A. B. Meacham, former Indian agent, famed for his just treatment of the Modocs; L. S. Dyer, another agent of character and standing; Riddle, an interpreter; and Winema, his Modoc wife, called Toby Riddle by the whites. With them, too, were Boston Charley and Bogus Charley, two of Captain Jack's warriors, who had gone to the soldiers' camp during the night to invite the commission out for the conference.

At the edge of the Lava Beds, in an open space near the foot of the bluff, a tent had been pitched. It was about halfway between the army lines and the Modoc lines, and its location was level enough so that a horse could be ridden to it. Three of Canby's party were, therefore, mounted—Meacham, Dyer, and the woman, Toby Riddle. Captain Jack met the commissioners with five braves, Schonchin John, Black Jim, Hooker Jim, Ellen's Man and Shacknasty Jim, who were joined by Boston Charley and Bogus Charley at the council tent.[1]

---

[1] The curious names of the Indians were not their native titles. They were named by the whites with whom they came into contact. Captain Jack was so called be-

331

It was observed that the Indians carried revolvers contrary to agreement—as a matter of fact, Meacham and Dyer also had derringers [2] in their pockets—but the consummately planned treachery was not suspected. Within fifty feet of the gully where the council was held were hidden twenty armed warriors, awaiting a signal to begin killing.

The parley opened. Canby's terms were that the Modocs should surrender the murderers and return to their reservation. Captain Jack, as before, insisted upon the removal of the soldiers and stoutly refused to give up his followers. He should have turned over those cowardly murderers without a moment's hesitation. The very men he thus defended were to be his eventual undoing. Hooker Jim's actions were insolent throughout. Several short speeches were made, the commissioners growing more and more nervous. Suddenly two Indians, named Barncho and Slolox, jumped forward from the ravine where the warriors were concealed, carrying three guns, while Steamboat Frank and another Modoc appeared from another direction.

Captain Jack gave the prearranged signal, "*At-we!*" (All ready) —and shot General Canby full through the face.

Instantly the hollow was filled with bounding Indians. Reverend Mr. Thomas was shot in the left breast by Bogus Charley. With the fear of death in his eyes, he staggered to his feet and ran, followed by two savages. A rifle shot stretched him dead within a few yards. Canby, horribly wounded by a ball which tore a ghastly hole under his left eye, fell but rose and tried to get away. Ellen's Man, one of the Modoc warriors, shot him and Captain Jack stooped over him to see if he was dead. The great-hearted general, friend of the men who were murdering him, groaned. At that feeble moan, Cap-

---

cause of his fondness for brass buttons. Hooker Jim had worked for the Hooker family. Shacknasty Jim's shack was always in an unclean condition. Boston Charley was light in color, hence like the white men or "Boston People." Black Jim, on the other hand, was very dark. Scarface Charley had a deep, ugly, three-cornered scar on his right cheek which disfigured him. Schonchin John was the brother of Old Schonchin, the chief. And so on.

[2] A derringer was a small, single-shot, pocket pistol very popular at one time in the West. It was named after the American gunsmith who invented it.

tain Jack plunged his knife again and again into the prostrate back, until Canby lay still and lifeless. Meacham was missed by the first bullet, although Schonchin John fired at less than four feet. The former agent whipped out his derringer and fired back, but missed. Then a second ball struck him in the head and he fell unconscious to the lava floor. Riddle, his ear burned by a rifle bullet, and Dyer, the agent, ran for their lives with Hooker Jim in pursuit. At about two hundred yards Dyer pulled out his derringer and pointed it at the Modoc. He did not fire, but Hooker Jim drew back and permitted the two to escape.

Only brave Toby Riddle, the Indian squaw, remained behind. Slolox, one of the warriors who had been hiding in the ravine, hit her across the back with his rifle, but Captain Jack harshly ordered her left alone. The Modocs were stripping the clothing from the dead. Boston Charley stooped and began to scalp Meacham.

"Soldiers! Soldiers!" It was Toby Riddle's voice. Boston Charley desisted and ran for cover. The shooting had been heard by soldiers at the army camp. Troops were actually coming at the double-quick, although Toby had not seen them when she called. The quick-witted woman used the ruse to save Meacham from being scalped.

As the troops approached, Scarface Charley, posted at the edge of the Lava Beds, shot down Lieutenant Sherwood. In spite of that the soldiers came right on. The Indians slipped away to their retreats like ghosts.

In the little hollow which was to have been dedicated to peace the ghastly wreckage of treachery was found. A few feet apart lay the bodies of General Canby and Reverend Mr. Thomas. Further on was Meacham, wounded five times and partly scalped. It seemed impossible that he should recover, but he finally did so. The dead and wounded were carried back to camp. Lieutenant Sherwood died three days later.

THE BEGINNING OF THE ATTACK

The army was crazy for revenge. But revenge, it was to find, was hard to obtain. Colonel Alvin Gillem, who took command at Canby's death, took prompt action. Mortars were brought up on

March 14th, and all next day shells were thrown into the lava fields. A few Indians were killed.[3] Then the troops went through three days of fighting exactly like that experienced by Wheaton at the start of the war.

It was hard—terribly hard—but bull-dog tenacity finally had its effect. Captain Jack was forced at last to withdraw to another part of the Lava Beds. On the morning of March 17th, three months after the fighting began, the soldiers entered the Modoc Caves, and found them deserted. A small Modoc rear guard fired a few derisive shots and disappeared. In the three days' attack the troops had lost eight men killed and seventeen wounded. They found the bodies of three warriors and eight squaws in the stronghold which had been so gallantly defended.

And where were the Indians now? It was six days before the Modocs were found—and when the soldiers found them they had cause to regret that they had done so. A party of Warm Springs Indians [4] headed by their interpreter, Donald McKay, reinforced the soldiers and took charge of the scouting. By this time the over-confidence of the soldiers had been converted to a respect which was almost fear.

Early on the morning of March 26th, Captain Evan Thomas, with eighty-five men, began a reconnaissance of the Lava Beds, to try to discover if mortar batteries could be taken far enough into them to shell the new Modoc stronghold which had been discovered just three days before.

Thomas marched toward a sand hill which he had marked near the center of the Lava Beds as a possible artillery emplacement. He was not hunting for Indians at all, but he found them. As the command halted for lunch at noon, a sudden, completely unlooked-

---

[3] The chief damage was due to the Modocs' own curiosity. One of the shells failed to explode. The Indians gathered around and examined it. One tried to draw the fuse plug with his teeth. The shell exploded and blew the group into eternity. This was shortly before nightfall on the 16th.

[4] These Indians, from Warm Springs, Oregon, are not to be confused with the Warm Springs Indians of New Mexico. The Oregon Indians were excellent scouts, but were extremely religious. They were Christians and absolutely refused to scout or fight on Sunday, which considerably impaired their effectiveness since the Modocs possessed no such scruples.

for volley lashed into them from the ridges about. The soldiers found themselves in a valley of doom. On both sides lay the hidden Modocs, their bullets cutting the troops down.

There was a panic. "We're surrounded!" was the cry. Commands were not heeded. Some of the men sneaked away and retreated to the main camp. The rest took refuge on the sand hill near them.

With a handful of soldiers, Lieutenant Wright advanced toward a ridge on the west. Lieutenant Cranston with five soldiers attempted to reach another ridge to the north. Every man in Cranston's detachment was killed. The rest of the troops, about thirty including the surviving officers, followed Wright within a few minutes. They could hear heavy firing. By the time they reached Wright the Indians had cut his platoon to pieces. As the main body came up to a hollow which he was supposed to occupy, it was greeted by another death-dealing Modoc fusillade.

About this time McKay and his Warm Springs Indians, who had been scouting far out ahead, slipped back and attempted to join the soldiers. But the fear-stricken troops, mistaking them for Modocs, began shooting at them. The scouts tried every possible device to show who they were. They even captured an escaping bugler and at the points of their rifles forced the craven to sound the whole gamut of bugle calls. Thomas' men could not understand. McKay's Indians had to remain concealed between two fires, until the fight was over. Miraculously not one of them was hit.

Only twenty men now remained with Thomas. The captain kept steadying the survivors. "We're surrounded, but we can die like brave men," he said over and over. Although they fought as best they could behind the volcanic rocks, the Modocs had them at their mercy. Thomas was killed. Lieutenant Howe also fell dead. Lieutenant Harris was already dying from a wound.

But help was coming at last. Major Green had heard the firing and was rushing all available reinforcements to what was left of Thomas' command. The relief reached the battle ground late in the afternoon, in time to save the remnant. All that night they held the position, yet in spite of their watchfulness the snake-like Modocs crawled through the lines to scalp the dead and rob the bodies. In the morning the Indians were gone. The troops also retired, carrying their dead and wounded.

In that day's fighting, eighteen enlisted men had been killed and seventeen wounded. Captain Thomas was dead as were Lieutenants Cranston, Wright and Howe. The only other line officer, Lieutenant Harris, died in a few days, and Surgeon Semig, who heroically performed his duties without regard to flying bullets, suffered a shattered knee which necessitated the amputation of his leg.

The most astonishing thing about the affair, as the whites later learned, was that the Modocs had only twenty-one warriors in the fight. Not one of them was hit. With less than one-fourth of the total number of their enemies, they had inflicted a crushing blow, and had killed or wounded nearly twice their number of foes.

GENERAL DAVIS TAKES COMMAND

Within a few days General Jefferson C. Davis arrived at the Lava Beds to take command. He found the troops dispirited, half convinced that they could not whip the Modocs. The utter invisibility and silence of the Indians were fearsome. Davis spent days rebuilding the morale of his men. Then he went to work to squeeze out the Modocs.

Fortune favored him. Hooker Jim, who had been one of the leading advocates of war to the hilt, was tiring of it. Some time early in May he separated from Captain Jack. Davis drew his cordon tighter each day. Numerous skirmishes were fought. Finally Captain Jack resolved to leave the Lava Beds for the open country.

A pair of friendly Indian squaws first reported the departure. Soon afterward the news was confirmed by the Warm Springs scouts. Then came word that the Modocs had captured a supply train of four wagons outside of the Lava Beds near Tule Lake, wounding three of the escort. Major H. C. Hasbrouck, with two squadrons of cavalry and some Warm Springs Indians, rode in pursuit.

He camped the night of May 10th near Sorass Lake. At dawn the same fierce warriors who had so often defeated the white men charged down upon him. Captain Jack himself, clad in General Canby's uniform, led the rush. Behind him were thirty-three warriors.

Momentarily in confusion, the cavalry soon rallied and fought back. The first charge scattered the troopers' horses and pack mules, but Hasbrouck led a counter-attack which drove the Modocs from the adjacent hills. Most important, a pack train of twenty-four mules, carrying practically all the Indians' ammunition, was captured. And all this with the loss of but three killed and seven wounded on the white side. One Modoc was killed.

The Modocs, who had fought well together in victory, now began to find how much harder it is to stand defeat. After Hasbrouck's repulse of their attack, there was a violent quarrel between Captain Jack and Hooker Jim. The latter accused his leader of being tyrannical. All of the Indians concerned in the murders of the settlers during the march from Lost River to the Lava Beds at the start of the war, sided with Hooker Jim. The separation, already begun, became final. Hooker Jim, with the men whom Captain Jack had defended and in whose behalf he had committed the act of treachery which made him a marked man, went away, deserting their leader. There were thirteen warriors and sixty-two women and children in this band. The best part of the fighting men, however, thirty all told, with fifty-two women and children, remained staunchly with their chief. This separation occurred about May 15th.

As soon as the split in the Modoc band was discovered, Davis ordered pursuit. The trail of Hooker Jim's band was picked up by Hasbrouck, who overtook the Indians after a hard march of fifty miles. For seven miles the Modocs kept up a running battle before they scattered. Next day, May 22nd, all of Hooker Jim's followers came in and surrendered.

Where now was the resolution which the Indians had shown in the three months' heroic resistance under Captain Jack? Hooker Jim, Bogus Charley, Shacknasty Jim and Steamboat Frank, all involved in the murders which had caused Captain Jack to refuse

Canby's peace terms because he did not wish to see them hanged, displayed overweening eagerness to be of service to the white man. One after another they suggested that they be allowed to go to Captain Jack's camp to secure his surrender. On Willow Creek, where the turncoats found the chief and his people, there was a stormy interview. Captain Jack was full of intense scorn.

"You are cowards and squaws," he hurled at them. "You got me into this war and now you desert me. Kientpoos will never surrender; he will die with his gun in his hand."

Back to the troops slunk Hooker Jim and his partners. The next day they were leading the soldiers to the hiding place of their fugitive leader—traitors to him and their people.

At 2 o'clock on the afternoon of May 29th, Hasbrouck's cavalry struck Captain Jack's camp. Rifles rattled briefly. Then Boston Charley came out of the brush with his hands up. Seven women, including "Princess Mary," the chief's sister, were captured. The rest of the band escaped by running down a canyon where horses could not follow.

But the end was very near for Captain Jack. His band, harassed and pursued by the cavalry, was captured, one by one. The inevitable came at last. With but two faithful warriors and several women and children, the chief was surrounded a few miles above the mouth of Willow Creek, by Captain Perry's cavalry squadron on June 1st.

There was nothing to do but surrender—Captain Jack saw that. One of his two warriors was sent forward with a flag of truce, a white rag tied to a stick. He told Captain Perry that Kientpoos wished to give himself up. Perry consented.

A few more minutes and a solitary figure stepped from the woods. He gazed about him with an expression of utter hopelessness, then came forward and held out his hands for the manacles to be put upon them.

"My legs have given out," was all he said.

With him surrendered the last of the Modocs, two warriors, fifteen squaws and seven children.

CAPTAIN JACK'S EXECUTION

That ended the Modoc War but it did not complete the tragic drama. The Indians had dealt a stunning blow to the white man's prestige.[5] Examples must be made. General Davis was for hanging the leaders out of hand, but was stopped by a telegram from Washington ordering their trial by a military commission. That body sat at Fort Klamath from July 5th to July 9th. And here occurred the crowning act of infamy on the part of Hooker Jim and his worthies—they turned state's evidence.

The Indians arraigned were Captain Jack, Schonchin John, Black Jim, Boston Charley, Barncho and Slolox. Ellen's Man was dead. Hooker Jim had bought immunity with his promise to testify. The prisoners were charged with the murders of General Canby and Reverend Thomas, in violation of the rules of war.

The Modoc prisoners saw the men they had defended sitting with the tribunal as their accusers. They knew there was no mercy there. In spite of the fact that the trial was conducted with the utmost fairness, the verdict was a foregone conclusion. Little testimony was introduced by the Indians.

Captain Jack made one halting speech in his own defense. Not gifted with any natural eloquence, he tried to tell the commission about his early life.

"I have always lived like a white man and wanted to live so," he said. "I have always tried to live peaceably and never asked any man for anything . . . have never gone begging; what I have got I have always got with my own hands, honestly . . . I don't know

---

[5] The summary of losses in the Modoc War is as follows:

Whites	Killed	Wounded
Officers	8	5
Enlisted men	39	60
Civilians	16	—
Scouts	2	—
Settlers	17	18
	82	83
Indian (Men) killed	5	

Several women and children were also killed.

how white people talk in such a place as this; but I will do the best I can."

Told by the Judge Advocate to "talk exactly as if you were at home, in council," he went on to say that the whole trouble was caused by Captain Jackson's attack; that his people feared treachery and fled. When he reached the place where he had given in to the demands of the murderers, he choked and could not finish—emotion strange for an Indian. Then he asked the court to adjourn until next day. The request was granted.

By the next day his full composure was restored. Captain Jack was every inch the warrior again. Short, sharp and pointed were his words. He pointed out that his accusers—the wretched, spineless tribesmen, who to save their own worthless lives had turned state's evidence and given their leader to the gallows—were the very men he had refused to surrender to the commission to be tried for murder.

That was all. It was inadequate. The prisoners were found guilty and sentenced to death.

At 10 o'clock on the morning of Friday, October 3rd, 1873, Captain Jack, Schonchin John, Boston Charley and Black Jim were hanged before the assembly of Klamaths and their own people. The sentences of Barncho and Slolox were commuted to life imprisonment on Alcatraz Island.

The four condemned men met their deaths with typical Indian stoicism. As he stepped out on the gallows platform, Captain Jack took one last, long, lingering look which swept far to the horizon of the country he loved and for which he had fought. His eyes descended from the hills and rivers of his beloved land to a high stockade at the foot of the gallows. In it he saw the faces of his people—penned up like cattle to see his execution. He must have seen his wives and children there, children he loved with the deep fervor of fatherhood, a fervor which induced him to kill the man who failed to save the life of one of his little ones.

Not a word did he speak, although there was much, very much, which clamored to be said. The treachery of Ben Wright still went unpunished. One of the men who stood with a noose about his neck beside the chief—Schonchin John—could have told first-hand of that massacre. Other wrongs heaped upon the Modocs by the white man cried for utterance. Captain Jack was silent. His was not the gift of tongues.

The hoods were adjusted over their heads. At a signal the traps were sprung. There was an involuntary cry of horror, even from the spiteful onlooking Klamaths, as the men died.

The prestige of the white man was upheld.

But was it quite upheld?

14: THE DEATH CAVE

COCHISE SURRENDERS

WHILE the events described in the past two chapters were taking place in northern California, the Apache War, with varying fortunes, still swung back and forth in the Southwestern deserts. After a decade the celebrated "Extermination Policy" had failed. And when, in July, 1871, the government decided to try a policy of conciliation, the situation was very bad.

Cochise, chief of the Chiricahuas, was in particular a problem. In May, 1871, he ambushed and killed Lieutenant Howard B. Cushing, one of the ablest, most tireless, and most successful Indian fighters of Arizona.[1] In three years the young officer had led his 3rd Cavalry detachment over thousands of miles of desert mountains and desert country, fought scores of skirmishes, killed a number of Indians, and destroyed several *rancherias,* laying waste to the small fields planted by the squaws, wherever they were found.

But Cochise at last stopped his campaigns.

It was May 5th. With twenty-two men Cushing was following like a blood-sleuth on the trail of Cochise. The track led toward the Bear Springs in the Whetstone Mountains. There lay Cochise, the serpent-like. In spite of all his experience, Cushing ran right into the trap, laid along the sides of a canyon leading to the springs.

Before a shot was fired, the whites were surrounded. Sergeant

[1] Cushing came from a famous family. One of his brothers was renowned for his exploit in blowing up the Confederate ram "Albermarle" during the Civil War. Another died in the repulse of Pickett's charge at Gettysburg. Still another had a distinguished service record in the U. S. Navy. This member of the family was typical of the lot. His relentlessness in fighting Apaches was due to the death at their hands of a close friend, Lieutenant Franklin Yeaton, in the fall of 1869. Cushing brooded over this and was positively ferocious in his pursuit of the Indians.

John Mott, a veteran Indian fighter, first detected the presence of the Apaches and called Cushing's attention to it. The warning came too late. At the first tearing volley from the bushes, Cushing dropped, a bullet through his body. Down the sides of the gorge bounded the Apaches. It was hand to hand. Mott finally extricated a few survivors from the canyon, but he left behind the bodies of the lieutenant and several men. Days later troops from Fort Crittenden found the mangled corpses. By then Cochise and his warriors were safely across the international boundary in Mexico.

On July 21st, 1871, President Grant appointed Vincent Colyer his personal representative in Arizona and sent him to the Southwest with plenary powers to "locate the nomadic tribes upon suitable territories, and bring them under control of the proper officers of the Indian Department." [2] Colyer knew the President's kindly attitude toward the Indians. He worked hard, trying to conciliate them and actually succeeded in bringing about friendly relations with some. But the Camp Grant massacre, the Pinal Treaty, and the Extermination Policy were too fresh in the minds of most Apaches to permit them to listen to white promises of peace.[3] Had Colyer gone to Arizona ten years earlier, he might have had much greater success.

Most important of the chiefs who quit the war path under Colyer's policy was Cochise himself. After some negotiations, he met a peace commission headed by General Gordon Granger at the Cañada Alamosa, early in September. The great Apache appeared with his warriors around him. Apparently he at first suspected treachery, but he finally joined the council circle and blew a cloud of smoke with General Granger. The conversation was in Spanish.

Granger told the chief he must stop raiding, expressed the Presi-

[2] Order of authorization from the War Department, July 21, 1871.

[3] "This report shows plainly that . . . the Apache Indians were the friends of the Americans when they first knew them; that they have always desired peace with them . . . the peaceable relations continued until the Americans adopted the Mexican theory of 'extermination,' and by acts of inhuman treachery and cruelty made them (the Apaches) our implacable foes; that this policy has resulted in a war which, in the last ten years, has cost us a thousand lives and over forty millions of dollars, and the country is no quieter nor the Indians any nearer extermination than they were at the time of the Gadsden purchase."—Report to the Board of Indian Commissioners on Peace with the Apaches, made by Vincent Colyer, 1871.

dent's great desire for peace, and ended by offering the mountains and valleys in which they were then conferring as an all-time reservation for the Chiricahuas. It was part of their favorite country, and the terms were acceptable to Cochise. Dr. A. N. Ellis, who was present, thus describes him as he looked that day:

"While he was talking we had a fine opportunity to study this most remarkable man. Evidently he was about fifty-eight years of age, although he looked very much younger; his height, five feet, ten inches; in person lithe and wiry, every muscle being well rounded and firm. A silver thread was now and then visible in his otherwise black hair, which he wore cut straight around his head about on a level with his chin. His countenance displayed great force." [4]

Cochise's speech was a striking example of Indian oratory and logic. The essential sadness of the red man and his perplexity in facing the unsolvable problem presented by the white encroachment were all included. Toward its conclusion he said:

"When I was young I walked all over this country, east and west, and saw no other people than the Apaches. After many summers I walked again and found another race of people who had come to take it. How is it? Why is it that the Apaches want to die—that they carry their lives on their finger nails? They roam over the hills and plains and want the heavens to fall on them. The Apaches were once a great nation; they are now but a few. . . . Many have been killed in battle. . . . Tell me, if the Virgin Mary has walked throughout all the land, why has she never entered the lodge of the Apache?" [5]

He ended his extraordinary address by saying firmly that he would never go to the Tularosa reservation in New Mexico.

"That is a long ways off," he said. "The flies in those mountains eat out the eyes of the horses. The bad spirits live there. I have drunk of these waters. . . . I do not want to leave here."

In spite of the specific promise made by General Granger, Cochise was ordered within a few months to take his people to the hated Tularosa reservation. The Chiricahuas went into galvanic action.

[4] Kansas Historical Society Collections, Vol. XIII, p. 391.
[5] The full text of this speech is well worth reading. It is quoted by Dr. Ellis in his article in the Kansas Historical Society Collections, Vol. XIII, pp. 387–92.

Cochise took to the mountains and war flared all over the Southwest. Less than half of the sixteen hundred Apaches at Cañada Alamosa traveled to Tularosa. The rest followed Cochise. And even those who did go had to be transferred soon to Ojo Caliente, New Mexico.[6] In exactly a year, September 1st, 1871, to the same date in 1872, the Apaches made fifty-four separate attacks, killed forty-four persons, wounded sixteen, and ran off much livestock. The white man's inability to keep his promises was reaping its usual harvest.

THE TONTO BASIN

General George Crook, known to the Indians as Nan-tan Lupan (Chief Gray Wolf), took command in Arizona in July, 1871. He was an experienced Indian fighter and knew the red men thoroughly. His attitude toward the Apaches was refreshingly different from that of his predecessors. Said he: "I think the Apache is painted in darker colors than he deserves and that his villainies arise more from a misconception of facts than from his being worse than other Indians. Living in a country the natural products of which will not support him, he has either to cultivate the soil or steal, and as our vacillating policy satisfies him that we are afraid of him, he chooses the latter, also as requiring less labor and being more congenial to his natural instincts." [7]

Crook's first act was to call the troops of his department together for an inspection and practice march. When he assembled them there were just five troops of cavalry and one of scouts. The general had planned an immediate move against the hostile Apaches, but Vincent Colyer was then in Arizona, with powers from the President which exceeded those of the army. Crook marked time while long conferences took place and nothing was accomplished. The general took advantage of this delay to reorganize his forces for hard campaigning.

Lieutenant Cushing had employed friendly Apaches as scouts

---

[6] This occurred in 1874.
[7] Annual Report of the Secretary of War, 1871, p. 78.

against their hostile relatives to some extent, but Crook amplified and worked out this branch of the service in a manner never before conceived. In its ranks he put Navajos, Apaches, Opatas, Pimas, Yaquis, Pueblos, Mexicans, Americans and half-breeds of all kinds and pedigrees. This corps was to prove tremendously effective in the months to come. Skillful as he was it is doubtful if Crook could have accomplished much without his scouts. There were hatreds among the Apaches and after the days of Mangus Colorado they never presented a united front to the white man. This was taken advantage of by Crook.

The general also reorganized the pack train service to the highest state of efficiency it had ever known. He knew mules and he knew packing and he insisted on the utmost efficiency from his men. As a result of his care in this department the pack trains of his troops gave the finest service in the entire army.[8] By the time Colyer's policy late in 1871 had been proved impractical, Crook was ready to strike.

Well to the north in Arizona is the famed Tonto Basin. It is really a mountain plateau, surrounded on all sides by the high ranges of the Mogollons, the Mazatals and the Sierra Ancha, heavily timbered and snowy topped. Into this area, then comparatively little known, many of the hostile Apaches had retreated.

After Colyer had been given every chance to try persuasion and had given up his project, Crook announced in September, 1872, the new policy of "proceeding at once to punish the incorrigibly hostile." He knew that there were Tontos, Coyoteros, Yampais and Hualapais in the Tonto Basin, and that they were led by various daring chiefs, such as Del-she, Chuntz, Nata-totel, and Naquinaquis.

---

[8] On one occasion a packer who had never seen Crook was visited by the general, who was in the habit of personal inspections. The packer saw an individual dressed in the ordinary manner, who looked able bodied, and the following conversation ensued: Packer—"Say, mister, do you understand packing mules?" General Crook —"I think I do." Packer—"Have you had any experience in that line?" General Crook—"Well, considerable, here and there." Packer—"I'll give you forty dollars a month and grub to help us in this campaign." General Crook—"I'm much obliged for the offer, but I already have a job." Packer—"Is that so? What kind of a job is it?" General Crook—"Well, my friend, I am at present commander of this department."

For several reasons he set November 15th as time to start the campaign. It marked the beginning of winter, making it harder for the enemy to climb into the higher mountains because of the snow; causing the Indians to be unwilling to move if they could avoid it; and making campfires necessary, with resultant smoke which could be spotted by the keen eyes of Crook's scouts.

Promptly on the day, Crook started. The troops marched on plateaus where cold weather had already set in so hard that all the springs and small streams were frozen solid, making it difficult to water stock. Each morning the sleeping soldiers were aroused at 2 o'clock. By 4 the whole command was on the march and they did not halt until late in the afternoon.

Crook's plan was to sweep the Tonto Basin clean of hostile Indians by sending out several converging columns, each self-sufficient, but all cooperating in a central scheme. The orders were simple: The Indians were to be induced to surrender wherever possible; where they would not surrender, they were to be hit hard and hunted down until the last one in hostility was killed or captured; every effort should be made to avoid the killing of women and children; no excuse was to be accepted for leaving a trail; if horses played out, the enemy was to be followed on foot.

The Tonto Apaches were among the most dangerous of the Indians in the basin, and Crook especially wished to find the *rancheria* of Chief Chuntz, a fierce and tireless raider. This particular task was assigned to Major William H. Brown and his battalion of the 5th Cavalry. Somewhere Crook had found a young Apache called Nantahe, who had been a member of Chuntz' band and knew his favorite lairs. The general sent this scout with Brown. As events transpired, Nantahe was destined to be the decisive factor in the success of this expedition.

In addition to Nantahe, there were forty Apache and a hundred Pima scouts, the latter deadly hereditary enemies of the Apaches, under their crafty, daring chief Bocon (Big Mouth). All told, including the scouts, Brown had three hundred and twenty fighting men, with whom he set out to capture a band—as it was later learned —of ninety-four men, women and children.

THE FIGHT IN THE SALT RIVER CANYON

Brown's men spent Christmas Day on the march, cold, pinched and tired. On the night after Christmas, December 26th, the command began to ascend on foot the rugged gorge of the Salt River Canyon in the Mazatal Mountains. The night was exceptionally frosty and the men, who had left all unnecessary baggage and clothing behind them, climbed fast to keep their blood circulating. After a time a whispered command was passed back to lie down and remain silent. Far up ahead the Indian scouts had discerned the flickering of distant campfires. The scouts returned shortly with word that the fires were at an abandoned camp, where they also found fifteen foot-sore horses, recently stolen from the Pima villages on the Gila and abandoned as useless.

Again the advance began. Every precaution was taken to avoid making a noise.[9] Toward morning of December 27th, one of the scouts, ranging far ahead, smelled smoke. No Apache, knowing an enemy was on his trail, would have been guilty of so colossal a breach of woodcraft as to kindle a fire. But these Indians did not dream of the proximity of their pursuers. The keen nostrils of the scout—sensitive almost as those of a blooded hound—caught the telltale taint while the command was still a mile away. Nantahe now took charge of the troops' movements.

They were within a few minutes' climb of a cave where Chuntz' band often camped. Nantahe asked Major Brown to send a detachment of picked men with him to climb over the precipice up the canyon and head off escape from above. The officer whispered his instructions. Within an hour every man was in his place.

[9] To illustrate the wonderful perceptive powers of these Indians, during the march up the canyon, in blackest night, Nantahe suddenly threw both arms around Major Brown and stopped him from stepping forward. The Apache's moccasined foot had fallen on a depression in the trail and although he could not see it, he *knew* it was a footprint. With his fellow scouts holding blankets over him to screen the light from any possible watchers of the trail, Nantahe lay down, lit a match, and inspected the sign. In a moment he was up again, grinning in the dark. It was not a human track but a bear track, very similar in size and shape. The wonderful thing about the incident is that the Indian, although he could not see a foot ahead of him, could tell in an instant that he had stepped into a track which was like a human footprint.

Lieutenant William J. Ross led the men who went over the precipice. And it was he who opened the battle. Creeping to where he could see, Ross descried in plain view a large rock shed, in which were many Apaches engaged in their early morning activities. The sun had just risen and he could see women cooking, children playing about, and men smoking. On a sort of shelf in front of the cave a party of returned raiders was dancing. So peaceful was the scene that it required an effort of mind to realize that here was as bloody a band of savages as the world contained.

By now the unsuspecting Apaches were all "bottled up". Ross' men chose the warriors as their targets and the lieutenant gave the order to fire. The crashing volley, which re-echoed a dozen times from the canyon walls, was the first intimation the Indians had that danger was near. Six of them, killed instantly, never knew what enemy had fired.

It was wonderful how quickly and smoothly the Apache mind worked in a crisis. Without stopping to take a look in the direction of the shooting, warriors, women and children sprang for the one haven of safety—the cave, which had a natural parapet of boulders along its front. Not a moment's hesitation, not a bit of confusion, but before the troopers could fire a second volley, the face of the cliff was vacant except for six huddled heaps of rags and gaudy finery which represented the corpses of six men who had a moment before been full of life.

Now Nantahe, calling out in the Tonto tongue, shouted across the canyon a summons to the Indians to surrender. A yell of defiance was the reply. With the first shots sputtering out the battle began.

Brown's experienced eye saw at once that a direct charge and an attempt to scale the parapet would be too costly. The rock wall was at least ten feet high at its lowest point and smooth and slippery as well. The Apaches could have clubbed the climbing soldiers as they mounted, even had the Indians not possessed modern firearms with which to shoot them.

Assault was out of the question. Attrition seemed the better plan. At vantage points on the wall of the canyon opposite the cave,

Brown placed six sharpshooters. A first line of battle was arranged, in a sort of half moon, with flanks resting on the canyon's rocky walls, about fifty yards from the Indian position. Back of this line were more marksmen, carbines ready, watching to prevent the escape of a single warrior.

The men in the first line could not reach the Apaches by direct fire. Brown directed them to aim against the granite roof of the cave so that the bullets would glance down among the Indians massed behind the rampart. It was like shooting with the eyes shut, but the men opened fire with enthusiasm and results were soon apparent. The Apaches, goaded into desperation by the glancing bullets, began to return the soldiers' fire. Squaws loaded the warriors' guns. Now and then a baby's wail or a woman's cry showed that the leaden hail was taking effect on others besides men behind the bloody rampart.

After thirty minutes of continuous firing, Brown gave the order to cease. Again the Apaches were offered a chance to surrender or let their women and children come out unharmed. In the silence which followed, a peculiar chanting sounded from the cave. Nantahe listened intently. "Look out! That's their death song; they're going to charge!" he cried sharply.

At the words, twenty almost naked brown figures catapulted over the rampart, their hair bound back from their faces by red turbans, their bodies splashed with war paint. They came shooting. Half stood upright on the rocky wall and blazed away at the soldiers below as rapidly as they could work the levers on their guns. The others went bounding like catamounts down the slope toward the right flank. For a moment it looked as if they might break through. But the troopers flung themselves into a hand-to-hand mêlée. Six or seven men were killed in a space only a few feet square. The sortie was over. Back into the cave ran the survivors. In a few minutes only the blank wall of the parapet presented itself to the eyes of the besiegers.

One of the charging Indians did break through. He got beyond the first line and, not seeing the second line behind him, was in the act of giving a war whoop of encouragement to his friends, when he saw death staring him in the eye. Twenty carbines were concentrated upon him. In an instant it was over. The poor devil tried to say something: "No! No! Soldados!" was what it sounded like, but the twenty guns rang out and the warrior was dead. His body was almost pulverized by the volley, and the force of the bullets was such that he seemed to be lifted clear off the ground and hurled back by them.

Brown redoubled the fire on the cave. Feebler and feebler was the Apache reply. And now came the turning point. Captain James Burns, with two men, climbed the canyon above the cave. By leaning over they could see the Apaches behind the rock wall which jutted out somewhat from the cliff. Burns had an idea. Sending for more men, he reverted to stone-age warfare. Within a few minutes he had his men throwing and rolling boulders down on the rampart. Many of the rocks hit on top of or directly behind the wall. The havoc was fearful. Men, women and children were smashed into wet pulp beneath the huge, bounding stones.

That boulder barrage ended the battle. After ten minutes the soldiers stopped rolling rocks, and skirmishers cautiously advanced from below. Corporal Hanlon, of Troop G, was the first man over the top. Even to the hardened old soldier, the sight was sickening. In an indescribably shocking mess, the wretched Indians lay mangled, dead or dying. Only eighteen persons, all women or children, were found living and practically all of these were wounded or injured by the boulders. Seventy-four were dead. Brown had carried out his orders. The band was wiped out.[10]

---

[10] Six or seven young women escaped at the start of the fight and made their way to their friends in other bands. They had been sent to examine a mescal pit at dawn and the first volley warned them not to return. One other person escaped. A warrior, badly wounded in the leg, had lain down behind one of the great slabs of stone which leaned against the rear wall. As the fight progressed more and more corpses piled about him, and when the soldiers entered, they completely overlooked him. After they left, he improvised himself a pair of crutches and crawled and hobbled to Tonto Creek where he met and turned back another band of Indians which might have run into the soldiers.

15: CONCENTRATION

WHILE it was by far the most crushing blow given by Crook's forces during the campaign, the destruction of Chuntz' band was only one of several victories for the soldiers. Chuntz himself had escaped—a big disappointment to Crook. Warned, either by the escaping girls or by the wounded warrior, he was able to elude Brown, having been away when the soldiers struck. The following day after the fight in the cave, he joined Del-she's band with the few warriors left to him. But in doing so he selected anything but a haven.

There still remained, in the Tonto Basin, two strongholds where Crook believed large bodies of Indians were lurking. One of these was the almost inaccessible top of Turret Butte. The other was in the fastnesses of the Superstition Mountains.

Brown marched toward the last named place. With all the care which had characterized his former efforts, he combed this area, but the Apaches were alert. Time after time they eluded him. Once, in the early morning of January 15th, 1873, he "jumped" a small *rancheria* and captured it, killing three Indians and capturing thirteen, all women and children. But the main body escaped.

It was bitter cold and the troops suffered in the high mountains. Still Brown grimly held to his purpose. Three days after the capture of the *rancheria*, some yells were heard from the high shoulder of a mountain near the trail. Like hounds slipped from their leashes, a dozen or more lean Apache scouts detached themselves from the column and melted into the underbrush. The soldiers halted. Every ear was strained for the opening reports of the rifles. Minutes stretched into half an hour or more. Still not a sound was heard. It was as if there were nobody on that mountain side, yet every man in the detachment was morally certain that there were scores of Apaches there.

Suddenly the sibilant, warning scout hiss: "Tssit! Tssit!" sounded down the trail. Every eye turned in that direction. The bushes parted and the scouts stepped into view—with a captive.

But what a captive! The cruel faces of the scouts expanded into broad grins. In their midst was a tiny, black-eyed boy. Not more than eight years old was he, yet he carried himself with the pride of a chief. And well he might—he was the emissary of his people, sent down by them to interview the white commander. With all his pride the lad was badly frightened. He trembled as he confronted the major. Yet there was an edge of defiance to his voice as he delivered his message: His people wanted no more war, but wished to make peace.

It was Brown's turn to grin. Food was brought to the youngster, and then tobacco with which the eight-year-old filled a pipe and puffed away with all the gravity and satisfaction of an octogenarian. Having filled the young emissary's belly with beans and given him a smoke, Brown provided him with an old army blouse—the boy was naked to the waist in that bitter weather—and sent him back to his people, with a message that while the lad was too young to talk with men, he could see for himself that the troops would receive favorably real peace talk, and not harm any Indians who were sincere about wanting to surrender.

Up the mountain side scurried the boy, mightily relieved to be out of the reach of the white men. An hour later the soldiers in Brown's column heard another series of shouts. This time it was unnecessary to send out scouts. It was the boy again. He brought with him a wrinkled old squaw to talk with the major. Once more Brown refused to discuss terms with anyone less than a warrior. The squaw in turn was fed and sent back.

For the third time shouts up the mountain warned of an envoy. This time it was an aged and very decrepit old man. Down the slope he came, using a long walking-stick to support his feeble body. And now Brown consented at last to talk. He told the old chief that Nan-tan Lupan was determined to bring every Apache to peace or hunt him down, and indicated that only an immediate surrender would save the Indians. The old man replied that his band could not surrender on the instant. It was scattered too widely to be assembled at once, having separated in every direction at the approach of the troops. He added that if the soldiers would march directly to Camp Grant, he would gather his people together and they would follow, catching up at the junction of the Gila and San Pedro Rivers, and there surrender.

Major Brown agreed. He marched slowly across the mountains to the appointed place. But there was not a sign of an Indian. It was a bitter disappointment. The army saw itself tricked again. But the Indian scouts were unperturbed. "Wait and see!" said they.

Just at evening, the old chief came cautiously sidling into camp, accompanied by a few warriors. He wanted to know what would be done with his people when they surrendered. Brown replied that only Crook himself could decide that. Another smoke, and the Apaches vanished again into the mountains.

Next morning as the troops started up the San Pedro there was not an Apache in sight. But as the march progressed, a furtive Indian appeared from behind a cluster of mesquite and slipped in among the scouts. Another and another emerged from behind sagebrush, or *palo verde* or cereus cactus. Each newcomer's face was a study in anxiety and fear. "*Sisquism*" (My brother) was the greeting of each, uttered in a manner half supplicating, half defiant. By the time the troops reached Camp Grant, one hundred and ten men, women and children had joined the column. It was a decisive and bloodless victory and cleared the Superstition Mountains of hostile Apaches.

THE CAPTURE OF TURRET BUTTE

Meanwhile a blow almost as crushing as the debacle at the Salt River Canyon cave had been struck by Major George M. Randall of the 23rd Infantry.

After Chuntz joined Del-she's band, the Tonto Apaches raided south again, toward Wickenburg, near which they overwhelmed a party of young Englishmen, headed by a man named Taylor, who, lured by visions of wealth in cattle raising or mining, had recently crossed the ocean. The Indians killed most of the party immediately, but two were captured and tortured to death.[1]

Following their usual tactics, the Tontos retreated rapidly to their coverts, across the Bradshaw Mountains, then to the Tonto Basin. They had twenty-four hours' start of the troops, but Randall knew where he was going, and what he would do when he got there.

Turret Butte is named from the fact that it is shaped much like the turret of an old-style battleship or castle, with steep walls and a comparatively flat top. It was almost inaccessible, and the Apaches, believing themselves secure there, neglected to take their customary precautions against surprise. At the base of this Gibraltar of savagery, Randall and his battalion, weary with a long march, arrived the night of April 22nd. Randall understood his danger in climbing that natural fortress. If warned, the Apaches could easily hold it. Even boulders, rolled from the top, would be deadly weapons on the treacherous slope. Everything depended upon his making the climb without the knowledge of the enemy above.

Leaving every bit of superfluous baggage at the foot, the men began the crawl up the steep slope in the darkness. Every soldier was cautioned to take the greatest care not to dislodge a stone, or even strike the metal barrel of his rifle against a tree or rock. For hours they scrambled upward. Every minute was tense. It seemed almost impossible for so large a body of men to make the climb without being discovered. But in some way they did. At last they were on the top.

It was midnight and off to one side Randall could see the red eyes of campfires at the Apache village. It was a welcome sight. It meant that his quarry was still there. The soldiers had to sit down and wait until daylight, since in the night it would have been easy for most of the Indians to escape. So with what patience they could muster the men shivered through the long hours before dawn.

The sudden, brazen blare of a bugle, sounding the charge, was the first knowledge the Apaches had that the troops were upon them.

---

[1] "The assailants . . . tied two of them to cactus, and proceeded deliberately to fill them with arrows. One of the poor wretches rolled and writhed in agony, breaking off the feathered ends of the arrows, but each time he turned his body, exposing a space not yet wounded, the Apaches shot in another barb."—John G. Bourke, "On the Border With Crook," p. 208.

With startled yelps they ran this way and that. But Randall's men cut off every retreat.

A few ripping volleys. The Indians knew they were helpless. They could not escape or even fight. Some of the warriors in despair leaped over the edge of the precipice near their camp and were dashed to death hundreds of feet below. But the rest of the band surrendered. Among the captured were the chiefs Chuntz and Delshe.

The Turret Butte fight completed the cleaning out of the Tonto Basin, and abated forever the threat of the Tonto Apaches. They never again as a tribe went on the war path.

Crook as usual dealt fairly and yet firmly with the Tontos. Most of them were sent to Fort Apache. The Apache-Mojaves, under Chali-pun, surrendered early in April. Their chief appeared with his head men at Camp Verde, and took Crook by the hand with the words, "*Demasiados cartuchos de cobre*" (Too many cartridges of copper). He meant that he had never been afraid of fighting the Americans but that they had too much fixed ammunition while most of the Apaches were still using antiquated muzzle-loading guns, or bows and arrows.

The problem of how usefully to employ his captives was Crook's next study. He set them to work under military supervision, building irrigation ditches and breaking the ground for farms. He also arranged for a cash market for their products, so that the Indians had the comfortable assurance that when their products were harvested they would receive real money for them. The Indians worked with astonishing zeal. They seemed relieved to find something to which they could turn their hands. Since they had no tools or implements of their own, Crook let them use every axe, spade, pick, hatchet and shovel not in actual service in the army cantonments. These the Apaches supplemented with sticks, pointed and hardened in fire. With their crude implements, by infinite labor, they dug a ditch five miles long, averaging four feet wide by three feet deep. The men dug; the women carried away the earth in their conical wicker baskets.

SEVEN HEADS ON THE PARADE GROUND

Crook kept under the most rigid observation the Indians on his several reservations. There was a system of tagging under which each male old enough to bear arms wore a numbered disk and was checked at the agency periodically. This did much to prevent parties of outlaws from slipping away from the reservations. When small bands did go on raids, it was possible to find who the guilty ones were.

The scouts who had served Crook so faithfully and efficiently in the Tonto Basin remained on the payroll as police. Nan-tan Lupan called the chiefs of the various tribes into council and talked to them about maintaining order in their purlieus. The white man, he explained, forbade crime among his own people, and if any committed offenses against the law, was quick to punish. The Indians must do the same with their people. The appeal to the Apache race pride was a master stroke. Its results were soon forthcoming.

There was plenty of reason for discontent on the reservations. Many Indians objected to the tagging. Others resented the infringement on their liberties. But most of the bad feeling was caused by the grafting, unscrupulous white men who buzzed about every reservation like blowflies around carrion, using political influence to enrich themselves at the expense of the helpless red men.

A good example of this was the fate of the Camp Verde Indians. The labors of the Apaches to make that place habitable have already been described. After the Indians dug with sharpened sticks and a very few old implements an irrigation ditch, they began to cultivate a patch of ground. Some fifty-three acres were put under water. On this the Apaches soon had squashes, melons and other garden stuff. Directed by two army officers, Colonel Julius W. Mason and Lieutenant Walter S. Schuyler, both of the 5th Cavalry, they began next to plant corn, barley and other grains on a large scale. The outlook was brighter than it had been in years for the Indians.

And then the maleficent hand of the white man's graft showed itself. At Tucson there existed a political ring of federal officials, contractors and other interested persons. This gang of racketeers saw with alarm that under Crook's management the Indians at Camp Verde would soon be self-supporting. It meant that the white contractors would cease to furnish the government inferior supplies and thin cattle at exorbitant prices, to feed these Indians. But the Tucson ring had its own methods. Political influence was exerted at Washington. One day a peremptory order came to remove all Indians from Camp Verde to the barren San Carlos reservation.

The despairing people were once more driven out into the desert. From their melon patches and corn fields, the Apaches, shepherded by their only friends, the army officers, began their long, dusty journey to San Carlos. Overnight they changed from interested, industrious, cheerful people, into sullen, treacherous savages once more. Small wonder that the old, old cycle of death began to reappear in the desert.

The Camp Verde case is cited merely as an instance. There were many others. Chuntz, Chaun-desi, and Cochine [2] repented of their surrenders. On May 27th, goaded to desperation, Chaun-desi tried to stab Agent Larrabee of San Carlos with a lance. Another Indian, Yomas, prevented him from doing it. Then Chaun-desi seized a gun and killed Lieutenant Jacob Almy. With their people the three chiefs took to the hills.

Crook called the remaining chiefs on the reservation together and told them the matter lay in their hands. They would have to trail down and bring in the outlaws, dead or alive. The leaders looked at each other and departed.

One day a group of scouts, carrying a large sack, presented themselves before the general. As he looked, they dumped at his feet seven bloody, grinning human heads. Then they explained. A few nights before a wagon train had halted near San Carlos and some of the teamsters gave whiskey to the Apaches. The Indians got ugly drunk. When the teamsters refused the Indians more liquor, every man in the train was killed.

The Apaches took to the wilds. But the reservation chiefs and scouts had their orders. Without even reporting to Crook they took the trail. The outlaws were surrounded. When they refused to sur-

[2] Not to be confused with Cochise, the Chiricahua. Cochine was a Tonto.

render, the scouts simply killed them all. There was no other way of proving that they had disposed of the renegades, so they severed their heads, put them in a sack and dumped them at Crook's feet.

Meantime the hunt continued for the outlaw chiefs. One by one they were killed. Cochine was first. He was shot in the mountains May 26th, 1874, a year after he fled the reservation. Chaun-desi met his death June 12th of the same year. And finally Chuntz came to his end on July 25th. Del-she, too, after an abortive attempt at revolt, was brought to bay and killed by his own people on July 27th. The Tonto Apaches had entered a new era in their relations with the white man.

CONCENTRATION CONTINUES

But unbearable injustices persisted. The Tucson Ring kept its sinister forces at work in Washington.[3] Whenever a promising start was made by the Indians, the fruit of their labor was taken away from them and they were herded elsewhere. Wrote Captain John G. Bourke:

"Just as soon as a few of the more progressive people (Apaches) begin to accumulate a trifle of property, to raise sheep, to cultivate patches of soil and raise scanty crops, the agent sends in the usual glowing report of the occurrence, and to the mind of the average man and woman in the East it looks as if all the tribe were on the highway to prosperity, and the first thing Congress does is to curtail the appropriations. Next we hear of 'disaffection,' the tribe is reported as 'surly and threatening' and we are told that the 'Indians are killing their cattle.' But, whether they go to war or simply starve on the reservation effects no change in the system; all supplies are bought of the contractor as before, and the red man is no better off, or scarcely any better off, after twenty years of peace, than when he surrendered." [4]

[3] The following significant paragraph from the annual report of General Schofield, in 1871, throws additional light on some of the motives and methods of the Tucson Ring:

"It is worthy of remark that these Indians (the Apaches) paid for a large part of the rations issued them by supplying hay and wood to the military posts, and the wood and hay thus furnished cost the government much less than before paid to contractors, and that the contractors, their employees and customers, thus lost the profits heretofore realized. It has been suggested that this may explain the Camp Grant massacre."—Report of the Secretary of War, 1871, p. 87.

[4] "On the Border With Crook," p. 223.

In spite of all these circumstances, Arizona was now nearer to peace than it had been for generations. So much so that on January 6th, 1875, Governor Safford said in his message to the legislature:

"At no period in the history of Arizona have our Indian affairs been in so satisfactory a condition. Comparative peace now reigns throughout the Territory, with almost a certainty that no general Indian war will ever occur again."

Among the prophets of modern times, the governor must stand out as one of the worst. There was going to be trouble, and that in plenty. And the "Concentration Policy," so called, as adopted by the Indian Bureau, was responsible.

The reservations of Arizona were transferred from the War Department to the Department of the Interior. The Indian Bureau at once began to concentrate its Indian wards. The fate of the Camp Verde Indians has been told. Next to go were the White Mountain Indians, who were driven down out of their healthful mountains to San Carlos, in the stifling valley of the Gila. Then the Indian Bureau turned its attention to the Chiricahuas. While Crook had been busy in the Tonto Basin, General O. O. Howard, guided by an intrepid white frontiersman, Captain Jeffords, made peace with Cochise. Howard pledged his solemn word that the Chiricahuas should be allowed to remain among their own mountains. Cochise died in peace, never dreaming that his treaty with the white men would be broken within eighteen months of his death, which occurred in June, 1876.

One fortunate circumstance there was. A man of exceptional tact, firmness and understanding, was made agent at San Carlos, destined to be the danger point for all the Arizona country. This man, John P. Clum, took his post in 1874. He served until 1877. During his term of office he handled, always with judgment and justice to the Indians, some tremendously difficult situations. With his company of twenty-five Indian policemen, he time and again walked right into a camp full of bitter, maddened savages and quieted them.

But no one man could make up for the accumulated wrongs heaped up by a whole bureaucracy. Very speedily was Governor Safford to see his optimistic prophecy proved futile and fatuous.

VII
The Hunting of Victorio
1877-1880

16: SUCCESSOR TO MANGUS COLORADO

CROOK LOOSES HIS GRIP

IN THE middle of March, 1875, General Crook was transferred to the Department of the Platte, far to the north where already ominous signs foretold the outbreak of the Sioux. His place in Arizona was taken by General August V. Kautz, who found his hands immediately filled with complications arising from the myopic policy of the Indian Bureau.

The Chiricahuas were deeply disgruntled. Cochise's death had left them without a real leader. The true Chiricahuas were headed by Tah-sa, the old chief's son. The Mogollon division of the tribe recognized Juh, an old-time lieutenant of Cochise, as its chief. Over on the Ojo Caliente reservation in southwestern New Mexico, was Geronimo, born a Mimbreño, but now living with the Chiricahuas. With him on the same reservation was Victorio. Each of these men had his following.

Only a spark was needed to stir these ready elements into con-flagration. That spark was supplied by an incident which took place in April, 1876. At Sulphur Springs, in the Dragoon Mountains, stood one of the stations of the Overland Stage route. The agent, a man by the name of Rogers, had been warned frequently against selling liquor to the Indians, but the temptation of easy profits was too great. He made quite a little side income by bootlegging whiskey to the Apaches.

That April the Chiricahua agent gave some of the warriors per-mission to take their families to the Dragoons to hunt, because their supply of food was exhausted. During their somewhat lengthy stay in the mountains, the Indians became acquainted with the slippery

Mr. Rogers, and bought from him some liquor. Alcohol always had a bad effect on Apaches. It made them ugly and brought to the fore their undeniable talents for killing. The reaction in this case was typical. That night the Indians got drunk and had a fight among themselves which ended in the deaths of two men and a child. Next morning, nursing a terrible hangover and mourning the deaths of their friends, most of them dragged themselves back to the agency. A small band of a dozen warriors and their families, headed by a sub-chief named Eskina, remained in the mountains.

After Rogers found out what had happened in the Apache camp because of his liquor selling, he was probably apprehensive. And he was anything but joyful next day when two of Eskina's warriors, a sub-chief named Pi-hon-se-ne and his nephew, rode up to the stage station, demanding more liquor. The Indians, by their bloodshot eyes and irritable manner, still showed the signs of their debauch of the previous night. Rogers had grown cautious. Perhaps he began to fear word of this might reach the ears of the authorities. He sold the two warriors small drinks but refused to give them any large quantity of whiskey.

Pi-hon-se-ne and his nephew stood in the stage station, drinking the driblets the agent gave them and growing uglier and more sullen every minute. Presently Rogers quit selling them any liquor at all. He grew peremptory, told them they could have no more whiskey, and ordered them to leave the station. Pi-hon-se-ne and his nephew thereupon raised their rifles and shot the station agent dead, then killed his assistant, a man named Spence.

With all the liquor, horses and ammunition they could collect, the two Apaches rode back to Eskina's camp where the whole band got wildly drunk that night and decided to go on the war path. They killed a white man next day, wounded another, and stole four horses. A company of cavalry was sent to drive them back on the reservation, but failed to overtake them. And so, because a profit-greedy station agent refused to obey the laws of his own nation, another bloody Apache war began.

Eskina's warriors raided several ranches. Early in June they were on the Chiricahua reservation again, trying to persuade the rest of the tribe to join them. Tah-sa, the chief, refused. In a fight which followed, six men were killed and three wounded. Eskina was among the dead and Pi-hon-se-ne, shot in the shoulder by Tah-sa, was among the wounded.

As a climax to this dangerous situation, officials from the Indian Bureau arrived with orders for the Chiricahuas to move to the hated San Carlos reservation. It was a tense hour. Tah-sa, unwilling to comply, but seeing the futility of resistance, at last agreed to go.[1] But on June 7th seventy-five or eighty warriors, with their women and children, some three hundred people in all, suddenly left the reservation and fled south into Sonora, killing as they went. They were led by Geronimo and Juh.

The war, now well started, progressed bloodily. Not less than twenty persons were killed on the United States side of the international border in the next few weeks. And the record will never be complete of those who died at the hands of the stealthy Apaches in Mexico.

Not until the spring of 1877 were any of the hostile band apprehended. Then Agent Clum, with his faithful agency police, surprised Geronimo and Pi-hon-se-ne at Ojo Caliente and arrested them. Geronimo was lodged in the guard house at San Carlos to await trial. But the machinations of the Indian Bureau had grown too much for the intelligent, fair-minded Clum to stomach. He resigned. In the confusion which followed his replacement, Geronimo was freed.

THE MESCALEROS

The outbreak of Geromino, Pi-hon-se-ne and Juh was watched with eager interest by the Mescalero Apaches. Since the days of Gian-na-tah, who will be remembered by the reader as an ally of Mangus Colorado, that people had suffered tragically at the hands of the whites. This, viewed from the white man's standpoint, was largely their own fault, because the Mescaleros never were what

[1] Shortly after this Tah-sa was taken to Washington by Agent Clum. He died on the trip.

one might term tractable. They insisted upon their right to the land and continued to view the white men as interlopers.

After Gian-na-tah surrendered to Kit Carson, as described in an earlier chapter, the Mescaleros were held for some time at the Bosque Redondo. But the Navajos, more numerous than the Mescaleros and arrogant in their numbers, were soon moved down there. These newcomers made life so unbearable for the Apaches that by 1867 all the Mescaleros had left the reservation and wandered out on the plains of Texas and among the mountains of New Mexico, committing frequent depredations. It was not until four years later, in February, 1871, that Captain Chambers McKibben, by negotiating with the sub-chief La Paz, induced the tribe to go on to the reservation at Fort Stanton.

They soon saw that they had made a mistake. The white settlers began charging that the young braves were leaving the reservation and raiding. If the Indians did so, they could at least say that there were plenty of vivid examples in cattle and horse theft set for them by the whites.[2] There is no doubt that much of the "rustling" in the territory, which was blamed on the Indians, was committed by white men. Add to this situation the fact that the Mescalero reservation was soon drained of game and the people were virtually starving, while at the same time unscrupulous white traders from La Luz and Tularosa constantly bootlegged whiskey to them,[3] and it is to be wondered why there was not more trouble than there actually was.

In the fall of 1874, a mob of white citizens crept up on a camp of Mescaleros, which was situated well within the borders of the reservation. Several women, children and men, peacefully sleeping in their tents, were massacred. The rest of the band, panic-stricken, fled to the mountains. Captain E. G. Fechet was sent with a detach-

[2] The Mescalero chiefs made frequent protests to W. D. Crothers, their agent, that white thieves were stealing their horses, in the fall of 1874. Crothers tried to catch the thieves, but was unsuccessful. (See Report of W. D. Crothers, in "Annual Report of Commissioner of Indian Affairs," 1875, pp. 329–330.)

[3] According to F. C. Godfroy, Mescalero agent from 1876 to 1879, the Apaches were so crazy for liquor that they frequently would trade a horse for a single quart and the unscrupulous traders sold them only the most inferior grade of whiskey, at that. ("Annual Report of Commissioner of Indian Affairs," 1876, pp. 105–109.)

ment to bring the Indians back. Instead of trying to bring them peacefully to the reservation, he slipped up on the band, launched a surprise attack which killed more of them, and captured most of their horses. These same Indians were later induced by two men, an Indian scout and an agency employee, to surrender without any use of arms.[4]

Still the Mescaleros were hectored and abused. Once more, in 1877, a body of the fragrant gentry who at that time infested the Texas border, made two raids on the reservation in which they ran off some forty horses belonging to the Indians. Again the Mescaleros saw the hopelessness of depending upon the government for protection and took to the hills. Some of them wandered as far north as the Staked Plains and joined the Comanches in their war against the buffalo hunters that year.[5] But at last the bulk of the tribe was induced to come back to the reservation by a new agent, S. A. Russell, who even managed to bring Victorio there for a time.

Numbers of the Mescaleros refused, however, to surrender to Russell and continued to rove the wilderness. A ceaseless campaign was waged against them by Colonel B. H. Grierson and General Edward Hatch. One band of the Indians fought and defeated a detachment under Captain S. B. M. Young near San Carlos on October 28th, 1877. But the following year even these were driven on the reservation.

VICTORIO

Among the old guard of warriors trained under the great Mangus Colorado was the Mimbreño chief Victorio. He had been one of the Red Sleeves' lieutenants, and was thoroughly grounded in every detail of Apache fighting tactics. In the years after his leader's

[4] "On their return (to the reservation) it was heart rending to see a class of human beings so destitute of the common necessities of life; many of them were almost naked and bearing marks of an outraged class of human beings."—W. D. Crothers' report in 1875, p. 330.

[5] Captain P. L. Lee, with his detachment of the 9th (Colored) Cavalry, killed four and wounded several other Indians in a fight at Lake Quemado in 1877. He attacked what he thought was a Comanche camp. But some of the Indians killed were Mescalero Apaches.

death, Victorio was a constant menace to the white man and was frequently out on the war path. He agreed to settle on the reservation in 1877, but was soon thoroughly tired of his agreement.

At the time Clum arrested Geronimo and Pi-hon-se-ne, he had a talk with Victorio, who told him he would far rather die than go to San Carlos. All the Indians hated that place, and word was beginning to creep around among them of the "Concentration Policy" and its baleful significance.

Victorio's worst fears were realized in April, 1879. He was notified then that he and his people were to be moved to San Carlos. That was enough for the Mimbreño. Between sunset and sunrise he disappeared with thirty of his braves. Never again did he return.

With the troops hot on his trail, Victorio fled for Mexico, swinging around south of El Paso, and crossing the Rio Grande into the Big Bend country of Texas, south of Fort Quitman. There he received reinforcements. Caballero, the aged chief of the Mescaleros, inspired by Victorio's bold move for freedom, also left the reservation with two or three hundred of his people and joined the Mimbreños.

Victorio now had more than a hundred warriors. He began at once a series of the most baffling movements the United States army ever had to combat in Indian campaigns. The Mimbreño leader was a perfect master at deception. He pursued a settled policy with the Mexican sheep herders and small ranches in the country over which he ranged. They were permitted to live on sufferance. So long as they furnished him with arms, food, and ammunition, just so long he allowed them to exist.[6] All of them knew this. Their lives were pitiable; they were in constant terror. When the grim brown warriors with their steel-trap mouths rode up to the little adobe *casas*, the owners came forth with anything they demanded and were glad to get off with their lives. Replenishing his supplies

[6] Colonel Grierson complained about this as follows: "There seems to be a tacit understanding between Victorio and many Mexicans, that so long as he does not make war upon them in earnest, he can take whatever food and other supplies he may need for his warriors."—Report of Colonel B. H. Grierson, 1880, Old Records Section, A. G. O., War Department.

in this manner and knowing every foot of the country, Victorio matched his wits against the best in the United States and Mexican armies and won for many months.

As soon as he entered Texas, the chief learned through his scouts —who probably never had superiors in the history of any warfare —that Captain Nicholas Nolan, with a detachment of the 10th (Colored) Cavalry, was headed toward him. Too weak to fight any such body of troops, the Mimbreño retreated. He turned and twisted, trying to shake off the soldiers, but finally was forced to cross to the south side of the Rio Grande when Colonel George W. Baylor [7] and a company of Texas Rangers pressed him too closely.

But it was only for a short time. In September the Apaches appeared again—this time in New Mexico. Victorio never moved more secretly than he did that time. The first hint anybody had that he was north of the border was a message of blood. Captain Ambrose E. Hooker's company of the 9th Cavalry was camped near Ojo Caliente. Victorio passed that way, headed north to give some of the Mescaleros and Mimbreños still on the reservation a chance to join him. But he needed horses and, when he saw the troop herd grazing under a guard on the night of September 4th, he turned aside from his direct line of march. Victorio's shadowy skirmishers stole through the gloom. Orange flashes spurted out in the darkness as the rifles chattered angrily. With yells which sounded sharp and clear above the thunder of the stampeding horses, the Apaches were gone in a smother of dust.

Eight troopers were killed in the brief, bloody little battle, and forty-six of Uncle Sam's cavalry horses found themselves between the knees of Indian riders. Victorio did not lose a man.

The troops groped frantically through the desert for the Apaches but Victorio's people were gone almost as if they had disappeared into the air. Ten days later they struck again, suddenly, savagely.

It was near Hillsboro, New Mexico, this time. A posse of citizens,

---

[7] A former Confederate officer and the brother of John R. Baylor, one-time Confederate governor of Arizona, who proposed the original policy of extermination for the Apaches and was removed from office as a result by Jefferson Davis. Colonel George W. Baylor hated the Indians as much as did his brother. He was one of the great figures among the Texas Rangers of the period.

THE APACHE COUNTRY
1822~1886

SANTA FE

BUQUERQUE

BOSQUE
REDONDO

FORT
SUMNER

TERRITORY

ORT
ANTON

Rio Hondo

Rio Tularosa

Rio Penasco

SACRAMENTO MTS.

Sacramento R.

an
k

GUADALUPE MTS.

Salt Fork

Double Mountain Fork

Colorado R.

STAKED PLAINS

POPES
WELLS

PECOS

Pecos R.

RATTLE SNAKE
SPRINGS

RT
TMAN

EAGLE SPRINGS

FORT
STOCKTON

Rio Grande

FORT
DAVIS

RIZAL

IUA

res Castillos
ctorio killed
Oct., 1880

PRESIDIO
del NORTE

Rio Grande

C

O

HUAHUA

Rio Conchos

EAGLE
PASS

ranchers and miners had taken the trail. Victorio turned on them with a snarling fury which caught them unprepared. Ten of them were killed and all their horses were captured by the raiders.

All this time warriors were flocking to join Victorio, slipping away from their reservations and meeting him in the wilderness. He now had about one hundred and forty braves, including the Mescaleros under fierce old Caballero.

Lieutenant Colonel N. A. M. Dudley, with two troops of the 9th Cavalry, rode hard to cut the Indians off following the Hillsboro fight, and found them on September 18th, in the canyons at the head of Las Animas Creek. Dudley attacked at once. But Victorio's desert wolves were posted in almost impregnable positions among the rocks.

The rattle of rifles had scarcely started when Captain Charles D. Beyer galloped up with two more troops of the 9th, making a total of four companies in action. The Apaches were now badly outnumbered, but in spite of this the soldiers could not drive the Indians out of their position. Throughout the day the constant roar of the battle echoed through the hills and canyons. When night fell, Dudley discovered that in the day's fighting, from rock to rock and bush to bush, he had lost five enlisted men, two Navajo scouts and one civilian white scout killed, a number wounded, and thirty-eight horses killed or crippled. The troops did not know of a single Indian they had killed. It was clear to Dudley that Victorio was too strong for him in his present position. In the darkness the soldiers withdrew from the field, carrying their dead and wounded. Victorio had won a convincing victory.

The chief's purpose was now fulfilled. He had fought and beaten the white men three times, had killed twenty-six of them, captured a large number of horses, and picked up much booty. More important, he had been joined by a good many warriors from the reservations. He therefore began a retreat toward the border.

But the troops were still in the field. With one hundred and ninety-eight officers and men of the 9th Cavalry, Major Albert P. Morrow struck Victorio near Ojo Caliente, and in a two days' running fight killed three Indians and captured sixty horses and mules, among them twelve of the animals taken from the hapless Hooker.

Four nights later prowling Apaches crept close enough to his picket lines to kill a sentry walking post. But Morrow kept on the trail. With the aid of a captured squaw he found and captured Victorio's camp. But the victory was an empty one. The cunning chief had vacated the camp before the troops arrived. That was on October 1st, 1879. Morrow followed the Indians across the border into Mexico and fought another skirmish October 27th, near the Corralitos River, a night fight in which he lost one scout killed and two men wounded.

But the troops were at the limit of their endurance. They had been without water for three days and nights and their ammunition was nearly exhausted. If Victorio had counter-attacked he might have wiped Morrow's forces out. The troops were glad to retreat back to the border, reaching Fort Bayard on November 3rd, completely worn out.

17: THE DOUBLE MASSACRE

OVER in Texas the settlers and soldiers were congratulating themselves on having, for the time at least, rid themselves of the Indians. News came of the fighting in New Mexico and at last word was received that Major Morrow had driven Victorio down into Old Mexico. The frontier breathed freely again.

But late one afternoon the stage coach from Fort Davis dashed in to Fort Quitman with the driver and one passenger dead and arrows still quivering in the woodwork of its sides. Next came a report that the telegraph wires were cut and the poles chopped down between Fort Davis and Eagle Springs. The truth dawned on Texas: Victorio had in some manner eluded the troops who literally plastered the border those days, and was back in the Big Bend.

Colonel Grierson, at Eagle Springs, believed the Indians were headed for Fresno Springs and, knowing that this was an isolated watering place, he made a forced march by a short cut to get there first. He succeeded. When he reached the springs there was no sign of recent Indian visitation there. Grierson wasted no time. Soldiers were carefully posted around the springs in such a way that when the Indians came they could be permitted to reach the water, then surrounded and killed or captured. There were nearly a thousand troops concealed about the springs, and Grierson did not think that Victorio had more than one hundred and fifty. It looked as if the old wolf was reaching his finish at last.

Shortly before 11 o'clock next morning, the first cautious scouts of the Apache advance were seen. Grierson's men were nearly suffocating with excitement, but he held them in check while the Indians came slowly toward the spring.

Suddenly out of nowhere a wagon train appeared, also crawling toward the springs. The Indians took to cover at the first hint of this unexpected arrival. Helplessly the concealed soldiers watched the unfolding of an ambush within an ambush as the Apaches, wholly unconscious of Grierson's proximity, prepared to overwhelm the train. As the minutes passed it became increasingly apparent that unless Grierson rescued them the teamsters who had thus blundered into the situation would be massacred to a man.

Angry and disappointed, the colonel gave the order which sent his men to avert the attack on the wagons. The appearance of the troops, riding over the rise toward them was a complete surprise to the Apaches. But now they saw the trap into which they had almost fallen and began to retreat in earnest toward the Rio Grande. Grierson, before he took up the pursuit, probably used some warm language on the wagon master of that blundering train. In spite of his best efforts he could not overtake the Apaches, although he was so close behind them that his advance could see the Indians on the other side of the river when it arrived at the bank. There the soldiers were forced to turn back.

Victorio moved slowly down into Chihuahua. As they went south the Indians swept the country clean as far as the large ranches and prospectors were concerned, although they continued to observe the policy of sparing the sheepherders and small farmers. The first stop was at the Santa Maria River, where there was an abundance of rich grama grass, together with plentiful wood and water—the three essentials of an ideal camping place. The location, however, did not satisfy the nervous Indians. It was too open and Victorio knew that Mexican troops might be expected at any time. In his present position he could easily be reached by them, and would be in a poor place for defense.

So Victorio ordered his people to break camp and moved them over into the wild and rugged Candelaria Mountains. There he took up a position which once more proved his genius as a leader. The new camp was not only perfectly located with regard to range for his horses and water and wood, but was beautifully strategic.

It was situated among almost inaccessible steeps, which would have been extremely difficult to attack successfully without serious loss to the enemy. Equally important, it afforded two or three towering peaks from which Victorio and his hawk-eyed scouts could see for twenty or thirty miles in every direction. Added to these advantages was the fact that it was near to the public road which ran between the city of Chihuahua and the Presidio del Norte—the Juarez of today—and all traffic could be observed.

THE FIRST MASSACRE [1]

Word of Indian depredations among the neighboring ranches soon reached Carrizal, the nearest settlement. Cattle and horses had been stolen and atrocities reported. The Mexicans at Carrizal deduced correctly that there was a band of Indians operating from some *rancheria* in the Candelaria Mountains. But they failed to grasp the idea of how powerful a band it was, or that it was led by the redoubtable Victorio himself. Had Carrizal realized this, the tragedy which followed might have been averted.

The general notion was that there was only a handful of Indians to deal with—possibly a dozen or even fewer, of the "broncho" [2] savages who were always wandering through the desert country. Early in November, Don José Rodriguez, one of the principal citizens of Carrizal and a member of one of the large land-owning families, organized a posse to scout for the Indians and if possible exterminate them. The expedition confidently set forth on November 6th, apparently failing to comprehend the peril of its mission. Most of its fifteen members were from the better families of the district. It was a sort of a lark—dangerous but good hunting.

From his lofty watch tower in the Candelaria peaks, Victorio saw

---

[1] The word "massacre" is used because it is popularly applied to this affair, although it was not a massacre at all, but a battle in which all the members of one party were killed. No women or children or unarmed persons were involved. All the Mexicans fought until they were dead. The slaughter of Apache women and children by Mexicans and Americans at Santa Rita del Cobre and Camp Grant were true massacres. An Indian speaker once aptly phrased the common attitude in this respect when he said: "In the Indian wars, white treachery was always stratagem, and white massacre was always a victory; Indian stratagem was always treachery and Indian victory was always a massacre."

[2] "Broncho" Apaches were outlaws who held no allegiance either to the United States or to the Mexican government, or to any of the recognized chiefs among their own people. There were always a few of these bands on the prowl during this period.

the small party of Carrizalistas while it was nothing but a tiny dust cloud, a score of miles away. That was November 7th. The Mexicans were coming up an old beaten track which led from the Santa Maria River to a big "tank" [3] on the northern slope of the mountains in which the Apaches were camped. The possemen were riding along carelessly enough, but Victorio knew that if they continued that line of march, they would be certain to strike the main trail made by his band when he moved it into the Candelarias. Once they saw the breadth of that trail, there was no chance of ever luring the Mexicans any farther—and he wanted those rash Carrizalistas.

A delicate situation. But Victorio was equal to it. Calling forty or fifty of his warriors together, he laid a trap for the oncoming Don Rodriguez and his *compadres*. The trail led through a deep canyon which passed between two of the taller Candelaria peaks, both of which had done the Apaches good service as watch towers. In this gorge Victorio prepared as clever an ambush as ever an Indian devised; an ambush which was a psychological as well as a military masterpiece.

At the north side of the trail, among some large boulders, he posted some of his best marksmen—not many, but enough for his purpose. These would be the first to come into contact with the Mexicans, and Victorio counted on them to spring the real trap which was laid on the other side of the canyon, somewhat back from the trail itself.

On came the jaunty Mexicans, slouching in their saddles, chattering and smoking their corn-husk cigarettes, not dreaming of peril. A sudden spray of bullets from the boulders to the north greeted them. To the south of the trail lay some inviting rocks which would make excellent shelter. It was natural for them to seek the cover of these boulders—and that was exactly what Victorio had planned. Knowing human nature, he had not placed any braves among those particular rocks, but had posted his men *higher*, and back so that the very friendly hospitality of the boulders should convert them into

[3] A "tank" in the Southwestern desert, was one of the infrequent places where rain water sometimes gathered in small pools or ponds, affording water until it dried out.

a death trap worthy even of his sinister intelligence.

As Don Rodriguez and his men threw themselves behind the shelter, preparing to fight the Indians on the north side of the canyon, beady-eyed warriors watched them from behind. They had the Mexicans at their mercy, and knew it. At the perfect moment the first rifle sounded from above—possibly Victorio's own—and the slaughter began. There was no escape and no protection from the terrific fire which broke from the higher cliffs.

One poor devil of a Mexican managed to squeeze into a crevice where his body was protected, but his legs protruded; there was no room for them inside. The Apaches turned their rifles in that direction and began deliberately, remorselessly to shoot those legs to pieces. How the helpless wretch must have writhed and screamed as his twitching limbs were struck again and again by the bullets of those pitiless marksmen. It was the sort of thing which appealed to the macabre Apache sense of humor. The twitching ceased after a time. The Mexican had bled to death. But the Indians kept on firing until they literally shot both legs off at the knees.

By that time every member of Don Rodriguez' party, including that elegant *hacendado* himself, was dead. As they vainly tried to find cover, they had been picked off coolly and deliberately from above. Their horses, plunging and rolling in their death struggles, added to the confusion by breaking their lariats and crashing down into the deep canyon to the east, in a smother of dust far below.

After a time the shooting ceased. Then the first of the furtive Indians stole forward from rock to rock. No rifle sounded to greet him. Others came down, one by one, until Victorio's warriors all stood among the slain, looting the bodies and making sure that there were none left living.

THE SECOND MASSACRE

The failure of Don Rodriguez' party to return to Carrizal, caused grave alarm. As the days passed, the fear grew into a conviction that the men had met some terrible fate. There was no proof of this, however, and at last a party of fourteen citizens of the town volunteered to try to find what had happened to their kinsmen. It was a dangerous thing to attempt, but they probably counted on the fact that the Indians seldom lingered long near the scene of a fight.

Following the trail left by Don Rodriguez, they too disappeared into the mountains. Days passed. They failed to return. When, after a reasonable time, the party had not made its reappearance, Carrizal went wild with excitement, rage and grief. It dawned upon the town that the Apache menace in the mountains was far more serious than had been supposed. A courier was sent to the Presidio del Norte, to beg for help. While he was making his report to Señor Ramos, in command at del Norte, Colonel Baylor of the Texas Rangers in El Paso, on the American side of the Rio Grande, heard of it and crossed the river to offer the services of his hard-riding, straight-shooting dare-devils—an offer which was thankfully accepted.

With true Latin courtesy, Señor Ramos offered to Baylor the command of the united forces, but the Ranger declined because the campaign was to be on Mexican soil. Then Ramos placed Don Francisco Escajeda of Guadalupe, a seasoned and experienced soldier, at the head of the allied array, giving second command to Baylor. A force of one hundred well-armed, well-mounted men was soon on its way south toward the Candelarias.

Straight south rode the rescue party. It halted beyond Samalayucca where scouts were pushed forward to reconnoitre. There was going to be no blundering into ambush this time. Night fell, bitter cold. Deep in the canyons where they could not be seen by watchful eyes in the peaks ahead, some of the men kindled fires of greasewood and mesquite and there tried to warm themselves.

The scouts returned late in the night. Going to the bivouac of Don Escajeda and Baylor, they reported they had not seen a sign of Indians. The commander immediately ordered his men to mount. It was an all-night march this time, and the foot of the Candelarias was reached early the next morning.

Shortly after dawn, for the first time, they saw Indian sign. A great, broad trail it was, whose width and plainness indicated that it was made by a very large band. It looked fresh. The scouts examined it and pronounced it only two days old. It led toward Lake

Santa Maria to the north. Evidently the Indians were gone. Still, no chances of a trap were taken. As the command entered the canyon between the two Candelaria peaks, a detachment was sent over the crest to the south while another took the northward steeps. The rest then proceeded down the gorge itself.

Not far had the beaters in front progressed when a shout brought the stragglers hurrying up. Scattered about in the rigid and awkward poses of death, lay the bodies of the unfortunates from Carrizal. The scouts looked here and there, then pieced together from the signs, the story of the battle.

And now the consummate cunning of Victorio revealed itself. The first ambuscade had been cleverly planned and executed. But when did it ever before occur to an Indian leader to use the victims of one victory as bait with which to trap a second party? This is exactly what Victorio had done. The manner in which the Apaches had destroyed the second Carrizal party, as deduced by the scouts, was as follows:

When the rescue expedition from Carrizal, looking for Don Rodriguez and his companions, arrived at the scene of the battle, there was not an Indian in sight. The Mexicans had every reason to believe the Apaches had been gone for several days. Therefore they relaxed their vigilance and began to gather the bodies of their kinsmen and place them together for burial.

The assumption that Victorio's warriors were gone was tragically wrong. All the time that the Mexicans were carrying the corpses of their friends to a central burying place, fierce eyes were fixed on them from above. Grieving, the Carrizalistas went about their sad work, oblivious of the fact that almost over their heads death awaited only the signal of the leader. Not until the bodies were all collected and the fourteen living Mexicans had gathered around their dead friends did the Apaches fire.

It was a repetition of the first fight. Nor is it likely that it lasted long. The Apaches were too numerous and too well situated. Presently the Indians once more descended into the valley and bent over the dead. Carrizal would never again see the faces of her sons.

Escajeda and Baylor, reconstructing the events which took place in that bloody gorge, had only one thing to do—bury the dead. The bodies were collected and a disquieting thing was learned. The first Carrizal party had numbered fifteen. The second contained fourteen men, a total of twenty-nine in the two parties, which had ridden into the jaws of Victorio's trap. Only twenty-seven corpses were found.[4] What had become of the other two Mexicans? No trace of the missing pair was ever discovered, but everyone knew what had happened to them. Too thorough, too sure was the Apache leader to have permitted them to escape. Somewhere along the trail, these two men, captured alive, suffered out their mortal hours, perhaps hanging head down over a slow fire . . . perhaps staked out, their mouths pried open with sharpened skewers, on some ant hill . . . perhaps twisting and writhing against the poisoned spikes of a tree cactus, lashed by green rawhide bands which, drying in the sun, bound them ever tighter and tighter against the torment. . . .

[4] Singularly enough, although the twenty-seven corpses buried had lain on the ground for nearly two weeks, they were all in an excellent state of preservation, and had not been touched by an animal or a buzzard. The Texans had a strange belief about the bodies of Mexicans. Says one Texas writer of this incident (C. G. Raht, "Romance of Davis Mountains," p. 266): "Neither wild animals nor birds had touched the bodies and it is said to be a strange fact that no wild animal or bird of prey will ever touch the body of a Mexican. If they had been Indians, negroes or whites, the coyotes, buzzards and carrion crows would have eaten them the first day and night."

18: WHAT HAPPENED TO THE MESCALEROS

AFTER his double *coup* in the Candelaria Mountains, Victorio pressed northward as fast as his horses could carry his people. Early in January he again crossed the border and stood on the soil of New Mexico. His old enemy, Major Morrow, took prompt and strenuous action. Every body of cavalry in the section was set in motion. Victorio found himself in a veritable hornets' nest. Even his matchless skill could not forever keep his people clear of the thronging multitudes of soldiers about him.

Near the head of the Puerco River, on January 9th, he fought a stand-off engagement with Major Morrow and a battalion of the 9th Cavalry. Several of his warriors were hit and on the white side one enlisted man was killed and a scout wounded. Victorio drew off toward the San Mateo Mountains, where Morrow attacked him again on January 17th. It was another inconclusive fight, but a brave young officer, Lieutenant J. Hansell French, was killed and two scouts wounded.

After that Victorio once more disappeared. The troops searched blindly for him through the barren mountains and across sun-smitten flats, but for nearly three months they never were near enough to see the dust cloud raised by his tireless marchers. Back and forth he swung, leaving a smoking wrack behind him. The chief seemed to grow more savage as the relentless pursuit continued. Some of the scenes the soldiers stumbled upon as they followed him endlessly, stirred black rage in their hearts. Women were found by their charred homes, torn limb from limb. Little children were discovered, looking as if wolves had worried them to death. And many men, prospectors, stage drivers, and cowboys, died horribly in the hills, leaving their mangled corpses as mute evidence of the bottomless cruelty of the Apaches into whose hands they had fallen. In that bloody raid Victorio killed upward of a hundred persons who are accounted for and enumerated. But there were dozens of others never heard from, who met their end at the hands of his desert killers.

Not until April 8th did the soldiers find Victorio. Then it was the old story—an indecisive fight, with no results to show for it. Captain Henry Carroll, 9th Cavalry, and seven enlisted men were wounded during General Hatch's fruitless attempt to drive the Indians out of the strong position they had taken high up in the San Andreas Mountains. Three Indians were killed. Victorio drew off toward the east. Hatch, who took the trail the following day, decided that he was headed for the Mescalero reservation.

It was too disappointing, too disheartening. Something had to be done about it.

DISARMING THE MESCALEROS

Those were sad days for the wretched Mescaleros who remained on the reservation near Fort Stanton and tried to keep the peace. They were caught between two fires. On one side were Victorio and their old chief Caballero, inciting them always to the war path, sometimes losing patience with their pacifistic ways, and doing spiteful deeds against them. On the other side were the soldiers who never believed them when they protested their innocence of trouble making, never gave them any rest if they as much as wandered outside of the confines of the agency.

Their one friend was their agent, S. A. Russell, who protected them all he could, advised them, and tried to stand between them and the military. Russell was hampered by the presence among the peaceful Indians of many malcontents who were always stealing supplies and smuggling them to the hostile bands. These supplies appeared frequently when camps of outlying raiding parties were captured, and gave rise to the charges that "The Mescalero Agency . . . largely served as a base of supplies and recruits for the raiding parties of Victorio." [1]

[1] "Record of Engagements With Hostile Indians," p. 94.

Captain Thomas C. Lebo, on March 6th, 1880, surprised and captured the *rancheria* of some "broncho" Indians at Shakehand Spring, about forty miles south of Penasco, Texas. Lebo's men killed a chief of the band, captured four squaws and one child, and the livestock and supplies of the camp. Much material from the Mescalero Agency was found in this camp, in which, incidentally, a captive Mexican boy, Coyetano Garcia, was rescued and later restored to his parents near del Norte.

Because of this evidence, Generals Pope and Ord, commanding the departments of Missouri and Texas, ordered on March 24th that the Mescaleros remaining on the reservation should be disarmed and dismounted. General Hatch and Colonel Grierson were given the task. Hatch took four hundred men from the 9th Cavalry, sixty infantrymen, and seventy-five Indian scouts. Colonel Grierson had under him two hundred and eighty officers and men of the 10th Cavalry and the 25th Infantry, making a combined force of eight hundred and fifteen officers and men. The two commands were to meet at the agency.

In the meantime, a band of peaceful Mescaleros, not knowing of these plans, asked permission of Russell to leave the agency on a hunt. Russell granted the permission. He told the Indians they might camp on the Rio Tularosa, several miles west of the agency limits. This was a common procedure. Years before all the game had been killed off on the reservation and in view of the type of supplies issued by the government to the Mescaleros, the agent thought it no more than fair that they be allowed to eke out their larders with what game they could occasionally kill.

Camping, in accordance with the agent's instructions, near the head of the Tularosa, this band of Indians was "discovered" by Grierson, April 12th, when he appeared through the Sacramento Mountains. The colonel had found many Indian trails on his march. He assumed that these trails were made by "marauding Indians." Just why they should be "marauders" is not clear, unless it was the officer's assumption that every Indian should be placed in that category. Without knowing anything about the band on the Tularosa or bothering himself to ascertain why they were camped there, he prepared at once to attack them.

It was early in the morning. Most of the Mescaleros were still asleep as Grierson surrounded the camp. All was ready for the charge which would be sure to kill many Indians when a messenger came spurring up with a message from Russell. The agent notified Grierson that these Indians were peaceful and were camping there by his special permission. He added that he had just ordered them back to the reservation and they had not yet had time to obey.

There is not much doubt that the Mescaleros in this camp were saved from a dreadful experience by the timely arrival of that courier. Another Camp Grant affair was averted.

Grierson, more or less grudgingly, marched on to the reservation as soon as he saw that the Indians were actually moving. General Hatch had already arrived. The Indians were quiet. Hatch decided he did not need all the troops he had brought. He began to send some of them west, leaving three hundred and fifty or so with Grierson. Russell summoned the chief Nautzilla [2] and told him the purpose of the troops.

The disarming was scheduled to take place on April 16th. Rifle firing was heard south of the agency at about 10 o'clock that morning. The Indians were thrown into a minor panic. Word came in shortly that Lieutenant Charles B. Gatewood had come upon some braves "driving off stock," had killed two of them, and was now bringing the livestock back to the agency. Russell was indignant. It appears that the stock in question had strayed away from the agency and the Indians had been sent by him to bring it back. While they were carrying out this errand, Gatewood had attacked them, with two fatalities resulting. Small wonder that the whole tribe seemed to have a bad case of nerves as Grierson began to disarm them.

It had been agreed between Grierson and Hatch that if more troops were needed than were then at the agency, three signal shots

[2] Following the government policy of "making" and "breaking" chiefs, Russell "promoted" Nautzilla to the chieftainship of the Mescaleros when Caballero joined Victorio. Nautzilla was a friend of the agent and Russell counted on him to help in the disarming.

should be fired. Grierson saw that the Mescaleros were sullen and frightened. Some of them even began to slink away. He decided he needed the other troops. The signal shots rang out on the clear air.

Those shots crystallized the panic. In every direction the Indians rushed to escape. The confusion was enhanced by the sudden arrival of Hatch's troops, who tried to halt the Apaches and speedily found themselves fighting. Ten Indians were killed. Two hundred and fifty surrendered.[3] But scores got away and made a bee line for Victorio's camp, where they became among his most vindictive fighters.

THE TEXAS CAMPAIGN

With these reinforcements, Victorio began a southerly retreat. He fought a couple of sharp engagements, but was back in Mexico by early June. There he was temporarily safe. The Mexican government refused to permit United States troops to cross its borders.

A breathing spell was all the Mimbreño wanted. On July 31st Captain Coldwell of the Texas Rangers, on an inspection trip to Ysleta, Texas, began a journey to Fort Davis. Riding in the mail stage coach, of the type called a "jerky" on the frontier, he passed through Quitman Canyon, where he discovered that Indians had cut off the stage coach from the other direction, killing its driver, E. C. Baker, and a passenger, Frank Wyant. In this manner Texas learned that Victorio was back within her borders.

And now began one of the biggest man-hunts in the history of the frontier. An agreement was made between General Ord, commanding the Department of Texas, and General Trevino, commanding the Mexican troops in northern Chihuahua, whereby the two nations were to cooperate in a campaign to run down Victorio. Trevino notified Grierson that about six hundred Mexican soldiers

---

[3] "The Indians who surrendered were told that they would be taken care of; that though they must give up their arms . . . they would be properly rewarded if they would submit peacefully. This agreement was not kept. Those who surrendered were placed in a large stock pen, in which horses and cattle had been kept. The refuse from the pens was not even removed and the disconsolate Indians were forced to put up with this indignity. When they would ask concerning the return of horses, guns, etc., and their own release, noncommittal answers would be given."
—C. C. Rister, "The Southwestern Frontier," pp. 198–199.

were ready to pursue the Indians south of the border, with additional troops coming. Grierson threw every soldier he could get into the campaign. Within the next few weeks, Victorio, whose forces never exceeded one hundred and seventy-five or eighty warriors, had to fight or dodge at least two thousand United States soldiers, and an equal number of Mexican troops, not to mention hundreds of cowboys, miners and ranchers.

With only six men Grierson was at the spring of Tanajas de las Palmas, on the day Victorio's invasion was discovered. His young son, out West on a summer vacation from college, was with him "looking for excitement."

Learning that the Apache camp was within ten miles of him, the colonel sent to Eagle Springs and to Fort Quitman for reinforcements for his small escort, and daringly remained with his half dozen men to watch the movements of the hostile Indians. His order was misunderstood at Fort Quitman where nothing was known of Victorio's proximity. The commanding officer there thought Grierson merely wanted an escort to bring him back to the fort. Lieutenant Leighton Finley was sent with fifteen men—a woefully inadequate force. At once another courier was dispatched by Grierson with peremptory orders for more troops and an explanation of the situation.

Grierson, occupying his exposed position far out in the desert, saw Victorio's advance guard approaching him at about 9 o'clock on the morning of July 31st. His twenty men were in a position as strong as they could find. The Indians observed this and instead of charging, they scattered about the place, ignorant of the fact that a courier had gone for help. Victorio planned to wipe out the whole force, in the Apache manner, with the least possible loss to himself.

Lieutenant Finley was ordered by Grierson to take ten men and prevent this enveloping movement if possible. The carbines began to crackle as the young officer attacked a vastly superior force of the Indians and for more than an hour held them in check. This was probably not so much due to the Apache fear of him, as to the fact that they thought they had all the time in the world and were prepared to carry out their battle plans at leisure.

That hour proved the saving of Grierson. As the men lay among the rocks with the bullets whining overhead, or smacking among the stones and kicking up spiteful jets of sand and dust, blue uniforms appeared over the rise from the direction of Fort Quitman. It was Captain Charles D. Viele, with a troop of cavalry.

The Apache fire slackened. But Viele's troops, coming up, mistook Finley's advance detachment for Indians and opened fire on it. Nobody was hit although the bullets skipped most disconcertingly among the men. To avoid being riddled by his own friends, Finley ordered a retreat to Grierson's main position. The Apaches sprang in pursuit as he withdrew, hoping to prevent Viele from joining Grierson. But Viele now saw his mistake. He deployed his men and sent them forward among the rocks so fast that the Indians, in their own immediate danger, forgot all about Finley.

All up and down the field, heated like a blast furnace under the brazen sun of late July, the fight became general. Although there were now about a hundred troopers against him, Victorio pressed them hard. He might have punished them severely, were it not that Captain Nicholas Nolan arrived with another company of cavalry from Fort Quitman.

Outnumbered and half surrounded, Victorio at last retreated. The engagement had lasted four hours. Seven warriors had been killed and others wounded and carried back to the rear by the Apaches. The Mimbreño chief's force was too scanty to permit of such losses. On the white side, Lieutenant S. R. Calladay was wounded and one enlisted man killed.

Victorio rapidly fell back to the Rio Grande and recrossed into Mexico. But within four days the tireless raider was across the border into the United States again, heading with his warriors for the Van Horn Mountains. Brushing off one detachment of soldiers, he eluded Grierson's main command, which tried to pin him at Bass's Canyon, and on the evening of August 4th was in the passes of the Van Horns.

Grierson guessed that Victorio was heading for Rattlesnake Springs. He made a forced march to that important point, riding sixty-five miles during the next twenty-four hours, a terrific march considering the heat. The soldiers reached the springs well ahead of the Indians. Captain Viele had two troops in ambush. The Indians arrived at about 2 o'clock the next morning. They were greeted by a surprise volley and as the rest of Grierson's force came up, they were driven from the springs, losing several warriors.

Undaunted, Victorio fell back toward Bowen's Springs in the Guadalupe Mountains. But again his arch-foe, Grierson, anticipated his movements. The chief found Captain William B. Kennedy's force waiting there. In the brush which followed, two Indians and one soldier were killed. The Apaches now retreated toward the Sacramento Mountains. There they came into contact with another of the swarming detachments, this time under Captain Lebo.

The border was crowded with soldiers as never before. Every way Victorio turned, he met troops. At last, about August 18th, he gave up the attempt to remain in the United States, and once more led his people into Mexico.

19: THE END OF THE HUNTING

HUNTED like a mad wolf from mountain range to mountain range and from desert tank to alkali spring, Victorio and his faithful followers pushed southward from the Texas border and took refuge in the Tres Castillos Mountains of northern Chihuahua. September and October passed. The chief, now about sixty years old, was tired. But his young men were not. As the month of November opened, a large party of the younger braves went north again, while a second, somewhat smaller band, led by old Nana, Victorio's chief lieutenant, raided through Mexico. The older warriors and all the women and children remained with Victorio in the mountains.

News that the Indians were in the Tres Castillos district quickly reached Colonel Joaquin Terrazas at Chihuahua. He planned immediately a major operation against them. The colonel had spent some time in organizing a body of irregular troops, made up of men from such towns as Ascension, Janos and Casas Grandes, which were called the *Seguridad Publicos,* or, more familiarly, the "S. P.'s." In their duties and semi-military nature, they were patterned after the Texas Rangers. For scouts, Terrazas enlisted a company of Tarahumari Indians from the mountains of that name. These Indians, while lacking the extreme deadly vindictiveness of the Apaches, were little their inferiors in most respects, and in one respect they were the superiors, not only of the Apaches, but probably of every living race of mankind. They were, and still are, peerless foot racers. Their name signifies that and their warriors were able to boast with truth that they could outstrip any horse in a race sufficiently long. It was nothing for them to cover as much as one hundred miles in a day, and they could jog along, kicking a small ball before them, at a speed which carried them forty miles in six or eight hours with the greatest ease.[1]

[1] For further description of this remarkable people, see Hodge, "Handbook of American Indians," pp. 692–693.

Terrazas sent a message to Ysleta, Texas, asking Colonel Baylor of the Texas Rangers to cooperate with him, and marched north with his S. P.'s and Tarahumari scouts.

Meantime Grierson's men were on the trail of the young warriors who were raiding into Texas without Victorio as a leader. Captain Theodore A. Baldwin had a short fight with them near Ojo Caliente, Texas. Four of his men were killed, but the action prevented the Apaches' immediate return to the main band which awaited them in Tres Castillos. That delay was fatal. It is hard to believe that Victorio would have remained in one place for the length of time he did, had he not promised his young men to keep a rendezvous with them there. The great chance had come for Terrazas.

The Mexican leader had been joined by several bodies of fighting men from the United States. Colonel Baylor brought twenty of his Rangers. Lieutenant James A. Manney appeared with twenty Negro troopers. And Captain Charles Parker came to Terrazas' camp with sixty-eight Chiricahua Apache scouts. The combined expedition found Victorio's trail and followed it until all doubt that it led to the Tres Castillos was gone. Then Terrazas made a surprise announcement.

He blandly requested his American allies to return to their own side of the border, giving as his excuse his belief that Captain Parker's scouts were too wild and too nearly related to Victorio's people for safety. To the Americans it looked simply as if the Mexican, having made sure of his quarry, jealously wished to take all the glory to himself for the victory which had been made possible, in large part, by the scouting of the very Chiricahuas to whom Terrazas objected. There was nothing they could do about it, however, except to return. Reluctantly and thoroughly angry, the American detachments marched north and crossed the border.

THE APACHE WOLF DIES

At one place the Tres Castillos Mountains form a deep basin, which can be entered only through a box canyon. This spot had long been a favorite camping ground for the Indians and thither Terrazas led his command. When he arrived on October 14th, no Apaches were there, and he camped for the night.

Frantic signalling from his pickets posted on the peaks of the mountains overlooking the plain, warned him that something important was afoot. Soon a soldier came running to say that a large dust cloud could be seen coming toward the canyon. Terrazas himself climbed a lookout peak and with his powerful field glasses made out definitely that the dust was raised by a large band of marching Apaches.

Here was unlooked-for good fortune. The Mexican commander hastily deployed his men to places of advantage. All traces of his campfires were concealed. In the cliffs around the basin, the soldiers and the Tarahumari scouts lay, with every foot of the interior covered by their rifles.

For once Victorio was caught napping. The chief had no idea that troops were in the vicinity. Without fear or hesitation, he led his band, consisting largely of noncombatants, through the gullet of the box canyon and into the inviting valley beyond.

Then, when the Apaches were all inside, the rocks echoed to the reports of the rifles of Terrazas' men until the uproar was deafening, the canyon walls grew hanging curtains of drifting smoke, and the Indians died in a blight of lead and fire.

As has been said, Victorio's best warriors were away on a raid. He was greatly outnumbered. But the Apache was always dangerous, never more so than when he was cornered. Ringed completely around with rifles, and with the bullets cutting his people down about him, the chief summoned the survivors to make their going memorable.

Darkness fell. Throughout the night the continued crashing of rifles echoed through the basin and spurts of fire lit the crags with lurid flashes. At early dawn the few remaining Apache warriors were still fighting, but their ammunition was almost all gone. About an hour after sunup their guns were silent at last. Now the Mexicans charged forward, brave in the knowledge that their enemies were out of cartridges.

Victorio had been wounded more than once during the battle,

but still he rallied his braves. Creeping forward with Terrazas' scouts was a Tarahumari Indian named Mauricio, famed for his skill with the rifle. Some time during the battle, he caught a glimpse of Victorio directing his few defenders. The black eye of the Tarahumari gleamed down the barrel; for an instant the sight pricked out the bronze figure of the Apache chief; then the trigger finger pressed.[2]

And so Victorio died—instantly, in the heat of battle, as he would have wished. His was a character difficult for the white mind to comprehend. He was an implacable enemy and his cruelty was notorious. But his long fight against the white man, carried on for years in spite of the heartbreaking odds against him, was inspired by something akin to what we call patriotism.[3]

Most of Victorio's band died in the basin of the Tres Castillos with him. The few who escaped were harried wildly through the mountains. They were without leaders; surely Apache resistance was at an end.

[2] So delighted was the Governor of Sonora by Mauricio's feat in killing Victorio, that he later caused the state to present the Tarahumari with a handsome nickel-plated rifle in recognition of the event.

[3] "He (Victorio) outwitted two generals of the American army and one in command of the Mexican forces. He captured from the Governor of Chihuahua, in one campaign, over five hundred horses. He and his warriors killed over two hundred New Mexicans, more than one hundred soldiers and two hundred citizens of the Mexican Republic. . . . This war was the result of the greed of the settler and the corrupt policy of the government in the management of the Indian affairs in the Southwest. If Victorio had been permitted to remain at Ojo Caliente it is more than likely that the terrible devastation following his removal to San Carlos would never have occurred."—Ralph Emerson Twitchell, "Leading Facts in New Mexican History," Vol. II, p. 440.

20: THE RAID OF OLD NANA

AFTER VICTORIO'S DEATH

VICTORIO was dead. That was a fact of prime importance. You cannot replace, with a mere wave of the hand, a man with the gifts of leadership, courage and fighting qualities possessed by the great Mimbreño. The Apaches south of the Mexican border recognized this fact. After the hue and cry following the Tres Castillos fight died down, such sub-chiefs as were left alive thought hard upon who should take the place left vacant, but without successful conclusion. The Apaches were still unconvinced that the white man was all-powerful, but they looked about in vain for a leader of Victorio's stature.

In the months following they roved in small, scattered bands, rather than the single large body which had followed Victorio in his day. Their raids were individual efforts. There was not the plan and the purpose behind them which was characteristic of every move made by the late chief.

Among the sub-chiefs remaining to the wild tribes in the south was one who, although many years Victorio's senior, had always served in a subordinate capacity—old Nana. Under Mangus Colorado he was a simple warrior. Under Victorio he was a lieutenant only. When the Tres Castillos debacle took place, Nana was about eighty years of age,[1] a short, fat and wrinkled old man, much troubled by rheumatism which practically crippled him. Usually he

---

[1] This is the estimate of both Charles F. Lummis ("The Land of Poco Tiempo," p. 183) and Britton Davis ("The Truth About Geronimo," p. 115). Of course Nana, like most Indians, did not know his own correct age. He had a clear memory of the events of Mangus Colorado's time, as he showed in conversations with Lieutenant Davis.

moved slowly, almost feebly. But on occasion he was capable of displaying tremendous sustained energy—as events were to prove. Superannuated he was and there was reason to suppose that his days of activity as a warrior were over. But a strange, belated glory was to be his. After most men, red or white, would have retired to the comfort of a sheltered fireside, to live in the memories of the past, this unimpressive little octogenarian suddenly flamed across the sky of the desert country to write bloody history.

Nana had been Victorio's friend. Hunched in his blanket, he sat high among the mountains, biding his time and gathering his people. Here and there he found them, one or two at a time, where they lurked, terrified and despairing, like wild beasts who knew that the hunter was upon them. In some way Nana gave back to these people their confidence. Then he set about slowly instilling in them again the old fighting fury. It took more than half a year to do it, but by July, 1881, Nana was ready.

There were only fifteen warriors with the old man as he crossed the international line—all that he could gather of Victorio's old fighting array. But loyalties run deep among the Apaches. On this old Nana counted, and with reason. Within a few days after he entered New Mexico, he had been joined by twenty-five more deep-chested, narrow-eyed, fierce-visaged warriors, Mescaleros all, eager to fight the white man once more.

In wide skirmish order, the forty Apaches drifted through the country, headed for the Alamo Canyon. They slew the sheepherders and ranchers as they went. Nana was an embittered old man. He cared nothing for policies, least of all for mercy. There was to be none of Victorio's easy way with these people on the present raid.

The Alamo Canyon was reached—just when is not known. Up to this time the troops had only the vaguest information that the Indians were in the country. On July 17th, however, a few of Nana's scouts ambushed the pack train of Lieutenant John F. Guilfoyle's 9th Cavalry command, wounded Chief Packer Burgess and captured three mules after a hot little skirmish. That was the first real indication as to Nana's whereabouts. Guilfoyle hurried a message to General Hatch at Fort Stanton and, with his Negro troopers and a detachment of friendly Apache scouts, swung into pursuit of the Indians.

The trail was plain enough. It led west through the Canyon del Perro, the famous "Dog Canyon," where the Mescaleros had suffered a terrible defeat in 1862, as described in an earlier chapter. Now, however, the Indians had learned a different kind of warfare. There would be no catching of Nana in any such place.

The trail left the Canyon del Perro. Hot on the track, two days later, Guilfoyle's Indian scouts came suddenly upon thirteen Apaches at a small ranch house near the Arena Blanca. They had just finished butchering two Mexican men and a woman. So obsessed were they with the work of slaughter, that they might have been taken easily. But the scouts were overeager. Their first shots were from such long range that they were ineffective. Worse, the raiders had ample warning and skipped up among the high hills where it was impossible for Guilfoyle's men to overtake them.

Once more the soldiers patiently took up the trail. This time it led toward the San Andreas Mountains, once a favorite camping ground of the dead Victorio. Was it some sentiment which drew the aged Nana thither, to look once more upon the scenes his old friend had loved? Guilfoyle's scouts, puzzling out the trail on the slopes of the San Andreas peaks, located a *rancheria* there, on July 25th. This time, profiting from the lesson at Arena Blanca, they showed some prudence. Instead of a premature rush, they stalked the place as they would have stalked a herd of deer. At the psychological moment they charged. Dashing through the smoke of their own volley, the troops rounded up fourteen captured horses, gathered together a number of blankets and some provisions. But Nana was gone again.

The soldiers thought they had wounded two of the Apaches in the brief fight, and Guilfoyle so reported. But if such was the case the wounds were not very severe. Apparently unhampered, the hostiles danced ahead, leaving a mocking trail, but nothing more; then turned suddenly south and crossed the Rio Grande below San José. On the way they caught and killed two miners and a Mexican herder.

THE DISCOMFITURE OF MITCHELL

And still the bloody game of tag went on. Next news of the ghastly wanderings of the band came on July 30th, when the bedraggled and blood-spattered bodies of four Mexicans were found in the foothills of the San Mateo Mountains. It was a definite clue and the troops started west again. Two days later came still more conclusive evidence that Nana was really prowling in the San Mateos.

Too impatient to await the arrival of the soldiers, a rancher named Mitchell, who had found an Indian trail, gathered a posse of thirty-six men and pursued the Apaches. The posse had little organization and like most civilian bodies of the type, its members were probably plentifully braced up with alcoholic courage. Nana did not make much of an effort to disguise his trail and the posse followed it right up the Red Canyon of the San Mateos. The cowboys were cheerful and nonchalant, but they were ignorant of one circumstance which would have sobered them considerably had they known it. All the time they rode up the canyon, the eyes of Apache warriors were upon them. Later evidence showed that their entire march must have been paralleled by Nana's wraith-like scouts.

At high noon, August 1st, Mitchell, now well up the canyon, called a halt for dinner. There was not much concern about the Indians. The horses were unsaddled and turned loose to graze. A careless guard lounged near the herd and kept a lacklustre eye upon it, while the rest of the party sat down to eat.

A series of wild yells, the drum-roll of a rifle volley, and with blankets waving, a swooping dash of Apache riders broke out of an adjacent gorge. No Western horses were ever able to stand a combination of sights and sounds like that without going into hysterics. This herd bolted down the canyon in a cloud of flying dust and pebbles, leaving the guard staring foolishly after it. Mitchell's men were on foot.

There was a brief, red-hot exchange of rifle shots. The Indians had the range and could see the white men, while the cowpunchers had no idea where the Indians were. One after another, eight of

Mitchell's men crumpled to the ground. The posse fought bravely enough. But had Nana wished to do so he could have finished them all. Just now his chief interest was in the horses. In a few minutes he left Mitchell and went off to round up the stampeded herd. The cowboys counted their casualties. One man was dead. Seven more were badly hit. The Indians were gone. Carrying its wounded, the posse began a crestfallen return on foot to the settlements. Nana had taken thirty-eight first-class saddle horses—every head of stock in the party.

Two days after the Apaches' contemptuous noon-day raid on the Mitchell party, Lieutenant Guilfoyle reached the San Mateos and took up the trail in Red Canyon where the posse had, perforce, abandoned it. He speedily found where Nana had left the gorge—sure evidence, in the form of a Mexican's mangled corpse. Guilfoyle drove his flagging command to the limit of its endurance, and was almost rewarded. On August 3rd he actually caught up with the hostile band—for a minute. But it was only a minute. The Indians were near the Santa Monica Springs. What followed could scarcely be called a fight. A couple of volleys and the Apaches were gone. Guilfoyle again reported the wounding of two of the enemy. And he captured eleven worn-out horses, abandoned by the Indians, to gether with some blankets. But wily old Nana had slipped away again.

Crippled by rheumatism and bent with old age, the chief had already ridden hundreds of miles with his young men, keeping ahead of the best cavalry in the Southwest, and still he showed no signs of giving out. Cool and crafty as ever, he considered the situation. He knew by now that the entire military establishment of New Mexico was swarming through the mountains and across the deserts to corner him. Nana really had ample reason to feel flattered. General Hatch had put every available soldier in the field. According to army records there were at this time eight troops of cavalry, eight companies of infantry, and two companies of Indian scouts, all hunting for the tiny Apache band. Nana had lost some warriors through wounds and desertions. He had now only about twenty or thirty braves left. But he was undaunted and confident as he prepared to circumvent every plan and resource the soldiers opposed to him.

Without pausing, except to gather up horses wherever possible, he traversed the desert to La Savoya. There, on August 11th, eight days after the brush at Santa Monica Springs, Guilfoyle, still following, came upon the grim signs of Nana's recent presence to which he was by now becoming so accustomed—two Mexicans, their bodies bearing the unmistakable and horrible mutilations of Apache hatred. The troops learned later that two Mexican women had been carried off from this same place.

In spite of his utmost efforts, efforts which well-nigh killed his command, Guilfoyle was falling far behind. What cavalry could follow these raiders? It is a rule of army tactics [2] that twenty-five miles a day is the absolute limit which cavalry can stand in continuous overland marching. Guilfoyle exceeded that every day of his campaign. Some days he did forty miles or more. Yet, Nana, old and crippled, rode away from the troopers as if they had been infantry.

Of course the Indians had a number of advantages. Whenever their horses wore out, they changed them—their remount depots being the nearest ranches or settlements. They carried practically nothing but their arms and ammunition. Their commissary was the country—the mescal, the mesquite bean, and the prickly pear. For meat they occasionally shot a deer, but the usual repast was a horse or mule, slaughtered when it could run no longer, and cut up almost before life was extinct, to be roasted and gorged by the warriors. The Apaches knew every spot where water could be found, no matter how small and inaccessible. But they did not need water like the white man. With a pebble under the tongue to keep the saliva flowing, one of Nana's raiders could go without water under the blaze of the desert sun two days longer than a white man could survive.

And so Nana left Guilfoyle plodding through the sand, eliminated from further consideration as an antagonist. But another adversary came cutting across at an angle—Captain Charles Parker, who had seen some of the hardest campaigning in the Victorio War.

[2] Upton's "Cavalry Tactics," p. 477.

Parker had with him only nineteen 9th Cavalry troopers, but, about twenty-five miles west of Sabinal, on August 12th, he ran squarely into the Apaches. It was foolhardy for the nineteen soldiers to try conclusions with the deadly Apaches who, though reduced in numbers, still outnumbered them. But without hesitation the colored troopers went into action.

There could, of course, be but one outcome to such a contest. Nana's warriors spread out and melted through the underbrush, like the pouring coils of a great serpent. The cavalrymen also took to cover. There was a period of blind shooting. Then, as suddenly as they had appeared, the Apaches were gone. Parker checked his losses. One trooper was dead and three wounded. And one man was missing. There was small doubt that he had been carried off by the Indians. The thought of his fate, somewhere back in those barren hills, when the Apaches had the leisure to devise for him a new way of dying, brought a shiver even to these veteran soldiers.

Parker, of course, was helpless. There was no pursuit—the little command had been too roughly handled in the brief time it had felt Nana's teeth, and, for the time being, nobody wished any further experience of the same kind.

SAFE OVER THE BORDER

Again the Apaches distanced the troops. During this raid they sometimes rode as much as seventy miles a day, with old, rheumatic Nana at their head. They had fought off three separate detachments of pursuers now, but southern New Mexico was swarming with soldiers. Within four days of his fight with Parker, Nana again tasted the mettle of the army.

This time it was Lieutenant Gustavus Valois, with another troop of the ubiquitous 9th Cavalry. Nana knew they were dogging his trail. Not far from Cuchillo Negro, named after the famous Mimbreño chief, the old warrior turned viciously. Always from cover, with never a sign of where they lurked, except for frequent spurts of fluffy rifle smoke, the Indians snaked through the mesquite and cactus. Courageously the troopers fought back. They gave a good account of themselves, but they could not deal with this enemy. They were facing the finest skirmishers in the world.

Lieutenant George R. Burnett, second in command, was wounded twice. Two enlisted men were killed. And a good share of the troop's horses were killed or crippled by the Apache fire. Nana, once he was satisfied that he had left the detachment so it could not follow him, withdrew as quickly as he went into action. Beating off a sally from the flank by Lieutenant F. B. Taylor and another troop of the 9th, the Apache raiders moved rapidly toward the Black Range.

In addition to three or four hundred civilians, General Hatch had approximately a thousand soldiers swarming through the country. Yet Nana with his handful laughed at the efforts to catch him.

Satisfied at last with his raid, the old chief turned back toward Mexico after his fight with Valois and Taylor. But before he left the United States he stopped to teach the white man a final lesson.

With a detachment of twenty 9th Cavalry troopers, Lieutenant G. W. Smith was toiling on the Indians' trail, near McEver's ranch, on August 18th. George Daly, a rancher, brought a party of cowboys to help the soldiers and see the fun. The combined force far outnumbered Nana's warriors. But the odds failed to worry the old Apache. He chose his ground, and his dusty fighters took to cover. The drifting smoke from their rifles and the staccato rattle of their volley, were the first hint the white men had that they had caught up with their foes.

That Apache fire was wickedly deadly. Daly, leader of the cowboys, was killed. Here and there troopers dropped as the heavy bullets from the Indians' rifles found their marks. Finally the gallant young Lieutenant Smith, in the act of directing his men to a more efficient disposal of their force, crumpled dead in the sagebrush.

That ended the fight. Six men were dead, including both the cowboys' and soldiers' leaders, and others were wounded. Neither the Negro troopers nor the white ranchers cared to go any further into the matter with Nana. The Apaches drew off and continued their course, unimpeded, to the border. Late in August they reached Old Mexico and rejoined their people in the mountains.

One may search long for a duplicate to this raid. In less than two months, Nana, handicapped by age and physical disabilities, led his handful of braves over a thousand miles of enemy territory, maintaining himself and his followers in the country as they went. He fought eight battles with the Americans, winning them all; killed anywhere from thirty to fifty of his enemy, wounded large numbers more; captured two women and not less than two hundred horses and mules; eluded pursuit by more than a thousand soldiers, not to mention three or four hundred civilians—and did it all with a force which numbered only fifteen warriors at the start and never exceeded forty braves.

Not even Victorio himself ever equalled that record.

21: THE PUNISHMENT OF LOCO

CHATO and Nachite, with their handful of Chiricahuas, squatted in the heights of the Sierra Madre and stared northward across the border. Those pallid mauve shadows of distant ranges they saw over the horizon, were in the United States. Between stretched the dun-gray desert with dark masses of intervening mountains forming opaque blotches on its harsh surface.

The two chiefs presented a vivid contrast. Nachite was the son of the great, dead Cochise. He was said also to be the grandson of the mighty Mangus Colorado, by a daughter of his marriage to a Mexican girl.[1] If this was so he inherited more of the blood of the Mexican beauty than of the Apache bull. He was a tall, loose-jointed, graceful Indian, a dandy in his dress, with a handsome, almost effeminate face, and slender, elegant hands. One thing he did inherit from Mangus Colorado—his magnificent height. Nachite stood six feet, one inch tall in his moccasins. Fonder of drinking and feminine society than of war, he lacked the stubborn force of leadership. Still, he was the hereditary chief of the Chiricahuas, and as such maintained a ranking position in council.

Chato, on the other hand, was an Apache of Apaches. He was short, barrel-chested, with wiry legs and a bull neck. His face was marred by a flat nose, due to his having been kicked by a mule. That was the significance of his name, Chato—Flat Nose. With this disfigurement, his features were a mask of impassivity, and he possessed to the full the right Apache lust for fighting.

Behind the two chiefs sat their lean, dark-visaged warriors, also looking northward. Come nightfall, the danger would begin. It had been months since the Apaches had raided on the American

---

[1] The Mexican girl referred to is the one for whom Mangus is said to have fought his famous double duel. One of her daughters by him was given to Cochise as a wife. This was to cement diplomatic relations between the Mimbreños and the Chiricahuas.

side of the border. All knew of the perils and the success of old Nana's wild ride in the summer of 1881. But this was April, 1882.

It was a bold move the Indians were planning. Somewhere on the other side of the mauve ranges lay the heated flats of the San Carlos reservation. There lived others of their people—Chiricahuas, Mimbreños and Tontos, chafing in impotence, eating out their hearts like wild animals caged in a zoo, crazy to be free again. Chato and Nachite were going to free them.

The plan was simple but audacious in the extreme. They would strike north at dark, cross the border, and head for the reservation. Once across the line, all knew, every moment would be fraught with peril. United States soldiers patrolled nearly every foot of the border. There were thousands of them, reinforced by hundreds of Apache scouts—trailers and fighters as keen, as tireless, and as deadly as the hostiles themselves. Yet so sure were Chato and Nachite of their own ability, that they considered their coming raid anything but a forlorn hope.

Dusk fell at last. Like lethal spectres the Apaches left the heights, mounted their ponies and began their march. Two days later, on April 20th, every telegraph key in every military post on the border was clicking. The Chiricahuas had struck—struck so suddenly and so stunningly that the first notice of their presence was the blow itself. A sudden attack at San Carlos, and back toward the border headed the raiders, accompanied by Loco, chief of the reservation Mimbreños, and several score of the imprisoned Apaches.

Loco was one of the last of the old followers of Mangus Colorado. He was naturally a good-humored man, but he had lost an eye, either through trachoma or some accident, and this gave him an unpleasantly sinister appearance which, those who knew him said, was belied by his true character. He had, for several years, remained peacefully on the reservation, in spite of the almost unsupportable indignities he had to suffer. Even as he rode south with Chato and Nachite, his heart was filled with misgivings. Indeed he would not have come at all had not the raiders threatened him with a rifle and forced him to mount and ride.

Within an hour after the raid at San Carlos troops at all the border posts were ready to move. By dawn next day soldiers and their Indian scouts were on the march everywhere. Arizona was full of them. The fact that many women and children from Loco's band were with them, was a serious handicap to the Apaches. It had been a very dry spring. Most of the streamlets and desert tanks, as well as the springs, were waterless. Cumbered as they were, the Indians must stick to the river courses. Not even Apache women and children could stand the dread *jornada* across the desert without water. They rode along the line of the Gila River which took them over into New Mexico.

Lieutenant Colonel George A. Forsyth,[2] commanding at Fort Cummings, New Mexico, knew the condition of the country and shrewdly guessed the route of the raiders. As soon as word of the attack reached him, he sent a scouting party under Lieutenant C. S. Hall down to the Hatchet Mountains, in the extreme southwest corner of the Territory, and followed at once with six troops—about four hundred men—of the 4th Cavalry.

MCDONALD IS AMBUSHED

Along the eastward border of the Steins Peak Range rode the cavalry. Ranging far off to the side, at the base of the mountains themselves, was Lieutenant D. N. McDonald, with a few Yuma and Mojave scouts and a corporal, trying to "cut" any Indian trails which might lead up into the hills. On the morning of April 23rd, three days after the San Carlos fight, McDonald sent word that he had struck a small trail about twelve hours old, leading toward the Gila. A little later a second message informed Forsyth that another, larger party had joined the first. The colonel was now worried about McDonald. He continued his march but sent two enlisted men back with the messenger. The little party of scouts was at this time about sixteen miles west of the main column. Both bodies were moving in a northwesterly direction.

[2] Forsyth was a frontier hero. He it was who, with fifty white scouts, held off the combined forces of Cheyennes and Sioux in the bloody battle on the Arickaree River, in eastern Colorado, during the fall of 1868. Forsyth knew Indians. His deductions in this case were perfect.

It was terrifically hot. The dust mounted in stifling clouds, so thick that it was almost impossible to breathe. The hats, uniforms, faces and moustaches of the men were gray with a thick layer of it. Tears from their eyes, caused by the blinding fog, made rivulets of pure mud down their cheeks. Above them a dun cloud mounted in a dense column and hung for minutes after the horses had passed.

A sudden shout at the rear of the column and through the screen of dust the men descried an Indian scout—one of McDonald's men —lashing his horse across the desert at full speed. In another minute he was with them. By words and signs he told them: McDonald had been ambushed. At least four of his scouts were dead. The lieutenant and his surviving men were besieged, fighting for their lives.

Bugles blared. In perfect order the squadrons wheeled, each in its position, and started off at an angle. "Gallop" sang the bugles. Four hundred horses broke into a run. It was a sixteen-mile gallop across the stifling plain. There was ample reason to fear that the horses could not stand the pace, but with Forsyth grimly leading, stand it they did.

As they neared the mountains, the distant clatter of rifle fire reached their ears. They were in time, then. A few minutes later Forsyth's troopers cheered hoarsely. A man had appeared high up on one of the spurs of the range, waving his carbine. It was McDonald himself. Very soon, breathless but ready for trouble, they reached him and he made his report to Forsyth.

It had been a typical piece of Apache cunning. And it was a bit of carelessness, very rare for these Indians, which prevented the killing of every man in the scouting party. Moving close to the foot of the range that morning, the chief scout, Yuma Bill, pointed out to the lieutenant a wisp of smoke up a gorge. They halted. Were there Indians up there, or was it the dying campfire of some prospector or hunter? McDonald had to find out. Up the defile he cautiously led his men. They found the remains of a camp high up in the gorge—evidently of a considerable number of Indians. No Apaches were there. But the scouts were warned. Save for this discovery, they might have walked later right into Loco's well-laid trap.

The march was resumed at the foot of the mountains. It was a plain trail now, leading toward the Gila. Suddenly, with a sharp exclamation, Yuma Bill stopped them. He had caught a glimpse of a movement up ahead. In a moment they all saw—two men on the mountain side. Rifles came forward; but they were lowered in a moment. The men were white prospectors. They had hidden in the underbrush and Loco's Indians by some miracle had passed by without noticing them. Perhaps they were too preoccupied with getting back to Mexico. Not one of them investigated the hiding place. They passed on, gaunt, grim, and deadly, and disappeared.[3]

McDonald sent the prospectors on to Lordsburg and proceeded. Again Yuma Bill stopped and pointed to the rocks above. "Two Injun!" he grunted. Sure enough. A pair of Apache warriors. The scouts dropped out of sight. Cautiously Yuma Bill raised his head above the boulders.

"Watch out, McDonald!" he shrieked. The words were punctuated with a blast of rifle fire which burst almost in their faces. Fourteen or fifteen Apaches lay on the other side of the very rocks behind which the scouts were concealed. Three of McDonald's Indians were killed by that volley. Yuma Bill was badly wounded.

Down the slope galloped the survivors—for life. A bullet sang through the lieutenant's hat and another singed his neck. Yuma Bill did not follow. He sat his horse where he was, gradually buckling forward in his saddle, until he pitched to the ground, dead. The six remaining scouts and the corporal, as well as the officer, owed their lives only to atrocious shooting by the Apaches. Not one was hit as they galloped away.

Extending out from the main range was a high, rocky spur, terminating in a small hill. There McDonald halted. He looked around for a man to ride for help, selected Qua-de-le-the-go

---

[3] McDonald said that these two prospectors were the most abjectly terrified men he ever saw. They seemed to think that his Indians were part of the hostile band and it took an almost brutal tongue lashing from the officer to bring them to a realization that they were among friends. Small wonder they were frightened. If ever death passed close to men, it passed close to these two as the Apaches rode by. (See General George A. Forsyth, "Thrilling Days of Army Life," pp. 93–94.)

(Blood), his youngest scout, and sent him speeding away to find Forsyth.[4] The others began piling rocks in front of them. McDonald knew that he had run into the main body of hostiles. The Indians were so sure of finishing the scouting party that they did not at once advance. First they gathered the bodies of the four dead scouts into a pile and built a bonfire on them.

This was more than McDonald could stand. He crept forward three hundred yards, took meticulous aim under a low-spreading mesquite bush, and brought down one of the Apaches. Still the hostiles delayed their attack. McDonald decided on another retreat. He and his men began to ride down the spurs of the mountain, pursued now by the savages. Forsyth arrived just in time to save them.

THE BATTLE OF HORSE SHOE CANYON

Loco, watching from the heights which his Apaches occupied, must have viewed with considerable distaste the sight on the plateau below him. His warriors occupied the high bluffs on both sides of Horse Shoe Canyon, a deep cleft in the Steins Peak Mountains. As he viewed the advance of the troops, his harsh visage must have scowled and the single eye in it gleamed with ferocity.

It was true that his warriors were of the best. But there were not enough of them to oppose the masses of United States soldiers deploying before them. Old in the game of war, Loco and Chato could estimate the numbers of opposing forces as well as anybody. There were four hundred soldiers there, to which the Apaches could oppose only seventy-five braves. And the enemy had all the advantage of ammunition and arms, as well as being unencumbered with noncombatants.

The helpless women and children in his train were what made Loco's problem difficult. Clearly there was no advantage to be

---

[4] The scouts were fortunate in having the troop race horse with them. This animal "Jumping Jack," a very fast runner, really saved all their lives. Qua-de-le-the-go killed him in the terrific ride to Forsyth, but a slower steed might not have taken the message through in time. As it was the rescuers did not arrive a minute too soon.

gained by fighting the troops. He would much rather have withdrawn as quickly as possible. But he had to cover the retreat of his people.

Dismounted, with carbines in hand, the soldiers were already beginning their climb up the mountain. Well, blood would have to be spilled. Loco, who had gone on the war path unwillingly, prepared to do the best he could, now that battle was thrust upon him.

The deep-cut Horse Shoe Canyon possessed some natural features of which the chief took prompt advantage. To the right were some lofty cliffs. In the middle of the gorge stood a mass of huge rocks, forming a small peak joined to the wall on the right by an escarpment about thirty feet high which formed a causeway over to the central rocks. On these vantage points Loco placed his warriors. Colonel Forsyth later commented upon the dispositions of the Apaches: "The position occupied by the hostiles was a capital one." [5] But just now he was most interested in driving them out.

Two flanking parties, containing two troops of dismounted cavalry each, were formed by Forsyth, with a fifth troop as a horse guard, and the sixth under himself in the center. Major Wirt Davis, commanding the right wing, opened the battle. Carefully Loco watched the advance of the soldiers. His warriors fought warily. As the vastly superior forces of his enemy enveloped his positions, one by one, his braves retreated. Occasionally an Apache crashed down from his perch in the cliffs. But the defense was stubborn. In spite of the tremendous fire superiority the troops maintained throughout the fight, it took hours for the soldiers to dislodge the savages. But step by step Forsyth drove the Indians back. As evening fell the last of the hostile warriors were so far up the canyon that they could not be reached. Then the troops rested.

There were thirteen dead Apaches in that hard-won canyon. And others were wounded. But Loco had succeeded in the one thing which concerned him most. His warriors had held back the white men until the women and children got away. In doing so they had killed three troopers and four scouts, besides wounding eight or ten men. Considering the disparity in numbers, the honors were

[5] Forsyth, "Thrilling Days of Army Life," p. 105.

very much with Loco.

Time was an essential. Leaving Forsyth entangled in the gorge, the Apaches moved swiftly over the range, down on the other side. Across the San Simon Valley they went, toward the Chiricahua peaks. Forsyth extricated his command from the canyon and followed. Next morning he was joined by Captain Gordon and Lieutenant Gatewood, with a troop of cavalry and a company of Indian scouts. If he could only catch up with the hostiles now—

But there was no overtaking them. Carrying their wounded, the Indians crossed the border, killing a number of people in the valley as they went.

COLONEL GARCIA'S VICTORY

For years the Apaches had scoffed at the Mexicans. The Indians lived in the mountains of northern Mexico practically unmolested. But now the Mexicans were to prove themselves as deadly as tarantulas. Colonel Lorenzo Garcia, of the 6th Mexican Infantry, with two hundred and fifty men, was patrolling the border when he heard that the Chiricahuas under Chato and Nachite, had crossed to the north on their raid into Arizona. As brave and skillful a soldier as the Mexican army boasted, Garcia made his plans at once to strike the Indians when they returned. He knew that on their way back the Apaches would be so occupied by the thought of pursuit that they would be unlikely to think of danger ahead.

His scouts, near the western edge of the Janos Plain, brought word to him April 27th that they could see a cloud of dust, made by a large party and traveling fast, coming up the valley from the north. Garcia concluded that it must be the raiding Apaches returning to Mexico.

The trail led up a mountain canyon. Using the Indians' own tactics, he laid an ambush. While he did not know the exact numbers of his enemy, with his two hundred and fifty soldiers he had reason to believe himself numerically superior.

The plan worked out better than he dreamed. Oblivious of danger ahead of them, the Indians came on as they never would have done in the days of Mangus Colorado or Victorio. The women, children and old men were ahead. Far behind hung back the warriors, watching Forsyth's dust cloud, many miles to their rear. The first hint of danger came too late. Like a clap of thunder among the hills the Mexican volley crashed out. The Apache caravan writhed like a shattered snake. It was the noncombatants upon whom the Mexicans had fired. Dropping loot and camp bundles in the trail, the brown figures bolted for the nearest cover. There was something more than loot lying on the trail. A thick cluster of bodies showed where the bullets had cut their swath. As the gray pall of smoke drifted away from in front of Garcia's men, scores of women and children lay stricken.

The Mexicans sprang in pursuit of the fleeing survivors. But now the rocks began to spit fire as the Apache warriors, hurrying up, fought back. There was one death spot in particular. An old Apache, long past his prime, had burrowed into a small depression behind a thick clump of cactus. Venomous as a snake he fought there. Time after time as Garcia's soldiers tried to circle him or rush him, his rifle spat death. Eight Mexican soldiers were killed by him before his ammunition gave out. Then the soldiers killed him.

The fight was still raging. Bullets kept crying like banshees as they struck rocks on the mountain sides and ricocheted. But the advantage was all with the Mexicans. They had four rifles to the Apaches' one. They were in better position. Slowly the Indians retreated down the canyon, until at last they disappeared.

Garcia had lost two officers and nineteen men killed, and three officers and thirteen men wounded, a total of thirty-seven. But the Indians had received a crushing blow. There were seventy-eight dead among the rocks, chiefly women and children. Moreover, there was a huddled group of more than a score of captives, all women and children.[6] It was the most terrible reverse the Apaches had suffered in years.

[6] One of these was Loco's daughter. She told the Mexicans her father had been forced to accompany the raiders against his will. This story has been repeated over and over again until the writer believes it was true. Loco may have been forced to go on the war path, but he entered fully into the spirit of the affair once he embarked upon it.

But the Mexican victory was by no means complete. A disproportionate number of the dead and captured were noncombatants. Most of the warriors—the deadly, vicious killers—escaped. And among these were Loco, Chato and Nachite. Mexico and the United States were to hear more from them.

Next day Garcia had a delicate duty to perform. Ignoring instructions to the contrary, Forsyth pursued the Indians right across the border into Mexico. Garcia had to stop him.

The two commanders met at a small ravine. The Mexican was courteous but firm. He said his government had ordered him to oppose any invasion of its territory by the Americans. Forsyth was equally polite. But he insisted on pursuing the Apaches, who, he said, had murdered many people in Arizona and New Mexico, besides burning homes, stealing livestock and causing great property damage. Then Garcia sprang his surprise.

"If your sole object is the punishment of this band of marauders," he said, "it is already accomplished. My command fought, routed, and scattered them yesterday." [7]

Forsyth had not an argument left. He asked permission to visit the battle field, and Garcia himself took him there. The scattered dead, still lying unburied where they had fallen, were sufficient proof. The American saluted his soldierly acquaintance and with his command started back for the United States.

[7] Forsyth, "Thrilling Days of Army Life," p. 118.

22: THE BLUNDER OF NAN-TIA-TISH

AFTER Crook chastised the White Mountain Apaches in 1872, they were exemplary in their conduct for nearly ten years. But in August, 1881, the medicine man Nok-e-da-klinne, by his prophecies and magic working, which convinced the Indians that he was divine, stirred up a deep current of unrest among them.

Nok-e-da-klinne was believed to have the power of bringing the dead to life. He held ceremonial dances to repopulate the country with Apaches and drive out the whites.[1] The situation was reported as "very serious" to General E. A. Carr, commanding at Fort Apache, and late in August he sent a runner to summon Nok-e-da-klinne to a conference. With some of his followers the medicine man came to the fort where General Carr advised them to give up the dances, warning them of serious trouble if they continued to incite the Indians.

But by this time the Apaches were fanatical and when Nok-e-da-klinne returned to his village on Cibicu Creek, about forty miles back in the Indian country, they continued their dances. Up to this time there had been no hostilities, although the excitement was growing constantly.

Carr considered the condition so serious that on August 30th, after talking with Agent Tiffany, he ordered Captain E. C. Hentig, 6th Cavalry, to proceed to the Cibicu country and arrest the medicine man. Hentig took two troops of cavalry and a company of Indian scouts under Lieutenant Thomas Cruse.

The arrest order was a mistake. Nok-e-da-klinne was an impostor, but he had attained great influence among his people. Some of those

---

[1] It is strange how similar this trouble was to the Ghost Dance trouble among the Sioux in 1890, although on a much smaller scale. The same claim, of repopulating the country with Indians and driving out the whites, was made; dances were the chief features of the ceremonies in both cases; and bloodshed was the result of each.

who believed in him most profoundly were the very scouts whom Cruse took to make the arrest. Moreover, the act made a martyr out of the medicine man, and some saw in it evidence that the white men feared his powers.

Nok-e-da-klinne was at his home, peacefully preparing to plant corn, where Hentig arrested him. The forty-mile journey back to the fort began. There was a queer, strained atmosphere among Cruse's Indian scouts. For days they had been acting strangely, so much so that on August 17th the lieutenant had temporarily disarmed them, and Carr in a telegram on that date to General Irwin McDowell, spoke of the "general belief in their disposition to treachery." The whole command marched about five miles back toward Fort Apache and camped for the night. Almost immediately scores of Apaches from Nok-e-da-klinne's camp appeared on the scene, glowering and threatening.

A tense situation. Hentig felt the electric atmosphere and ordered the scouts to camp at a distance from the soldiers who had charge of Nok-e-da-klinne. Dusk fell. Without a word of warning, Cruse's scouts, who had served faithfully, even heroically, in the Indian campaigns, mutinied.

The overt act came when one of the scouts approached too close to the soldiers' camp. Hentig shouted an order at him to move away. This Indian, Mosby, had been followed by other scouts. As the captain called out his order, he turned to pick up a rifle.

All in a moment the peaceful valley woke to tumultuous action. Guns crashed. Captain Hentig and Privates Bird, Sullivan, Miller, Levingston, Amick, and Sondergass were killed by that first, sudden volley. Private Foran died later from his wounds. Sergeant Mc Dowell and Private Betty were wounded. The place was a shambles

Three of Cruse's scouts, Deadshot, Dandy Jim, and Skitashe, made a daring attempt to release the medicine man from the soldiers' camp during the height of the fighting. But Bugler Ahrens saw them, ran up, and pumped three bullets from his army Colt into Nok-e-da-klinne's head.

Nine men were dead or dying and several had been wounded in the brief minutes of furious shooting. The Indians retreated.

Lieutenant W. H. Carter, upon whom the command devolved at Hentig's death, posted sentries and everybody stood to arms during the night. A detail was told off to bury the dead. Sergeant John A. Smith was in command of the squad. While the graves were being dug, Smith observed a movement. Running to where the corpses lay, he saw the horrifying spectacle of the medicine man, Nok-e-da-klinne, the blood and brains oozing from the bullet holes in his head, hitching himself along the ground. The old Indian was blinded, probably shattered mentally by the lead slugs in his brain, but the invincible Apache determination to live drove him to crawl slowly along the ground toward where instinct said safety lay. Smith glanced about. A shot would alarm the command. But an axe lay near. The sergeant seized it, bent over the creeping horror. Once, twice the steel head rose and fell. Smith stepped back. Nok-e-da-klinne crawled no more.[2]

At Fort Apache, meantime, the troops had learned in no uncertain way of Apaches' resentment. The government telegraph line was cut, and from all about the fort the savages opened fire. Lieutenant Gordon was wounded. There were five or six thousand Indians on the reservation and it was feared they would all join in the revolt. Timely arrival of reinforcements under Major Gorden, from Fort Thomas, saved Carr's troops. The Indians sullenly retreated to their homes. Three freighters whose wagon train had been cut off, two civilians who had left the fort against orders, three soldiers who had been detailed to guard the Black River ferry, a rancher named Fibs, shot in his own shack, and a mail carrier—these were the casualties of the fighting which resulted from the arrest of Nok-e-da-klinne. Eleven soldiers and seven civilians were dead. So far as has been learned, the medicine man himself was the only Indian fatality.

A month after the Cibicu affair, things were complicated at San Carlos when part of the Chiricahuas, refusing to move from Camp

[2] As a trophy Smith took from the dead man's neck a medal commemorating the peace established by Colyer. On the obverse side of the medal was President Grant's head and the words: "United States of America. Let us have peace. Liberty and justice." On the reverse was the globe with a number of implements signifying agriculture and the sentiment, "On earth peace, good will to men. 1871." The irony of such phrases on the dead man's breast seems not to have struck anybody at the time.

Goodwin to Fort Apache, killed Albert Sterling, chief of the Indian police, and tried to kill the sub-agent, Ezra Hoag. Then they cut the throats of all their dogs, that they might not be betrayed by the barking, stabbed their old or ailing horses, to avoid being encumbered by them, and, leaving behind every bit of camp equipment that was bulky or unnecessary, hurriedly and silently fled to the Sierra Madre of Mexico.

They fought one skirmish on the way, with two troops of the 6th Cavalry, at Cedar Creek, killed a sergeant and two men and escaped to the mountains where they were a constant menace.

Subsequently a military tribunal dealt sternly with the Cibicu mutineers. Five of the scouts were tried by court martial. Two were sent to prison on Alcatraz Island. The other three, Dandy Jim, Deadshot and Skitashe, were hanged at Camp Grant, on March 3rd, 1882.

It was thought the trouble was ended. But it was far from that. In April, 1882, little more than a month after the execution of the mutineers. Five of the scouts were tried by court-martial. Two were Loco and his band to accompany them, as described in the preceding chapter, and fought their way back across the border. All these events combined to keep the White Mountain Apaches very much stirred up. Yet they remained peaceful in spite of their execrable treatment by the Indian agents, who seemed to be in league with the malodorous Tucson Ring.[3]

Trouble should have been expected, but when it came it surprised everyone. Without any warning, on July 6th, fifty-four White

[3] The following excerpts from the report of the Federal Grand Jury of Arizona, October 24th, 1882, will give some idea of conditions:

". . . never until present investigations . . . laid bare the infamy . . . could a proper idea be formed of the fraud and villainy which are constantly practiced in open violation of law. . . . Fraud, peculation, conspiracy . . . seem to be the rule on this reservation (San Carlos). . . . In collusion with the chief clerk and storekeeper, rations can be issued *ad libitum* for which the government must pay while the proceeds pass into the capacious pockets of the agent. Indians are set to work in coal fields, superintended by white men; all the workmen and superintendents are fed and frequently paid from agency stores and no return of the same is made. . . . All surplus supplies are used in the interest of the agent. . . . Government contractors . . . get receipts for large amounts of supplies never furnished. In the meantime, the Indians are neglected, half-fed, discontented, and turbulent."

Mountain Apaches, led by Nan-tia-tish and Ar-she, swept down on the San Carlos Agency. They kidnaped a dozen or more squaws. Then they rode wildly up the San Carlos Valley, killing as they went. A few miles from the agency, they ambushed J. L. (Cibicu Charley) Colvig, who had succeeded Albert Sterling as agency police chief. With Colvig died seven of his Indian scouts.

The Apaches now rode north, past the city of Globe, across the Pleasant Valley, and on, leaving behind a trail of blood and smoking ruins. These Indians were the Cibicu White Mountain Apaches, the same who had believed devoutly in Nok-e-da-klinne. Never had they forgiven the arrest and murder of their prophet. As this band rode up the San Carlos and over to the Tonto Basin, it raided every ranch it passed, destroyed property worth many thousands of dollars and killed six ranchers.

With the army's usual promptness, fourteen companies of soldiers, with strong details of Indian scouts, took the field. There was especial anxiety about this outbreak, since the Apaches were headed north and might get into the Navajo country. But they were found to have gone to the Tonto Basin, where they attacked the Sigsbee ranch, killing Bob Sigsbee and Louie Houdon.

THE BATTLE OF CHEVELON'S FORK

By the morning of July 17th, ten troops of cavalry were converging on the Indians' trail, with others close behind. Yet they might not have overtaken the marauders, had it not been for a blunder by Nan-tia-tish, leader of the hostile band.

Nan-tia-tish fancied himself a war chief. Thirsty for fame, he conceived a plan of ambushing the leading troop of cavalry, which chanced to be Captain Adna R. Chaffee's white horse troop of the 6th Cavalry. Those white horses were easy to descry on the back trail. The hawk-eyed Apaches kept them under surveillance, knew their exact number, and every detail of their movements. So interested were the Indians in Chaffee and his white horses, that they quite overlooked the fact that other soldiers on less conspicuous horses were following behind him. Nan-tia-tish set his trap, basing his plans on his optimistic but sadly mistaken belief that the white horse troop was alone on his trail.

As if a giant axe had split the mountains, a canyon, variously known as Chevelon's Fork of the Canyon Diablo, or the Big Dry Wash, cuts it way through the Mogollons. Only seven hundred yards wide at the top, it drops away fully a thousand feet deep, its sides so steep that they actually overhang in places, with pine trees growing wherever they can find a precarious foothold. At the bottom is a fair-sized mountain stream which appears to be a mere trickle from the heights above.

Here Nan-tia-tish prepared his ambush. Marksmen lay along the side of the canyon in such a way that when the soldiers descended into it, as they must do if they followed the trail which the Indians had purposely left, they would be caught almost helpless. Toward this trap, Chaffee, hot on the track, came riding July 17th, 1882.

On the evening before Captain George L. Converse, with his command, had joined Chaffee. By merest chance Converse's troop was also mounted on white horses. So incompetent was Nan-tia-tish that he did not even notice the increased numbers as the combined force advanced. Victorio or Nana would instantly have seen the change. But the White Mountain leader lacked their calibre. Fatuously confident that he had to deal with only one troop, he proceeded with his plans.

Even with his increased force, Chaffee would have been severely handled had he gone into the canyon as Nan-tia-tish planned. But he had with him Al Sieber, chief of the Arizona scouts, and Lieutenant George H. Morgan, with eight Tonto Apache trailers. The uncanny eyesight of these Indians really unmasked the trap.

As soon as Chaffee was shown the situation, he dismounted his men on the brink of the canyon opposite the position of Nan-tia-tish and waited. He knew, as the Apaches did not, that Colonel Evans was right behind with the main body of the troops. Shortly Evans rode up and Chaffee made his report. The colonel, with generous courtesy, told him to take charge of the fight, as he had found the Indians and deserved the credit. Chaffee was delighted. In the battle which followed, he handled his men like a born general.[4]

At his order Converse's men dismounted and crawled forward to the brink of the canyon, where they opened a heavy fire across the chasm. Lieutenant Frank West took his own troop and that of Chaffee, together with Al Sieber and part of the Tonto scouts, far to the east, looking for a place to cross over the canyon. At the same time Chaffee sent the remaining troops under Captain L. A. Abbott along the canyon wall in the opposite direction. Morgan and the rest of the Tontos accompanied this detachment. The pack train and cavalry horses remained under a guard.

A spitting, snarling rifle duel was already in progress between Converse's troop and the Apaches across the gorge. Early in the engagement a bullet from the hostiles split on a rock and half of it penetrated Converse's eyeball. He suffered intense pain from this wound, but survived.

The Apaches were so busy shooting at Converse's men that they did not observe the two flanking detachments. Far down the canyon West at last discovered a steep pathway by which his men could descend to the bottom and then climb the other side. It was a desperate scramble, real danger every foot of the way. All they could hope was that the situation would remain uncomplicated by their being discovered by the Indians as the troopers hung by their toes and fingernails. Luck was with them. Unchallenged, they reached the top and moved forward in skirmish order through the pine woods.

Abbott's column, meanwhile, had an easier time finding a way across and got into action first. Evans and Chaffee heard the rippling crash of the first volley soon after Abbott departed on his detour. The Apaches had not discovered West's detachment at all. They turned their attention toward Abbott and went swarming through the trees to fight him. While the battle roared in that direction, Sieber and his scouts, closing in from the east, ran right into the herd of Indian ponies. So busy were the Apache horse guards watching in the direction of the battle noise that they did not realize the scouts

[4] Chaffee was to rise to supreme command of the United States Army, becoming chief of staff in 1904, after a brilliant record, his military career having begun as an enlisted private.

were upon them until the first point-blank volley wiped them out. The soldiers rounded up the ponies and sent them to the rear.

Let us return now to Abbott. He had run into the Apaches quite unexpectedly. The men climbed down into the canyon and were almost at the top on the other side, when Morgan's scouts warned of a band of hostile Indians coming. The Apaches were headed down the very path up which the soldiers were going. They had no idea, apparently, that the white men were anywhere near. Still fondly supposing that Chaffee was alone, they were slipping down into the canyon with the intention of taking him from the rear. Right into their surprised faces burst the soldiers' first volley. Several Indians were hit. The rest ran for the pines on the crest.

They soon reached their main body which had been fighting the long-range duel with Converse's men across the canyon. Abbott's steady advance continued. The whole band presently began to retreat along the wall of the gorge, slowly toward the east. Suddenly they ran right into the arms of West, Sieber and their men, and were greeted by another murderous blast of fire.

Their line of retreat was cut off but the Indians were not daunted. As the soldiers slipped forward from tree to tree, the Apaches redoubled their fire. Lieutenant Morgan of the scouts was shot through the side. Sergeant Conn and several enlisted men were hit. But Sieber and his scouts had the range now and were dropping one hostile warrior after another. Lieutenant Thomas Cruse led a charge through the woods. Under the cover of some deadly shooting by that same group of scouts, he broke the Apache line.

It was nearly dark. A heavy rain had set in. The Indians scattered in every direction—those who could move. The White Mountain band was almost wiped out. Of fifty-four Indians who started the fight, twenty-one were found dead on the battle field, including the blundering Nan-tia-tish. Five died later from wounds. Few, if any, escaped unscathed. The survivors soon slipped back to the reservation, their stomach for fighting gone.[5]

[5] The loss to the troops in this battle was surprisingly light. One scout and one enlisted man were killed, two officers and five enlisted men wounded.

CROOK RETURNS

Two things of prime importance to the Apaches occurred shortly after the Chevelon's Fork fight. On July 29th, 1882, a treaty was signed between Mexico and the United States, permitting soldiers of each country to cross the borders of the other in pursuit of hostile Indians. No longer was the invisible international line to be a bulwark of safety for fleeing raiding parties.

The second event was the return to Arizona of General George Crook, who, since 1874, had been in the north fighting the Sioux. Crook took command on September 4th. He found conditions bad. The desert which he had left almost peaceful was at war again. And of the reasons for this, one of his officers, Captain Bourke, wrote as follows:

"But there was a coincidence of sentiment among all people whose opinion was worthy of consultation, that the blame did not rest with the Indians; curious tales were flying about from mouth to mouth, of the gross outrages perpetrated upon men and women who were trying faithfully to abide in peace with the whites. . . . No one had ever heard the Apaches' story, and no one seemed to care whether they had a story or not." [6]

Crook set about patiently and skillfully to knit up the ravelled sleeve of affairs. He reorganized the agency police and enforced the rule that the male Indians on the reservations be counted regularly. He went out into the hills, riding his old mule "Apache," to talk with the people who were hiding out there. One warrior, Alchise, who had served loyally as a scout during the Tonto Basin and other campaigns, told Crook:

"When you left . . . we were all content; everything was peace. The officers you had here were all taken away and new ones came in—a different kind. Perhaps we were to blame, perhaps they were, but anyway we hadn't any confidence in them." [7]

Other chiefs such as Cha-lipun, Eskimo-tzin, Santos, Chiquito, and Huan-klishe also interviewed the general. Although he had been gone for years, Nan-tan Lupan still had their confidence. They

[6] "On the Border With Crook," p. 434.
[7] *Ibid.*, p. 436.

told him their grievances without reservation. He acted as promptly as possible in their behalf. Trusted officers were placed over them; they were encouraged to start growing crops again—an activity which had been abandoned completely. On October 5th, he laid down his policy toward the Indians in his General Orders, issued at Fort Whipple:

"The commanding general, after making a thorough and exhaustive examination among the Indians . . . regrets to say that he finds among them a general feeling of distrust and want of confidence in the whites, especially the soldiery; and also that much dissatisfaction, dangerous to the peace of the country, exists among them. Officers and soldiers . . . are reminded that one of the fundamental principles of the military character is justice to all—Indians as well as white men—and that a disregard of this principle is likely to bring about hostilities, and cause the deaths of the very persons they are sent here to protect. In all their dealings with the Indians, officers must be careful not only to observe the strictest fidelity, but to make no promises not in their power to carry out; all grievances arising in their jurisdiction should be redressed, so that an accumulation of them may not cause an outbreak."

Crook's next official action was to expel all squatters and unauthorized miners from the reservations. He announced also that he would oppose further curtailment of the lands of the Indians. He even started an investigation which resulted in a reorganization of the Indian Department and the discharge of some agents and even officials higher up.

His efforts to make the Apaches self-supporting were viewed by the Tucson Ring of government contractors, with the greatest distaste. They knew that, should the Indians ever start to feed themselves, profits to the Ring would immediately be erased. At once began the long-drawn and devious political battle, which was to end only when Crook left the Arizona Territory. But that was not until the Southwest had seen some drama-filled days.

23: THE SIERRA MADRE CAMPAIGN

GERONIMO

CROOK almost succeeded in pacifying the Apaches. By judicious use of presents, promises and threats, he brought first one band, then another back to the reservations. But a new leader had arisen among the Apaches, destined to be the most famous of them all. His real name was Go-ya-thle (He-Who-Yawns), but he was known throughout the whole Southwest on both sides of the border as Geronimo.

In the later Apache wars, Geronimo was a potent, menacing figure always. Crook called him "the human tiger." General Nelson A. Miles referred to him with deepest sincerity as "the worst Indian who ever lived." He was cunning, bloodthirsty, and his cruelty was a bottomless pit; and he did more to resist the white man than any of his people since Victorio.

Geronimo's hatred for all people other than Apaches dated from early manhood. He was born high in the headwaters of the Gila River in June, 1829. Writers have called him a Chiricahua Apache, but he himself said that he was born into the tribe of which Mangus Colorado was chief, the Mimbreños. His grandfather, Maco, was a Mogollon chief, but Geronimo's own father married into the Mimbreño tribe, thus, according to Apache law, becoming a Mimbreño himself.

Geronimo grew up a care-free, pleasure-loving young buck, with no abnormal cruelty or hatred in his heart. His name, He-Who-Yawns, probably was the indication of a rather indolent, good-natured character. In 1846, when he was seventeen, he was admitted into the council of warriors and married a pretty Apache maiden with the lovely name of Alopé. By her he had three children, and with his widowed mother, they made a happy household.

The Apaches were at peace with Chihuahua in 1858, so Mangus Colorado led his people south that year to trade. Their destination was Casas Grandes, but on the way they camped near the Presidio del Janos. All was peaceful. The Mimbreño warriors went unconcernedly into the town, leaving their women and children in the camp.

At this time General Carasco was military governor of the neighboring Mexican state of Sonora. He was a harsh, strenuous dictator, who impressed into service as soldiers the poor of his state, and forced the rich to supply the money for his campaigns. Carasco learned that a large band of Apaches was at Janos. He had no authority in Chihuahua, but ignoring the boundaries of the two states, he reached Mangus Colorado's camp by forced marches one day while all the warriors were in the town, trading.

There followed scenes of horror which beggar description. The blood-maddened Mexicans weltered in slaughter. Scores of Indian women and children were massacred and ninety were taken prisoner, to be sold later into slavery in southern Mexico. Then Carasco withdrew as quickly as he had come.[1]

The Mimbreño warriors returned from Janos to find their camp sacked, and most of their people butchered or carried away. In the shambles Geronimo discovered his mother, his wife and three children, all dead. The young warrior went nearly insane with grief. Long years after he told in his own simple words his sensations in discovering the terrible tragedy:

". . . without being noticed I silently turned away and stood by the river. How long I stood there I do not know, but when I saw the warriors arranging for council, I took my place.

"That night I did not give my vote for or against any measure; but it was decided that as there were only eighty warriors left, and as we were without arms . . . surrounded by Mexicans . . . we could not hope to fight success-

---

[1] For this act of treachery, Governor Medina of Chihuahua complained to the general government of Mexico, but the administration upheld Carasco. The Mexicans might better have handed him over to the Apaches to wreak their vengeance on him, for the people of Sonora and Chihuahua were destined to pay for decades as a result of his act. Years later Carasco, whose tyranny had grown unbearable, was poisoned by his own people.

fully. So our chief, Mangus Colorado, gave the order to start at once in perfect silence for our homes in Arizona, leaving the dead upon the field.

"I stood still until all had passed, hardly knowing what I would do—I had no weapon, nor did I hardly wish to fight, neither did I contemplate recovering the bodies of my loved ones, for that was forbidden. I did not pray nor did I resolve to do anything in particular, for I had no purpose left. I finally followed the tribe silently, keeping just within hearing distance of the soft noise of the feet . . ." [2]

From that day Geronimo's hand was against the world. He was sent by Mangus Colorado on more than one occasion to stir up other tribes to join the Mimbreños in war expeditions against the Mexicans. Gifted with eloquence and carrying his well-known wrongs as a grievance, he persuaded both the Chiricahuas and Mogollons, under Cochise and Juh, to join with Mangus Colorado in bloody raids. From 1858 to 1873 there was scarcely a year which did not see Geronimo lead at least two or three war parties into Mexico. On one of these, in 1863, he captured a whole town, the hamlet of Crassanas, forty miles west of Casas Grandes, and looted it. On another occasion, in the summer of 1865, he led his warriors clear to the Gulf of California. In 1876, Geronimo led an uprising against the white men, and was later arrested by Agent John Clum and taken in chains to Fort Apache. But fortune was with him. Clum resigned, and with nobody to press the charges against him, Geronimo was freed. After two or three flights to the mountains and cautious returns, Geronimo and Juh, on the night of September 30th, 1881, fled once more to Mexico, after killing Albert Sterling, chief of the agency police and whipping a detachment of the 6th Cavalry. The sinister struggle known as the Geronimo War was on.

Geronimo was a combination of many talents. He had the cunning of his race intensified to the highest degree. When he could get them, he took full advantage of the white man's latest weapons. He was courageous, although he gave an impression of cowardice with his skulking tactics. Of his appearance, Charles F. Lummis says:

[2] This story was told by Geronimo to S. M. Barrett, at the time superintendent of schools at Lawton, Oklahoma, near Fort Sill. It is quoted by him in his book, "Geronimo's Own Story of His Life," pp. 45–46.

"He was a compactly built, dark-faced man of one hundred and seventy pounds, and about five feet, eight inches in height. The man who once saw his face will never forget it. Crueller features were never cut. The nose was broad and heavy, the forehead low and wrinkled, the chin full and strong, the eyes like two bits of obsidian with a light behind them. The mouth was a most noticeable feature—a sharp, straight, thin-lipped gash of generous length and without one softening curve." [3]

CHATO'S SECOND RAID

This was the new force with which Crook had to reckon. With Geronimo in the fastnesses south of the border were a number of other redoubtable fighting chiefs. Old Nana was there. So was Juh. And so were Chato, Nachite and Loco.

It was Chato who struck the first blow. With twenty-six men he left the border on March 24th, 1883, accompanied by Mangus, the son of the old giant, and swept through Arizona and New Mexico, seeking chiefly to capture ammunition. Several persons lost their lives in this raid, but it is most memorable because of the murder by Chato's band, of Judge H. C. McComas and wife, and the abduction of their little son Charley. This tragedy occurred in Thompson's Canyon, near the Gila River, on the morning of March 28th. The McComas family was on its way from Silver City to Leitendorf, a mining camp near Lordsburg. Mrs. McComas, cultured and accomplished, was a sister of Eugene F. Ware, the then popular poet "Ironquill."

The bodies of the judge and his wife were found by Jim Baker, a stage driver. Signs on the trail showed that Judge McComas had leaped from the buckboard, giving the reins to his wife, and had attempted to stand off the Indians while she whipped the horses into a run, trying to escape. The judge was killed where he stood. There were seven bullet holes in his body when he was picked up.

The buckboard traveled less than fifty yards from where the Indians killed the jurist, before one of its horses was shot. Mrs. McComas was clubbed to death and the little boy Charley, just six

[3] "The Land of Poco Tiempo," p. 181.

years old, was carried away by the Indians. For days posses scoured the country, fruitlessly trying to find the child. The incident created a national sensation because of the prominence of the persons concerned.

A few days later Chato safely crossed the border into Mexico again, having won back some of the laurels lost in the ill-fated expedition which ended in the Garcia fight, when Loco's band was nearly destroyed in April, 1882.

It was Crook's turn to move. Taking advantage of a new international treaty, he led a troop of cavalry under Captain Chaffee and a battalion of one hundred and ninety-three Indian scouts under Captain Emmett Crawford, 3rd Cavalry, across the boundary line on May 1st. Somewhere to the south five hundred or more hostile Indians were lurking, the remnants of Victorio's Mimbreños under Nana; Loco's band; the Mogollons and Chiricahuas under Juh, Chato, Nachite and Geronimo, and a few scattered "broncho" Apaches of various tribes.

By May 8th Crook was in the Sierra Madre. The country was so rough that the command lost several pack mules which rolled over precipices. Everybody was walking and leading his horse.

Crawford and his Indians surprised a *ranchería* high in the mountains on May 15th, defeated the hostiles and captured several prisoners.[4] Eight days later, Nana, Chato and two hundred and sixty other Indians voluntarily came to Crook's camp and surrendered, saying they were tired of war. That made two hundred and eighty-five prisoners, including forty-eight warriors. Shortly after this Geronimo, Nachite, and Loco also surrendered, and reported that

[4] After this fight there was partial news of what became of Charley McComas. He was in the *ranchería* when it was attacked. During the fight according to the Indians, the little fellow wandered off into the woods and either starved or was killed. Five Mexican women and one small child were recaptured from the Indians. It was at first thought the child was Charley McComas. He was, however, a Mexican boy, the son of Señora Antonio Hernandez, who was also a prisoner. There should have been no mistake in this case as the rescued child was only two years old while Charley McComas was six. The Mexican women were the wives of Mexican soldiers and were captured almost in full view of their husbands, whom they were following on a march, near El Carmen, on the Mexican frontier. They had been prisoners fourteen days when rescued.

Juh, with a few of his bitter-enders had gone far west to the Yaqui country to live, hoping thus to escape further pursuit by the troops.[5]

Crook conferred with the chiefs and agreed to return to the United States with the women, children and old men, allowing the warriors time to round up their stock and follow. By this time other Indians were furtively stealing in from the mountains. When the general reached San Carlos, June 23rd, he had with him fifty-two warriors and two hundred and seventy-three women and children. Among the braves were old Nana and Loco, the Mimbreño chiefs.

Crook ordered Lieutenant Britton Davis to wait at the border with a company of scouts, and meet the rest of the hostiles as they came over. Nobody in Arizona believed the Indians would keep faith with the general. There were anxious days as they waited to learn the result of his experiment in making a gentleman's agreement with Apaches.

But Crook knew the Indians. One afternoon Nachite and Zele came riding into Davis' camp with thirty or forty of their band. They were taken to San Carlos.[6] There was another weary wait. Then, six weeks after Nachite's surrender, Geronimo came over the border driving along a large herd of cattle.[7] There was every reason to believe the cattle were stolen, but it was necessary to avoid all trouble. Davis started the band, of approximately eighty-five

[5] Juh met a sordid end. In the summer of 1886 he became unromantically drunk, and while attempting to ford a river near Casas Grandes, fell from his horse and was drowned.

[6] On this march a couple of women suddenly dropped out of the line and went off into the bushes. Davis asked one of the scouts where they were going. The Indian laughed. "Bimeby baby," he said. Sure enough, within a few miles the women caught up with the caravan—and the younger was carrying a newborn infant in her arms. What is more, she rode right along on the march and appeared to think nothing of it, to such degree was her body attuned to the hardships of her existence.

[7] A very curious story is told by Davis ("The Truth About Geronimo," pp. 82–83), of how Geronimo's arrival was foretold by a Tonto-Mojave medicine man. After the command had waited for weeks with no sign of the chief, the Indian scouts called on the medicine man to tell how soon he would arrive. There was a day and night of incantation, the burning of *hoddentin*, the sacred pollen, and other charms, then he announced that Geronimo was three days away, riding a white mule with a great herd of horses. Five days later Geronimo arrived, with a large herd of stock and *mounted on a white pony*.

persons, to San Carlos. They were met at Sulphur Springs by a United States marshal and a customs collector, who wished to arrest the whole body of Indians for smuggling cattle across the border without paying duty. It was so stupid that it was almost laughable, but it was serious.

Young Davis did some rapid thinking. A brother officer came along and Davis put the Indians under his charge. That night, while the marshal and the customs collector were snoring at a ranch house near, the Indians were started silently away and by morning were far on the road to San Carlos which they reached safely. The marshal and customs collector found only Davis himself at the Indian camp next morning, waiting solemnly to answer their subpœna. They were furious at first, but the frontier was always ready to laugh, even when the joke was on the person doing the laughing, and the whole thing ended in an uproarious burst of mirth with the marshal congratulating the lieutenant on his resourcefulness.

24: ULZANA'S RIDE

In their camp on Turkey Creek on the San Carlos reservation, most of the five hundred or more hostile Apaches who had surrendered, lived in peace and apparent content for two years. Lieutenant Britton Davis was their special agent, and he made long strides toward winning back their trust in the white man.

The Indians had brought to the reservation one bad habit which prior to their coming had almost been stamped out among the peaceful Indians already living there. This was the making and drinking of *tiswin*[1] Crook ordered the manufacture and use of this native Indian intoxicant to cease. There was an immediate flare of rebellion, headed by one Ka-ya-ten-ne, the turbulent young leader of a small band of the wildest Apaches. But Davis, with the troops at his back, arrested Ka-ya-ten-ne and the trouble maker spent eighteen months in Alcatraz Island prison, before Crook obtained his pardon. It was believed that the trouble was over.

In December, 1884, however, a new agent appeared at San Carlos and there was immediate friction between the Indian Department and the army. The Apaches, quickly sensing this change, grew more and more unruly. *Tiswin* drinking, which had practically ceased after the arrest of Ka-ya-ten-ne, reappeared again. The time was ripe for an explosion. Geronimo touched the match to the magazine.

The chief had never been satisfied with conditions on the reservation. As time passed he built up a circle of followers who were ready to do anything he proposed. On May 15th this group of chiefs defied Davis to stop their *tiswin* drinking. Davis telegraphed to Fort Apache for instructions but received none. Two days later, on May 17th, Geronimo, Chihuahua, Nana, Nachite, and Mangus, with thirty-two warriors, eight well-grown boys, and ninety-two women

[1] *Tiswin* was a sort of native beer, made out of fermented corn mash. It was fairly intoxicating and had a serious effect on its addicts, making them quarrelsome and irresponsible. Hence the government's efforts to stop its use.

and children, left the reservation.

Davis pursued with his scouts, and had a long-distance fight with part of the band under Chihuahua on May 27th. The Apaches surprised a small camp of soldiers, killed a sergeant and two men, captured all the horses, and burned the wagons and tents. The war was on again in all its bloody earnest. Expeditions under Major Wirt Davis, Captain Emmett Crawford and Captain Dorst traversed the mountains, hunting the hostile Indians. Their lack of success was almost tragic. A woman was killed in an attack on a small *ranchería* near the Bavispe Mountains, June 23rd. Two warriors were ambushed by Davis' scouts and killed in the Hoya Mountains of Mexico, July 29th. Nine days later three braves, a squaw and a child were killed in the Sierra Madre by the same scout detachment. And more than a month later one warrior was shot by the scouts on the Bavispe River. That was the extent of the achievements of the army—six warriors, two women and a child killed in four months of campaigning. Meantime the Apaches had slaughtered scores of white men and Mexicans.[2]

Among the warriors who went to Mexico with Geronimo was Ulzana, a brother of Chihuahua, and known as a dour fighter. He was not a chief, but he had at one time served with the government scouts against Nana. In that war of 1881, Ulzana learned much about the arts and tactics of raiding from Nana, the old past-master, by following him with the troops and observing his methods and stratagems. And now, in 1885, the former government scout suddenly launched a raid of his own which in many respects threatened to surpass even Nana's exploit.

Early in November he, with ten warriors, slipped across the line and started up into Arizona. He knew that every water hole was guarded, so he deliberately avoided them. The Apaches had developed a technique in handling water which enabled them to disregard mere stationary guards. A horse, having gone as far as it could stumble, was killed, and the small intestine taken out. Cleaned

---

[2] The records show that seventy-three American settlers and soldiers were officially listed as killed during this time. Twelve reservation Indians were also killed and an unknown number of Mexicans.

—very sketchily according to white standards, but satisfactorily to the rudimentary Apache notion of cleanliness—this receptacle was filled with water and thirty or forty feet of it wrapped around the body of a led horse. It contained enough water to last a band of Apaches for days. Carrying his water in this manner, and traveling only over the most difficult parts of the mountains, in the full knowledge that two thousand troops waited to cut them off and exterminate them, Ulzana and his raiders began their perilous invasion of the United States.

Ulzana guessed correctly as to the hue and cry which would be raised as soon as it was learned the Apaches were in Arizona. From every post expeditions set out in pursuit of him. But traveling only at night and spending the days in the rocky ridges, he led his tiny band north to the Gila River. There he and his warriors, pressed too closely, scattered and disappeared completely. A puzzled soldiery marched back to its cantonments. No human wisdom or foresight could predict what Ulzana would do next. The troops could only await his pleasure.

For nearly three weeks nothing was heard from the Apaches. During that time Ulzana was hiding in the mountains of New Mexico, planning his campaign.

THE BLOODY TRAIL

His first stroke was stunning in its unexpectedness. Prowling through the dark, the Apaches descended upon Fort Apache. On the way they caught and killed two settlers, William Waldo and Will Harrison, whom they found November 24th, on Turkey Creek.

Chill and black came the night of November 26th. Suddenly guns began to thud and white-hot flashes lit the gloom around the White Mountain Apache village near the agency. There were wild yells and scurrying figures in the darkness. Then Ulzana's band was gone. It left in its wake the dead bodies of twelve White Mountain Indians and one of its own number, killed during the fight by an axe in the hands of a reservation Apache.

From that hour Ulzana's band, now numbering exactly ten warriors, had a thrilling and bloody career. As the first news of the appearance of the Apaches was flashed by telegraph, troops took the trail from Fort Apache, San Carlos, Fort Thomas, Camp Grant and Fort Bowie. But the Indians were as elusive as so many fleas. On November 29th they left a bold marking of their trail in the dead bodies of W. H. Clark near the sub-agency, McAllister at Bear Springs, and Thomas Johnson at Black Rock.

Ulzana now seemed to decide to make for the Mexican border again. He took a straight southerly course, toward the Gila River, arriving near Solomonville on December 2nd, an event he signalized by the killing of two brothers named Wright near that town, and of Dick Mays the next day on the Coronado ranch.

The usual route back into Mexico was the valley which lay between the Dragon and Whetstone Mountains. But Ulzana had too clear a picture of what was going on. He did not need to be told that the valley was literally alive with soldiers. As a matter of fact, according to Crook's later report, five troops of cavalry were ambushed in that very locality. Laughing at such clumsy planning, Ulzana turned east and traveled up the Gila Valley. He entered New Mexico with the soldiers swarming on his rear. But Ulzana did not fear pursuit. He stopped long enough on December 9th and 10th, to kill four ranchers on the upper Gila. Then once more he disappeared completely, as if into the air. He abandoned his horses and much of the plunder he had picked up. His braves scattered like so many coyotes, and nobody could tell where they would reassemble.

Wildest panic prevailed in Arizona and New Mexico. Efforts were made both by the government and by private citizens, to notify all ranches, farmers and prospectors of the presence of the Apache death in the country, but it was impossible to do so.[3] Never for one moment did Crook relax his pursuit. Captain Crawford was called

[3] "Many of the persons killed were found on roads or trails, at a distance from points of communication. Every possible means was taken to give warning and afford protection, but even had the whole army been employed for the purpose, it would have been impossible to get word to every prospector, farmer and teamster near their (the Apaches') course."—Crook's report, January 11th, 1886.

back from Mexico, to lead the chase.

Ulzana, in his own good time, made his presence known again on December 19th, when he and his warriors fought a brief battle with a detachment of the 8th Cavalry, killing Dr. Maddox and four men in the Dry Creek Canyon. Troops were rushed to the place at once. It was ascertained that the hostiles were once more headed south. Crawford and Crook guessed that they would pass through the country between the Chiricahua and Peloncillo Ranges. Four troops of the 10th Cavalry and one of the 4th Cavalry were posted in those areas in hope of trapping the ten hostile Apaches as they came down. Behind the Indians came Lieutenant Scott, puzzling out the trail, and pushing Ulzana hard, with a company of Navajo scouts.

Two more white men were killed by the Apaches on November 26th. They were named Snow and Windham, and they were slain near Carlisle, New Mexico. On that same day the raiders crossed over into Arizona and butchered two more men near Galeyville. One of these was Caspar Albert. The other was never identified.

Ulzana showed evident knowledge of the army's plan when he hesitated long before entering the passes between the Chiricahuas and the Peloncillos. Now was the time when Scott should have closed in on him and forced him to go forward into the waiting ambush of soldiers. But Scott's Navajos did not remain staunch. At the critical moment, very fortunately for Ulzana, they refused to go farther. That night a heavy snowstorm fell, lasting for three days. There was no further possibility of trailing the Indians. Some time during the next few days Ulzana reached Mexico, by a mule trail over the mountains into Sonora.

Summing up this raid, it would be difficult to believe some of its figures, were they not attested by the military report of General Crook himself, who certainly had no wish to exaggerate the exploits of this band of Indians against him. In four weeks Ulzana and his ten warriors traveled not less than twelve hundred miles through enemy country, maintaining themselves as they went. They killed thirty-eight persons, captured and wore out two hundred and fifty horses and mules, changing mounts at least twenty times during the raid; and, although they were twice dismounted, they eventually got back safely to Mexico. And all this with the loss of only one brave—killed by the White Mountain Apaches near Fort Apache.

25: THE TRAGEDY OF CRAWFORD

ON GERONIMO'S TRAIL

ULZANA's raid proved to Crook that his cavalry was not capable of catching the Apaches. He reorganized his whole fighting system. Two battalions, largely of Indian scouts, were formed to take up the trail and follow it to the end. One of these, commanded by Major Davis, consisted of one hundred and two Indians and a troop of cavalry. This organization was so handicapped by its white contingent that it accomplished little. The other battalion, however, was formed almost exclusively of lean, bronzed Indian warriors— Mimbreño and White Mountain, with a sprinkling of friendly Chiricahuas. There was much shaking of heads as this body was organized, and free predictions of treachery were made. In spite of that several fine officers volunteered to accompany Captain Crawford, who was to command. Lieutenants Marion P. Maus, W. E. Shipp and S. L. Faison were selected, together with Assistant Surgeon T. B. Davis. Shipp and Maus commanded a company each of approximately fifty Indians and Faison was adjutant of the little force.

They left Fort Bowie November 11th and a few days later crossed into Mexico near Fronteras. It was interesting to the white officers to watch the methods adopted by their Indians in scouting the country. There was no need to give orders. Their system of flankers and advance guards was perfect. When they went into camp, outposts were at once put out, noiselessly and smoothly as if the command was a unit of long experience. Yet most of these Indians had never been on the war path together before. They were following the lessons of a lifetime. It showed Crawford and his lieutenants what might be expected from the hostile Apaches.

For clothing each scout wore only a faded soldier's blouse and a light loin cloth. His hair was bound under the inevitable turban and he scarcely made a sound in his moccasins. The Indians were

434

keen as hounds, tireless and deadly as the wolves they resembled.

Across the Sierra Madre went the expedition and deep into Mexican territory, following a rumor picked up in a Mexican village. There it was found that Geronimo with most of the hostiles had gone far south into Sonora. Crawford called a council of war and decided to leave, under a small guard at the camp, all equipment not absolutely essential, and march on with the bulk of his force. H. W. Daly, chief packer, with most of the packers and six scouts, were detailed to remain with the baggage.

That night the Indians held a medicine dance. Lieutenant Maus afterward described what an impression that ceremony made on him, how the wild and stern mountains seemed to tower above, how the old medicine man, No-wa-zhe-ta, unrolled the sacred buckskin he had carried since he left Fort Bowie, how the dance, with its weird incantations, was followed by each warrior's kneeling before the old man and pressing his lips to the sacred buckskin while he received No-wa-zhe-ta's blessing.[1] Next morning, leaving the camp and the weaker members of the party, seventy-nine men, with twelve days' rations on the toughest mules they could find, crossed the Haros River and took up a well-marked trail which they found on the other side.

Moving mostly by night and suffering extreme hardship, the expedition marched toward some extremely rugged mountains, the Espinosa del Diablo or "Devil's Backbone," so called because the broken outline of peaks resembles a series of jagged vertebræ. The topography of the country changed rapidly. Soon they were in almost a tropical land. Palm trees were seen in the river bottoms and once a jaguar, spotted like a leopard, bounded away.

Noche, the chief Apache scout, commanding the advance guard, sent a runner back at sunset on January 9th, 1886, warning Crawford that he had located a *rancheria*. That was a cheering message. The stern Indian warriors looked to their rifles and discarded their surplus clothing as they always did when going into a fight. All that night they toiled over the mountain trails, crossing and recross-

[1] Maus' very graphic description of this expedition may be found in General Nelson A. Miles' "Personal Recollections," pp. 460–471.

ing a turbulent river that led down the gorge in which the hostile village was supposed to be situated. Captain Crawford was so nearly exhausted that for the last few miles of the march he had to be assisted by an Apache scout on each side.

Just at dawn they heard the braying of burros. Like the geese of Rome, as Maus afterward said, those watch-dogs of the Indian camp saved their masters from surprise.

The still, dark canyon was lit by orange flashes of rifle fire and echoes sprang like thunder-claps from the cliffs. Down the gorge the ghostly figures of Apaches scurried. But the scouts took it with a rush, their flank guardians high on the bluffs, fending the depths below from ambuscade above. One horse was killed by Crawford's men, but the enemy was gone. One by one the scouts returned from the pursuit. The village, and its supplies of meat and other food, was destroyed. In the chill dampness of the early morning, the disappointed command gathered around small fires the scouts built, now that necessity of concealment no longer existed.

Within a few minutes an old squaw crept up to this camp. She brought a message from Geronimo and Nachite, saying they wanted to talk. Crawford, surprised and delighted, told her he would see the chiefs next day. The place for the conference was set. It seemed that fortune, who had so far averted her face, was about to smile at last.

CAPTAIN CRAWFORD'S DEATH

But that conference was never to take place. Throughout the campaign, Crawford had been troubled by the hostility of the Mexicans in the district through which he traveled. Two or three scouts in other expeditions had even been shot by the very persons they were trying to protect from Geronimo's braves.

Early on the morning of January 11th a detachment of Mexican irregulars—the same *Seguridad Públicos* who had brought Victorio to his end—encountered some of Crawford's outposts. They were hunting the same quarry as the American expedition was, and thinking the scouts were hostile Apaches, they fired upon them, wounding three. Crawford and Maus, with Tom Horn, the white chief of scouts, hurried to avert a battle. Out between the lines walked the gallant American captain, holding up his hand and calling "Don't shoot!" Major Corredor, the Mexican commander, seemed equally anxious to stop bloodshed, crying *"no tiran,"* to his men. The Apache scouts lay with their heads peering over the rocks, and the click of their breechblocks sounded clear in the morning mountain air.

At that moment, a single, loud report rang out from off to one side. A group of Tarahumari Indian scouts had crept up unseen from that direction. As the report echoed among the rocks, Captain Crawford fell forward upon his face.

Instantly the whole front of the American line blazed. Crawford was the idol of the Apache scouts and they were filled with a single consuming desire—revenge. Major Corredor fell, shot through the heart. A lieutenant, Juan de la Cruz, was riddled by thirteen bullets. Two more Mexicans were killed. The rest fled.

With Dutchy,[2] one of the scouts, Maus went forward and brought Crawford into the lines. A ragged bullet hole showed in his head and the brains were running down over his face. He was still breathing, but the surgeon said his death was a matter of only a little time.[3]

The command could not stay where it was. The Mexicans outnumbered the Americans two to one. Maus fixed a litter and placed the unconscious captain on it. Another litter carried one of the scouts who had been seriously wounded. The retreat began.

The Mexicans drew off after insolently demanding food and

[2] Dutchy was a Chiricahua with a bloody reputation. At the time he enlisted, he was being sought by civil authorities for the murder of a white man near Fort Thomas. During the march, a marshal from Tombstone, Arizona, who had plenty of nerve, walked into Crawford's camp one day, and in the midst of the scouts served a murder warrant on Dutchy. He had followed their trail for two hundred miles to make the arrest. Crawford convinced him that he could not arrest an enlisted man during a campaign, and the marshal returned without his prisoner. In spite of his reputation, this Indian was one of the best and most faithful of the scouts.

[3] Raht says the man who fired the fatal shot was Mauricio, the Tarahumari who is credited with killing Victorio. ("Romance of the Davis Mountains," p. 271.)

other concessions. Maus, who went to pacify them, was held a prisoner for a time, and gave them six mules as indemnity before they would release him.

Only two or three miles were made by the scouts the first day. That night Geronimo himself met Maus outside of his lines and talked with him. Of course the conference was fruitless. The Indian, who had been all ready to surrender, saw the white man in retreat. So he contented himself with outlining his grievances. Maus promised him that General Crook would meet him, to discuss his surrender, in two moons near the San Bernardino Springs. He further agreed that Crook would bring no escort of regular soldiers. After this conference old Nana, now thoroughly tired of war, came to Maus' camp and voluntarily surrendered with eight other Indians, including Geronimo's wife. They accompanied Maus back to the United States, reaching the border February 1st. Captain Crawford died on the march. The expedition had failed just when it seemed sure of success because of a piece of blundering, to call it by its easiest name, or international treachery, to call it by its worst.

THE APACHE DOUBLE CROSS AND CROOK'S RESIGNATION

As soon as Crook learned of Maus' promise to Geronimo, he prepared to attend the conference as agreed. The place designated was the Canyon des Embudos, twenty miles southeast of San Bernardino Springs, near the Arizona line in northeast Sonora. Thither, on March 25th, went Crook with Captains Charles Roberts and John G. Bourke, and Lieutenants Maus, Faison and Shipp, their Indian scouts, several white and Mexican interpreters, and some other Indians, including the chief Alchise and the recently released Ka-ya-ten-ne. They were met by Geronimo, with Chihuahua and Nachite as well as a number of sub-chiefs.

The Apaches were nervous and suspicious. With the exception of the few who actually took part in the council, they hid themselves in the beautiful ravine, with its lovely stream and cool, shady glades. Geronimo was the chief spokesman.

That was a long talk. As has been said, Crook knew Indians.

"Treat them as children in ignorance but not in innocence," were his instructions to his men, and these instructions he followed himself. He sat patiently upon the ground to wait through what he knew would take place—hours upon hours of talk, much of it apparently meaningless. Out of it all he had to sift the few grains of meaning and truth, and from these derive the facts wherewith to drive a bargain with these Indians which should bring them peacefully upon the reservations.

Geronimo began to speak. Indian-like, he devoted much time to a recital of his wrongs, some of which the general knew to be true, and some of which were clearly imaginary. Every once in a while a significant sentence or phrase would drop in the midst of this conversational flood.

"I have several times asked for peace, but trouble has come from agents and interpreters." [4] How well Crook knew the truth of that statement.

"Whenever I meet you I talk good to you and you to me, and peace is soon established; but when you go to the reservation you put agents and interpreters over us who do bad things."

"To prove to you that I am telling the truth, remember I sent you word that I would come from a place far away to speak to you here, and you see us now."

"What I want is peace and good faith."

Thus the chief talked endlessly during the first day, these sentences being the only statements upon which Crook could lay hold out of his almost interminable speech. They parted in the evening. The next council was two days later, on March 27th. This time there were several to speak for the Apaches. Chihuahua, Nachite and Geronimo all harangued at length. Finally Geronimo abruptly made his decision.

"Two or three words are enough," he said. "I have little to say. I surrender myself to you." Here he shook hands with General Crook. "We are all comrades, all one family, all one band. What others say I say also. I give myself up to you. Do with me what you

---

[4] This and the following quotations are all excerpts from the official transcription of the interpreted speeches, made during the conference at the orders of General Crook.

please. I surrender. Once I moved about like the wind. Now I surrender to you and that is all." Again he shook hands with Crook.

And so the conference ended with a few words by the scouts Alchise and Ka-ya-ten-ne. Geronimo was quite evidently sincere. With a free mind the general prepared to leave for Fort Bowie, the Apaches to follow.

But once more the evil influence of the money-grabbing white man spoiled everything. The night before Crook departed, an American bootlegger named Tribolet, who lived on the San Bernardino Springs ranch, sneaked into the Indian camp and began selling liquor to the wild Apaches. Faithful old Alchise and Ka-ya-ten-ne came to the general's tent shortly before daylight of March 28th, with word that the warriors of Geronimo's band were howling drunk. They asked permission to take a squad of their own men and deal with Tribolet. Crook refused permission. One almost wishes he had granted it. The Apaches had a singular flair for dealing unpleasantly with those whom they thought deserving of punishment.

Some of Crook's officers started at once for the Indian camp. By the time they reached the canyon where it stood, the woods and grass were afire, and the Apaches were riding about on their horses and mules, crazed with liquor.

It began to rain, a steady, drizzling downpour. That night Geronimo, Nachite and twenty warriors, thirteen women and six children, stole through the spattering showers and rode again for the fastnesses of the Sierra Madre. They feared the consequences which might follow their drinking Tribolet's liquor. Thus the whole careful plan for ending the war came to nothing. A frontier racketeer had set in motion a new horror which was to cost additional scores of human lives.

Most of the Apaches, including the chief Chihuahua and his brother, the ferocious Ulzana, remained true to their agreement to surrender. Eighty of them accompanied Lieutenant Faison back to the reservation, reaching Fort Bowie on April 2nd.

Meantime an unlooked-for complication arose. Crook who knew the people with whom he was dealing, and at the risk of his life had made certain definite agreements with them to surrender, wired the terms of this agreement to General Phil Sheridan, then at Washington.

Sheridan, who knew nothing about Apaches, and whose attitude toward the whole Indian question is summed up by the statement often attributed to him: "The only good Indian is a dead Indian," telegraphed back disapproval of the terms. He directed Crook to receive the Apaches only on unconditional surrender. This was a direct violation of Crook's word to the Indian. The general was not the man to allow his honor to be smirched.

The escape of Geronimo, the hated and dreaded, moreover aroused a storm of criticism in Arizona. The malodorous Tucson Ring which had long chafed under Crook's rule, set about its machinations with renewed energy. The Tucson Ring did not obtain Crook's removal, as it had been plotting for years to do, but there is small doubt that the unpleasantness it made contributed strongly to his decision in what followed.

On April 1st, the man who had done so much to bring order out of chaos in the Southwest, sent a long message to Sheridan, carefully outlining his policy of fairness to both red men and white, describing his plan of campaign and ending with these words:

"I believe that the plan upon which I have conducted operations is the one most likely to prove successful in the end. It may be, however, that I am too much wedded to my own views in this matter, and as I have spent nearly eight years of the hardest work of my life in this department, I respectfully request that I may now be relieved from its command."

The very next day, April 2nd, General Nelson A. Miles, then stationed at Fort Leavenworth, Kansas, was assigned to the command of the Department of Arizona.

26: TREACHERY AT FORT APACHE

GENERAL MILES was the most famous and successful Indian fighter in the United States Army. He was the conqueror of the Kiowas, the Comanches, the Sioux, the Nez Percés and other great plains tribes in wars extending over more than a decade. Now he was suddenly sent south to deal with the Apaches. The order putting him in command in Arizona, was a surprise to him and no welcome assignment. Crook and he were friends and he knew of the efficiency of the former's administration. But Miles had no choice but to obey.

With characteristic energy he applied himself to the problem of catching Geronimo. There were five thousand soldiers under his command, and to these he added approximately five hundred Indian scouts. In twenty-five detachments he sent these troops to combing the entire desert country.

"Commanding officers are expected to continue a pursuit until capture, or until they are assured a fresh command is on the trail," was the order.

Every waterhole in Arizona, no matter how small, was guarded. Every ranch had its garrison. The Mexican international boundary line meant nothing, since the treaty with Mexico, and the troops crossed over at will.

But Miles' study of Crook's methods showed that it would be useless to attempt the subjugation of the Apaches with ordinary soldiers. Therefore he devised a flying column, similar to those of Crook's day, composed of picked desert men and Indian scouts, who were to carry on the final hunt. In command of this column he placed Captain H. W. Lawton, a desert athlete who knew the Indians and the Indian country, and who had a curious strain of bulldog determination which prevented him from ever knowing when he was beaten.

With this flying column Miles introduced an innovation—the heliograph. This device, the invention of a British army officer, had been used successfully in India. It consisted of a mirror which reflected the sun in flashes of greater or less length for the dots and dashes of the Morse code. Arizona's atmosphere was clear and bright, and experiments showed that messages could be flashed through it for fifty miles or more. The use of the heliograph entailed the establishment of twenty-seven stations on mountain peaks from twenty-five to thirty miles apart. So expert did the heliographers become that once they transmitted a message eight hundred miles over inaccessible mountain peaks, in less than four hours. They handled two thousand, two hundred and sixty-four messages during the months from May 1st to September 30th, 1886.[1]

Thus Miles prepared to hunt down Geronimo and his tiny band. But before he was fully ready the campaign was precipitated by Geronimo himself, with a raid which swept north across the border and into the United States on April 27th.

Up the Santa Cruz Valley went the Apaches, killing. They captured the Peck ranch, butchered several cowboys, and compelled the rancher, Peck, to witness the torture of his wife until he went temporarily insane. The crazed man was later freed by the superstitious Apaches and so he lived. But they rode away carrying with them the youngest Peck girl, about thirteen years old.

Lawton pursued. The raiders were far ahead and would easily have escaped him had they not run into a band of seventy Mexican irregulars and fought a brief battle with them. One Apache woman was killed. A bullet dropped the horse of the warrior who was carrying the Peck girl. In the confusion she got away, crawling and running through the bushes to safety. The girl was eventually found by rescuers and returned to her father, who recovered his sanity after a few days.

In the meantime the whole Apache band had escaped from the

[1] After Geronimo's surrender, Miles put on a demonstration of the use of the heliograph for his benefit. He asked for some information about the chief's brother, who was held prisoner at a distant fort. The immediacy of the reply stunned Geronimo. He sent word at once to Nachite, who was still hanging out, to "come in and come in quick; there was a power here which he could not understand." Nachite surrendered within a few hours. (See Miles, "Personal Recollections," p. 524.)

Mexican force, with the single exception of the dismounted warrior who had been carrying the Peck girl. The Mexicans scattered about his hiding place and tried to get him. But the single savage fighter was more than a match for the entire seventy. He killed seven of them and drove the rest back.[2] Then he made his own escape.

On went Geronimo's band. The Indians slaughtered five or six Mexican placer miners at a camp a little farther on, killed seven wood choppers next, and left a trail of blood nearly every mile of their way back toward Mexico.

The veteran Captain Lebo was hunting for them with his troop of the 10th Cavalry, when, on May 5th, Geronimo finally halted in the Pinito Mountains, in northern Sonora, thirty miles south of the border. Lebo attacked him immediately. Smoke plumed out from the rocks above as the soldiers struggled forward across the rugged boulders. The Indians lay in heights which formed a sort of half-moon, occupying almost impossible terrain. Very soon the troops had to fall back.

Out in the open, where the bullets of the Apaches combed the ground, lay the prostrate form of Corporal Scott, so badly wounded that he could not even crawl for cover. His comrades, by keeping up a heavy fire on the Indian position, did their best to protect him, but everybody could see that it was only a question of a few minutes until the wounded man would be killed.

Lying behind some sheltering rocks, Lieutenant Powhatan C. Clarke, fresh from West Point, stood it as long as he could. All at once, without saying what he was going to do, he jumped up and ran toward the wounded trooper. A hail of lead from the Apache rifles literally churned the ground around his feet, but still he kept on. He reached Scott. Lifting him, Clarke turned and staggered back. He was now a target for every rifle in the heights. How he ever reached his own lines is a mystery. But not a single bullet touched him and he deposited the wounded corporal behind a boulder where he was safe from further injuries.

[2] Captain Lawton, who arrived at the scene of this fight only a few hours after it took place, examined the bodies of these seven Mexicans. Every one of them had been shot through the head, showing the exceptionally deadly marksmanship of which some of the Apaches were capable.

There was no question now in Lebo's mind as to the strength of the Indians and their ability to hold him. As Geronimo drew away, the troops made no effort to follow.

NEVER-ENDING PURSUIT

The Indians rode southward, while behind the pursuit thickened hourly. It was a black situation for them. Five thousand American soldiers, hundreds of Mexican regulars and irregulars, five hundred Indian scouts, and thousands of ranchers and other civilians were in the death hunt. Geronimo and Nachite had only eighteen warriors now. Two of the original twenty had been killed. And they were encumbered by their women and children. But with small evidence of fear or discouragement, they trotted along, alert, wolfish, deadly always.

Ten days after Lebo's skirmish, on May 15th, Captain C. A. P. Hatfield stumbled on the hostile camp in the hills between the Santa Cruz and San Pedro Rivers. His charge captured the village and the entire herd of ponies. But it was a short-lived triumph. As he tried to make his way out of the rough country, Geronimo ambushed him in a box canyon, killed two men, wounded two more, and recovered every one of the captured horses, with no loss to his own band.

By now Lawton's flying column had taken the trail in earnest. It was a hand-picked body of men. Every one was a veteran and physically fit. On one occasion they marched twenty-four hours without stopping, for the last eighteen hours without water. Yet even so they were no match for the Indians.

It was the heliograph system which really was the decisive factor. Flashing all day long from mountain top to mountain top, the mirrors kept Lawton and the other commanders continually informed of the progress of the Apaches. Geronimo had not a moment's rest. Ceaselessly he had to keep on the move. As he shook off one pursuing detachment of soldiers or scouts, another would cut his trail. Twist and dodge as he would, he was never free.

But, driven as he was, Geronimo took time to busy himself with the people of the country through which he passed. Apache hate, embittered by the aggravating pursuit, translated itself into slaughter. Lawton picked up as many as ten butchered Mexicans a day during his long chase, and Governor Louis E. Torres of Sonora reported that around five or six hundred of his people were killed during the campaign.[3]

Days dragged into weeks. Doggedly, wearily, Lawton crossed and recrossed the mountains, following the elusive Apache trail. The continual discovery of new instances of Geronimo's grim handiwork in the maimed and disfigured corpses which he left in his wake, set a harder, bitterer look on the faces of white officers and Indian scouts each day as they tramped on and on, to end the prowl of the human tiger.

It was June 6th before Lawton overtook Geronimo. On that day a small detachment of the scouts under Lieutenant R. S. Walsh struck the hostiles. Only the briefest kind of a running fight took place, but the detachment took what satisfaction it could out of the capture of the Apache camp with the food supplies, most of the ammunition, and the herd of ponies. That was a serious blow to Geronimo. He was in sore straits.

Far south into Sonora the bloodhound Lawton followed the Indian trail. The hardships his men underwent were almost unbelievable. One day they would scale an eight or nine thousand foot peak; the next day they would drop down into a desert flat, where the heat was so intolerable that at times the hand could not be placed on the metal work of a gun. Pack trains had to be abandoned because the mules could not keep up in the terrific temperatures. Once the men went for five days without any food except what game they could kill. On another occasion, so terrible was their torture from hours of burning thirst, that some of the men opened the veins in their own arms to moisten their lips.[4]

---

[3] This figure sounds almost incredible, yet it is quoted by General Miles himself. ("Personal Recollections," p. 508.)

[4] Miles, "Personal Recollections," p. 491. This was the second time that men under Miles used their own blood to relieve their thirst. The other instance was when his command was caught without water in the Sweetwater country of Texas, during the Kiowa-Comanche War of 1874.

Lawton's persistence was again rewarded on July 13th, when his advance, under Lieutenant R. A. Brown, discovered the hostile village near Tonababu. But the attempted surprise failed as usual and the Indians escaped. Still, something was accomplished. Brown captured most of their remaining horses and supplies.

Once more the endless pursuit dragged on, this time toward the Torres Mountains. Geronimo used every thinkable device to throw Lawton off his trail. In the rough mountain country his people frequently crossed the ranges jumping from rock to rock. Yet Lawton's faithful Indian scouts would pick up the trail and the hunt would continue, the weary, hollow-eyed men, worn to shreds, toiling remorselessly along.

THE FORT APACHE INCIDENT

Throughout all the troubles south of the border the great bulk of the Mimbreño and Chiricahua Indians near Fort Apache remained peaceful. Scores of them, in fact, did more. They enlisted as scouts in Miles' army, and served faithfully, courageously and skillfully in the hazardous and terrifically rigorous campaigns. Among these none had a better record than Chato. When he left the war path, the Flat Nose lived up to every word of his agreement with Crook. He was a first sergeant in the company of scouts commanded by Lieutenant Britton Davis in Crook's campaign against Geronimo, and much of the success in that operation was due to him. Others also had fine records.

In spite of this, military authorities continued to fear these reservation Indians. Miles called them a "turbulent, desperate, disreputable band." Early in his administration he recommended their removal to some other state, preferably the Indian Territory. But how was he to round up four or five hundred Indians without precipitating another outbreak which would make those which had gone before seem trivial incidents by comparison?

The solution to this problem was suggested by Lieutenant James Parker. In June, 1886, while talking to Miles at Fort Huachuca, Parker mentioned the system in effect at Fort Apache, where the peaceful Indians were living. Whenever there was news of a raid, he said, the Indians, in order not to become involved in the fighting, went in to the post and were quartered in the quartermaster corral.

Parker suggested that a false report of a raid be spread and when the Apaches came to the corral, they should be surrounded by troops, disarmed, taken to the railroad and shipped east.

Miles stared at him. "Why that would be treachery," he said at last. "I could never do that."

But the thought had been planted.

Word came from the Secretary of War that the general's scheme of removing the Indians from Arizona to some territory in Texas, New Mexico, or Kansas, could not be carried out under the existing laws. Miles' next step was to send a delegation of the leading Indians to Washington, hoping so to impress them with the power of the government that they would return and recommend to their people that they go without resistance wherever they were told.

He placed Chato at the head of this delegation. The Apaches journeyed to Washington and viewed the wonders of the *rancheria* where the Great White Father lived. But for some reason they remained unimpressed. In spite of the pressure brought to bear upon them, the delegates sturdily refused to accede to the demands made upon them. Instead they asked to be taken back to Arizona. As they began their return journey, Captain Dorst, who had accompanied them, wired Miles that the Indians were still defiant. Immediately Miles ordered them held at Fort Leavenworth. Then he notified Dorst to tell the delegates that they must either become "treaty Indians," and work among their people for the wishes of the army, or they should consider themselves prisoners of war.

And so Chato and his companions received still another insight into the strange, incomprehensible villainy of the white man. But they were Apaches and true to their blood. Faced with imprisonment, they refused to betray their people. That was August 20th. Four days later Miles received word from Washington that if he could take into custody the Indians on the reservation, they could be "accommodated" at Fort Marion, Florida.

Miles at once put into operation the very plan suggested by Lieu-

tenant Parker, and denounced by himself as "treachery." Colonel
J. F. Wade was in command at Fort Apache. The Chiricahuas and
Mimbreño Apaches were told to come in to the agency to be counted,
as was the custom when a raid was reported in the section. Unsuspecting, they trooped in.

It was Sunday. Used to seeing the soldiers at the fort go through
their inspection on that day, the Indians paid no attention as the
regulars marched out and took positions which commanded every
point of egress from the place.

Not until too late did the Apaches sense that something was
wrong. Observers at the fort saw the warriors leap to their feet as
if at a command, and stand looking about with wild, startled eyes.
Then Colonel Wade walked boldly into the crowd, calling to everybody to sit down. The Indians were helpless and they knew it. One
by one the grim warriors squatted, until not one remained standing.
In the silence of despair they listened as Wade told them that they
were to be removed, that they were to part from their desert homes,
leave their few pitiful little fields of growing crops, and their friends
and familiar scenes, and go away into the unknown as prisoners of
the white man, who thus rewarded their peaceful lives and their
service to his flag.

A little later they were herded like cattle on trains and, with the
women and children wailing and the men staring in stony silence at
the panorama of their beloved country whirling behind the flying
wheels of their cars, they began the long journey to hot, damp
Florida.

27: THE END OF THE TRAIL

FINAL SURRENDER

But Geronimo and Nachite were still free. And Lawton and the rest of Miles' soldiers were still after them. For three months the hunt had continued. No Indians had been killed, but one soldier died and another was wounded, and many Mexicans gave up their lives under the knives of Apache warriors.

The hostile band was traced south of the Yaqui River, where it captured a Mexican pack train and remounted itself after Brown set it afoot July 13th. Next it was reported near Fronteras.

And now came good news for Miles. Two squaws stole into Fronteras to talk with José Maria, a Mexican whom they knew, as he had once been a captive among them. The man was gone—he was with Lawton as an interpreter for the scouts—but his wife was home and she sent word to the military authorities that the hostiles wanted to give themselves up.

Near Fort Apache lived a Chiricahua named Ka-e-ta, who had deserted the hostiles and voluntarily returned to live peacefully under the white man's authority. Miles decided to send this man with a message to Geronimo. With him went one Martiné, a Chiricahua sub-chief, who had never been on the war path and whose loyalty was unquestioned. Next Miles looked around for a white officer to accompany these two. He chose Lieutenant Charles B. Gatewood, best liked by the Indians of all the officers in Arizona since the death of Crawford.

It was an assignment fraught with desperate danger. Gatewood knew that he was putting his life into the hands of Geronimo and his warriors, but he instantly prepared to go. First he and the two emissaries from the reservation went to Fronteras to pick up the trail of the two squaws. With him was Tom Horn, formerly chief of scouts under Crawford. He also obtained the services of the interpreter José Maria of Fronteras, who had been with the hostile

Apaches as a prisoner, and whom the squaws had come to Fronteras to consult. Gatewood learned that the prefect of that city had made plans to lure the Apaches to the town, make them drunk, and then massacre them all in the cheerful Mexican manner. The lieutenant was anxious to avert this.

With Horn and José Maria, he and the two Indians began a perilous invasion of the hostile country. They carried before them constantly a piece of flour sacking, tied to a stick, as a flag of truce.

Growing plainer each day, for three days the trail of the squaws led them on. On August 23rd, Martiné and Ka-e-ta, scouting far ahead, discovered Geronimo's camp on the Bavispe River.[1] They approached it boldly. The "broncho" warriors let them in, then closed upon them, rifle hammers clicking. But the scouts were unafraid. To Geronimo's very face they delivered Gatewood's message. The chief pondered. At last he gave orders that Ka-e-ta should be held as a hostage, while Martiné returned to the white men with a message that he, Geronimo, would speak with Gatewood alone, unaccompanied by any soldiers. With this message, Martiné reached Gatewood's camp in the canebrakes at sundown.

Lawton's advance guard under Brown had just overtaken Gatewood. But, following the instructions of Geronimo, the lieutenant went to an intermediate meeting place early next morning, accompanied only by Horn, José Maria, and Martiné. Smoke signals were sent up and guns were fired from time to time, to reassure the Indians, who replied in kind.

They met in the river valley. One or two at a time, the Apaches rode up, unsaddled their ponies and allowed them to graze. Geronimo was among the last to arrive. His thin scar of a mouth was thinner than ever as he faced the officer. Pipes were lit and a cloud blown. Then the chief asked what Miles' word was. There was no hesitation in Gatewood's answer, though he knew his words might be his own death warrant.

"Surrender, and you will be sent with your families to Florida,

[1] Geronimo had been watching Gatewood and his men all the way, although they did not know it. He later told the lieutenant that he could not make out what kind of fools comprised such a small party dogging his trail. He did not notice, or did not understand the significance of, the flour-sack flag of truce.

there to await the decision of the President as to your final disposition. Accept these terms or fight it out," he said.[2]

As to the voice of doom the Apaches listened in dead silence. Finally Geronimo passed his hand over his eyes and, as he did so, Gatewood saw it tremble. The iron chief was shaken at last.

But it did not take him long to recover his composure. He asked for time to talk with his warriors, then went into conference with Nachite and others. Presently he was back with a counter-proposition: that they be taken to the reservation and there given the little land they needed, or else they would fight to the death.

The moment was tense. But Nachite, the easy-going, stepped in and smoothed things over. Gatewood now had a chance to tell them of the shipping of their friends and relatives to Florida. That was a stunning piece of news to the Apaches. Again they conferred. When they finished Geronimo returned to Gatewood and said with intense meaning: "We want your advice. *Consider yourself not a white man, but one of us;* remember all that has been said today and tell us what we should do."

"Trust General Miles and surrender to him," was Gatewood's instant reply. Geronimo asked the night to think things over.

Next morning the Apaches had made their decision. They told the lieutenant they would go with him to meet Miles and surrender. That very day, August 25th, the northward trip began.

Almost at once a complication arose. The bloody-minded prefect of Fronteras appeared suddenly with two hundred soldiers. Lawton and his scouts held the Mexicans off while the Apaches, accompanied by Gatewood, fled to the hills. After suitable explanations, the prefect departed, and the Indians were gathered up again and started once more northward.

The end came finally, at a place named as if by inspiration for just such a scene—Skeleton Canyon. There, on September 3rd, Geronimo and Miles met at last—the sole remaining fighting chief of the Apaches, and the representative of the great nation of sixty

---

[2] These conversations are from Gatewood's own story, as contained in the Arizona Historical Review, Vol. IV., No. 1, pp. 36-38.

million people which had finally conquered him. They talked for a time, the fine, handsome, soldierly white man, and the squat, broad-shouldered Indian with the steel-trap mouth. Then Geronimo returned to his village.

Next morning he and his people came in and delivered themselves into Miles' hands. The Apaches as a tribe had ended their resistance.

PEACE IN THE DESERT

It was a desperate band of savages which Miles had cornered in Skeleton Canyon. So long had they been hunted that they had become almost wild animals. His description of them gives an idea of how they looked:

"The Indians that surrendered with Geronimo have probably never been matched since the days of Robin Hood. Many of the warriors were outlaws from their own tribes, and their boys from twelve to eighteen were the very worst and most vicious of all. They were clad . . . to disguise themselves as much as possible. Masses of grass, bunches of weeds, twigs or small boughs were fastened under their hat bands very profusely, and also upon their shoulders or backs. Their clothing was trimmed in such a way that when lying upon the ground in a bunch of grass or at the head of a ravine, if they remained perfectly quiet, it was as impossible to discover them as if they had been a bird or serpent . . . An unsuspecting rancher or miner going along a road or trail, would pass within a few feet of these concealed Apaches, and the first intimation he would have of their presence would be a bullet through his heart or brain." [3]

Troops met them at Fort Bowie and loaded them on a train; within a short time they had started their long journey east. And here occurred the crowning infamy. Ka-e-ta, who had risked his life and had been held as a hostage by Geronimo while Martiné carried the message to Gatewood; and Martiné himself, whose record of friendliness to the white man was exemplary, were loaded on the same train with the hostile Indians, and sent to Florida with them. Protests availed nothing. Ka-e-ta and Martiné were Indians. Like

[3] Miles, "Personal Recollections," p. 525.

Chato, their services were already forgotten.[4]

Of this cynical act of the government's Captain Bourke wrote:

"Not a single Chiricahua had been killed, captured or wounded throughout the entire campaign—with two exceptions—unless by Chiricahua Apache scouts, who, like Chato, had kept the pledges given to General Crook in the Sierra Madre in 1883. The exceptions were: one killed by the White Mountain Apaches near Fort Apache, and one killed by a white man in northern Mexico. Yet every one of those faithful scouts—especially the two, Ki-e-ta (Ka-e-ta) and Martinez (Martiné) who at imminent personal peril had gone into the Sierra Madre to hunt up Geronimo and induce him to surrender—were transplanted to Florida and there subjected to the same punishment as had been meted out to Geronimo. And with them were sent men like Goth-kli and Toklanni who were not Chiricahuas at all, but had only lately married wives of that band, who had never been on the war path in any capacity save as soldiers of the government and had devoted years to its service. There is no more disgraceful page in the history of our relations with the American Indians than that which conceals the treachery visited upon the Chiricahuas who remained faithful in their allegiance to our people." [5]

Two thousand miles to the east, the Apaches were finally brought to their prison home.[6] Years passed. Interest in their case was

[4] Ka-e-ta and Martiné were actually held as *prisoners of war* for twenty-six years. In 1931 they made demand upon the government for their back pay as scouts, at $2.00 a day for their entire period of imprisonment. The Secretary of War admitted that they had undoubtedly rendered service of great value to the nation, but said that there were no funds available to pay them for it.

[5] Bourke, "On the Border With Crook," p. 485.

[6] One member of Geronimo's band escaped on the way to Florida. Miles thus describes the incident: "Just after they passed St. Louis, one Indian contrived to make his escape from the train despite all precautions which had been taken. True to his wolfish nature he succeeded in avoiding settlements and people who would be likely to arrest him, and though it took him a year to work his way back to the San Carlos reservation, he finally succeeded in doing it. Like a hyena he occasionally, at long intervals, stole down upon the Indian camp at San Carlos, captured an Indian woman, carried her back up into the mountains, kept her back for several months, then cruelly murdered her and returned to repeat the same crime. This he did several times, and his movements were as secret and stealthy as those of a reptile. One Indian girl whom he had captured made her escape and told of his habits and cruelty. This man was afterwards reported killed."—Miles, "Personal Recollections," p. 529.

Surely nobody but an Apache could have equalled the feat of this unnamed Indian warrior. He escaped from the prison train in a thickly settled part of the country. He had to find food and a hiding place each day. He crossed Illinois, Missouri, Oklahoma, Texas and New Mexico. It took him more than a year to make the trip. Yet in that entire period not a single human eye was ever laid on him. Without weapons, without a map, with only his unerring homing instinct guiding aroused through the nation as a result of the efforts of Herbert Welsh, secretary of the Indian Rights' Association. His investigations showed that although Miles' definite promise was that the surrendering Indians should be sent with their families to Florida, they had been separated and kept at hard labor without them for three years. Under pressure from interested persons all over the United States, the Apaches were removed to Alabama. Some seven hundred of them had been taken to Florida in 1886. When they were transferred to Alabama, they were very much reduced in numbers. Later they were moved again, this time to Fort Sill, Oklahoma. At that time only three hundred and eight of them were left alive. Finally, in 1907, through the efforts of Dr. Henry Roe Cloud, a full-blooded Winnebago, then a student at Yale University, and later superintendent of Haskell Indian Institute, the remnants of the tribe, then numbering only two hundred and fifty, were permitted to return to New Mexico, where they settled on the Mescalero reservation.

．　．　．　．　．　．　．　．　．

There is peace in the desert today. Not, however, because the Apache has in one whit abated his fiery spirit. Old Chato died just a few years ago, August 16th, 1934, at the age of ninety. His passing was at the Mescalero Agency hospital. And about his grave still lingers the aura of hate.

South of the international boundary line, outbreaks continue to occur occasionally. As recently as April 10th, 1930, Apaches from the Sierra Madre raided a settlement and killed three persons only a few miles from Nacori Chico, in northern Sonora.[7]

But on the United States side of the border, the Indians keep a

---

him, he journeyed straight to the desert and reached there some time in the fall of 1887. If history records the fellow to this exploit it has so far escaped the writer's attention.

[7] The following news dispatch published in the press of the United States April 23rd, 1930, tells the story of the most recent Apache outbreak:

"Tucson, Ariz., April 22 (INS)—Riding out of their wilderness hideout, high in the Sierra Madre Mountains, a band of wild Apache Indians scalped three persons, April 10, in a settlement near Nacori Chico, Sonora, Mexico, it was reported today by V. M. White, a mining engineer.

"The three victims were Mexicans who opened fire on the marauders while the sullen, dogged peace. If the white man was too strong for them in the days of Geronimo, what would now be their fate, in the day of the machine gun and the airplane?

What men must do, they do.

---

latter were looting the village.

"Armed parties immediately set out to trail the painted savages and attempt to engage them in battle before they reached their impregnable and historic cliffs.

"The Apaches are believed to have been led, White said, by Geronimo III, the grandson of the Geronimo who was chased by the U. S. Army for three years during the '80's in Arizona."

BIBLIOGRAPHY

Arizona Historical Review, 1928–1934.

Arizona Legislative Assembly, "Memorial and Affidavits Showing Outrages Perpetrated by the Apache Indians in the Territory of Arizona, for the Years 1869 and 1870," San Francisco, 1889.

Bancroft, Hubert Howe, "History of Arizona and New Mexico," San Francisco, 1889.

Barrett, S. M., "Geronimo's Own Story of His Life," New York, 1906.

Bartlett, J. R., "Personal Narrative of Explorations," New York, 1854.

Bourke, Captain John G., "An Apache Campaign in the Sierra Madre," New York, 1886.

Bourke, Captain John G., "On the Border With Crook," New York, 1891.

Brady, Dr. Cyrus Townsend, "Indian Fights and Fighters," Garden City, 1912.

Brady, Dr. Cyrus Townsend, "Northwestern Fights and Fighters," Garden City, 1910.

Branch, E. Douglas, "The Hunting of the Buffalo," New York, 1929.

Brininstool, E. A., "A Trooper With Custer," Columbus, 1925.

Brininstool, E. A., "Chief Crazy Horse, His Career and Death," Nebraska Historical Magazine, December, 1929.

Brininstool, E. A., "Fighting Red Cloud's Warriors," Columbus, 1926.

Brininstool, E. A., and Hebard, Dr. Grace Raymond, "The Bozeman Trail," Cleveland, 1922.

Bronson, E. B., "Reminiscences of a Ranchman," Chicago, 1910.

Browne, J. Ross, "Adventures in the Apache Country," New York, 1874.

Carrington, Frances Courtney, "My Army Life," Philadelphia, 1910.

Carter, Captain R. G., "The Old Sergeant's Story," New York, 1926.

Cochise County, Arizona, "Resolution Adopted at Meeting of Residents of Cochise County, Regarding Outbreak of Indians from San Carlos Reservation," Washington, D.C., 1885.

Colyer, Vincent, "Peace With the Apaches," Report to the Board of Indian Commissioners, Washington, D.C., 1872.

Cook, James H., "Fifty Years on the Old Frontier," New Haven, 1923.

Cook, John R., "The Border and the Buffalo," Topeka, 1907.

Cooke, General P. St. George, "The Conquest of New Mexico and California," New York, 1878.

Cremony, Captain John C., "Life Among the Apaches," San Francisco, 1868.
Custer, Elizabeth Barrett, "Boots and Saddles," New York, 1885.
Custer, General George A., "My Life on the Plains," New York, 1874.

Davis, Lieutenant Britton, "The Truth About Geronimo," New Haven, 1929.
De Barthe, Joe, "Life and Adventures of Frank Grouard," Sheridan, 1894.
Dixon, Olive K., "The Life of Billy Dixon," Dallas, 1927.
Dodge, Colonel Richard I., "Our Wild Indians," Hartford, 1885.
Dunn, J. P., "Massacres of the Mountains," New York, 1886.

Finerty, John F., "War-path and Bivouac," Chicago, 1890.
Folwell, Dr. William Watts, "A History of Minnesota," publication of the
    Minnesota State Historical Society.
Forsyth, George A., "Thrilling Days of Army Life," New York, 1900.
Frazier, Robert, "The Apaches of the White Mountain Reservation," Phila-
    delphia, 1885.

Grinnell, George Bird, "The Fighting Cheyennes," New York, 1915.
Grinnell, George Bird, "Two Great Scouts and the Pawnee Battalion," Cleve-
    land, 1928.

Hafen, LeRoy R., and Ghent, W. J., "Broken Hand," Denver, 1931.
Hare, Bishop W. H., "Chief Joseph's Own Story," North American Review,
    April, 1879.
Heard, Isaac V. D., "The Great Sioux War," New York, 1863.
Hodge, Frederick W., "Handbook of American Indians," Bulletin 30, Bureau
    of American Ethnology, Washington, D.C., 1912.
Howard, General O. O., "My Life and Experiences Among Our Hostile In-
    dians," Hartford, 1907.
Hyde, George E., "Rangers and Regulars," pamphlet, Denver, 1933.

Indian Affairs Office, Annual Reports, 1876–1886.
Inman, Major Henry, "The Old Santa Fé Trail," New York, 1896.
Irwin, General B. J. D., "The Apache Pass Fight," Infantry Journal, April,
    1928.

Jackson, Helen Hunt, "A Century of Dishonor," Cambridge, 1885.
Johnson, W. Fletcher, "The Life of Sitting Bull," Chicago, 1891.

Kansas Magazine, New Series, 1886–1888, Kansas City, Kansas.
Kansas State Historical Society Reports.
King, Captain Charles, "Campaigning With Crook," New York, 1890.

Laut, Agnes C., "Pioneer Women of the West," Outing Magazine, March, June, July, 1908.
Linderman, Frank, "American," New York, 1930.
Lockwood, Frank C., "Pioneer Days in Arizona," New York, 1932.
Lummis, Charles F., "Land of Poco Tiempo," New York, 1893.

Manypenny, George W., "Our Indian Wards," Cincinnati, 1880.
Marcy, General R. B., "Thirty Years of Army Life on the Border," New York, 1866.
Mazzanovitch, Anton, "Trailing Geronimo," Los Angeles, 1926.
Miles, General Nelson A., "Personal Recollections," Chicago, 1896.
Minnesota State Historical Society Collections.
Mooney, James, "The Ghost Dance Religion," Bulletin 14, Bureau of American Ethnology.

Nebraska State Historical Society Collections.
New Mexico Historical Society Records.

Parkman, Francis, "The Oregon Trail," Boston, 1872.

Raht, Carlisle Graham, "Romance of Davis Mountains and Big Bend Country," El Paso, 1919.
Read, Benjamin M., "Illustrated History of New Mexico," Santa Fé, 1912.
Rister, C. C., "The Southwestern Frontier," Cleveland, 1928.
Ruxton, George Frederick, "Adventures in Mexico and in the Rocky Mountains," New York, 1848.

Sheridan, General P. H., "Record of Engagements With Hostile Indians, From 1868 to 1882," Official Army Compilation, Washington, 1882.
Shields, G. O., "The Battle of the Big Hole," New York, 1889.
Stone, Charles Pomeroy, "Notes on the State of Sonora," Washington, 1861.
Sumner, Colonel E. V., "Besieged by the Utes," Century Magazine, October, 1891.

Twitchell, Ralph Emerson, "Leading Facts in New Mexican History," Cedar Rapids, 1912.

Vestal, Stanley, "Sitting Bull, Champion of the Sioux," Boston, 1932.

War Department, Annual Reports of the Secretary of War, 1846–1891.
"War of the Rebellion; a Compilation of the Official Records of the Union and Confederate Armies," Washington, 1880–1891.

Welsh, Herbert, "The Apache Prisoners in Fort Marion, St. Augustine, Florida," report to the Indian Rights Association, Philadelphia, 1887.
Wheeler, Colonel Homer W., "Buffalo Days," Indianapolis, 1923.
Wood, Major C. E. S., "Chief Joseph the Nez Percé," Century Magazine, May, 1884.

INDEX